THE AZANDE

History and
Political Institutions

Namarusu

THE AZANDE

History and
Political Institutions

———

E. E. EVANS-PRITCHARD

OXFORD
AT THE CLARENDON PRESS
1971

Oxford University Press, Ely House, London W. 1

GLASGOW NEW YORK TORONTO MELBOURNE WELLINGTON
CAPE TOWN SALISBURY IBADAN NAIROBI DAR ES SALAAM LUSAKA ADDIS ABABA
BOMBAY CALCUTTA MADRAS KARACHI LAHORE DACCA
KUALA LUMPUR SINGAPORE HONG KONG TOKYO

PRINTED IN GREAT BRITAIN
AT THE UNIVERSITY PRESS, OXFORD
BY VIVIAN RIDLER
PRINTER TO THE UNIVERSITY

PREFACE

I

IN 1937 my only substantial monograph on the Azande people of Central Africa was published.[1] In that book I wrote: 'If I have paid no particular attention to Zande history this is not because I consider it unimportant but because I consider it so important that I desire to record it in detail elsewhere.'[2] That I have not till now accomplished this task is due to a number of circumstances, among them being that I undertook at the request of the Government of the Anglo-Egyptian Sudan a study of the Nuer and Anuak peoples and that, when I was returning to the writing up of my Zande material, the Second World War broke out and I was involved in military service for the greater part of it. At the end of the war I was for some years engaged in different interests. I was afterwards able to take up my Zande studies again and I gave my first attention to their history.

It soon became evident that in the absence of adequate historical documents and with the limitations of verbal traditions anything like a systematic history of the Azande could not be written. All that could be attempted was a piecemeal presentation of various aspects of their history in a series of articles treating of one or other aspect and for the most part in one kingdom, the one in which I did by far the greater part of my field research. These articles, each of which bears a relation to the others, are now brought together in this volume. Nothing more is likely to be recorded of the history of this people before European domination of their country, or even after it. Therefore the historical material here presented may be regarded as definitive, though interpretations of it may differ.[3]

---

[1] Since then a small volume has appeared entitled *The Zande Trickster*, 1967.

[2] *Witchcraft, Oracles and Magic among the Zande*, 1937, p. 19.

[3] Since this was written there has appeared *Les Zande dans l'histoire du Bahr et Ghazal et de l'Equatoria* by A. Thuriaux-Hennebert, 1964. This book covers some of the same ground as part of the present volume, using the same historical sources.

2

The articles, which have been subjected to minor editorial adjustments, mainly to avoid too much repetition and inconsistencies in format, are based on my own research in the field, carried out between the years 1926 and 1930, and the observations of early travellers, ethnologists, missionaries, and administrators. The literary sources are referred to in footnotes and in the Bibliography, but comments on the more important of them will be in place here. Of these the earliest was Carlo Piaggia, who resided among the Azande during the years 1863 to 1865. He delivered a lecture at Lucca on the Azande—only a few pages—in 1877,[1] from which we learn little. He was an ill-educated man, a gardener by profession. A fuller account of his adventures was composed from his verbal information by his friend and fellow hunter and trader the Perugian Marchese O. Antinori.[2] Many years later his memoirs were published;[3] but these must be accepted with critical reservations, for there are discrepancies between the memoirs and earlier versions. Literary friends appear to have influenced his presentation. Georg Schweinfurth, an eminent Russo-German botanist, spent about three months travelling through the most easterly districts of Zandeland in 1870.[4] Valuable though his information is, we have to bear in mind that he could not speak Zande, that he was in the company of an enormous Arab caravan in disturbed conditions which must have prevented him from having opportunity to establish close relations with the Azande; that, though he did not realize it, he was travelling through country occupied by peoples who were not, in a sense shortly to be explained, strictly speaking Azande at all; and that he lost his original notes in a fire in December 1870. A more trustworthy authority is Wilhelm Junker, a doctor of medicine and like Schweinfurth a Russo-German, who spent over ten years, from 1875, exploring Central Africa, most of them among the

---

[1] Carlo Piaggia, *Dell'arrivo fra i Niam-Niam e del soggiorno sul lago Tzana in Abissinia*, Lucca, 1877.

[2] O. Antinori, 'Viaggio di O. Antinori e C. Piaggia nell'Africa Centrale', *Boll. Soc. Geog. Ital.*, i, 1868, 91–165.

[3] A. Pellegrinetti, *Le memorie di Carlo Piaggia*, 1941.

[4] Georg Schweinfurth, *The Heart of Africa*, 2 vols., 1873; *Im Herzen von Afrika*, 1878 and 1922. *See also* K. Guenther, *Georg Schweinfurth*, 1954.

Azande.[1] Another of our sources of the explorer genre is the Italian officer and cartographer Gaetano Casati, who was in Zandeland or in neighbouring areas from April 1881 to August 1884.[2] His notes were also destroyed, and he was much given to embellishment. These are our main early sources. There are others who will be mentioned from time to time, but they are not such valuable witnesses. All—good, bad, or indifferent— had little understanding of Zande institutions: they were, for example, ignorant of the fact that the Azande have totemic clans.

I would like to say in parenthesis that one of the fascinations of the study of early exploration of the Southern Sudan is the cosmopolitan characters of the persons engaged in it. For example, Miani, Piaggia, Antinori, Casati, and Gessi were Italians; Schweinfurth, Emin (Schnitzer), Junker, and Heuglin were Germans; Petherick was a Welshman; Potagos was a Greek; Pruyssenaer, Schuver, and Miss Tinné were Dutch; the Poncet brothers were Savoyards; Kleincznick and Marno were Austrians; Baker was English; De Malzac, Peney, Vayssière, and Lejean were French; Andrea DeBono was Maltese; Chaillé-Long was an American.

I now mention the more important later sources. For the history of the Azande the most remarkable of these is de Calonne-Beaufaict's book.[3] De Calonne was a Belgian administrator in the Uele region from 1905 till his death in 1915. He was deeply interested in the peoples of this region, among whom he had travelled widely, and he had already to his credit books on the Ababua and Bakongo when he devoted himself to an intensive study of the Azande. It is most unfortunate that he died before he had completed his labours and before he had published his material. In de Calonne's posthumous work *Azande*, his editor, Col. Bertrand, says that a great part of his notes appear to have been lost after his death, and this would seem to be confirmed by the table of contents at the end of the book, in which he presents a plan for a general ethnographic treatise on the Azande. All that was found, however, were the notes, in every stage of development, which Col. Bertrand put

---

[1] Wilhelm Junker, *Travels in Central Africa*, 3 vols., 1890, 1891, 1892 (trans. from *Reisen in Afrika*, 3 vols., 1889, 1890, 1891).

[2] Gaetano Casati, *Ten Years in Equatoria and the Return with Emin Pasha*, 2 vols., 1891.

[3] A. de Calonne-Beaufaict, *Azande*, 1921.

together to form *Azande*, and some linguistic material which has not, as far as I can discover, been published. Most of our knowledge of Zande history is derived from de Calonne and Armand Hutereau. Hutereau, a career soldier, served the État Indépendant du Congo, mostly in the region of the Uele, from 1896 to 1909. He had always interested himself in the history and customs of the African peoples among whom he served and had already published an ethnographic monograph,[1] dealing largely with the Azande, before he undertook in 1911–12, on behalf of the Minister for the Colonies (Belgian), an ethnographical mission to the Congo. He then returned to military duties and was killed, fighting with great gallantry, in 1914. His detailed account of Zande history was published posthumously in 1922.[2] The Polish ethnographer Dr. Jan Czekanowski has also provided us with some excellent information on the Azande of the Congo.[3]

So far as I am able to judge, none of the men whose names I have cited understood the Zande tongue, either at all or to more than a very limited extent. This is not the case with later sources. I have made use of C. R. Lagae and V. H. Vanden Plas's studies.[4] These two Dominican Fathers spent many years in that part of Zande country which lies in what used to be the Belgian Congo. It will be noted that the books which constitute our principal sources, those of Hutereau, de Calonne, and Lagae and Vanden Plas, all appeared in 1921 and 1922 and may therefore be regarded as independent authorities; and the same may be said of Czekanowski. I pay tribute also to the researches of an old and lamented friend, Major P. M. Larken, who spent over twenty years among the Azande of the Sudan and spoke their language fluently.[5]

I have cited only our main historical sources. I have used them with due caution, but often, since they treat of areas of

[1] Armand Hutereau, 'Notes sur la vie familiale et juridique de quelques populations du Congo belge', *Ann. Mus. Congo belge*, 1909.

[2] Idem, *Histoire des peuplades de l'Uele et de l'Ubangi*, 1922.

[3] Jan Czekanowski, *Wissenschaftliche Ergebnisse der deutschen Zentral-Afrika-Expedition 1907–1908, unter Führung Adolf Friedrichs Herzog zu Mecklenburg*, Bd. 6, 2: *Forschungen im Nil-Kongo-Zwischengebiet*, 1924.

[4] C. R. Lagae, and V. H. Vanden Plas, *La Langue des Azande*, 2 vols., 1921; C. R. Lagae, *Les Azande ou Niam-Niam*, 1926.

[5] P. M. Larken, 'An Account of the Zande', *Sudan Notes and Records*, 1926; 'Impressions of the Azande', ibid., 1927.

Zandeland with which I am little or not at all acquainted, the information they give has to be to some extent accepted on trust, though not entirely so since one authority can be weighed against another. On the topics with which this volume is concerned I regard the major sources as fairly reliable, on some other topics less so. A detailed criticism of the sources on all that they report would require a long essay, a task I must defer to a later opportunity.

3

In trying to make a historical reconstruction of a people like the Azande where the literary sources are sparse and, though not necessarily unreliable, are limited in scope and inadequate and in some respects are incomprehensible, we have very often to interpret the past by what we know of the present in the light of anthropological field research. So we are inclined to start with well-authenticated information about the present situation and then to try to explain it by what we can glean of the past from verbal traditions and literary sources, rather than vice versa, starting from some point in the past and working from it to the present. This may seem like standing history on her head but such must to a large extent be the procedure in a reconstruction of the history of primitive peoples. The historian of, shall we say, medieval England cannot proceed in this manner: he cannot do field research, in the anthropological sense, in the year 1300 to interpret what his authorities say about what happened in the year 1200. Hence the unusual presentation in this book. It starts in Part 1 with essays describing the present situation with regard to distribution of clans and related topics. In Part 2 it then discusses how the ethnic admixture which has brought about Zande society such as we know it today is to be seen also in a culture derived from many sources. In Part 3 it discusses how the Azande themselves see the development of some of their institutions and how, on such evidences as we have, they have arisen. Some historical sketches, in particular of the kingdom of Gbudwe in the Sudan, conclude the book. I can only regret that I did not pay more attention than I did to traditional history. Much more information could have been obtained had I tried harder to collect it. On the

other hand, I am thankful that I obtained what I did, for, in
the anthropological climate then prevailing, I might have
regarded their traditions as of merely antiquarian interest and
therefore not worth recording. Today it would be impossible to
gather the traditions here recorded.

4

Besides trying to present a partial history of the Azande I
have wished to show in these essays (now chapters) how confused and complicated the institutions and culture of such a
people can be and therefore how necessary it is to have an
understanding of their historical background. We have to
account for the political consistency given to a very heterogeneous ethnic, social, and cultural amalgam by the institutions
of the Avongara–Ambomu. Part 3 gives some account of the
way in which the amalgam was organized. Part 2 is therefore a
counterpart to Part 3 in that it shows how cultural assimilation
was related to political absorption.

5

When I say that the past must be interpreted in the light of
what we know of the present, both 'past' and 'present' may
require comment. The past does not go back very far. Traditions, and literary sources recording them, take us back about
two hundred years at most, the facts becoming less certain the
further back we go. De Calonne tried to reconstruct the history
of the Uele region much further back, but his evidences are
inconclusive and his interpretation of them most speculative,
and I have not followed him in his reconstructions, preferring
to be on firmer ground.

We have also to recognize that it is impossible to write a
general history of the Azande, because they were divided into a
number of different kingdoms, each of which had its own
history, requiring detailed reconstruction—this has been done
only in a very elementary way—before anything more general
could be attempted, and it is now too late to do what is required.

With regard to 'present' I speak of the period in which I did
my research among the Azande of the Sudan, between the years
1926 and 1930. Their political life had by that time been

disrupted and much had already disappeared, but also much remained and could be observed; those who gave me information about the past had lived in it and their thoughts, values, and sentiments were still of it. No effective administration was established in Gbudwe's kingdom—though a military administration of a kind dated from 1905—till about 1920, a few years before my own research was carried out in that region.

6

As this book is intended primarily for students I do not feel that it is necessary to introduce the Azande, for to the student of social anthropology they are a well-known people. They have been famous in the literature of the subject for over a century; and a general account of them has been published in C. R. Lagae's *Les Azande ou Niam-Niam* (1926) and another, based almost entirely on my own research, in a book by C. G. and B. Z. Seligman.[1] All that requires to be known by way of synopsis is that the Ambomu people under the leadership of their Avongara royal house migrated eastwards from their homeland in what used to be French Equatorial Africa and conquered vast areas and many peoples, on whom they imposed their language and institutions. That migration and its consequences are the theme of this book.

7

This will be my third book on the Azande, and I have also published a number of articles on some of their customs and beliefs.[2] I hope that I may be able to present further volumes on their domestic institutions and rites. Then I shall have carried out my duty—forty to fifty years late.

8

There are incongruities in the spellings of names and places. This cannot be avoided because I have had to follow the

[1] *Pagan Tribes of the Nilotic Sudan*, chap. xv, 1932.
[2] Some of these have been brought together in *Essays in Social Anthropology*, 1962, and *The Position of Women in Primitive Societies and other Essays in Social Anthropology*, 1965.

spellings of my authorities. I would wish, however, to disarm criticism on one point, the spelling of the same word sometimes with an *r* and sometimes with an *l*. This is a complicated matter and one in which I am not in agreement with the phoneticians; but where *l* occurs, *r* can be read by those who take their view.

ACKNOWLEDGEMENTS

I HAVE received much help in making a book of the essays contained in it from Dr. Eva Krapf-Askari, Mr. Garrett Barden, and Mr. André Singer, to all of whom I express my thanks. In the final stages of publication I have had the further help of Miss Juliet Blair, for whose assistance I am indebted to the Social Science Research Council.

I make acknowledgement to the Editors of the Journals in which the essays first appeared: *Man*; *Anthropological Quarterly*; *Southwestern Journal of Anthropology*; *African Studies*; *Zaïre*; *Africa*; *Cahiers d'études africaines*; *Anthropos*.

I thank the British Academy for financial assistance in the preparation of this book.

CONTENTS

LIST OF PLATES

LIST OF MAPS AND FIGURES

PART ONE

INTRODUCTION

THE leit-motiv of this part is the complexity of Zande society. The true Azande are divided into two categories: the noble or Avongara clan, and the commoner or Ambomu clans. The Avongara provide the kings of the various sections of Zandeland and most of their provincial governors within each kingdom. The Ambomu form only about 38 per cent, on a rough estimate, of the commoner population, for, besides these true Azande, it is also composed of foreigners, *Auro*, who outnumber them. These foreigners and their descendants belong to many different clans. Zande society as a whole is, then, divided into three categories: nobles, commoners who are of true Zande stock, and commoners who are of foreign origin. In Chapters I and II the distribution of persons of these categories in one of the Zande kingdoms—that of King Gbudwe—is set out. In Chapter III the composition of the categories is worked out in greater detail. Chapters IV, V, and VI illustrate how this diversity is manifested in the names and totems of the clans. The following three chapters on Zande culture show how this ethnic diversity is again mirrored in several aspects of Zande life from cultivation of crops to forms of institutions.

I

THE DISTRIBUTION OF CLANS
IN THE SUDAN

THOUGH I was able during the twenty months or so that I spent among the Azande of the Sudan to get a rough idea of the distribution of their clans in the course of my travels and by taking samples here and there, I was unable myself to spare the time to study it in such detail and on so wide a scale as was required. I therefore instructed my clerk, Reuben Rikita, to take, during my absences in England in 1929 and 1930, as broad a census as he could of the adult males in the old kingdoms of Gbudwe, Ezo, and Tembura. For a part of the time he was assisted by another youth. The census was far from complete, and it was more thorough in some areas than in others; but on the whole it served its purpose. The districts were listed separately, and the name of each man was taken down with his clan, his totem, and the ethnic group to which he belonged. In the circumstances then obtaining, this was not a difficult task, for the Azande had no reluctance to being listed. They had accustomed themselves to the procedure of a census during sleeping-sickness inspections and settlement along government roads. Doubtless there are errors in these lists, but, apart from such possible minor errors, I have no reason to regard them as other than reliable. Reuben was an honest recorder; there could have been no motive for a man to conceal or falsify his name, clan, or totem; and I was able to check Reuben's lists against my own few samples.

For the purpose of comparison, the area covered by the inquiry has been divided into four parts. The central region, A, between the Sueh and the Lingasi, was the realm of King Gbudwe *minus* the domain of his second son Mange, and it also corresponds roughly with the realm of Gbudwe's father, Bazingbi. Area B, roughly between the Lingasi and the Mongu, was the old kingdom of Gbudwe's elder brother Ezo. To the north-west of this, area C is that part of the old kingdom of Tembura, of a different dynasty from that of Ezo and Gbudwe, ruled at the time of the survey by his son Renzi. Area D, to the east of the Sueh and extending to the east of the Iba, was once the principality of Mange, son of Gbudwe. My own researches in the Sudan were almost entirely restricted to area A. All these areas could be broken down into smaller districts, and some further conclusions might be reached by this more detailed treatment, but it is not required for the very broad results aimed at here.

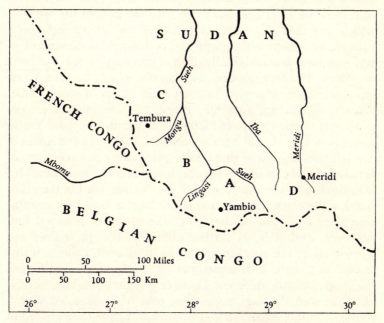

I. SKETCH-MAP OF SUDAN-ZANDELAND.

With a few exceptions, only those clans are listed whose members in the registers numbered at least 25. The remainder, all of foreign stocks, are entered as 'unclassified'. Some of them show only a few entries in the table, and I cannot say whether the clan names are in such cases invariably correct. I did not myself carry out research in the areas in which they were for the most part recorded; and some of them would not have been heard of by a Zande of Gbudwe's kingdom. Reuben was, it is sometimes evident, puzzled to know how he should write such outlandish names.

Some entries are names of ethnic groups and not of clans, e.g. Apambia, Abangbinda, Abarambo, and Auma. Doubtless a further clan name could have been given, but the people who gave the name of their ethnic groups as that of their clans and then *auro*, foreigners, as an ethnic designation may very well have thought of the group as corresponding in the context of inquiry to a clan. This introduces a very complex problem which will be dealt with later.[1] Suffice it to say that it is possible that some of what are today regarded as clans in the sense in which one uses this word to translate the Zande *ngbatunga*, exogamous groups with a supposed or assumed common ancestry, may have been originally distinct ethnic groups. It has been suggested, I believe erroneously, that the ruling clan, the Avongara, was such a group; but the Adio group of clans (Adio, Akowe, Abananga, Andebili, Apise, etc.) undoubtedly were a distinct ethnic group. It follows that when an ethnic group appears in the table, it does not mean that this is a statement of the full composition of that ethnic group, for other members of it may be, and certainly often are, listed under clan names. This is undoubtedly the case, e.g. with the Abarambo. On the other hand, some clans must consequently have a larger representation than is shown in the table; the numbers involved are, however, negligible. A further difficulty, though it does not greatly affect the conclusions drawn, is alluded to but not discussed at length. It is sometimes uncertain whether different spellings indicate different clans or phonetic variations, e.g. Bananga and Banangi, Apambage and Abambage, Abakumo and Abaikumo, Abambai and Abangbai. I have been guided in this matter by what seems to me to be the bias of probability; but, here again, the numbers involved are negligible. A related, more serious, and perhaps insoluble, problem has been brought about by assimilation or by a veritable babel of tongues, resulting perhaps in a confusion of collective prefixes—Sudanic, Nilotic, and Bantu. I am not able to say for certain, being ignorant of the areas concerned, whether, for example, the following should be listed, in each case, as two clans or as a single clan or whether

[1] See Chap. III.

those who belong to them would speak of themselves as a single clan or as separate clans: Akowe and Abakowe; Aboro and Ababoro; Muru, Bamuru, and Babamuru; and Banga and Babanga. I have sometimes listed them together and sometimes separately, but not, I must confess, on any clear principle. Fortunately, once more, the issue is of little numerical importance.

TABLE I

	Clan	A	B	C	D	Totals
1.	Avongara (Akulongbo)	520	468	93	301	1,382
2.	Agiti	763	193	93	245	1,294
3.	Akalingo	414	179	81	53	727
4.	Avunduo	430	143	79	159	811
5.	Angbadimo	293	107	67	59	526
6.	Akowe	446	22	41	118	627
7.	Abandogo	487	289	37	42	855
8.	Aubali	88	56	138	7	289
9.	Amiandi	138	31	0	15	184
10.	Angbapiyo	324	167	18	32	541
11.	Angumbe	410	51	4	47	512
12.	Abiama	164	1	0	99	264
13.	Avundukura	86	15	11	18	130
14.	Avotombo	258	72	7	72	409
15.	Ameteli	356	13	0	24	393
16.	Abadara	228	78	7	47	360
17.	Angbaga	206	182	58	31	477
18.	Abakundo	239	81	13	37	370
19.	Agberenya	94	2	0	105	201
20.	Abazaa (Babaza)	100	38	26	120	284
21.	Angbaya	183	76	6	46	311
22.	Abakpuro	164	189	14	219	586
23.	Abangombi	291	66	1	37	395
24.	Aremete	146	49	6	12	213
25.	Angali	216	10	2	83	311
26.	Akurungu	66	64	3	2	135
27.	Aboro	134	31	5	26	196
28.	Abawoyo	125	92	11	155	383
29.	Abangbara	227	32	10	118	387
30.	Agbunduku	48	19	9	37	113
31.	Amuzungu	110	14	1	28	153
32.	Agbambi	469	146	20	30	665
33.	Abale	50	0	0	6	56
34.	Avokili	39	3	20	4	66
35.	Adio	43	23	24	38	128
36.	Abakpoto	107	0	2	69	178
37.	Abapia	79	3	19	48	149
38.	Akpongboro	21	83	21	0	125

	Clan	A	B	C	D	Totals
39.	Abadugu	3	30	125	107	265
40.	Abakpa	3	84	97	0	184
41.	Amogba	0	88	55	4	147
42.	Avumaka (Abumaka)	230	0	0	12	242
43.	Abakpara	142	3	0	39	184
44.	Ambata	178	24	2	63	267
45.	Abalingi	69	84	27	31	111
46.	Abatiko	104	309	35	6	454
47.	Ababanduo	2	0	0	171	173
48.	Abagende	0	0	0	279	279
49.	Abawoli	217	57	12	106	392
50.	Abaigo	12	181	33	14	240
51.	Avokida	71	14	16	12	113
52.	Ametanga	2	226	32	13	273
53.	Abananga	115	397	60	191	763
54.	Abisiaka	22	0	0	36	58
55.	Abangboto	42	48	7	0	97
56.	Agoro (Abagoro)	0	11	68	0	79
57.	Akenge	127	10	1	12	150
58.	Abakaya	8	93	3	219	323
59.	Abauro	115	10	8	44	177
60.	Abayali	5	0	0	250	255
61.	Amegburu	45	196	11	0	252
62.	Amegbara	95	93	2	14	204
63.	Avonama	3	10	24	0	37
64.	Abagbate	95	28	5	18	146
65.	Avudima	0	65	57	0	122
66.	Avuzukpo	0	28	44	0	72
67.	Avugioro	0	156	23	0	179
68.	Apambia	23	4	5	3	35
69.	Abakpanda	3	0	0	198	201
70.	Angbuki	59	89	9	13	170
71.	Abakangba	17	120	10	3	150
72.	Abangere	63	35	8	26	132
73.	Abaningba	45	38	4	3	90
74.	Abaanya	179	18	6	110	313
75.	Andabili	74	5	3	19	101
76.	Abamunga	21	0	0	135	156
77.	Ambare	192	121	2	10	325
78.	Abagua	59	32	24	4	119
79.	Akpurandi	24	123	23	0	170
80.	Abasiri	55	105	98	0	258
81.	Akpura	140	8	12	4	164
82.	Avuruwa	0	5	28	0	33
83.	Abangbaya	30	0	0	140	170
84.	Anguli	16	230	21	2	269
85.	Abanziwa	0	31	13	0	44
86.	Avumai	1	30	20	0	51
87.	Andungu	0	2	20	0	22
88.	Amenguna	68	37	2	1	108
89.	Akangani	32	0	0	13	45

	Clan	A	B	C	D	Totals
90.	Abagbangi	137	28	5	42	212
91.	Abangbinda	8	84	7	58	157
92.	Avodai	0	0	31	0	31
93.	Avodangba	0	75	14	0	89
94.	Augu	0	42	10	0	52
95.	Avungbadi	35	90	15	7	147
96.	Ababaya	18	52	1	13	84
97.	Abani	30	3	8	0	41
98.	Avombili	2	23	17	0	42
99.	Abadumbo	0	9	26	0	35
100.	Auma (Bauma)	0	8	17	0	25
101.	Apambage (Abambage)	0	30	11	1	42
102.	Abakpakili (Akpakili)	0	4	18	0	22
103.	Abatukpo	150	121	6	2	279
104.	Abagbaga	37	79	0	0	116
105.	Abaningo	34	0	1	59	94
106.	Abakupa	31	0	0	38	69
107.	Ababili	33	9	6	37	85
108.	Ababaimo	2	0	0	144	146
109.	Ababiro	0	1	2	70	73
110.	Abakango	1	0	0	168	169
111.	Abadigo	103	4	0	97	204
112.	Abaturu	0	0	0	92	92
113.	Afutu (Abafutu)	18	2	10	0	30
114.	Abandiko	157	52	1	12	222
115.	Avonamangi	0	0	22	0	22
116.	Aduruwe	7	28	6	1	42
117.	Abandia	1	0	25	0	26
118.	Abamburo (Abangburo)	203	40	4	37	284
119.	Ababali	0	0	0	165	165
120.	Apise	34	5	3	2	44
121.	Abandagburu	0	0	0	50	50
122.	Abamage	2	0	0	76	78
123.	Abarambo	2	24	30	0	56
124.	Abagiamu	0	4	13	4	21
125.	Avuduma	70	10	0	0	80
126.	Abakumo (Abaikumo)	18	30	10	44	102
127.	Akudere	30	0	0	0	30
128.	Abambai (Abangbai)	37	1	1	10	49
129.	Amadi	73	0	0	15	88
130.	Ababioro	0	39	0	0	39
131.	Abangbere	0	0	0	78	78
132.	Abagiali	0	0	0	74	74
133.	Abadugumu	0	0	0	68	68
134.	Abangau	35	25	4	56	120
135.	Amabenge	14	0	0	55	69
136.	Abanzuka	37	0	0	1	38
137.	Avubanga	0	123	10	0	133
138.	Abangbandili	0	0	0	87	87
139.	Abaruvuro	0	0	0	96	96
140.	Avoando (Avando)	34	53	11	3	101

	Clan	A	B	C	D	Totals
141.	Abalingua	0	27	1	0	28
142.	Abambiti	16	2	2	37	57
143.	Abakianga	25	36	8	1	70
144.	Abaipi	0	0	0	39	39
145.	Amigano	25	54	5	1	85
146.	Amizoro (Amiforo)	63	53	7	0	123
147.	Abagbuto	10	1	5	87	103
148.	Abaiwo	63	0	0	0	63
149.	Abadangasa	0	0	0	38	38
150.	Abanguri	34	0	0	2	36
151.	Agbuku	19	0	0	1	20
152.	Ambaragba (Abambaragba)	2	15	17	0	34
153.	Abagbaya	0	29	12	83	124
154.	Agilibo (Abagilibo)	0	0	0	21	21
155.	Abanyere	0	0	0	30	30
156.	Abagbo	18	2	0	20	40
157.	Abakowe	0	29	28	0	57
158.	Ababanga	0	58	14	0	72
159.	Abara (Abare)	1	69	36	1	107
160.	Ababoyo	0	0	0	73	73
161.	Abanzuma	53	12	0	3	68
162.	Abangbata	0	109	0	0	109
163.	Abadangba	0	9	9	0	18
164.	Abadanga	0	25	8	1	34
165.	Ambari	38	0	0	2	40
166.	Abamerenge	0	0	0	26	26
167.	Ababangali (Abagbangali)	0	0	0	29	29
168.	Avumangu	0	31	5	0	36
169.	Amuru (Abamuru, Ababamuru)	1	0	0	19	20
170.	Abangoro	24	35	2	0	61
171.	Abanguoto	22	0	0	2	24
172.	Abambaradi	0	0	0	52	52
173.	Abangapere	0	0	0	25	25
174.	Ababoro	0	3	17	0	20
175.	Abazibo	0	17	0	0	17
176.	Amorongono	0	0	0	28	28
177.	Abangbia	0	0	0	32	32
178.	Avozaba	0	40	0	0	40
179.	Abatambu (Abatangbu)	0	23	0	0	23
180.	Abayoro (Abayaro)	19	0	0	1	20
181.	Adogo	45	0	0	11	56
182.	Agbutu	55	3	0	8	66
183.	Abuda (Ababuda)	12	0	0	5	17
184.	Amego	27	0	0	5	32
185.	Abanganya (Abaganya)	3	0	0	24	27
186.	Abangbuka	0	0	0	22	22
187.	Ambura	0	16	0	0	16
188.	Abaika	0	13	10	0	23
	Unclassified	375	592	455	764	2,186
	Totals	13,711	8,767	2,988	8,169	33,635

What conclusions may we draw from the above table? First, we may say that it confirms what Azande themselves say, that when the original nucleus of the present-day Azande, the Ambomu under their Avongara royal house, conquered the territories which the Azande now occupy they were scattered far and wide among the conquered peoples, and also, though the table in its presentation here does not show this, that they preferred to reside in districts directly ruled over by their kings rather than in areas administered by royal representatives.[1] It must be admitted that there is a certain difficulty here, and one which in Zande eyes is somewhat delicate, for people are not always prepared to acknowledge that their clans are of foreign origin, and therefore, by implication, socially inferior. I do not pursue this question further, for it is sufficient to know that everybody recognizes as true Ambomu such clans as the Abakundo, Agiti, Agbambi, Angbapiyo, Aboro, Angbadimo, Ambata, and Akalingo, all of which are found in all four regions in, in most cases, relatively large numbers. I do not attempt to estimate more than in a very rough and general way the proportion of Ambomu to the total population when I hazard the opinion that, even if all claims to pure Mbomu descent were to be accepted, in none of the areas would the Ambomu clans much exceed half the population. This would be more apparent had more or less solid blocks of foreigners still speaking their own languages—Auma, Basiri, Bongo, Babukur (Buguru), etc.—been included in the survey. Reuben evidently felt that this lay outside his directive, so such peoples have only been listed where they are individuals forming part of the general Azande amalgam and not where they are peripheral groups. My reasons for the opinion which I have expressed will be presented later,[2] when a division into Ambomu clans and *Auro*, or foreign, clans will be attempted and a numerical computation made on the basis of it.

Secondly, the lists show that whilst some of the conquered and politically absorbed peoples are also widely scattered, having in all probability been the earliest conquered and enrolled into the armies of further conquest, others are concentrated, except for a few individuals, in one or other of the four

[1] This is also suggested by Junker, op. cit., 1891, p. 469.
[2] See Chap. II.

areas or can at any rate be labelled western (B and C) or eastern (A and D) clans. A glance at the pages of the register is sufficient to tell one to which area they refer. If, for example, we find the clan names of Abayali, Ababanduo, Abagende, Abakpanda, Abakango, Ababali, or Ababaimo occurring several times, we may be sure that the lists refer to the old principality of Mange (D); or where we see the names Abakpa, Amogba, Avuzukpo, Avugioro, Abadumbo, or Avonamangi we may conclude that this part of the census was made in one of the western kingdoms (B and C). As will be seen from the table, in some cases a single entry is a sufficient clue to provenance. When the four areas are broken down into districts we find that the localization of these foreign clans is even more pronounced, certain clans being in the main restricted not only to one or other of the four regions of the table but to a particular district of that region. The geographical and political distribution of these clans undoubtedly reflects ethnic differences in the different parts of the Sudan into which the Avongara–Ambomu moved in the course of their northward migrations. It also suggests that some of the foreign peoples who now form part of the Azande amalgam submitted without putting up strong resistance and were left in their homes. Otherwise we might expect to find their clans more widely scattered. This suggestion is supported by the presence of foreign groups still culturally distinct in various parts of Sudan Zandeland, and by other considerations. The breaking-up and scattering of the indigenous foreign population seems to have been greatest in area A, where the Ambomu were most strongly represented, where the fighting against foreign peoples (mostly Amiangba and Amadi) is said to have been fiercest, and where the process of assimilation began the soonest and has probably been the quickest and, except in places on its northern and north-eastern limits, the most complete. Nevertheless, we may speak also of central clans, those found exclusively, or almost so, in areas A or B, or both A and B, and not at all, or only rarely, in the wing areas C and D, e.g. Akurungu, Abagbaga, Abatukpo, Avuduma, and Abangbata.

Thirdly, the figures on the whole substantiate the statement by Azande of the old kingdom of Bazingbi (A) that the majority of the Ambomu followed the fortunes of the House of Yakpati (Bazingbi's father), only a minority attaching themselves to the

House of Nunga and other royal houses. The crude figures do not show this, but if we take as a sample the eight Ambomu clans mentioned earlier, we find that their percentage of the total population of area A is about double (20 per cent) that of the total population of area C. It is also much higher than the corresponding figures for areas B and D, which is what one might expect, since these two areas are a spill-over from area A, area D, with the lowest percentage, being the area of most recent settlement.

Fourthly, the lists are useful in giving us an indication of the relative numerical strengths of the various clans, and they are particularly valuable in this respect in that they enable us to make an approximate estimate of the strength of the royal clan of the Avongara. It is possible that this clan was unduly favoured in the census in that its members may have taken special care that their names were recorded and perhaps sometimes the names of sons who would have been considered too young for inclusion had they not been nobles. Perhaps, also, my clerk, being himself a noble, had a greater interest to record membership of his clan than of commoner clans. The register sometimes gives this impression, blocks of Avongara names occurring as is seldom the case with commoner clans, but this may well be accounted for by the nobles having been together at court or having been given precedence in the order of recording. But even if there has been a slight bias in favour of the royal clan, it could have been only slight and does not lessen the significance of their numerical proponderance. This is a fact of great interest when compared with the size of other royal clans, e.g. in the Southern Sudan those of the Shilluk and the Anuak, a growth readily understandable where some superiority of status and wealth is combined with polygamy. It eventually leads in some degree to a differentiation of social class rather than of simple political status. Altogether, 1,382 Avongara were listed, making them the largest single clan in the Sudan, the Agiti, with 1,294, coming next. This means that they are just over 4 per cent of the total population registered. If they are in much the same ratio in other parts of Zandeland there must be at least some 4,000 adult male Avongara in the whole of Zandeland and therefore at a very minimum 10,000 Avongara of both sexes and of all ages. As all Avongara trace their descent from Ngura, a man who, if the genealogies are correct, lived eight generations ago, we might view the genealogy with suspicion or even reject it out of hand as spurious; but I would myself hesitate to do so on these grounds alone. All the more important members of the royal lineage had many wives; and one has seen in the Arab world, with some restrictions on polygamy, how the descendants of a dominant person have in the course of a few generations multiplied into something numerically comparable to clans. After the Avongara, it is the Ambomu, what we may perhaps call the privileged, clans which have most members, possibly for the same reason, that they have been able to acquire a greater number of women than members of clans of foreign origin.

The Avongara spread in all directions with the armies of conquest, and their harems were probably, almost certainly, as large in other territories as those who conquered Sudanese territory. It is therefore possible that in other parts of Zandeland they are as numerous as in the Sudan. This may be the case also with some of the Ambomu clans, but if what Azande say is correct, as I believe it to be, that the great majority of the Ambomu population followed the House of Yakpati, then we may expect to find that they are less numerous and form a smaller percentage of the population in all parts of Zandeland except those ruled by descendants of Yakpati, our areas A, B, and D and the old kingdoms of Wando and Malingindo, territories bordering A, B, and D to the south in what was till recently the Belgian Congo. Nevertheless, such clans as the Agiti, Agbambi, Akalingo, and Akowe must each number through the length and breadth of Zandeland several thousands. The foreign clans are for the most part more localized and much smaller. This is evident from the table, for which it can be asserted without doubt that all those with the smallest representation are of foreign origin. Their spread in the Sudan is usually restricted, and since they are descendants of peoples at one time independent in Sudanese areas, they are in most instances unlikely to be found in numbers elsewhere—clans of the Amadi, Amiangba, and Abarambo peoples being excepted; many members of these may be in the Congo, for some of them were resident there at the time of the Ambomu conquests and others seem to have turned southwards at the onslaughts of Yakpati and his sons. Some of the clans of area C may be, and probably are, distributed in what used to be French Equatorial Africa, though to what extent and in what numbers there is no means of telling.

The conclusions set forth must be regarded as tentative. If someone were to compile, if only as samples here and there, figures for Zande clans in what used to be the Belgian Congo and French Equatorial Africa, firmer and more general conclusions might be reached, and others might be substituted for what can at present be no more than conjecture. Since such figures are lacking, all that can be stated is that most of the important Ambomu clans of the Sudan are mentioned by de Calonne-Beaufaict, Hutereau, Czekanowski, or Lagae[1] in their works on the Azande as occurring in the Congo, though there are many other Zande clans listed by them, especially in Czekanowski's lists, which do not occur in my table, and many in my tables which are not listed by them.

[1] See under these names in the Bibliography.

CLANS AND SETTLEMENTS

THE previous chapter listed 188 Zande clans and showed the distribution of their members in the Sudanese part of Zandeland. However, the areas into which Zandeland was divided for the purpose of marking clan distributions were so large that it was possible for there to be much localization of clan members without this appearing in the figures given. I feel, therefore, that it is desirable to go a step further by demonstrating that there is very great admixture of clans on the neighbourhood level. It is important to establish this point because it illustrates strikingly how unimportant, by comparison with many primitive societies, kinship ties beyond those of the closest kin can be in politically more developed societies, and especially in one in which wars of conquest have led to widespread dispersal and great ethnic admixture and social and cultural assimilation; and how tenuous and more or less nominal clan relationship can be in such societies. This being the case with the Azande, I found, after taking down a few genealogies at the commencement of my studies, that, except in the royal clan, genealogical relationships between clansmen were very seldom known and usually quite untraceable, and that even first and second cousins were so widely dispersed that the relationships could have little significance for conduct. Consequently I took down no more of them.

What I now present are the clan affiliations of twelve Zande settlements. Before sleeping-sickness regulations forced them into settlements, the Azande of the Sudan, as those elsewhere, lived in dispersed homesteads. However, when they were forced to live in settlements they were able to live in which settlements they preferred and, in fact, the people who in the dispersed state lived in the same neighbourhood generally continued their neighbourhood relationship in the settlements. Further, the admixture of clans in the settlements was no more, as observation established, than in the districts where the people were still living in the traditional dispersed manner. To make this inquiry as representative as possible three settlements have been chosen from each of the four areas shown in the sketch-map (p. 3). The selection was a random one, but since making it I have taken the precaution of examining the clan representation in a large number of other districts to make sure that the examples are typical.

In the lists which follow 1 to 3 were in the old kingdom of Gbudwe (A) and in the areas ruled in 1930 by Princes Ngindo (headman, Badindo of the Agbutu clan), Gangura (headman, Kasia of the Agiti clan), and Zegi (headman, Debu of the Abaningba clan); 4 to 6 were in the old kingdom of Ezo (B) and ruled by Princes Iriwo (headman, Bapia of the Avubanga clan), Bakindo (headman, Tikimo of the Akpongboro clan), and Rikita (headman, Agebati of the Amegburu clan); 7 to 9 were in the old kingdom of Tembura (C) and ruled by his son Renzi (headmen, Kpitio of the Avuzukpo clan, Munzali of the Auboli clan, and Gbaki of the Avombili clan); and 10 to 12 were in the old province, almost an independent kingdom, of Prince Mange, Gbudwe's second son, and ruled by Prince Ngindo (headman, Degbe of the Angbadimo clan), Prince Sanango (headman, Bangeremenze of the Abangombi clan), and the important commoner governor Yangu (headman, Fotimbia of the Abowoyo clan).

TABLE II

(1) 263 individuals and 63 clans

Abawoli	15	Abandiko	5	Angali	2
Agiti	15	Amiandi	5	Akenge	2
Akowe	14	Angbadimo	5	Abazaa	2
Agbunduku	12	Abisiaka	5	Angumbe	2
Abangbara	12	Abapia	5	Avokili	2
Amenguna	11	Akpura	4	Abatiko	2
Ameteli	10	Angbapio	4	Abaaya	2
Abakundo	9	Avuduma	4	Agbambi	2
Ambata	9	Akulongbo	3	Abandogo	2
Abanduo	9	Ambare	3	Abakpuro	2
Akalingo	8	Abadigo	3	Avundugba	1
Abamburo	8	Angbaya	3	Avundukuro	1
Agbutu	8	Abakpoto	3	Amindamu	1
Abaiwo	8	Amizoro	3	Abasiri	1
Abadara	7	Angbaga	3	Abangere	1
Abangombi	6	Avumaka	3	Amigudo	1

Aremete	1	Akudere	1	Akurungu	1
Asekere	1	Abatukpo	1	Abakpara	1
Abamunga	1	Agberenya	1	Angbuki	1
Abawoyo	1	Abauro	1	Adogo	1
Avungbadi	1	Ababua	1	Amiandi	1

(2) 106 individuals and 32 clans

Ameteli	22	Avokili	2	Abadara	1
Agiti	14	Amigudo	2	Abanzuka	1
Akulongbo	11	Aboro	2	Ambata	1
Abamburo	8	Amego	2	Ambare	1
Akpura	7	Abakpara	2	Abanguli	1
Angbadimo	5	Abauro	2	Adio	1
Akowe	3	Andabili	1	Angumbe	1
Angali	3	Agbambi	1	Akalingo	1
Avunduo	2	Akenge	1	Abangpara	1
Abakpoto	2	Avotombo	1	Apise	1
Abangombi	2	Abangali	1		

(3) 54 individuals and 26 clans

Ambare	7	Abagbaga	2	Angumbe	1
Amenguna	6	Abanzuma	2	Abakundo	1
Abaningba	3	Abatukpo	2	Ambata	1
Abagbate	3	Abangboto	2	Abakpoto	1
Avundukuro	3	Avunduo	2	Abale	1
Abalingi	3	Aremete	1	Abangombi	1
Angbapiyo	3	Avoando	1	Ameteli	1
Akulongbo	3	Abakpuro	1	Akowe	1
Abamburo	2	Akenge	1		

(4) 126 individuals and 28 clans

Avubanga	33	Ametanga	4	Abatiko	1
Amegburu	10	Abaigo	3	Akulongbo	1
Abandogo	9	Angbingiwi	3	Avuba	1
Abangbani	8	Akpongboro	2	Avudima	1
Anguli	7	Avotombo	2	Akalingo	1
Avugioro	7	Afutu	2	Avungbani	1
Abiri	7	Abare	2	Abatambu	1
Abasiri	6	Abagoro	2	Abangbara	1
Abakianga	5	Abakure	1		
Avodokpo	4	Abaumo	1		

(5) 111 individuals and 51 clans

Abatiko	9	Abarumbo	3	Auboli	2
Agiti	7	Avungbadi	3	Avonama	2
Abandogo	6	Avugioro	3	Amegano	2
Angbaga	5	Apambage	3	Abamango	2
Abadara	4	Abaze	3	Abakangba	2
Akulongbo	4	Akparandi	3	Akurungu	2
Abangboto	4	Avudugba	2	Aboro	2
Ametanga	4	Avudima	2	Avumungu	2
Akpongboro	3	Abambaragba	2	Abire	1

Angbingiwi	1	Agbambi	1	Ambarawa	1
Abanduku	1	Abarunzo	1	Aburungbu	1
Abaigo	1	Abadangba	1	Abagbalimo	1
Abasiambu	1	Avundo	1	Abaanya	1
Abakaya	1	Anguli	1	Avuduma	1
Adio	1	Ababara	1	Angali	1
Abakpa	1	Amenguna	1	Angbadimo	1
Abadugu	1	Avugbate	1	Abagua	1

(6) 126 individuals and 41 clans

Amegburu	13	Akurungu	3	Agbaya	1
Abangbata	12	Agbambi	3	Abara	1
Abakpuro	8	Angbapio	3	Ababaya	1
Abatiko	7	Aduruwe	2	Amizoro	1
Amegano	6	Anguli	2	Amenguna	1
Abananga	6	Abangoro	2	Avunduo	1
Amegbara	5	Abagbaga	2	Ametanga	1
Augu	5	Abangombi	2	Angumbe	1
Abandogo	5	Abakundo	2	Akalingo	1
Akulongbo	5	Abarumbo	1	Avotombo	1
Abandiko	4	Avugioro	1	Abagbaya	1
Abaigo	4	Abangau	1	Akurungu	1
Aremete	4	Abangba	1	Abanzuma	1
Abaningba	3	Abakangba	1		

(7) 129 individuals and 48 clans

Avuzukpo	14	Abawiya	2	Amenguli	1
Abadugu	10	Amogba	2	Aupia	1
Auboli	9	Avukida	2	Amenguna	1
Ametanga	9	Abadanga	2	Angbadimo	1
Abakpa	7	Avokili	2	Abangau	1
Abananga	7	Agburuwa	2	Abavuru	1
Agiti	5	Abakangba	2	Auma	1
Abasiri	5	Akpongboro	1	Akalingo	1
Afutu	4	Abaga	1	Abarebu	1
Abadara	4	Abakunya	1	Abakpuro	1
Abambaragba	3	Avoando	1	Avudima	1
Avugioro	3	Ababanga	1	Abalingi	1
Avodai	3	Andogo	1	Abagbaya	1
Abadumbo	3	Ayama	1	Abangere	1
Avungbadi	2	Avubali	1	Abangbara	1
Abandimo	2	Abawoyo	1	Akulongbo	1

(8) 130 individuals and 53 clans

Abakpa	8	Amogba	4	Angbadimo	3
Avudima	7	Abakuma	4	Abakangba	3
Abananga	6	Avungbadi	4	Abarumbo	3
Avonamangi	6	Agiti	4	Apambage	2
Abatiko	6	Adio	3	Abanduru	2
Auboli	5	Abangbani	3	Abasiri	2
Abaigo	5	Avodai	3	Avudiko	2
Akulongbo	5	Avugbate	3	Abadugu	2

Angbuki	2	Abarambo	1	Ababaya	1
Abalingi	2	Avonama	1	Angbare	1
Angbapio	2	Abauro	1	Ametanga	1
Abagoro	2	Avubanga	1	Akowe	1
Avoando	2	Abangboto	1	Amegburu	1
Akalingo	2	Abangbai	1	Avuzukpo	1
Avumai	1	Avuruwa	1	Abakundo	1
Abanga	1	Anguli	1	Abandogo	1
Abarebu	1	Akpongboro	1	Abanziwa	1
Ababanga	1	Abara	1		

(9) 169 individuals and 63 clans

Angbadimo	11	Abakowe	3	Abagama	1
Agiti	11	Akalingo	3	Ababua	1
Angbaga	10	Abambaragba	2	Abangere	1
Akulongbo	8	Avunaze	2	Avukida	1
Akowe	7	Abalingi	2	Ambiro	1
Abasiri	7	Abara	2	Abanyoro	1
Avugioro	7	Abananga	2	Abanga	1
Avodai	7	Akparandi	2	Abandogo	1
Abawoyo	6	Abandia	2	Abakpoto	1
Abatiko	4	Avokagba	1	Abare	1
Avumai	4	Avombili	1	Abarambo	1
Avuruwa	4	Avodangba	1	Mbavilingo	1
Abangbinda	4	Abavuru	1	Agoro	1
Avunduo	4	Afutu	1	Apeneu	1
Abadugu	4	Abaza	1	Abawa	1
Abire	3	Akpongboro	1	Abaumbo	1
Abakundo	3	Akpakili	1	Abangengo	1
Avudima	3	Abakpa	1	Asangimba	1
Agbambi	3	Abungo	1	Amerengo	1
Andugu	3	Abakuma	1	Amosigbo	1
Auboli	3	Amogba	1	Ambare	1

(10) 99 individuals and 37 clans

Abaningo	9	Amabenge	2	Abakpuro	1
Abananga	8	Avunduo	2	Anyali	1
Abadigo	7	Angbadimo	2	Abayali	1
Ababiro	7	Abadara	2	Abaturu	1
Abangbandili	6	Abawoyo	2	Ambata	1
Abagioso	6	Abambiti	1	Ababaimo	1
Ababaza	6	Abuda	1	Abakupa	1
Abamunga	4	Angbaga	1	Akenge	1
Angali	4	Abalingi	1	Abakpangira	1
Abakangba	4	Akulongbo	1	Abagbatangbanga	1
Abakpanda	3	Abapia	1	Abanganzu	1
Angumbe	3	Angbapio	1		
Agberenya	3	Abandagburu	1		

(11) 62 individuals and 21 clans

Abananga	11	Ababaimo	6	Abangombi	4
Abakupa	7	Abangau	5	Abayali	4

Abiama	4	Abaigo	2	Ababangali	1
Akangani	3	Abagiali	1	Abakango	1
Abamunga	3	Akowe	1	Abaruvuro	1
Ababiro	2	Abawoli	1	Abangbara	1
Abagai	2	Abangbia	1	Ambiti	1

(12) 128 individuals and 36 clans

Abayali	15	Ababali	3	Abamunga	1
Abangbere	11	Agilibo	3	Adio	1
Abangbaya	10	Ababoyo	3	Ambuku	1
Abaipi	9	Abagbaya	3	Abia	1
Abaturu	8	Abarunzo	2	Angbaya	1
Abawoyo	8	Abadigba	2	Agiti	1
Abagende	6	Abangombi	2	Abaza	1
Ababanduo	5	Amundu	2	Abangoyo	1
Ababaza	5	Abanguru	2	Akalingo	1
Amorongono	4	Ababaya	2	Abagua	1
Abakaya	4	Ambata	2	Abagbuta	1
Abamage	4	Abandogo	1	Amuvo	1

On one point these figures speak for themselves: patrilineal ties beyond the family relationships of brothers and sons play little part in determining who lives where. What counts for more are maternal links, affinity, blood-brotherhood, personal friendship, a headman's reputation for generosity and good sense, and so forth. In Zandeland local groupings are not, except in the case of a few close neighbours, associated with clans or sections of clans, nor are they spoken about by any kinship reference. They are political and administrative units. What gives the group unity and distinctness is the common allegiance of its members to a king or prince through his representative in their community appointed by him to look after his affairs in that neighbourhood. It is only in this political sense that one can properly speak of local groups at all, for they are not otherwise distinct groups. The fact that in some cases the headman's clan is well represented in a community might suggest that his clansmen have settled near him on account of common clanship, but it may be chance, for it can equally bear the interpretation that because the clan is numerically prominent in the area the likelihood of a headman being appointed from it is greater.

It is of further interest to inquire what proportion of the men of the various settlements are true Azande (Ambomu) and what proportion are of foreign stock. To anyone acquainted with the

Azande it is at once evident that a number of foreigners are listed, for some men, instead of giving their clan name, have given a tribal name, e.g. Abasiri, Abare, Auma, Ababua, Amundu, Abangbinda, etc.; and had these tribal names been broken down into clan names the total number of clans would have been greater than those listed. Sometimes, as earlier suggested, a tribal name appears to have become a clan name, the original clan being submerged, or even forgotten. Many of the clan names also at once by their uncouth forms suggest a non-Zande origin. Nevertheless, it is a rather involved, and sometimes slightly embarrassing matter to determine with regard to other clans whether they are to be reckoned as being of original Zande (Mbomu) stock or of foreign origin. Azande tend to class their clans as (1) Akulongbo or Avongara, the ruling clan; (2) Ambomu, the original Zande clans who followed the Avongara in their conquests; (3) named foreign stocks, Adio, Abarambo or Amiangba, Amadi, and Abangbinda, all considerable peoples now assimilated to the Ambomu; and (4) *Auro*, a heterogeneous collection of clans of unspecified foreign peoples, also, when found in the present-day ethnic amalgam, assimilated to the Ambomu, but regarded by them more as foreigners than are the named stocks. Whilst there is no doubt who are *Auro*, there is not always agreement whether a clan belongs to the Mbomu cluster or to one of the four named peoples. Sixteen clans,[1] including the Akulongbo, I regard as undoubtedly Ambomu and I include also in this category five others[2] about which there was a difference of opinion.[3] This is an ethnic classification. A social classification would be somewhat different, since some of the Adio cluster are now regarded as being equivalent to Ambomu, and some of the Amadi, Abarambo, and Abangbinda as being more or less so. However, accepting the dubious cases as Ambomu and excluding on ethnic grounds those who are now socially in, or almost in, the Ambomu category,

[1] Akulongbo, Agiti, Akalingo, Angbadimo, Angumbe, Avotombo, Abadara, Angbaga, Abakundo, Ambata, Agbambi, Aboro, Akurungu, Abauro, Abatiko, and Angbapio.

[2] Angbaya, Aremete, Abagbangi, Abawoyo, and Avokili.

[3] I do not enter here into a complicated, and perhaps insoluble, problem. Some individuals and groups of foreign origin have attached themselves to Mbomu clans and claim membership of them, and when this has happened it cannot always be determined who is a true member and who is not.

we have the following approximate percentages of Ambomu for each of the twelve settlements: (1) 30, (2) 41, (3) 17, (4) 4, (5) 32, (6) 27, (7) 12, (8) 18, (9) 35, (10) 13, (11) 0, (12) 10.

It was established in Chapter I that the Ambomu are most numerous in area A, then in area B, and least numerous in areas C and D. The percentages for the twelve settlements are not, being a very small random sample, an entirely adequate representation of the situation in the areas as a whole. Using the same classification of clans, the approximate percentages of Ambomu in the four regions in which a census was conducted are: (A) 39, (B) 27, (C) 19, and (D) 17; and for all four areas 29. It remains to determine from the information recorded the degree of ethnic admixture on a provincial, as distinct from a kingdom or a district (settlement), level and, in particular, the correctness of the Zande statements that the Ambomu are most strongly represented in the province ruled directly by a king in person rather than in provinces ruled by royal representatives. This task has yet to be undertaken, as has also the more difficult task of attempting to break down the category of foreigners into its different ethnic elements and to compute their numerical contribution to the Zande amalgam.[1]

What has been attempted and shown here and in the previous chapter is that both in kingdoms and on the small-neighbour-hood level there has come about a most remarkable assimilation of different foreign peoples in Zande society, a product of conquest and of its political institutions. It has been, on a smaller scale, as considerable an achievement as can be claimed by, shall we say, the United States or Israel.

[1] Since writing the above a totting up of the census figures shows that easily the largest representation in the Sudan is that of the Abarambo (Amiangba), who are mostly to be found in area A of the sketch-map on p. 3 with a fair spill-over into B. The Adio and Bangbinda are mostly in A with a spill-over into D and with the Adio to a lesser degree into B. Such few Amadi as were listed were all in A or B. Those who gave their tribe as Bukuru were almost exclusively in D. The Pambia, the Basiri, and the Akare were mainly in B and C.

III

ETHNIC COMPOSITION OF
ZANDE SOCIETY

THE Zande language predominates from 23° to 30° Long.
E. and from 3° to 6° Lat. N. and in some places extends
beyond these limits.[1] As Professor Tucker[2] notes, it is
remarkable, considering the area covered by it and the number
of peoples belonging to different language-groups—Sudanic,
Bantu, Nilotic, and Nilo-Hamitic—who today speak it, that it
has developed only five, and those not very divergent, dialects.
It is also remarkable that, without any technological superiority,
those who built this empire were able to conquer such vast
territories and to weld their inhabitants into a single people.
That they succeeded was certainly due in the main to their
greatly superior political organization.[3] It was only when they
came up against peoples, the Abandiya and the Mangbetu, who
had a political organization comparable to their own that they
were unable to make headway. The other peoples who tried to
resist them and were defeated and displaced or subjugated
were, according to all the information we possess, ill organized
politically, having nothing like the Zande statal organs. On the
contrary, living in small communities at variance with each
other and lacking common direction, they sooner or later fell a
prey to the invader and became politically, and to an increasing
extent culturally, part of the great complex we know today as
the Azande. It is the purpose of this chapter to examine this
complex for the whole of Zandeland, so far as its ethnic composition is concerned, and to analyse its component elements.

Several of the early explorers of Zandeland remarked on the
great admixture of peoples comprising the population. Junker,[4]
for example, describes 'the motley mixture of broken tribes and
scattered populations', servile peoples (Amadi, Basiri, Augu,

[1] C. R. Lagae and V. H. Vanden Plas, op. cit., vol. i, 1921, p. 9.
[2] A. N. Tucker, *The Eastern Sudanic Languages*, vol. i, 1940, p. 17.
[3] See Chap. X.   [4] Op. cit., 1891, pp. 198–9.

and Maranga) with speech and habits and customs different from those of the Azande, in the comparatively small territory of Palembata (in the neighbourhood of 4° N. and 27° E.). He refers elsewhere[1] to Abarambo colonies among the Azande to the south of the Bomokandi and to Zande colonies among the Abarambo to the north of it, both peoples being in these areas subjects of the Zande prince Bakangai; and Casati,[2] speaking of the same prince, says that the population of his domains is composed of Azande, Abarambo, and Mabisanga. Junker again[3] says of the areas ruled by Zemio and his brother Wando in the Valley of the Mbomu that the ruling Azande class was greatly inferior in numbers to the other inhabitants (Akare, Basiri, Abarambo, and—whoever the following peoples may be, for Junker did not venture to determine their affinities— Shirwas, Ababullos, Embiddimas, and Apakelle). Then, once again:[4] 'As in many other northern lands, Linda's territory [about 5° 20″ N. and 26° 20″ E.] was occupied, besides the dominant Zandehs, by Bashirs, A-Barmbos, A-Biri, A-Pambia, and other subject tribes.'

It is not surprising that those who came after these explorers and could make their observations in easier circumstances have frequently remarked on the same phenomenon. The Polish ethnographer Czekanowski, for example, gave special attention[5] to the ethnic constitution of the Zande kingdoms, noting that the Zande conquerors are a sparse ruling class in vast areas, in many of which the greater part of the population are foreign peoples who have retained their distinctive character (Abarambo, Akare, Ampambia, Basiri, Makere, Mundu, Momvu, etc.). In the more thickly populated south, with which Czekanowski was personally acquainted, the 'serf' population includes peoples of many alien stocks who have been conquered but not yet assimilated: south of the Bomokandi scarcely a quarter of the population belong either racially or culturally to the politically dominant Zande elements, for the Makere, the greater part of the population, have kept their identity intact. In Bavungara's province, near Vankerckhovenville, the ratio

[1] Ibid., p. 466.　　　　　　　　　[2] Op. cit., vol. i, p. 198.
[3] Op. cit., 1892, p. 148.
[4] Ibid., p. 307. See also Von Wiese in Mecklenburg-Schwerin, *From the Congo to the Niger and the Nile*, 1913, p. 210.
[5] Op. cit., pp. 21–6.

is only about 80 male Azande to hundreds of Momvu, and in the neighbouring territory ruled by Bokoyo the situation is similar. He concludes[1] that the Zande clans stem mainly from these foreign stocks and that it has been the power of the Avongara ruling house that has integrated all these heterogeneous elements into the present Azande people.

When I have made statements without citing authority for them it must be understood that on those points our main sources are in agreement, the statements being a summary of the different records and confirmed in the areas known to me personally by my own experience. If I do not add much that is original to what others have said I can at least, in a condensed form, once more draw attention to the great ethnic complexity of Zande society. Czekanowski is one of my authorities for this chapter, but I have chiefly relied on Vanden Plas, and after him on Junker, de Calonne-Beaufaict, Hutereau, Larken, and Maes and Boone. The historical processes involved in, and the social consequences resulting from, ethnic amalgamations of this kind and on this scale (for they are found in many other African states) have not, I think, been sufficiently appreciated. The cultural effects have also been important, but they must await separate treatment.[2] Here little more is attempted than a brief review of the ethnic elements which constitute the present-day Azande.

The Avongara are the ruling aristocracy in by far the greater part of Zandeland. The Ambomu are their original subjects, and it is their language that the Azande speak. When one speaks of Azande one speaks of all those who use Zande as their mother tongue.[3] Nevertheless we have sometimes to distinguish in the area ruled by the Avongara between Azande of Ambomu descent (*Azande ni Ambomu*) and Azande of assimilated stocks (*Azande ni Auro*) who have been completely, or almost completely, assimilated culturally to the Avongara–Ambomu. A like distinction is doubtless made in Zande territories where the Avongara are not the rulers, but where they once were. We may speak of those peoples who still speak their own languages but are, within Zande territory or on its confines, politically under

---

[1] Czekanowski, op. cit., p. 43.   [2] See Part 2.

[3] Azande themselves use the word in such a sense, but they also use it in some contexts in the sense of 'commoners' in contrast to the Avongara.

Zande domination as subject peoples. They are, in varying degrees, in the process of becoming Azande. Some of these subject peoples are elsewhere independent. Some foreign peoples, although never subjugated by the Azande, were raided by them or came under their influence and have thereby contributed in a lesser degree to the formation of the ethnic conglomeration of the Azande people. The term 'Niamniam', a foreign, perhaps Dinka, designation, is best avoided as it has been used by Arabs and Europeans without much discrimination to refer not only to both Azande and their subject peoples but also to almost any people in the area under consideration. It was for some of them a very confused representation—cannibals, men with tails, etc.

The Avongara or Akolongbo, as they also call themselves, are today in speech and habits, if we except aristocratic modes of behaviour and mannerisms peculiar to their class, indistinguishable from their followers, and we have no evidence that they have ever been otherwise, though they themselves would not admit to being of Ambomu stock, saying that they are Akolongbo or Avongara of *Agbia*, 'noble', stock. In the first half of the eighteenth century—there seems to be little doubt about the broad outline of the facts—the Ambomu people, who at that time lived in the valleys of the Mbomu (hence their name) and the Shinko rivers, began to move, under Avongara leadership, first to the south-east and thence north, east, and south. These migrations, the causes of which we do not know, continued till checked by Arab and European opposition in the second half of the last century and in the first decade of the present century, and in the course of them the Zande people was formed. The Ambomu clans are consequently found in most, probably all, parts of Zandeland; but they are mostly, we have reason to believe as has earlier been noted, to be found in the territories ruled by the descendants of King Yakpati, on both sides of the Nile–Congo divide roughly between Long. 27° 30″ and 29° 30″. There they have a slightly enhanced social position in virtue of their descent from their conquering forebears, but it must be said that Azande do not attach great importance to whether a man is of Ambomu stock or not; there has been too much intermarriage for this to count much. What can be said is rather that the Ambomu have a long tradition of attachment

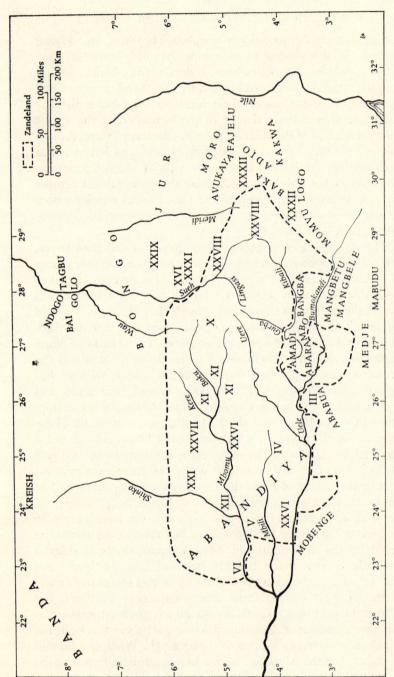

SKETCH 2. PEOPLES CONTRIBUTING TO THE ZANDE COMPLEX.

TABLE III

Peoples Contributing to the Zande Complex

Almost assimilated culturally		Still speaking own languages		Minor contributors to Azande	
SUDANIC					
I	Abandiya	X	Apambia	XXXII	Mundu
II	Adio	XI	Basiri	XXXIII	Avukaya
III	Abwameli	XII	Biri	XXXIV	Jur peoples
IV	Angada	XIII	Medje	XXXV	Moro peoples
V	Nzakara	XIV	Momvu	XXXVI	Logo
VI	Nzakara	XV	Mangbele		
VII	Abarambo	XVI	Mbegumba		
VIII	Amadi	XVII	Bongo		
IX	Bangba	XVIII	Golo		
		XIX	Tabbu		
		XX	Bai		
		XXI	Gobu		
		XXII	Kreish		
		XXIII	Banda		
		XXIV	Ndogo		
		XXV	Baka		
BANTU					
		XXVI	Ambili	XXXVII	Mabudu
		XXVII	Akare	XXXVIII	Ababua
		XXVIII	Abuguru	XXXIX	Mobenge
		XXIX	Huma		
		XXX	Abangbinda		
NILOTIC					
		XXXI	Mberidi		
NILO-HAMITIC					
				XL	Fajelu
				XLI	Kakwa

to their Avongara rulers and of familiarity with the polished life of courts, so that the standards of etiquette and manners obtaining at court are considered to be those of the Ambomu, and ignorance or contravention of them to be the behaviour of *Auro*, 'foreigners'.

Some peoples have entirely lost their cultural identity in the Zande amalgam but, through many vicissitudes, their ethnic distinctiveness and political independence have survived. This appears to be the case with the Sudanic Abandiya, who live in the most western part of Zandeland to the west of Long. 26° E. Junker[1] says that they moved into this area from the

[1] Op. cit., 1892, pp. 241–2.

Mbomu–Makua confluence when the Avongara–Ambomu left it to migrate to the south and east and that by this time they had already become vassals of the Arabo-Nubians. De Calonne[1] says that of their own accord they adopted not only the Zande language but also the Zande political institutions, but I find it difficult to believe that they would have done this so completely if they had not been at some period subject to the Avongara; and I find it easier therefore to accept Vanden Plas's statement[2] that they are an ethnically mixed people ruled by the Abaza (whose language a few old people still speak) who, after pro-longed combats, were finally subjugated by the Avongara, though, as was their policy in dealing with subjugated peoples, the Avongara left them their own Abaza rulers, with whom they made alliances. The Nzakara also only speak a dialect of Zande today, having lost their original Banda dialect. They appear to be strongly influenced by the Abandiya, on the limits of whose territory they live in two separated stretches of country towards the extreme western limits of Zandeland. The situation in this region is still, however, not entirely clear, and accounts vary.

There are a great many of the Adio people in the Zande population and they are found in all parts of Zandeland.[3] Some of them form a politically independent group (though cultur-ally in all important respects like other Azande and speaking only Zande) known as Makaraka or Azande-Bamboy, in the valley of the Tore, tributary of the Yei. They are thus the most easterly section (Long. 30° 30″ E.) of the Azande and, being isolated from the rest, have mixed much with neighbouring peoples. They are part of the Abile migration, as one of the Zande migrations came to be designated, and, I was told, adopted Zande speech and customs during the time they were conquered and ruled by the brothers and sons of Renzi, son of Yakpati, one of whom, Muduba, carried them with him in his

---

[1] Op. cit., p. 83.   [2] Lagae and Vanden Plas, op. cit., p. 14.

[3] Some people give Adio as their clan name. Clans of the Adio are the Akowe, Abananga, Andebili, Abangbai, and Apise. There may be others (Akudere, Ambari, Agbutu). De Calonne (p. 223) gives a list of Adio clans, but I do not find it acceptable. Vanden Plas (op. cit., 1921, p. 14) says that there are a people called Adiyo, fishermen on the Mbili, among the Abandiya who still speak their own Sudanic language, but these may be of a different ethnic group to those being discussed.

migration to the east. When, at Muduba's death, his men, faced with starvation, returned westwards, they left the Adio behind them where we now find them independent of Avongara rule. They would probably have been brought under it by Mange son of Gbudwe had not the Egyptian Government established military posts in the area.

De Calonne says[1] that there is another people, at one time closely associated with the Adio, the Abwameli, who, though they speak Zande, are not under Avongara rule. To escape subjugation by Ndeni son of Tombo, they fled into Ababua country, where they remain independent near the junction of 3° Lat. N. and 26° Long. E. The same author mentions other peoples who accompanied the Adio and Abwameli in their original migration. Whoever these people may have been, today they exist no more as distinct ethnic groups, with the possible exception of the Angada, who, though no longer a cohesive group, appear to be to some extent localized, though mixed with Avongara–Ambomu and speaking only Zande,[2] in a pocket in Abandiya country on the Mbili, north of Lat. 4° N. and between 25° and 26° Long. E. Elsewhere they have been scattered and absorbed by Azande and Abandiya.

Other peoples, or sections of them, have totally, or almost totally, lost both political and cultural identity and are entirely, or almost entirely, merged in the Zande amalgam, where they can be distinguished from the Ambomu only by their clan names and, so the Ambomu say, their boorish habits when they have not learnt to abandon them by contact with the polite society of courts. One of these is the Bantu Abangbinda, a once numerous people. After conquest by Yakpati and his descendants, their final resistance being broken by Gbudwe, they were almost completely absorbed by the Azande, though here and there in small groups their language is not entirely forgotten. I was able to take down vocabularies from some of the older people. They are one of the biggest elements of foreign origin in the Sudan to the east of the Lingasi.[3] Another

[1] Op. cit., p. 98.

[2] G. Van Bulck, and P. Hackett, *Linguistic Survey of the Northern Bantu Borderland*, vol. i, 1956, p. 101, say that a handful still speak their own tongue, but this statement is based on hearsay.

[3] The following clans claim to be of Abangbinda origin: Abiama, Abakpara, Abuda, Abani, Ambura, Abadigo, Amabenge, Abambiti, Abaanya, Abagbuto,

completely assimilated people, according to Vanden Plas,[1] are the Mabisanga, a section of the Medje who were at one time subjects of the Mangbetu. When the Mangbetu king Munza's kingdom was dismembered by the Egyptians, they were subjugated by Ngula-Mange son of Kipa. Emin,[2] de Calonne,[3] and Czekanowski[4] say that the Egyptian Government appointed Mbitimo son of Wando to rule them.

A large proportion of the Abarambo, or Amiangba, and of the Amadi peoples have also been almost totally absorbed by the Azande. These once numerous peoples were dispersed and fractionized by bitterly fought wars with the Azande ruled by the House of Yakpati. However, some Abarambo to the south of the Uele still speak their own language and are commanded by their own notables, though under Avongara suzerainty, in Junker's time in the person of Bakengai;[5] and they are an independent people between that river and the Bomokandi, for although Bakengai's father, Kipa, had ruled them on both banks of the Bomokandi, those to the north had by Junker's time reasserted their independence. They are probably the largest single foreign element in the constitution of the Azande of the Sudan,[6] where one can still find persons who remember their original tongue, though it is no longer spoken. Czekanowski[7] thinks that they are the largest foreign element among the Azande as a whole. The greater part of the Amadi people, whose ancient name, de Calonne says,[8] was Amago (Amego) or Aogo (Augu), settled, after wars and migrations, around the chain of hills on 27° Long. E., where Junker[9] found them and

Abaningo, Abagbo, Anguli, Abangbaya, Abamunga, Abagua, Avuduma, Abambai, and possibly also the Abangbara.

[1] Lagae and Vanden Plas, op. cit., p. 21.
[2] Emin Pasha, *Emin Pasha in Central Africa*, 1888, p. 204.
[3] Op. cit., p. 130.   [4] Op. cit., pp. 176–7.
[5] Op. cit., 1891, p. 335.
[6] Some of their more important clans, in the Sudan mostly found in the old kingdom of Gbudwe, are: Aubali, Abawoli, Abazaa, Avumaka, Avonama, Avundukura, Abakpuro, Amuzungu, Agbunduku, Abandogo, Abalingi, Avunduo, Abakaya, Amigbara, Abagbate, Agberenya, Akpurandi, Abapia, Akpura, Amiandi, Abangombi, Akenge, Abaale, Abaiwo, Abangburu, Amiteli, Abandiko, Angali, Angbuki, Ambare, Abangboto, Abisiaka, Abangere, Abanganya, Abakpoto, Abangau, Avuzigba, Amindamu, Avukida, and Amizoro. There are others. See also P. M. Larken, *Sudan Notes and Records*, 6, 1923, p. 240.
[7] Op. cit., p. 210.   [8] Op. cit., p. 120.
[9] Op. cit., 1891, pp. 317–18.

where they are still independent today, though all speak Zande as well as their own Sudanic tongue. The rest of this at one time considerable people were dispersed by Yakpati and his sons and were finally absorbed into the Zande complex, their descendants being found today widely distributed in all the central and eastern regions of Zandeland. In view of the fact that the principal battleground between the Amadi with their Abarambo allies and the Azande was in the valley of the Sueh, it is surprising that so few men claim Amadi descent there today.[1] One reason for this appears to be that after the severe hammering they received from the Azande in the north the main body turned towards the south. Also, those who were left behind seem to have become to a large extent confounded with the Abarambo, so some of the clans often said to belong to the Amiangba (Abarambo) may be Amadi in origin.

Another people who must, I think, have been partly assimilated are the Sudanic Bangba, who today mostly live to the south of the Uele–Kibali on Long. 28° E., where they sought refuge after a bloody defeat at the hands of Ukwe son of Wando I believe that some of this people must have contributed to the Zande population because Vanden Plas says[2] that besides their own language and Mangbetu some speak Zande, which is gaining ground, and, although the same writer says that none of this group of Bangba are subjects of Avongara, when they lived further to the north, Schweinfurth,[3] who met them there in 1870, tells us that they, or at any rate a powerful section of them, were subjects of Wando son of Bazingbi, most of them speaking Zande. It is highly probable, therefore, that they have contributed to the population of his old kingdom.

In addition to the peoples already mentioned, Vanden Plas mentions[4] others as being of foreign origin but now completely, or almost completely, submerged: Abubage (some dozens of individuals still stammer out their ancient language in the valley of the Gurba); Amuvumba (five or six families at most, who live in the valley of the Sekunde, tributary of the Gurba);

---

[1] Some of their clans are said to be: Avondawa, Augu, Abubage, Abatuwa, Akaya, Abaningba, Abanzuma, Amego, Abatambu, and Angatali, but some of these were also said to be Amiangba clans. De Calonne mentions others (p. 121). Some give their ethnic title, Amadi, as their clan.

[2] Op. cit., p. 23. [3] Op. cit., vol. i, 1873, p. 522.
[4] Op. cit., pp. 16–22.

Ngbwaya, Ngobwu, and Tokpwo (infinitely small groups about which information is now unobtainable); Abotupwe (met with in the valley of the Poko, tributary of the Bomokandi); Asibali (met mainly among the Apambia and the Abuguru); and Abangombi, Angombe, and Aholi (all completely absorbed). Of these, the Ngobwu are probably the Gobu or Gabu, still found among the Abandiya[1] and entered on Junker's map as 'Ngobbu' between Long. 24° and 25° and just south of 6° Lat. N. The others are probably all clans of peoples listed already or later, and not distinct ethnic groups: the Abubage, an Amadi clan; the Abotupwe (Abatukpo), an Abarambo clan; the Asibali (Asigbali), probably a Basiri clan; the Abangombi, an Abarambo clan; the Angombe (Angumbe), an Ambomu clan; and so forth. Hutereau[2] mentions a Ngara people, now absorbed by the Abandiya, and shows them on his map to the south of the Mbomu between Long. 25° and 26° E. Junker[3] and Emin[4] mention an Apagumba people who migrated to the east with the Adio but who had, even in their day, almost completely disappeared in the Adio (Makaraka) amalgam. I believe this to be an old name for the Avotombo clan of the Ambomu. Junker has on his map 'Mambelli, a Zande tribe', in Ngangi's old kingdom (between 28° and 29° Long. E. and 5° and 6° Lat. N.). Czekanowski also shows them, in the same position, in his ethnographic map and expresses the opinion[5] that they are of the same stock as the Ambili, who are mentioned later. If this people was once a distinct ethnic group, it has disappeared today. The same must be said of various groups mentioned by Junker—Marango, Amasilli, Shirwas, Abadullos, etc.—some of which may figure in this account under other names, while others seem to have disappeared.

When we speak of subject peoples it must be understood that, while there was certainly some discrimination and something of what Major Larken, in speaking[6] of the treatment meted out to the Apambia by the Azande, calls bullying, to say that these peoples were in a servile position would, at any rate usually,

---

[1] S. H. F. Capenny, 'The Khedivic Possessions in the Basin of the Upper Ubangi', *The Scottish Geographical Magazine*, 1899, p. 313. Tucker, op. cit., 1940, p. 17.

[2] Op. cit., 1922, pp. 317–18.   [3] Op. cit., 1890, p. 480.

[4] Op. cit., pp. 375–6.   [5] Op. cit., p. 23.

[6] Op. cit., 1923, p. 238.

be an exaggeration. It is true that the Akare and Basiri have been called slaves and serfs, e.g. by Schweinfurth[1] and Chaltin,[2] and it is possible that this was indeed the case in the west where under Arab influence trading in slaves seems to have been practised by some of the Avongara rulers,[3] but it was the traditional Zande policy to encourage submitted peoples to accept Avongara rule voluntarily, to stay in their homes, and to become Azande; and one of the main principles in that policy was indirect rule. We are told time and again by our authorities that once a people submitted they were left with their own chiefs. I have already cited Vanden Plas to this effect in the case of the Abandiya and the Abarambo,[4] and the same author speaks in the same manner of the Abangbinda and the Basiri.[5] Professor Tucker[6] asserts the same of the Mbegumba and the Mberidi, and other authors could be quoted in support of the contention, which is very much my own opinion from what I observed among the Bongo, Baka, Abuguru, and other peoples. All that was asked of the subject peoples was recognition of Avongara suzerainty, that they should keep the peace, and a payment of tribute in labour and in kind to their rulers which was no more than Azande commoners contributed towards the upkeep of the courts. Bit by bit Azande infiltrated among them and married with them. Commoners of standing settled among them and encouraged them to adopt Zande habits and to speak the Zande tongue by offering them hospitality—it is through *bakinde*, food, Azande say, that men are subjugated (*zoga*), and by justice. They say: *Azande na ra fu agbia mbiko gagama ae*, 'Azande subject themselves to the princes on account of the gifts they receive from them'. Finally some princeling was sent by his father to rule them or did so on his own initiative, and through his court the people became more familiar with Zande institutions. That such peoples as have retained their own languages and to some extent their own traditional way of life have been able to do so is doubtless in part due to the imposition of European rule but it is also in part

---

[1] Op. cit., vol. 2, pp. 395–6.

[2] L. Lotar, *La Grande Chronique de l'Uele*, 1946, pp. 250–1.

[3] Schweinfurth, op. cit., vol. 2, pp. 417–18 and 430.

[4] Op. cit., p. 21.   [5] Ibid., pp. 16–17.

[6] A. N. Tucker, 'The tribal confusion around Wau', *Sudan Notes and Records*, 14 (1931), p. 54.

due to the fact that Azande treated what they considered, in their sophisticated way, to be barbaric foreign usages with good-humoured tolerance, and also in part to the further fact that often, like so many small peoples in other parts of the world, these conies dwelt among the rocks: even the names of some of them indicate this, e.g. Apambia and Belanda both mean hill-men.

The three principal subject peoples in the north, all speaking their own languages as well as Zande (the first two, Sudanic tongues, and the third a Bantu tongue), but entirely under Zande domination, are the Apambia, the Basiri (Sere), and the Akare. Only the main areas of their occupation are mentioned. There are pockets of them elsewhere, and very many of them have been absorbed by the Azande. The Apambia live among the granitic hills forming the crest of the Nile–Congo divide to the north of Lat. 5° N. Tembura son of Liwa established his rule over them; and they form today a large element in the ethnic composition of the area ruled by his son Renzi and in the old kingdom of Ezo.[1] The two largest groups of Basiri are between the Boku and the Kere and to the north and south of the Mbomu between Long. 26° and 27° E. There are also pockets of them in the Sudan. Vanden Plas[2] remarks that of the peoples submitted to the Azande, they and the Momvu have been the most refractory to the culture of the conqueror; and de Calonne[3] notes that Zandeization is more advanced among such Bantu peoples as the Abangbinda and the Abuguru than among peoples culturally nearer to the Azande, such as the Basiri. However, Schweinfurth[4] says that many of them had been assimilated to the Azande by 1871. The Akare form a compact group on both banks of the Mbomu between 25° and 27° Long. E. In what was the French Congo they are, says Vanden Plas,[5] mixed with Banda, Gobo, and Nzakara.[6] In the same region there is a small people called Biri, apparently still

---

[1] Some of their clans in these regions are: Abadugu, Avuzukpo, Abakpa, Avon-amangi, Abakumo, Avugioro, Ambaragba, Abamerenge, Andugu, and Abakowe (Larken, p. 237, but my spellings). See also Von Weise in Mecklenburg-Schwerin, op. cit., p. 230.

[2] Op. cit., p. 16.   [3] Op. cit., p. 14.
[4] Op. cit., vol. 2, pp. 395–6.   [5] Op. cit., p. 15.
[6] De Calonne, pp. 225–8, lists some of their clans: Alibu, Apomboro (?Akpong-boro), Abanzika, Abangeli, Abakuba, etc.

speaking their ancient Sudanic tongue, to the east of the Mbomu–Shinko confluence;[1] they are also mentioned by Capenny[2] as dwelling on the middle course of the Warra.

Another people now completely under Zande domination are the Bantu Abuguru (Babukur), though they still speak Liguru as well as Zande. One section of them occupies the crest of the Nile–Congo divide between the eastern sources of the Sueh and the sources of the Meridi, and another occupies a stretch of country in the valley of the Sueh to the north of Yambio, the Azande having driven a wedge between the two sections. Smaller groups are found elsewhere.[3] They were first subjugated by Renzi and Bazingbi, sons of Yakpati. The Huma, who speak a language almost identical with Liguru, mostly live in the hills on the Sueh–Iba watershed, 70 miles to the NE. of Tembura. They were brought into subjection by Tembura.

A number of other peoples are in part ruled by the Avongara. Those in the south are members of the Mangbetu cluster. When the Azande began to push southwards from the Uele they met with strong resistance from the Sudanic Mangbetu, who at that time had a highly developed political organization embracing a number of peoples—Medje, Makere, Momvu, Mangbele, and others—ruled, like the Azande by the Avongara, by the Mangbetu aristocracy, which has given its name to the whole complex of peoples. Nevertheless, they made some advance and they took over further territories when, after 1870, Egyptian forces had broken the power of the Mangbetu kings. As recorded earlier, some of the Medje (the Mabisanga) have now become Azande, and it seems that others in the north are ruled by Avongara.[4] They were subjugated by the Zande king Kipa and placed by him under the rule of his son Bakangai. They are said to be, though much mixed with Azande, a compact group speaking their own tongue and speaking Zande only when it is

---

[1] P. W. T. Baxter and A. Butt, *The Azande and Related Peoples of the Anglo-Egyptian Sudan and Belgian Congo*, 1953, p. 33, on the authority of Von Weise and Kaiser-Walden.

[2] Op. cit., p. 313.

[3] Some of their clans found among the Azande, almost exclusively on or to the east of the Sueh, are: Ababaimo, Abakaya, Abagende, Ababanduo, Abayali, Abakpanda, Abakango, Ababali, Abamage, Abandagburu, Abangbandili, Abagiali, Abaruvuro, Abadugumu, Ababamuru, Abadangasa, and Abangbapere. To the east of the Sueh they are, on my calculations, over a quarter of the Zande population.

[4] Baxter and Butt, op. cit., p. 48.

required of them. In about 1885 Ukwe son of Wando, in a campaign against the Momvu, pursued them as far south as the Bomokandi, and subjugated them between that river and the Kibali. They have, however, kept their own language, manners, and customs, speaking Zande only when necessary. Their resistance to Zande influence may be due in part to the arrival of the Belgians shortly after Ukwe's campaign. Other sections of the Momvu are subjects of the Mangbetu, and yet others have retained their independence. A group of the Mangbele on the left bank of the Uele, from the lower Gada to the Mapuse rapids, were defeated by Kipa but later came again under Mangbetu rule. Some of the Mangbele are independent, and others are ruled by Avongara and Mangbetu. Originally a Bantu people, they now speak a Sudanic language.

Vanden Plas[1] speaks of the Ambili people, Bantu who have to a large extent become completely Zandeized. Those who live compactly in the region of Bondo (just west of 24° E. and just south of 4° N.) have kept their old language, though, having been subject to the Avongara for several generations, they also speak Zande. They seem to be part of the particular Zande complex known as the Azande–Abile.

A number of peoples living on the northern confines of Zandeland are, or were, wholly or in part, under Avongara domination. Two of these peoples have long been grouped together in literature as the Belanda, a Bongo term, and are referred to by the Azande as Abari. Though much intermingled, they are culturally quite distinct: the one, the Mberidi (Bor), being a Nilotic people related to the Luo; and the other, the Mbegumba (Bviri), a Sudanic people speaking a dialect of the language of the Basiri. One section of these peoples today lives between the Sueh and Iba rivers and Lat. 5° and 6° N. and other groups live between the Sueh and the Wau. Faced with Arab persecution from the north they chose to submit to the Avongara. Both peoples have preserved their languages and customs, though each speaks the language of the other as well as its own, and both speak also Zande and have been much influenced culturally by the Azande in other ways. Some of the Belanda settled permanently in Zande country, where they have been absorbed. The Bongo, a Sudanic people whom

[1] Op. cit., pp. 18–19.

Schweinfurth[1] reckoned in 1870 to number some 100,000 scattered over an area of nearly 9,000 square miles between Lat. 6° and 8° N., were unable to resist enslavement by the Arabs, and some communities fled to the south to seek refuge with the Avongara rulers Tembura, Gbudwe, and Mange. Others sought, by moving to the south, to escape the Arabs and also to preserve their independence, but were attacked by these Avongara and forced to accept their overlordship. Such Bongo speak Zande as well as their own language.

In Schweinfurth's day (1870–1) Azande were spread to the north roughly as far as Lat. 6° 30″, and they were in occupation of most of the same territory when Junker was in Zandeland ten years later; but the most northern areas, ruled in Schweinfurth's day by Mofio and Solongo, as he calls them, had been lost to the Avongara by about 1874,[2] so that such Azande as were there (known, Junker[3] says, as Diggas) no longer had a position of dominance but lived in common dependence on the Egyptian Government with peoples who had once been their vassals and with whom they were by this time very mixed. These were, in addition to groups of peoples already mentioned— Basiri, Bongo, and Pambia—the Golo and some of the Kreish (Gbaya); and to these peoples mentioned by Junker we must add the most easterly section of the Banda nation and some very small peoples—Ndogo,[4] Bai, and Togbu. All these peoples speak their own Sudanic languages but they also speak Zande with varying proficiency. Junker[5] tells us that some sections of some of these northern peoples had already by his time migrated to the south to seek protection in the powerful Avongara kingdoms from the Arabo-Nubians.

If the Zande expansion to the north on the whole met with weak resistance till countered by the Arab intrusion so that we can, with some latitude it is true, list the peoples of that region under the heading of subject peoples, in the east and north-east, resistance by some small peoples was not sufficiently, or on a large enough scale, overcome before the Egyptian Government established military posts in the area for us to describe them as

[1] Op. cit., vol. 1, pp. 257–60.   [2] Capenny, op. cit., p. 310.
[3] Op. cit., 1891, p. 112.
[4] Schweinfurth's 'Nduggo' are a Kreish tribe, not the Ndogo (Tucker, op. cit., 1940, p. 15).   [5] Op. cit., 1891, pp. 111–16.

subject peoples, except perhaps in the case of the Baka. De Calonne says that the Baka on the Aka and Garamba were subjugated by Wando, and even those who are independent of Avongara rule in the Sudan have been much influenced by Azande, whose tongue is widely known among them. Had it not been for Arab intervention they and the other peoples of the area would inevitably have been brought into complete subjection, for they were unorganized and disunited. As it was, they were raided and displaced by both the Avongara and the Adio, who took captives whose descendants are found among the Azande today. There must also have been some degree of social contact between them and the Azande, for it is seldom that one fails to find among them individuals who understand Zande.

The peoples raided and sometimes displaced by the Azande in this area but who cannot be said to have been subjugated by them to any extent, or even at all, are the Sudanic Mundu, Avukaya,[1] the so-called Jur peoples (Bell, Sofi, etc.), the Moro[2] peoples (Moro Kodo, Moro Meza, etc.), and the Logo; and the Nilo-Hamitic Fajelu and Kakwa. It would seem that individuals and perhaps sometimes small groups, of all these peoples have contributed to the ethnic composition of the Azande.

Some southern peoples who seem to have contributed, though in small numbers, to the formation of the Azande nation are briefly mentioned. De Calonne[3] says that the Mabudu, a Bantu people living today to the south of the Mangbetu cluster, were defeated by Kipa's sons, who, however, later withdrew northwards. The Ababua stoutly resisted the Azande, but the lack of unity among the communities of this Bantu people told against them, and they had already had to yield to the Avongara a stretch of their country to the north when the Belgian occupation stopped further encroachments. The Mayogo, of the Mangbetu cluster, appear to have had very limited contacts with the Azande. The Mobenge (Benge) form the most northern part of

---

[1] The Abakaya clan of the Azande, found in numbers to the east of the Sueh, may be this people, though it was listed by my informants as a clan of the Abuguru.

[2] The Amuru clan of the Azande, found almost exclusively in the most eastern parts of Sudan Zandeland, may be this people, though, here again, the clan was listed by informants among the Abuguru clans.

[3] Op. cit., pp. 73–4.

the Bantu Mobati, living just south of the Uele between Long. 23° and 24° E. Burrows[1] says that they are dominated by the Azande, to whom they pay tribute. Capenny[2] asserts that they were subjugated by Jabbir, 'a son of a Zande prince'.[3] Van Bulck and Hackett[4] say that they have been largely overrun by Abandiya and Azande. Zande domination of this people is not mentioned by other sources. The Bakango are riverains of the Uele between Bambili and Bondo. They do not, however, appear to be a distinct ethnic group, but sections of Azande, Ababua, and other peoples. Pygmies are sometimes met in the most southerly extensions of Zandeland, e.g. in the valley of the Poko, tributary of the Bomokandi.[5]

For convenience I have tabled the peoples who have in one way or another and in varying degrees contributed to the Zande complex, the table serving the further purpose of key to the sketch-map. Forty different peoples are listed. Some peoples who might well have been entered separately appear under a single title, the 'Jur' and 'Moro' peoples, for example, or the 'Medje' (the Mabisanga section are probably Bantu in origin). Had they been given separate entries and had some doubtful cases (mentioned by Junker, Vanden Plas, and others) been included, e.g. Apagumba, Mambelli, etc., we could assert that, together with the Ambomu, at least fifty different peoples have contributed to this vast ethnic amalgam; and it may even be, for we seldom have sufficient information to decide, that some of these peoples, as would appear to be the case with the Abandiva, were themselves composed of heterogeneous stocks.

In presenting, as I have done, the sketch-map (based on de Calonne's map of Zande distribution and with the location of peoples taken from the authorities mentioned in the text) I must emphasize that only the approximate locations are indicated.

Enough information has been given to indicate the great ethnic complexity of the Azande. Those who wish for further information may consult the authorities quoted. They will find it heavy going. It is indeed an exhausting experience to try to follow and reconcile their accounts. I may have made mistakes in this endeavour, and so may they in their reports; but this is

[1] G. Burrows, *The Curse of Central Africa*, 1903, p. 19.
[2] Op. cit., p. 312.   [3] Op. cit., p. 85.
[4] Op. cit., vol. i, p. 79.   [5] Czekanowski, op. cit., p. 25.

of little importance so long as the general presentation of the ethnic heterogeneity of the Azande is a correct one, and there can be no doubt about that. When we come, however, to consider the contribution of each people to this complex in terms of clans and their distributions and numbers, we are faced with difficulties far greater than any we have hitherto encountered, and only very rough approximations can be attempted. For most of Zandeland we have no record of the distribution or numerical strength of the clans, and we have also no record of the clans of most of the peoples represented in the Zande complex, and in the few cases where they are listed, mostly by de Calonne, they are scarcely reliable. De Calonne is not to be blamed for this, for he died before he was able to collate his notes and also because Azande are themselves vague and contradictory in their attachment of clans to ethnic groups. I have myself attempted, as will have been seen, to sort the matter out for Sudanese Zandeland, but without great confidence in the correctness of the results. All Azande I have consulted are agreed that certain clans are Ambomu, but about others there is uncertainty and dispute. Then, when all are agreed that a clan is of foreign stock, there is a diversity of opinion about to which stock it belongs. I have followed the advice of good informants in listing the clans of various peoples as I have done, but I must record that in some instances there was disagreement. Some men said a clan was an Amiangba one, others said it was an Abangbinda one, and yet others that it was an Amadi one. Generally Azande seem content to know that a people are *auro*, of foreign origin, and if pressed for further information they are inclined to put them into some category with which they are most familiar, their favourite in the area where I carried out my researches being 'Amiangba'. The truth is that in some cases nobody is quite certain, not even, I think, the clansmen themselves, what their origin is. What makes the matter even more complicated is that Zande clans split into sections with different names and, further, that totally different clans have fused together under a single name. Thus, to give a few examples, I was told that the Akpura clan, the Abakpuro clan, and the Amigano clan were all related offshoots from a common, single, original clan. The Abananga are said to be a true and original Adio clan from which some of them have separated out under the sobriquet of Akowe, and to these have attached themselves (*zi tiyo na* or *kpamia tiyo na*) some clans of totally different, probably Amiangba, origin (Abaranga, Apise, and Abakowe) who now claim to be genuine Adio. The Abaake, Abakpaku, Abainara, and other clans say, I was told, that they are sections of the Abadara, an Ambomu clan, but are really of foreign stock. The Angbaga clan are a composite group, it is alleged, consisting of an Ambomu clan with various foreign accretions; and the Aboro are likewise a *kpamiakpamia* clan, a coalition of various elements. All this is exceedingly confusing, and a study of totemic affiliations and the etymology of clan names only serves to increase the confusion.[1] The difficulties are perhaps insuperable. All I can say, therefore, is that if we accept the twenty clans I have listed as being Ambomu, as such then, as I have earlier noted, together with the Avongara they form some 29 per cent of the Zande population of the Sudan, a bigger percentage than we would be likely to find in other parts of Zandeland. This estimate is based on a census of 33,635 adult males made in 1929 and 1930.[2] Even if we allow all doubtful or disputed cases to count as Ambomu they would still not exceed half the total population.

What are the results which may be regarded as being of some social significance of this large-scale absorption of foreign peoples? One result is pointed to by the Azande themselves, and the evidences support their opinion. They say that it is where the foreign element is strongest that the Avongara rulers are the most autocratic. The colonialism of the Azande, as we might put it, has reacted on their own class structure, the paternalism of the Avongara, with its traditional intimacies and familiarities, tending to be replaced by a more distant and impersonal relationship between rulers and ruled, the Ambomu themselves becoming increasingly indistinguishable in the general mass. The result seems to have been that the word *vuru* lost some of its earlier sense of 'follower' and took on more of the tone of 'subject', and the cultural term 'Azande' came to be used in social and political contexts as synonymous with *avuru*, all alike being subjects of the Avongara whether they spoke only Zande or their own language as well. Whether the Ambomu clans ever had a more than vaguely social role cannot now be determined,

---

[1] See Chaps. IV, V, and VI.   [2] See Chap. I.

but Azande think of them as having been in the distant past corporate local communities which were to a large extent politically autonomous. What is certain is that they could have had no political significance after having been scattered over hundreds of miles and their members fused in community life with numerous foreign peoples. Clan affiliations could be only of negligible interest compared with political allegiances; and every effort was made by the rulers to eliminate slowly local and ethnic particularisms and to impress on all alike that personal loyalty to their masters and service at court and in the administration counted more than claims to good birth. An examination of the clans of administrative agents—commoner governors, deputies, captains of companies, etc.—makes it abundantly evident that loyalty and efficiency overrode all other considerations in appointment to public office.[1] Nevertheless, as I have mentioned earlier, descent does still play some part in social life. There has survived some feeling of Ambomu superiority, though it is expressed in terms of obligation and manners rather than of privilege or wealth. Boys and girls of Ambomu families are more strictly brought up; and their young men are taught to regard their attachment to their rulers as a hereditary right of service, a right conferred on them by generations of precedent.

A further consideration, which must receive separate treatment elsewhere,[2] would be the effect, difficult to estimate, of cultural borrowings brought about by ethnic fusion, borrowings of food plants, arts, institutions, etc. Without, however, discussing this aspect now, it may be suggested that the facts known to us about so great an ethnic and cultural amalgamation point to a further conclusion, hard though it be to define it or to prove its correctness: that the sophistication and, we might say, the cultural and social plasticity the Azande display in comparison with many primitive people derives from their historical experience. They have been a conquering people who have migrated and established themselves among foreign peoples, and have for generations been accustomed to hearing foreign languages and to seeing foreign ways of life and also to adjusting themselves to the processes of cultural assimilation and political integration. They have demonstrated through their institutions a remarkable capacity to absorb foreign stocks and foreign

---

[1] See Chap. XI.   [2] See Part 2.

customs. The resilience so acquired, it may be supposed, enabled them the more easily to come to terms with Arabs and Europeans and to support the humiliations and tribulations their presence imposed; for, in spite of all they had to endure, they were able, even their proud kings and princes, to adjust themselves to the new situation and by so doing to retain their essential values and institutions.

Lastly, attention may be drawn to the significance of the Zande empire in its latest historical phase, its significance for European dominion and administration. The Europeans, instead of being confronted with fifty different peoples, each with its own culture and institutions, took over a single people with a common culture, or at any rate a people advanced in the process of developing one, and with a common set of political institutions. This greatly facilitated their task, for, apart from being able to ignore many cultural diversities, they had at their disposal an organized and efficient administration through which they could operate their own, and, indeed, had no alternative but to do so. As Lelong says:[1]

Il est même permis d'apprécier certains bienfaits de l'expansion des Azande. Un de leurs partisans convaincus, comme ils sont nombreux parmi les administrateurs (il est plus facile de gouverner avec des chefs indigènes obéis et craints que de régenter l'anarchie), regrettait devant moi que l'occupation belge ne fût arrivée un peu plus tard. Elle a surpris, en effet, les Azande en plein mouvement d'expansion.

[1] M. H. Lelong, *Mes Frères du Congo*, 1946, p. 81.

IV

CLAN NAMES

WHEN Azande are asked why a certain clan has a certain name they usually, in my experience, say that they do not know. Older men will sometimes, however, offer some explanation of the name, though not always with any certainty or even, I think, conviction; they may add that they have heard it from someone or that people say that it is so. It soon becomes evident that, in most cases at least, the stories they tell of why these names were given to the clans are examples of what Max Müller called 'disease of language', stories invented by someone to explain the names, playing on the literal meaning of the words or of words to which their sounds bear a resemblance. The names are usually presented, however, as being nicknames, conventionally thought to have been given to the clans by the wives of their sons, bestowed on account of some characteristic or habit of their members. I give some illustrations.

The Akalingo clan are so called, it is said, because they used to behave badly to their fellows and kinsmen, not being able to abide that another should eat their food, and saying that when it was a matter of food or other goods, unless they were very close relatives indeed, they had no kinsmen. The last two syllables of their name, *lingo*, mean, when combined with the verb *de*, 'to cut kinship'; and we may conclude that the story that this clan were mean with their kin derives from this purely verbal association. In doing so, we reverse the construction of the Zande etymologists, that people of a certain clan behaved in a certain manner and therefore got a certain name, by saying that a chance identity or similarity of sounds has led to an explanation of the clan name and consequently to the attribution of certain characteristics to its members in the past. The Abakundo clan, who in Zande tradition were their chiefs in ancient days before the ruling Avongara clan of today became dominant, are said, with little respect for the composition of the word, to have got their name because when they killed an animal they used to put it for two or three days in a granary, since they liked to eat meat when it was high (*kundo*). The Angumbe clan bear a name which is the same word as that used to denote an oil-bearing gourd, and therefore it is attributed to them that in the past they were exceptionally industrious cultivators and that they chiefly planted in their gardens this gourd, which they preferred to all other food. The Abalingi clan are said to be so called because their ancestors displayed great meanness (*lingi*) in the matter of food. The Angbadimo clan were noted for their dislike of their sisters' sons and their sons' wives entering their huts, for these relatives are in the habit of appropriating anything which takes their fancy. When a sister's son visited them they would sit in the doorway (*ngbadimo*) of their huts till he departed, to deny him entrance. Hence their name.

The Abakpara were another clan who are said to have got their name on account of their lack of co-operation with others. They wanted to keep all their affairs, especially in the matter of food, to themselves and to separate (*kpara*) themselves in their activities from others. In the case of the Ambale clan the last syllable, *le*, has caught the ear, and it is said that when members of this clan used to kill an animal they could not bear that anyone but themselves should take its intestines (*le*), of which they were very fond.

Probably all these derivations are to be regarded as fictions, fanciful attempts, not taken very seriously by anyone, to account for the names of clans, which, assuming that, as is possible, they originally meant something, meant something quite different from the meaning given them in these aetiological stories.

That what we are considering is merely popular etymology is evident, apart from the violence done both to sound and grammar, from the manifest absurdity of some of the explanatory myths, wild guesses, as they would appear to be, at how names might have arisen. There is a clan called Abagua whose name, we are told, arose from their habit of killing in great numbers red grass rats, known to Azande as *agua*. People deceived them by telling them that these rats were not good to eat, so they threw (*ba*) them away—hence *Abagua*, 'the throwers away of red grass rats'. Likewise the Abatiko clan were the first to set traps for small birds, but when they found in their traps

a very tiny bird called *tiko* they did not take it home with them
but threw it away: hence their name *Abatiko* (*a*, pl. prefix; *ba*,
'to throw'; *tiko*, the bird of this name). The *ba*, which in these
two last examples is identified with the verb *ba*, 'to throw', and
forms the second syllable in the names of a fair number of Zande
clans, is presumably a plural prefix in the original languages of
peoples who today form part of the Zande ethnic and cultural
complex, the usual Zande plural prefix *a* having been joined
to it.

The Akurungu clan were the first to beat wooden gongs and
to spread news by this means. Now a wooden gong makes a
sound which, it seems, resembles to the Zande ear the cry of
the *kurungu* or blue-crested turaco, a bird found in thick forest
near streams. The old name of the Agiti clan was Agbembara,
'pullers about of elephant', because when they killed an
elephant they could not abide that anyone but themselves
should approach the carcass, which they pulled and chopped
about, struggling among themselves for the flesh.

Some of these interpretations are very far-fetched, one syllable
being emphasized and the rest ignored, sounds being forced
into a resemblance they scarcely bear, or some meaning the
words can be supposed to have being given a metaphorical
value which makes some, if little, sense when used in reference
to people. The Agbutu are so called from their habit of hiding
(*gbu*) their affairs from others; the Angali, because they played
games dangerously like the play of a dog (*ango*); the Avukida,
because they were always promising (*kida*) what they had no
intention of carrying out; the Abadala, because they hoed their
maize gardens where there grew a riverside grass called *dala*; and
the Akowe, whose original name was Abananga, because of the
unfaithfulness of their wives (*ko we*, 'to make fire by friction'—a
euphemism for sexual congress and hence for adultery). These
explanatory stories are manifestly absurd.

Even those Azande who seldom failed to give explanatory
commentaries on clan names when these were requested from
them were sometimes beaten by names which do not mean
anything and cannot easily be distorted into meaningful sounds,
for example, in the case of the Agbambi and Aubali clans. They
then generally said that the names bore no meaning because
they were originally clans of foreign origin, belonging to such

peoples as the Amiangba and the Abarambo, and that the
meanings of their names are either unknown to Azande or have
become lost to everybody with the disappearance of the languages to which they belonged. The Zande language has, they
said, become all mixed up with (*kpamiakpamia*) foreign tongues.
This is a true enough observation, but it ignores the fact that a
large number of clan names for which they put forward an
etymology are the names of foreign clans and are unlikely therefore to have originated in the way suggested, since although that
is what the words might mean in Zande the probability is that
they are not Zande words at all. This is the case with a number
of the clans I have already mentioned, and it is the case with
others. The Ameteli are, it is agreed by all, a foreign clan; yet
we are told that they got their name because they would say to
a man with whom they had quarrelled *mi a ta li ro na kina gi mi
ngbondo*, 'I will strike your head with my club'. So, because the
sounds in the word Ameteli bear some resemblance to the
pronunciation of the Zande words *mi*, 'I'; *ta*, 'strike'; *li*, 'head',
this clan is credited with having been the first to shape clubs and
use them in fighting. Another clan of *auro*, as Azande call all
foreigners, are the Angbaga, and here, if we consider the
phonetics of the word alone, the etymology appears more
reasonable, for there is a Zande word *angbaga*, meaning 'hoops'.
Hoops are made by twisting pliable withies into circles, and a
game is then played with them. The hoops are bowled at great
speed, and those along their course try to hurl spear-shafts
through their centres. We are told that the Angbaga got their
name through addiction to this sport. Another foreign clan are
the Akpura. There happens to be a Zande verb *kpura*, meaning
'to cook together oil and vegetable (usually manioc) leaves'.
This clan is therefore credited with having invented this cuisine.
There happens also to be a Zande noun *maka* which means a
coil of metal wire such as in the past Zande women used to
twist round their arms as an ornament, and so the foreign clan
of the Avumaka are said to be so called because they invented
this form of ornamentation—*vu* having to do service for *vo* or
voda, 'to bind'.

There are a number of other Zande clan names which begin
with the plural prefix *a* followed by *vu* or *vo*, and it is possible
that the second syllable *vu* or *vo* was, as has been suggested

earlier for the *ba* in other names, a plural prefix. This is a very involved linguistic question. What we have to note here is only that, just as when what follows the *ba* can by any stretch of the imagination be thrown it is taken to be the verb 'to throw', so when what follows the *vu* or *vo* can by any stretch of the imagination be bound it is taken to be the verb 'to bind'. Two further examples must suffice. The Avundukura clan are said to have originated the custom of tying (*vo*) a little bottle-gourd (*ndukura*) containing oil to their waists for purposes of toilet when going on long journeys. The second example is the ruling clan of the Azande, which Europeans have variously spelt Avongura, Avongara, Avongora, and in other ways, and as to the meaning of which they have speculated, not very convincingly. I was told by Azande a long and, to me, fanciful, if not fantastic, story about how a powerful bully called Ngora (or Ngara) was overcome and bound (*vo*) by a man who was consequently given the nickname of Vongora, 'the binder of Ngora', and whose descendants became known as the Avongora. V. H. Vanden Plas in his paper 'Quel est le nom de famille des chefs Azande?' played the same etymological game as the Zande etymologists, and, as he heard the clan name as Avongara, he put forward the suggestion that the name meant 'those who had "*lié-la-force*"' (*vo*, 'to bind'; *ngara*, 'force').[1]

It does not follow that in all cases, and necessarily, these explanatory myths, if they may be so called, are fictions, merely imaginative play upon words. In some cases the associations on which they are based may be sound. Thus the word designating all the true or original Zande clans and distinguishing them from assimilated foreign clans is 'Ambomu', and the statement that they are referred to by this word because their homeland, before they migrated eastwards, was the valley of the Mbomu river has much to commend it, for it is supported by a wealth of tradition and other ethnographical evidences. The word which means the oppositeto 'Ambomu' is *auro*, strangers or foreigners. That literally it means 'easterners' may readily be understood in terms of the eastwards movement of the Ambomu. The explanation of the name 'Adio', by which the most easterly Azande are known among themselves, that this people originated on the banks of a river (*dio*) may also appear adequate. But these three

---

[1] *Congo*, vol. i, 1921, p. 9.

names are ethnic rather than clan titles. A better example
would therefore be the Abandogo clan. They have as totems the
red field rat (*ndogo*) and the red pig (*zukubele*). They do not eat
the flesh of either animal, and their body-souls are thought to
pass into one or other of them after death. It does not try our
reason too far to accept that, as Azande say is the case, it is
because this clan have *andogo*, red field rats, for totem that they
are called Abandogo (or Andogo); though in view of what
we have learnt of other clan names we might wonder whether
the process could not have been the reverse—that they have
acquired the rat as totem because its name resembled, or was
the same as, part of their clan name, which may originally have
meant something quite different.

It may be surmised from what has been said in this chapter
that the etymology of clan names is a game anyone can play
who is skilful in the use of words, and that therefore we might
expect to find that different persons advance different interpretations. This is certainly sometimes the case in matters of detail
in the stories related, but the type of explanation is always
the same. That there are different interpretations is evident
from the writings of others about the Azande, for example
Mgr. Lagae.[1]

[1] Op. cit., 1926, pp. 29-31.

V

TOTEMS

MOST parts of Africa south of the Sahara display a great variety of animal and plant species, and since only some, usually only a very small proportion, of them are totems one may inquire whether any general conclusions can be reached about their selection and any principles be discovered in it. I set forth the full list of totems of the Azande and make some observations about them. It is essential that the list be as full as can be, because it is as important to know what are not totems as to know what are totems. The Azande are so numerous a people, are so ethnically mixed, and occupy so extensive a territory that it might be thought unwise to claim that all their totems are included in the list below, but the inquiry conducted by myself and my Zande clerk, Reuben Rikita, covered a large part, though by no means all, of Sudan Zandeland, and the clans of some thousands of men and their totems were taken down, so that, so far as this region is concerned, it is unlikely that many totems escaped the net. It may well be the case, however, that there are totemic creatures among the Azande of the then Belgian Congo and French Equatorial Africa which do not appear in the list below. That even in the Sudan alone it is possible to compile so formidable a list of totems is doubtless to be accounted for by the fact that many peoples of different ethnic origins have been assimilated, partially or entirely, in the Zande amalgam.

Mammals. 1. Lion (*bahu*). 2. Leopard (*moma*). 3. Hyæna (*gangbu*). 4. Hyæna (*zege*). 5. Genet (*mbili*). 6. Serval (*ngafu*). 7. Civet cat (*tia*). 8. Cat (*paka*). 9. Cat (*derimvugo*). 10. Cat (*dagbura*). 11. Ape, probably chimpanzee (*gazuru*). 12. Ape, perhaps the same as no. 11 (*bawamu*). 13. Ape, perhaps the same as no. 11 (*gadayo*). 14. Ape, perhaps the same as no. 11 (*tangua*). 15. Dog-faced baboon (*waku*). 16. Colobus monkey (*mvugo*). 17. White-nosed monkey (*rimo*). 18. Monkey, small grey (*mbiro*). 19. Monkey (*ngarangara*). 20. Monkey (*bagianya*). 21. Monkey, grey (*balibo*). 22. Buffalo (*gbe*). 23. Giraffe (*dikara*). 24. Water-buck (*mbaga*). 25. Bushbuck (*gbodi*). 26. Dig-dig (*gbafu*). 27. Mouse-coloured duiker (*mvuru*). 28. Gazelle (*gbangbalia*). 29. Bongo (*mangana*). 30. Reedbuck (*ngbandua*). 31. Roan antelope (*bisa*). 32. Rhinoceros (*kanga*). 33. Ant-bear (*garawa*). 34. Wart-hog (*zigba*). 35. Red pig (*zumburu*). 36. Red pig, probably the same as no. 35 (*zukubile*). 37. Domesticated dog (*ango*). 38. Jackal (*hua*). 39. Hunting dog (*waru*). 40. Otter (*ngurunguru*). 41. Mole (*tundua*). 42. Red field rat (*ndogo*). 43. Striped field rat (*sika*). 44. Field rat (*gbangata*). 45. Tree rat (*kuru*). 46. Cane rat (*lemvo*). 47. Rat, large-eyed (*tura*). 48. Rat (*bagbaya*). 49. Rat, evil-smelling (*ndari*). 50. Rat, short-tailed (*kandu*). 51. Ground squirrel (*badari*). 52. Ground squirrel, perhaps the same as no. 51 (*gambe*). 53. Hare (*ndakuta*). 54. Cricetus (*sumba*). 55. Bat (*fura*). 56. Water leopard (*moma ime*). 57. Thunder-beast (*gumba*).

Birds. 1. Vulture (*nguku*). 2. Vulture (*ranga*). 3. Vulture (*nguali*). 4. Vulture (*gbugbu*). 5. Greater bustard (*baziregbodi*). 6. Guineafowl (*nzengu*). 7. Domesticated fowl (*kondo*). 8. Black-crested hawk (*bigi*). 9. Black stork (*gonyo*). 10. Kite (*bakiki*). 11. Hornbill, black and white casqued (*ngongo*). 12. Hornbill (*ndasi*). 13. Blue-crested turaco or plantain-eater (*kurungu*). 14. White-crested turaco or plantain-eater (*kuruwa*). 15. Honey guide (*turugba*). 16. Green pidgeon (*baoto*). 17. Laughing dove (*mbipo*). 18. Pied wagtail (*ngbia* or *ngbiangbia*). 19. Cisticola warbler (*titi*). 20. Bronze mannikin (*nzoro*). 21. Dybowski's twinspot (*tindi*). 22. Small black and white bird (*kpiakpia*).

Reptiles. 1. Crocodile (*ngondi*). 2. Iguana (*kare*). 3. Tortoise (*basimaru*). 4. Tortoise (*dagado*). 5. Tortoise (*dukada*). 6. Gymnastic house lizard (*kokoso*). 7. Lizard, large (*tangandu*). 8. Lizard, small (*gara*). 9. Lizard (*kengua*). 10. Lizard, large (*bandugu*). 11. Spitting cobra (*basuru*). 12. Snake, loud hissing (*bagawege*). 13. Snake, grey and black (*ngbukpu*). 14. Black tree snake (*bikingi*). 15. Adder (*kpokowo*). 16. Adder (*mbirimvuru*). 17. Snake, black (*wo apipe*). 18. Green grass snake (*ngama*). 19. Python (*gbara*). 20. Snake (*rungbu*). 21. Snake, reddish-brown (*wo kpaga*). 22. Snake (*gbingbiti*). 23. Snake (*rungbura*). 24. Snake (*bilimi*). 25. Snake (*wo tura*). 26. Snake (*wo gumba*). 27. Water snake (*ngambue*). 28. Rainbow snake (*wangu*). 29. Slowworm (*magingi*). 30. Slowworm? (*kpurandu*). 31. Chameleon (*mvua*). 32. Toad (*dari*). 33. Toad (*nguro*). 34. Frog (*ndiko*).

Crustaceans. 1. Crab (*ngere*).

Insects. 1. Millepede (*kingoro*). 2. Red pinching ant (*dindo*).
3. Black soldier ant (*pipe*). 4. Fly (*zi*). 5. Hornet (*bando*). 6. Fire-
fly (*nzengue*). 7. Locust (*yere*). 8. Mosquito (*ngungu*). 9. Termite
(*ge*). 10. Species of termite (*asuo*). 11. Species of termite (*ang-
baimo*). 12. Insect or grub associated with pumpkins (*ngorombe,
gbiro boko*). 13. Butterfly (*fufurafu*).

As will be observed, it has not always been possible to give a
more precise description of the creature to which a name refers
than is contained in a statement of the family or species to which
it belongs, and even for some of these imprecise indications I am
indebted to dictionaries.[1] The compilers of these were often,
however, in no better position to go beyond native statements
than I was, the creatures not being easily seen or, if seen, identified; and such entries as 'species of small lizard' and 'une des
variétés de serpents' do not take us very far. Moreover, it is not
always certain whether two different names refer to different
species or to different varieties of a species or are different names
for the same species or variety: for example, whether *gazuru,
bawamu, gadayo*, and *tangua* are four different words for chimpanzee or refer to four different kinds of ape or monkey, and
likewise whether *dagado, dakada*, and *basimaru* are names for
different sorts of tortoise or different names for the same tortoise.
This uncertainty arises particularly among the Azande on
account of their being an ethnic amalgam in which not only the
Zande language but other languages are current, either in an
assimilated form or still, to varying degrees, spoken in addition
to the Zande tongue. Thus I have been told that *gbingbiti* is the
Miangba word for the slowworm, *bilimi* another foreign word
for it, while the true Zande word for it is *magingi*; but, if this is so,
all three words are current and all three were given as names of
totems. I decided, therefore, to list all the words given as
totems, even if this meant in some cases that the same creature
was listed more than once and that consequently there are more
totems listed than there are in reality; and I have done so partly

---

[1] C. R. Lagae and V. H. Vanden Plas, op. cit., vol. ii, 1922; Canon and Mrs.
E. C. Gore, *Zande and English Dictionary*, 1931. Some bird identifications were made
from a typewritten list compiled by Dr. H. W. Woodman. Four creatures were
identified by Mr. Raphael Zamoi. These are *balibo, gbugbu, kpiakpia*, and *kpurundu*.
For identification of the snake *bagawege* I am indebted to my friend Major P. M.
Larken.

also for the reason that in a certain sense the name, rather than what it refers to, is the totem for the person who holds it to be his totem, for Azande pay little, if any, attention to the totem animal itself. In a number of cases a man who says that such-and-such a creature is his totem may, on account of the movement of people from one latitude to another, rarely, or even never, have seen it. He has only heard its name, and this is necessarily the case where the totem is an imaginary creature.[1]

Some of the creatures may be supposed not to exist, though the experiences they stand for are, or may be, actual. The *ngambue*, a crested water snake, is an unlikely creature. The *wangu*, the rainbow snake, does not exist as a creature, nor, if we judge by Zande accounts of it, does the *moma ime*, the water leopard. Nor does the *gumba*, the thunder-beast, Azande speaking of thunder as though it were some sort of animal. However, in spite of their speaking of these imaginary creatures as creatures, Azande do not conceive of them as they conceive of ordinary creatures which they often see or which they know that others have often seen.

I have to make it clear that this chapter describes only the natural distribution of totems and not their social distribution. In my lists of Zande clans and totems some totems occur on almost every page, for example, the leopard, the colobus monkey, and the *rungbu* snake, whereas hundreds of entries may be run through without the appearance of others; and some only appear, in a list of some thousands of persons, two or three times. This means that whilst some totems are totems of large clans, or of several clans, and are represented also throughout Zande-land, others are totems of single clans which are also insignificant in numbers and restricted to small localities, or even of individuals or families of foreign origin living among the Azande (for example, the domesticated dog is probably a totem only of a few members of the Baka people, and the laughing dove of a few members of the Bongo people). We cannot therefore fully judge the significance of the natural distribution of the totems till the further and laborious task has been undertaken of determining the proportions of the total Azande questioned who regard each of the creatures as their totem and of mapping the

[1] I have discussed this point in reference to Nuer totems in *Nuer Religion*, Oxford, 1956, pp. 134 f.

territorial distribution of these persons. When presented, as here, simply as a list of totems, it cannot be said that any principle of selection is revealed unless it be the negative one that among the 127 totemic species listed there is not a single plant.

I have only to add that I have excluded from the list the elephant (*mbara*) as I can only find it recorded once in my notes and the entry is queried; that I have included the termite with reluctance because, though a few men gave it as their totem, it is probably not a totem in the same sense as the other creatures but belongs to a number of creatures whose names are avoided by certain clans on account of some misfortune connected with them; and that I have not been able to identify with any certainty a few entries in Reuben's lists. These uncertain names— uncertain because I neglected to check them at the time—are *ndurungbe*, *ngerepe*, *ngime*, and *bagayuge* or *yuge* or *bayuge*. *Ngime* means 'smoke' and *yuge* means 'wind', but, because these things are so unlike other Zande totems and because they appear in the lists so seldom, I exclude them till they have been confirmed by further inquiry.[1]

---

[1] Fr. F. Giorgetti tells me in a letter that *bagayuge* (*bayuge, yuge*) is another name for the snake listed as *bagawege*.

VI

CLANS AND TOTEMS

IN earlier pages I have listed 188 clans and 127 totems for the Azande of the Sudan alone (excluding the Azande of the former Belgian Congo and French Equatorial Africa). The figure for the totems is probably fairly accurate, but there are certainly many more small clans not listed. As a guess, for I have not counted them, I would say that there must be well over a hundred more; and were the Azande of other regions to be included they could amount to several hundred. In this chapter I undertake a broad survey of the totemic affiliations of some of the better-known clans in the Sudan, sample districts having been selected to represent all sections of the population from Tembura in the west to Meridi in the east.[1] Some observations are made which bear not only on the ethnic and social composition of the Azande but also on some features of totemism. In Table IV, the clans marked with an asterisk are either certainly or very probably of Mbomu (pure Zande) stock. The remainder of this chapter will consist of observations on this list.

1. In all cases except that of the Balingi clan individuals claiming membership of the same clan nevertheless gave different totems. Those are not secondary totems, except possibly in the case of the Abandogo clan (the red pig seems to be linked, perhaps for reasons of colour or perhaps because of a linguistic assimilation of the name of the animal—*ndogo*—to the name of the clan, with the red field rat). They are different totems given by persons who call themselves by the same clan name. This fact has long been noted. De Calonne remarked that, for example, the Aboro clan have the chimpanzee for totem in some areas and the snake *lumbu* (? *rungbu*) in other areas and that the Agbutu clan have the hornet in some areas and the viper in others, and he suggested that this might be an indication of

---

[1] In the areas ruled by Renzi in the old kingdom of Tembura, by Ngindo, Gangura, Rikita, and Dika in the old kingdom of Gbudwe, and by Ndoruma in the country once ruled by his father Mange. The survey was conducted between the years 1926 and 1930.

TABLE IV

Clan	1	2	3	4	5	6	7	8	9	10	11	12	13	14	15	16	17	18
1. *Agiti	225	40	21	2	1	0	0	0	0	0	0	0	0	0	0	0	0	0
2. Akowe	106	6	6	0	0	3	3	3	2	1	1	1	1	0	0	0	0	0
3. *Agbambi	115	2	6	0	0	0	0	0	0	0	0	0	0	2	0	0	0	0
4. *Angbaya	46	18	3	0	0	0	0	0	0	0	1	0	0	0	0	0	0	0
5. *Avotombo	37	29	11	0	2	2	0	15	1	0	2	0	11	0	3	1	1	1
6. Amiteli	61	50	25	2	1	0	0	0	0	0	0	0	1	0	0	0	4	0
7. Avunduo	72	65	6	0	0	0	0	0	0	0	0	0	0	0	0	0	3	0
8. Abandogo	0	1	1	0	0	0	0	0	0	0	0	0	0	0	0	0	0	0
9. *Angbaga	56	18	3	0	0	0	0	0	0	0	0	0	1	0	0	0	0	0
10. Auboli	5	40	5	0	0	0	0	0	0	0	0	0	0	0	0	0	0	0
11. Angali	17	10	8	0	1	0	0	0	0	0	0	0	0	0	0	0	0	0
12. Abangbara	21	7	48	0	0	0	0	0	0	0	0	0	1	0	0	0	0	1
13. Abaanya	9	6	4	0	1	0	0	0	0	0	1	0	0	0	0	0	1	0
14. *Akalingo	104	26	26	0	0	10	0	0	0	0	0	0	0	0	0	0	0	0
15. *Aboro	20	4	16	0	0	0	0	0	0	0	0	1	0	0	0	0	0	0
16. *Angbapiyo	0	1	64	0	0	0	0	0	0	0	0	0	0	0	0	0	0	0
17. *Angbadimo	70	1	5	0	1	0	0	0	0	0	0	0	2	0	0	0	0	0
18. *Abatiko	35	11	1	0	0	0	0	0	0	1	0	0	0	0	0	0	0	0
19. Akenge	12	5	1	0	8	0	0	0	0	0	0	0	0	0	0	0	0	0
20. *Abakundo	46	5	12	0	0	1	0	0	0	6	1	0	0	0	0	0	0	0
21. Akpura	0	41	0	0	0	0	0	0	0	0	0	0	0	0	0	0	0	0
22. Abakpoto	2	2	4	0	0	0	0	0	0	0	0	0	0	0	0	0	16	2
23. *Abadara	13	17	21	0	1	0	0	0	0	0	0	0	0	0	2	0	0	0
24. *Ambata	23	15	2	0	38	0	0	0	0	0	0	0	0	0	0	0	0	0
25. *Angumbe	100	0	2	0	0	0	0	0	0	0	0	0	0	0	0	0	0	0
26. Abiama	66	0	0	1	0	0	0	0	0	0	1	0	0	0	0	0	0	0
27. *Abawoyo	6	33	3	0	0	36	0	0	0	0	0	0	0	0	0	0	0	0
28. Abasiri	1	1	28	0	0	0	0	0	0	0	0	0	0	0	0	0	0	0
29. Abakpuro	6	1	5	0	0	0	0	0	0	0	0	0	0	0	0	0	0	0
30. Abangombi	6	58	1	0	0	0	0	0	0	0	0	0	0	0	0	0	0	0
31. Abananga	61	0	5	0	0	1	15	5	0	0	0	0	0	0	0	0	0	0
32. *Abagbangi	23	9	0	0	0	0	0	0	0	0	0	0	0	0	0	0	0	0
33. Abawoli	8	22	11	0	0	1	0	0	0	0	0	0	0	0	0	0	0	0
34. Ambare	34	6	0	0	0	0	0	0	1	0	0	0	0	0	0	0	0	0
35. Abatukpo	2	0	2	0	0	0	0	0	0	0	0	0	0	0	0	0	0	0
36. Abamburo	20	28	0	0	1	0	0	0	0	0	0	0	0	0	0	0	0	0
37. Avundukura	26	1	0	0	0	0	0	0	0	0	0	0	0	0	0	0	0	0
38. Abalingi	0	0	27	0	0	0	0	0	0	0	0	0	0	0	0	0	0	0
39. Abandiko	6	10	0	0	1	0	0	0	0	0	0	0	0	0	0	0	0	0
40. Avugioro	0	3	0	0	0	0	0	0	0	0	0	0	0	0	0	0	0	0
41. Abadugu	4	8	2	0	0	0	0	0	0	0	1	0	0	0	0	0	1	0
42. Abazaa	0	0	2	0	0	0	0	0	0	0	0	0	0	0	0	0	0	0
Totals	1,464	590	387	5	18	92	18	23	4	8	8	2	17	2	5	1	26	4

KEY TO LIST OF TOTEMS

1. Snake (*rungbu*). 2. Thunder-beast (*gumba*). 3. Leopard (*moma*). 4. Snake (*rungbura*). 5. Tree snake (*bikingi*). 6. Rainbow snake (*wangu*). 7. Vulture (*ranga*). 8. Red ants (*adindo*). 9. Millepede (*kingoro*). 10. Lion (*bahu*). 11. Spitting cobra (*basuru*). 12. Snake (*bagawege*). 13. Water snake (*ngambue*). 14. Hornet (*bando*). 15. Snake (*ngama*). 16. Lizard (*gara*). 17. Snake (*ngbukpu*). 18. Snake (*wo tura*).

Clans marked * are of Mbomu stock.

19	20	21	22	23	24	25	26	27	28	29	30	31	32	33	34	35	36	37	38	39	40	41	Totals
0	0	0	0	0	0	0	0	0	0	0	0	0	0	0	0	0	0	0	0	0	0	0	289
0	0	0	0	0	0	0	0	0	0	0	0	0	0	0	0	0	0	0	0	0	0	0	133
0	0	0	0	0	0	0	0	0	0	0	0	0	0	0	0	0	0	0	0	0	0	0	125
0	0	0	0	0	0	0	0	0	0	0	0	0	0	0	0	0	0	0	0	0	0	0	68
1	0	0	0	0	0	0	0	0	0	0	0	0	0	0	0	0	0	0	0	0	0	0	117
0	1	1	0	0	0	0	0	0	0	0	0	0	0	0	0	0	0	0	0	0	0	0	146
8	0	0	1	0	0	0	0	0	0	0	0	0	0	0	0	0	0	0	0	0	0	0	155
0	0	0	0	141	2	0	0	0	0	0	0	0	0	0	0	0	0	0	0	0	0	0	145
0	0	0	0	0	0	0	0	0	0	0	0	0	0	0	0	0	0	0	0	0	0	0	78
0	0	0	0	0	0	56	0	0	0	0	0	0	0	0	0	0	0	0	0	0	0	0	106
0	0	0	0	0	0	0	30	2	0	0	0	0	0	0	0	0	0	0	0	0	0	0	68
0	0	0	0	0	0	0	0	0	0	0	0	0	0	0	0	0	0	0	0	0	0	0	78
0	0	0	0	0	0	0	0	0	0	0	0	0	0	0	0	0	0	0	0	0	0	0	22
0	0	0	0	0	0	0	0	0	0	0	0	0	0	0	0	0	0	0	0	0	0	0	166
0	0	0	0	0	0	4	0	0	0	0	0	0	0	0	0	0	0	0	0	0	0	0	45
0	0	0	0	0	0	0	0	0	0	0	0	0	0	0	0	0	0	0	0	0	0	0	65
0	0	0	0	0	0	0	0	0	0	0	0	0	0	0	0	0	0	0	0	0	0	0	79
0	0	0	0	0	0	0	0	0	0	0	0	0	0	0	0	0	0	0	0	0	0	0	48
0	0	0	0	0	0	0	0	0	0	0	0	0	0	0	0	0	0	0	0	0	0	0	26
0	0	0	0	0	0	0	0	0	0	0	0	0	0	0	0	0	0	0	0	0	0	0	71
0	0	0	0	0	0	0	0	0	6	0	0	0	0	0	0	0	0	0	0	0	0	0	47
0	0	0	0	0	0	0	0	0	0	0	0	0	0	0	0	0	0	0	0	0	0	0	26
4	0	0	0	0	0	0	0	0	0	0	0	0	0	0	0	0	0	0	0	0	0	0	58
0	0	0	0	0	0	0	0	0	0	0	0	0	0	0	0	0	0	0	0	0	0	0	78
0	0	0	0	0	0	0	0	0	0	0	1	0	0	0	0	0	0	0	0	0	0	0	103
0	0	0	0	0	0	0	0	0	0	0	0	0	0	0	0	0	0	0	0	0	0	0	68
1	0	0	0	0	0	0	0	0	0	0	1	0	0	0	0	0	0	0	0	0	0	0	80
0	0	0	0	0	0	2	0	0	0	0	0	0	0	0	0	0	0	0	0	0	0	0	32
0	0	0	0	0	0	0	0	0	0	0	0	48	2	0	0	0	0	0	0	0	0	0	62
1	0	0	0	0	0	0	0	0	0	0	0	0	0	0	0	0	0	0	0	0	0	0	66
0	0	1	0	0	0	0	0	0	0	0	0	0	0	10	0	0	0	0	0	0	0	0	98
2	0	0	0	0	0	0	0	0	0	0	0	0	0	0	0	0	0	0	0	0	0	0	34
2	0	0	0	0	0	0	0	0	0	0	0	0	0	0	1	0	0	0	0	0	0	0	45
0	0	0	0	0	0	0	0	0	0	0	0	0	0	0	0	1	0	0	0	0	0	0	42
5	0	0	0	0	0	0	0	0	0	0	0	0	0	0	0	0	0	0	0	0	0	0	9
3	0	0	0	0	0	0	0	0	0	0	0	0	0	0	0	0	4	2	2	1	1	0	62
0	0	0	0	0	0	0	0	0	0	0	0	0	0	0	0	0	0	0	0	0	0	1	28
0	0	0	0	0	0	0	0	0	0	0	0	0	0	0	0	0	0	0	0	0	0	0	27
0	0	0	0	0	0	0	0	0	0	0	0	0	0	0	0	0	0	0	0	0	0	0	17
20	0	0	0	0	0	0	0	0	0	0	0	0	0	0	0	0	0	0	0	0	0	0	23
20	0	0	0	0	0	0	0	0	0	0	0	0	0	0	0	0	0	0	0	0	0	0	36
0	0	0	0	0	0	0	0	0	1	0	0	0	0	0	0	0	7	0	0	0	0	0	10
67	1	2	1	141	2	62	30	2	7	1	1	48	2	10	1	8	4	2	2	1	1	1	3,071

19. Colobus monkey (*mvugo*). 20. Serval (*ngafu*). 21. Snake (*gbingbiti*). 22. Snake (*wo apipe*). 23. Red pig (*zumburu*, *'zukubile*). 24. Rat (*ndogo*). 25. Chimpanzee (*bawamu*). 26. Pumpkin grub (*ngorombe*). 27. ? (*ngerepe*). 28. Tortoise (*basimaru*). 29. Blue-crested turaco (*kurungu*). 30. Python (*gbara*). 31. Cat (*paka*). 32. Genet (*mbili*). 33. Vulture (*nguku*). 34. Monkey (*ngarangara*). 35. Iguana (*kare*). 36. Squirrel (*badari*). 37. Toad (*dari*). 38. Monkey (*bagianya*). 39. Hyæna (*zege*). 40. Rat (*ndari*). 41. Slowworm (*magingi*).

different ethnic origins.[1] Mgr. Lagae was also well aware that persons with the same clan name give different totems.[2] It is evident from the information given by these two authorities that the situation in the Congo is the same as in the Sudan. To account for the fact we must, I think, accept the historical explanation of the Azande themselves. They say that in the course of war, migration, domination, and the displacement and fractionization of clans, individuals attached themselves to some clan, other than their own, of some standing in their vicinity, but, in some instances at any rate, carried their original totemic affiliation into it. This accounts for small minority totemic representations. They also say that in similar circumstances groups of foreign stock made similar attachments, either to the socially superior Mbomu clans or to some clan of another foreign people, eventually conquered and absorbed like themselves. This is what is called a *kpamiakpamia* clan, a conglomerate clan, such as the Akowe, the Abadara, the Angbaga, the Aboro, the Avundo, and other clans. Azande assert that it has been a common process in their history for sections of clans to lose touch with their fellow clansmen as a consequence of dispersal and in course of time to regard themselves as separate groups under the names of one of their elders (*i na sengi e ku ti bakumba*), and as such becoming new clans taking a new name after a nickname given to them by their daughters-in-law (*adiya agude sengi pai*), and then sometimes fusing with some section of a totally different clan and intermarrying with their original clan. Nobody seems to be very sure of the details of such splittings and fusions, and attempts to explain clan names are, as I have already shown, at least in most cases, quite obviously no more than popular etymology; but all are agreed that splittings and fusions were frequent. So much so, and for so long have they been going on, that uncertainty and contradictions between statements about them can readily be understood. Azande also say that some dispersed peoples have taken on in the process of dispersal the status of clans. The Abasiri are a case in point; the Adio are another. Abasiri and Adio, once distinct peoples with their own languages, are now often given as the names of clans. But the Adio were originally an ethnic group comprising a number of clans, among them the Akowe, and to the Akowe have attached

---

[1] Op. cit., p. 223.   [2] Op. cit., p. 371.

themselves various foreign elements (with totems different from that of true Akowe), now more or less regarded as Akowe, for difference in totem has no great social significance. It may be remarked upon, and it may be taken into consideration in questions of intermarriage or with regard to the obligation of kinsmen in the vicinity to bring beer to a man's feast, but Azande do not think it necessary, or polite, to inquire pointedly into a man's origins.

It must be noted that it is not just a matter of the totem linked to a clan being different in widely separated areas. In the clan census it was found that very frequently persons living in the same local community gave the same clan name but different totems. This may be due to secondary displacements, for Azande are very mobile, only the closest kin living near to each other, and sometimes not even they. It is understandable that in this state of flux and isolation de Calonne[1] should have come across Azande of foreign origin who were so cut off from folk of their own stock that they had not only forgotten their language but were often ignorant of their totems as well, an experience, however, which I have not myself had.

2. In addition to this constant movement other circumstances may have added to the confusion. Mgr. Lagae[2] says that many individuals declare that their clan has no totem, as also does de Calonne.[3] I have not myself met a Zande who said that he had no totem, but I would not dispute the statement of the two Belgian writers, for it would seem that some of the assimilated foreign peoples, for example the Abuguru and possibly the Abangbinda,[4] were originally not totemic, so it may well be that in some parts of the country they have remained so. This makes a further complication in that those of them who have adopted totems may have done so each man according to his taste. Another circumstance is the Zande dogma that a man's totem is that of his biological, not social, father. Consequently a man born of adulterous congress may, if it is known, be thought

[1] Op. cit., p. 190.   [2] Op. cit., p. 43.
[3] Op. cit., p. 192.
[4] Major P. M. Larken, whilst in agreement with regard to the Abuguru, says (op. cit., 1923, pp. 236–40) that the Abangbinda were totemic, as also the Abarambo, another people now completely assimilated in the Sudan to the Ambomu. When assimilation has reached an advanced stage it is difficult to be certain one way or the other in such matters.

to belong in a general social sense to his mother's husband's clan or to his maternal uncle's clan, as the case may be, while having as his totem that of his biological father's clan. Furthermore, there is some vagueness about the transmission of totems from parents to children which has not been noted by other writers about the Azande. A common, but not uncontested, statement made to me was that a man takes his totem from his father and a woman from her mother (an opinion which is consistent with a similar notion of inheritance of witchcraft). Then, I was told that it is quite usual for first-born children to change at death (which is what is supposed to happen to a kind of what has been called a body-soul, associated with the right hand) into the totemic creatures of the clans of their mothers' brothers, and it is a common opinion that all children of the daughters of members of the royal Avongara clan change at death into leopards, the totem of the royal clan, regardless of their fathers' clans. In neither case does the opinion appear to lead to a change of clan, totem and clan being thus divorced.

Mgr. Lagae[1] is of the opinion that clans have segmented and new clans have thereby come into existence through the adoption by some section of a clan of a new totem, and that this happens so frequently that we can find in it a sufficient explanation of the extreme diversity of clans. He thinks that this could come about by a man finding traces on his father's tomb of an animal other than that of his clan, of an iguana, for example, instead of the snake *rungbu*, and he would therefore conclude that his father must have been a child of adultery and consequently not a true member of his supposed clan at all (in the example, the Agiti clan). So he starts a new clan called after his bastard father. Much though I respect Mgr. Lagae's opinion, I must reject the hypothesis. I have myself been told that a man has sometimes found traces on a man's grave of the totemic creature of the dead man's maternal uncle (the totemic animal is thought to emerge from the grave, and the kin visit the grave from time to time to look for traces of it), but I doubt whether any Zande would reach a conclusion from spoor on a grave that his father was a bastard, nor can I imagine him telling people that his father was a bastard, even were he puzzled. Mgr. Lagae offers no evidence for such an event ever having happened, and he

[1] Op. cit., pp. 36–45.

does not even suggest that any Zande has ever offered this explanation of clan segmentation, leaving us to suppose that it is no more than a just-so explanation of his own. I received the impression from what Azande told me that they do not take inspection of the grave for signs of the totemic creature very seriously, nor are troubled if there are none. Besides, it is common sense that, especially since the graves are dug in, or close to, homesteads, there frequently cannot be traces of totemic creatures on them and that, when there are traces, they are quite likely to be of animals other than that of the dead man's totem, so that new clans would be formed almost daily, and there is no evidence that they are. Indeed, some totemic creatures, or their traces, could never be seen on graves or anywhere near them—some even do not exist—yet they continue to be totems. I have earlier remarked that Mgr. Lagae says that many individuals declare that their clans have no totems and he attributes this to the same cause. A man searches the grave of his father for traces of an animal in vain and concludes that his father was descended from someone who had no totem, so he starts a new clan without a totem. If this were really how a Zande would act there would be endless clans without totems, which is certainly not the case. And if there is no evidence that a change of totem has led to clan segmentation, there is equally no evidence that segmentation has brought about a change of totem; nor, it must be added, is such evidence likely to be found in a society where, outside the royal clan, few people know anything about their forebears, even their names, farther back than their grandfathers and probably nobody could state his descent back for more than three or four generations. In this respect the Azande are like most of us.

3. It will be evident from the table of clans and totems that it is by no means always easy to state categorically that the totems of such-and-such a clan is such-and-such a creature and that those who have different totems are assimilated elements. One can, however, combining numerical preponderance with Zande statements, legitimately speak of a certain animal as being the totem of a certain clan in some cases, as for instance those of the Akowe, the Agbambi, the Angumbe, and the Abananga; but not in other cases, as for instance those of the Avotombo, the Angali, the Abadara, the Ambata, and the

Abamburo; and here it must be pointed out that the clans selected as samples are not only among the best-known clans in the Sudan but also those with the highest numerical representation and also for the most part those considered to be the 'best' clans socially; and they are therefore those in which assimilation of foreign elements is most likely to have taken place, and on the largest scale. It will, moreover, at once be seen how fatal it can be to ask only a few persons, perhaps a single person, for the names of clan and totem and then to say that this clan has that animal for totem. A statement of the kind to have any validity must be based on a very wide survey, both numerically and geographically. Errors have undoubtedly been made by taking too small a sample. Thus it is simply not the case that, as de Calonne[1] says, the Aboro's totem is the chimpanzee and that of the Abadara the tortoise (his notes were in any case left in a very confused state; and he did not always distinguish between what he calls tribes and what he calls clans). Mgr. Lagae[2] says that the thunder-beast is the totem of the Avundo, the Agbambi, the Akowe, the Avundukura, the Angbadimo, and the Agiti among other clans, an identification of clan with totem certainly not borne out by the survey here presented. Dr. Czekanowski, whose studies in the Nile–Congo area have been of considerable ethnological importance, did not have the lengthy experience of Zandeland of de Calonne and was without the added advantage of Mgr. Lagae's knowledge of the Zande tongue and so, not being aware of the diversity of totems sometimes given by persons claiming to be members of the same clan, he has all the more easily fallen into the same trap. Thus he gives as the totem of the Abakundo the *gara*, lizard, as that of the Agbambi the thunder-beast, and as that of the Agiti the leopard; but naturally, on the other hand, and by good luck, he is very often right in his identifications.[3] However, his remark that the number of different totems is very small is, it must be said, wide of the mark. The early travellers in Zandeland—Piaggia, Schweinfurth, Junker, Casati, etc.—some of whom resided for years among the Azande, do not seem to have been aware that they have clans, far less totemic clans.

4. Although he was well aware of the almost insuperable

[1] Op. cit., p. 187.   [2] Op. cit., p. 37.
[3] Op. cit., pp. 43–6.

difficulties of the task, de Calonne thought it possible that the evidence of what he called the pseudo-totemism of the Azande might enable us to reconstruct some of their history, in that if one finds the same totem among different clans it could indicate a common origin, at least in the case of creatures like the chameleon, the hornet, and the monitor lizard, for he adds that other species are so frequent as totems and are found among peoples of so diverse origins that *'leurs croyances zoolatriques à ce sujet perdent toute valeur indicatrice'*.[1] It is necessary to agree with him on this last point, and I would go further and say that an attempt to reconstruct ancient history from the thousands of bits and pieces is a hopeless endeavour. Clans have been so broken up, and then their fractions have been so broken up again, individuals, families, and groups of kin being scattered in the course of a couple of centuries of movements, both of peoples and individuals, that it is no longer possible from present conditions to reach certain, or even probable, conclusions about clans of earlier times. Indeed, so considerably have the clans been shaken up that of the better-known ones probably the only one in which all the members give the same totem is the royal clan of the Avongara. No case was recorded in the samples examined of a member of this clan giving any other totem than the leopard. The reason for this is doubtless that it would be impossible for any commoner to identify himself with this aristocratic class. The historical importance of the confusion lies rather in the further evidence which it provides of the correctness of Zande traditions about their development, a political society emerging from wars, migrations, political domination, and cultural and social assimilation of the foreign peoples on a large scale; and also in the further fact that present circumstances of clans and their totemic affiliations cannot be understood without some knowledge of that development.

5. It will have been noted that no less than twenty-one out of the forty-two clans listed have (in the numerical sense already defined) as their totem *rungbu*, a long black snake with a narrow head, a fact which disposes of the idea that it is a function of totems to distinguish one clan from another, as is evident also in the case of other totems. Moreover it cannot adequately be accounted for by a hypothesis that the clans which have this snake for totem could be branches of a once single clan which

[1] Op. cit., p. 111.

have separated out from it, if only for the reason that, as can be seen in the table, while most of them are of Mbomu, or true Zande, stock, others belong to foreign peoples. It may be worth pointing out in this connection that a snake is the most appropriate totem among the Azande on account of their belief that the body-soul emerges in its totemic form from the grave of the deceased, a notion which it is easier to entertain in the case of snakes than, for example, chimpanzees or red pigs. However, suited to the belief though a snake may be, this would hardly account adequately for its preference as a totem; for snakes figure prominently, as totems or in other symbolic ways, in the thought of many African peoples who have no such beliefs. A psychological explanation is probably here required.

Whatever the explanation may be, it is a remarkable fact that twelve out of the twenty-one clans which have the *rungbu* as totem are probably Mbomu clans, while two others have the, presumably non-existent, rainbow-snake, as totem. This makes a snake, and especially the *rungbu* snake, the Mbomu totem *par excellence*. Of the Mbomu clans listed, only the Angbapiyo and the Abadara have non-snake totems—two out of sixteen. We may go further and say that the *rungbu* snake is the most representative totem of these forty-two well-known and numerically important clans; for it is also the totem of nine clans which are probably not of Mbomu, but of foreign origin, while a tenth (Abakpoto) has another snake (*ngbukpu*) as its totem. There is also what we might call a substantial minority representation of snake totems in clans which have a majority representation of some other totem. Altogether out of the sample of 3,071 individuals, 1,645—more than half—have snake totems, 1,464 of them the *rungbu* snake.

6. The lack of sharp differentiation between clans by totems, and the giving of different totems by persons claiming to be members of the same clan, are not only evidence of intermingling and dispersal of peoples on a vast scale, which we know to have happened, but also of the unimportance of totemism among the Azande, an unimportance that caused de Calonne to speak of pseudo-totemism. It must be appreciated in the light of the intermingling and dispersal, for it is difficult to see how clan totemism can have much meaning where there is so much mobility. As Mgr. Lagae remarks, '*Les Azande ne témoignent aucun*

culte, aucune marque de respect pour l'animal totem.[1] Almost all the
totems are either inedible or, where edible, belong to the class
of creatures called *nyakorokpa*, 'unclean', which are not eaten,
at least by any respectable person, unless he be very aged; and
those which are valued as food, such as the waterbuck, the pig,
the buffalo, and the domesticated fowl, are, I was informed, in
fact eaten by everyone, including those whose totems they are.
I admit that it was difficult to make certain of the accuracy of
the information, and it is true that in theory, whatever may
happen in practice, people are supposed to abstain from eating
their totems, as Mgr. Lagae[2] observes, though he admits that
they can kill them with impunity, which is certainly the case;
and if they kill them would such great lovers of flesh as the
Azande abstain from eating them? In any case, with the
exception of the red pig, the totem of the Abandogo, the other
animals habitually eaten by Azande appear in the census as
totems so rarely that they have little significance. Then, sharing
the same totem is in itself no bar to intermarriage, and here again,
though in theory having the same clan name and the same totem
is a bar, in practice such marriages sometimes take place,
though, apart from marriage within the royal clan, it would be
difficult to determine how often. On the other hand, not having
the same totem does not necessarily make a marriage permissible between persons with the same clan name. It may do so if
it is known that the spouses are of different ethnic origins; but
it will be remembered that it is a common opinion that men
take their totems from their fathers and women from their
mothers so that a man and his sister can have different totems,
so strictly speaking it would be said that even fellow clansfolk
do not have the same totem. Opinions on this matter are,
however, vague and lack unanimity. We may therefore agree
with de Calonne when he says that even in an isolated compact
group, as distinct from isolated individuals, knowledge of the
totem may *'passe au rang des préoccupations secondaires'*.[3] We can
readily understand this state of affairs when the totem is little
more than a word, or a name, and if this is possible with compact groups it is not at all improbable that individuals may be
uncertain about their totems—I have myself noticed hesitations

[1] Op. cit., p. 40.   [2] Ibid., p. 40.
[3] Op. cit., p. 192.

on the part of men asked for their totems—and that they may
therefore pass from one to another, for example, from one snake
to another, under the influence of their social environment,
difficult though it would be to prove this.

7. Absence of cult, absence of marks of respect, etc., may,
however, be regarded as signs, rather than as causes, of the lack
of significance which totems have for Azande. The cause is
undoubtedly that clans are not in any degree localized and have
no corporate functions. Clanship can have some general social
interest for the individual (he is expected to behave in certain
ways to not only all his own clansmen but to those also of his
in-laws, his mother's brother, his blood-brothers, his circumcision tutor, etc.), and a man may feel some contentment at
belonging to a Mbomu clan, not that that gives him any
privilege. But clans as such are so amorphous that they mean
little to Azande. If we except close kinsmen, who are seen as
kinsmen rather than as clansmen, and clansmen who are close
neighbours, seen as neighbours as much as clansmen, it would
be no more than a slight exaggeration, if that, to say that
membership of the same clan means little more to Azande than
to Scotsmen of today. There is little beyond the common name:
there are no lineages, and descent counts for so little that commoners neither know their descent nor feel embarrassed at not
knowing it. Zande society is essentially a political society in
which political status, authority, functions, office, and allegiance
count for more than membership of a clan, and in which clans
have no political status or functions. The only clan which is
important, as such, is that of the Avongara, and that is because
its members are everywhere the ruling aristocracy (for whom
the other Azande are all just commoners rather than members
of this or that clan) and here the importance of clan membership derives from class privilege and power.

Azande say that it was not always thus, that at one time the
clans, both Mbomu and foreign, lived each in its own locality
under its own elders. Then began the domination of the Mbomu
clans by the Avongara and afterwards the migrations and
conquests of the Ambomu under their Avongara rulers in which
all alike were scattered far and wide, such as we find them today.
Beyond question no one can reconstruct in any detail the history
of these movements, dislocations, and dispersals, but it is equally

certain that they took place and can be reconstructed in outline. Although it may be to some extent a romantic and distorted representation of the past when Azande picture their clans as once having been localized and politically autonomous, it corresponds in some measure to what we find among other Sudanic peoples who are without rulers. Moreover, the situation must at one time have resembled such a representation rather than the state of affairs in their more recent history, for it is difficult to see how totemic clans could have come into existence in conditions anything like those obtaining during the last two centuries or so. The present state of Zande clans and that of their totemic affiliations can be understood only in the light of the political development of Zande society, even though it can be for us only a glimmering light. Hundreds of thousands of people of different ethnic origins all jumbled up—the ethnologist in Africa may sometimes sigh for some neat little Polynesian or Melanesian island community!

PART TWO

VII

ZANDE CULTURE

THIS part is designed to give some indication of the extent to which the Ambomu (including the Avongara) have taken over foreign usages from peoples they subjugated or bordered, and of the complexity of the cultural amalgam which these borrowings have brought about.

To simplify the task I am restricting the inquiry in space, time, and cultural range. The Azande occupy a vast stretch of country and, though their language and basic institutions appear to be everywhere the same, there are regional diversities of culture, e.g. of food-plants or hut-forms, due to environmental or ethnic divergencies. I shall therefore consider only one portion of their country, that where I conducted most of my research, the old kingdom of Gbudwe, the most north-easterly extension of Zandeland, in the valley of the Sueh in the Sudan. Were I to use information recorded by others about Azande in other parts of their territory the list of cultural borrowings would doubtless be greatly lengthened, but, apart from the difficulties such an extension of the inquiry would involve, an examination of one particular area is all that is required to give the reader an appreciation of the Zande cultural complex and enable him to assess its significance. Moreover, the area chosen has the distinction of being one in which the Ambomu form a higher percentage of the population than in most, perhaps all, other areas, so that it may be supposed that they may have kept their culture there more intact than in other regions in which they are less well represented.

My researches in Zandeland were conducted between the years 1926 and 1930. The British controlled the country from 1905, but there cannot be said to have been any very effective administration till a few years before I first visited it, though there had, of course, been some social and cultural changes, especially in political affairs. I am not concerned here with those changes, which were mostly imposed on the Azande and are—when I use the present tense the reference is to the years 1926–30—not regarded by them as part of their way of life but something to be passively accepted or to be circumvented or ignored. To give one example: though the Administration compelled them to maintain wide roads, it was noticeable that when a group of Azande walked down them they did so in single file as they were accustomed to do along their bush paths. I am dealing with Zande culture as it was at the death of King Gbudwe (1905) and in the years immediately following that event, when what was borrowed from other peoples was taken over voluntarily and was absorbed into their way of life.

I have also been selective in choice of material. I wished to discover to what extent the Ambomu had borrowed from the foreign peoples whom they had conquered or who neighboured them. I did not pursue this inquiry into every department of their culture or into every detail, but I took soundings here and there over a wide area of it, consulting a number of persons whom I had found to be honest and well informed. Some of the detail so gathered has been omitted, it being thought that in certain cases a lot of Zande words referring to objects neither illustrated nor within my powers to describe would be superfluous and that sometimes a summary of the evidence would be sufficient.

How reliable is this evidence? This is a difficult question. It can be answered that whether what I was told was invariably correct or not, the information I was given shows how Azande themselves conceive of their culture as an amalgamation of elements taken from many different ethnic sources. We can, however, go further than that and show that the information given is sometimes substantiated by the records of travellers, by accounts of other peoples, and by environmental considerations.

We have first to recognize that the transmission of a cultural trait from one people to another is, as indeed is well known, a complicated process of assimilation and that the evidences of it may be obscured or entirely hidden. I give some examples from language and one from material culture. Others will be mentioned later. The Azande have had contacts of one sort or another with Arabs in all parts of their country for about a century and in the western part of it for an even longer period, possibly as early as the middle of the eighteenth century. It is very likely that Browne[1] was speaking of the Azande when he mentioned relations between Arab traders from Darfur, round about 1794, with the 'Gnum Gnum (a sobriquet)'. These contacts were least in the kingdom of Gbudwe and left no impression on the language there. However, after Anglo-Egyptian rule had been established in the Sudan, the young men of Gbudwe's old kingdom sometimes picked up Arabic words and phrases either in government stations in their country or in the course of employment elsewhere and incorporated these into their own tongue, but they were recognizable only if one knew Arabic, for they were transformed both phonetically and grammatically. Thus in the sentence *gimi asadu kina o*, 'I have witnesses', the word *asadu*, witnesses (the *a* is the Zande plural prefix), is the Arabic *shahid*, 'witness'. Borrowed words have been given both Zande prefixes and suffixes. Who, if he did not know Arabic, would guess that the verb in the phrase *mi ausunga gu pai te*, 'I do not want that talk', is not a Zande one but the Arabic *'awiz* 'to want'? In *mi atafatisinga rago tipa baso te*, 'I have not yet searched the place for the spear', the Arabic verb *fattish*, 'to search for', is concealed between the Zande prefixes *a* and *ta* and the Zande suffix *nga*. In sketches by early travellers Azande men are shown wearing straw hats. Schweinfurth[2] describes them as using 'a cylindrical hat without any brim, square at the top and always ornamented with a waving plume of feathers; the hat is fastened on by large hair-pins, made either of iron, copper, or ivory, and tipped with crescents, tridents, knobs, and various other devices'. The same kind of cylindrical, brimless, straw hat was still worn in 1906 when Geyer[3] visited the Azande of Tembura's kingdom and of the old kingdom of Ezo. This is the old Mbomu hat, called *kutuku*, and some of the older men still keep to a version of it. The hat which is today fashionable, and has been for some years, is of much the same shape but with two new features: black lateral patterns, often wavy lines, and a broad brim, the first being copied from the Mangbetu and the

[1] W. G. Browne, *Travels in Africa, Egypt, and Syria from the Year 1792 to 1798*, 1799, p. 310. [2] Op. cit., vol. ii, p. 8.
[3] F. Geyer, *Durch Sand, Sumpf und Wald*, 1914, p. 303.

second from the earliest Europeans. As we shall see, there is very often this kind of fusion of borrowed and indigenous elements.

We have also to bear in mind that Azande of Gbudwe's old kingdom may know, or think they know, or have been told, that something they now have did not form part of the original Mbomu culture but was taken over from some foreign people, without being certain of its precise provenance. They may then say, for example, that 'it came from beyond the Uele river' or that 'it was taken over from foreigners to the west', or they may use a blanket-term like 'Mangbetu', a word which covers a number of peoples ruled at one time by the Mangbetu family, or they may just fall back on a category like 'Amiangba', a people to whom there is a tendency to attribute borrowings believed to have been made from some assimilated people, the word sometimes being used in a rather broad sense to designate other foreign stocks besides the Amiangba (Abarambo), such as sections of the Amadi and the Abangbinda. Often, however, they are definite about locations.

After these introductory remarks I commence the survey with some observations on cultivated plants. Schweinfurth passed through the eastern extremities of Zandeland at a time when the Mbomu conquest and assimilation of various foreign peoples were still in process. In assessing his observations it has to be borne in mind that we cannot always be certain whether he was describing Ambomu, people partly assimilated to the Ambomu, or what may have been people still little influenced by Mbomu ways of life. When, therefore, he speaks of the Niam-Niam his remarks have to be interpreted in a very broad sense. He says:[1] 'The Niam-Niam may be designated as a tribe of hunters, which, as is proved by the small quantity of cereals grown, makes agriculture only a secondary object, it being exclusively assigned to the female sex. The products of the soil are, enumerated according to the quantity yielded, Eleusine, Cassaves (Manioc), sweet Potatoes, Yams, Indian corn, Sorghum, Tobacco, Sesame, Colocasia, Bananas, and Sugar-cane.' He says elsewhere[2] that 'the men most studiously devote themselves to their hunting, and leave the culture of the soil to be carried on exclusively by the women' and that the men 'do nothing for

---

[1] G. Schweinfurth, *Artes Africanae*, 1875, Tab. XI.
[2] Idem, *The Heart of Africa*, 1873, vol. ii, 1922, p. 12.

the support of their families beyond providing them with game'. Nevertheless, the people as a whole are agriculturists as well as hunters. Now, Schweinfurth travelled through Zande country during the rains, when today both sexes give most of their time to their cultivations, so seasonal conditions can hardly account for his remarks about division of labour between the sexes and also about the predominance of hunting over agriculture. He supports his observation on the latter point by drawing attention[1] to 'the small size and unpractical construction' of their mortars, used to bruise the hard eleusine grain, and it may receive some support from his drawings of granaries, which appear to have been smaller than those built today. Emin[2] also declares that hunting is the chief occupation of the Azande, and Piaggia[3] remarks that, except for rather casual cultivation of millet, the sole food-producing occupation of the men is hunting. On the other hand, Junker,[4] writing just over ten years later, says that though the Azande are keen sportsmen 'they by no means depend mainly on the products of the chase. They would be reduced to sore distress if corn did not form their staple food at least during certain seasons of the year.' Nevertheless, the impressions of Schweinfurth, Piaggia, and Emin may have been in the main correct, and, if it is so, then there has been an important change in Zande economy, for no one during the present century could have suggested that they are not primarily an agricultural people. The Azande are now, to quote one recent observer, 'pre-eminently agricultural'[5] citing the reports of Myres, who claimed that in one morning in a single Zande settlement (presumably an imposed governmental one composed of a fair number of homesteads) he collected specimens of no less than sixty-eight crops, all named and distinguished. It should be added here that the Azande have no domesticated animals other than dogs and chickens, as Kroll correctly states.[6] If there has been this change in modes of livelihood we are better able to understand the Zande migrations, for they are easier to understand given a basic hunting and collecting, and therefore mobile, economy. It is possible also that the increase

[1] G. Schweinfurth, *Artes Africanae*, 1875, Tab. XIII.   [2] Op. cit., p. 451.
[3] Antinori, op. cit., p. 127.   [4] Op. cit., 1891, p. 161.
[5] Crowther in J. D. Tothill, (ed.), *Agriculture in the Sudan*, 1948, pp. 489–90.
[6] H. Kroll, 'Die Haustiere der Bantu', *Zeitschrift für Ethnologie*, 1929, pp. 215 et seq.

in power of the Vongara ruling families and the assimilation of foreign peoples may be connected with the greater stability a growing dependence on cultivated crops might have brought about.

If we cannot go beyond conjecture in this matter we can at least say, if Zande statements are to be trusted, that a high proportion of their cultivated plants have been borrowed during the course of their conquests in the eighteenth and nineteenth centuries. The staple cereal of the Azande is eleusine or bird-seed millet, but the main varieties (*maduara, baliwa, ngbindo, bambiso,* and *bandikondo*) were all said by my informants to have belonged originally to Miangba culture; and it is possible that the cultivation of eleusine was learnt from this people. De Calonne[1] is of the opinion that the Azande borrowed eleusine from the Akare and the Basiri peoples. On the other hand, several of the more important varieties of maize (*baguga, mbuma, gbangagbodi,* and *andege*) are firmly claimed by Ambomu to have been cultivated by their forebears, while they obtained the *nabandai* variety from the Ambili people, that called *badali,* used together with eleusine in brewing beer, from the Amiangba, and those called *ngbaya putu* and *ngbaya mbira* much later from the Belgians or Africans who came with them. However, though some varieties may have been introduced much earlier than others, all must have been introduced and none could have been cultivated by the Ambomu, nor indeed by anybody else in Central Africa, till fairly recent times, for, as is well known, maize is a native of America. Probably, like manioc, it reached the Azande from the south-west. De Calonne[2] asserts that the Abarambo (Amiangba) learnt its use, as also the cultivation of sorghum, from the Azande. That maize, when introduced, may, as Azande suggest, have then become their staple crop, before they learnt to cultivate eleusine or at any rate to cultivate it on any scale, is the more likely in that we learn from the same author[3] that maize '*constitue la base de la nourriture des Abandya*', the people, that is, who live in, or nearest to, the old Mbomu homeland in the valley of the Mbomu; and further in that we are told by Burssens[4] that the chief plants cultivated in the

[1] Op. cit., p. 212.   [2] Op. cit., p. 212.
[3] Ibid., p. 210.
[4] H. Burssens, *Les Peuplades de l'Entre-Congo-Ubangi*, 1958, p. 74.

Congo-Ubangi district in 1933, the area being that to the west of the Azande and the Abandya, were maize, bitter manioc, and bananas, then sorghum, ground-nuts, sesame, pumpkins, yams, and rice. The red kind of sorghum or dura (*zamba vunde*)—probably of African origin—is said to be a plant of the Ambomu and the other varieties to be foreign, *roli* having been taken over from the Amiangba, and the varieties *mbilika*, *bawiligugo*, and *koya* from the Baka people to the east. De Schlippe[1] says that one variety (*mobioro*) is of Dinka origin. The sweet sorghum (*koko atara*) came from south of the Uele and its culture is said to have moved northwards from the Abudu (Mabudu) people who live to the south of the Mangbetu cluster. De Schlippe[2] says that the bulrush millet (*ngiria*), little cultivated and only in the most northerly regions of Zandeland, came from the north.

The Azande cultivate a number of plants from which oil is extracted. The ground-nut, or at any rate the small variety called *abalungbwandura* or *azuguzugu*, is thought to be an old Mbomu plant. Two varieties entered Gbudwe's kingdom from outside it, *bazamangi* from some foreign people in Tembura's kingdom to the west and *amangirimo* from an uncertain, but southern, provenance. Although Azande may think of the Ambomu as having brought at any rate one variety with them from the west, it is reasonable to suppose that they must have acquired it in the course of their migrations, for it is a native of South America, and de Calonne, who was in the northern Congo from 1905 to 1915, says[3] that it was then only extensively cultivated by the Momvu and had among the Azande secondary importance as an oil-bearer to sesame, suggesting that it had made only limited progress even by that time; so we may conclude that its present importance is very recent. We may have greater trust in that conclusion in that that indefatigable student of plant life, Georg Schweinfurth, nowhere mentions ground-nuts among the principal Zande crops, though he says[4] that peoples who live to the north of the Azande of the Sudan cultivated them extensively (he believed it to be an African plant). The facts recorded by Schweinfurth may perhaps be

---

[1] P. De Schlippe, *Shifting Cultivation in Africa*, 1956, p. 54.
[2] Loc. cit.   [3] Op. cit., p. 212.
[4] G. Schweinfurth, *The Heart of Africa*, 1873, vol. i, p. 250.

accounted for by a guess that the ground-nut came to the Azande late—De Schlippe[1] says in the second half of the nineteenth century—from Angola through the Congo, whereas it reached the more northern peoples earlier from European settlements in north-west Africa. Sesame of the kind called *bagara* and an oil-seed cucurbit called *bangumbe* are old Mbomu plants, but other oil-bearing plants are said to have been borrowed: a melon called *detiro*, the gourd *kpagu*, the cucumber *koforo*, and the hyptis or hard sesame (*andaka*), a plant of American origin, from the Amiangba; a sesame of the kind called *bura* from the Baka people; and another called *Anzongbo* from the Adio, who probably took it over from their neighbours. The Azande bordering the Belanda (Mberidi and Mbegumba) appear to have borrowed from them the sesame called *bura* and another oil-bearing plant called *gali*, the nature of which I cannot determine. The Azande of Gbudwe's kingdom imported palm-oil from the south but they do not seem to have at any time attempted to cultivate the palm. Czekanowski says that these palms are numerous among the Azande of the Mbomu river.[2]

The Ambomu are said to have taken over from the Amiangba the chief pulses they now cultivate, the nettle bean or mung bean (*abakpa*) and two varieties of the earth-pea (*abandu*)— *zambara*, the red ones, and *abakabu*. De Schlippe[3] says the nettle bean is an old—though it could not be very old—introduction from the Nilotic peoples to the north. I was told that the black variety of the earth-pea or earthnut (*bi abandu*) had been recently introduced by the *Amusungu*, a somewhat vague term, of Bantu origin, indicating both the Belgians and such followers and influences as came in with their conquest. The varieties of the cowpea (*abapu*) called *akurungu*, *adungu*, and *awangu*, are said to be Mbomu plants, and those called *aura*, *amanzinzi*, and *awilinduemuduba* to be Amiangba plants, the last being a plant of the most easterly of that people, as is perhaps suggested by its name: 'toes of Muduba', Muduba having been a king of that area at one time. The variety called *arubiya* came from one of the foreign peoples subject to King Tembura to the west, and that called *abedi* also. De Schlippe[4] says that the climbing Lima

[1] Op. cit., p. 58.   [2] Op. cit., p. 29.
[3] Op. cit., p. 56.   [4] Loc. cit.

bean (*akpokoworo*), of South American origin, as its English name tells us, is probably of recent introduction to Zandeland.

The Zande reserve or famine crop is the starchy root of the manioc or cassava. Some varieties of this plant (*mazaranguya, bayuko, magburu* or *magbodo*, and *mbili*) are said to be Mbomu. Others came from what the Azande of the Sudan call *mbitiyo*, 'on the other side', that is, to the south of the Uele river, the Mangbetu, the Ababua, and the Bakongo being mentioned as peoples from whom they were borrowed: *babua* (after the Ababua people) or *bakango* (after the Bakongo people), *gbanda gisasa, gbanda nyoki*, and others. Two varieties (*bagbanda* and *mbirambira gbanda*) are said to be of Miangba origin. That kind which contains enough prussic acid to be highly poisonous till soaked (*gbazamangi*) came from one of the subjugated peoples to the west. Junker[1] says that the Azande mostly cultivate this, the bitter, kind of manioc. My informants were surely right in giving a southern origin to various kinds of manioc, and if the Ambomu, as they say, already possessed others before they reached what was Gbudwe's kingdom they would most likely have come from the same direction. Manioc is a South American plant which could scarcely have entered Africa before the sixteenth century. Schweinfurth[2] is doubtless correct when he says that very probably it found its way from Angola, where it was first planted by the Portuguese, north-eastwards through the Congo. He noted[3] that in 1870 it was as yet unknown to the Bongo and other peoples bordering the Azande to the north, as were also the sweet potato and colocasia. The probability therefore is that it reached the Azande not before the nineteenth century and that such varieties of it as are said to be Mbomu were acquired from the south during their migrations. This conclusion seems to be supported by Jones's discussion[4] of the introduction and spread of manioc in Africa. Of the varieties of sweet potato, a plant of South American origin, now much culti-vated in Gbudwe's kingdom, the red sort (*abazamba*), the small white sort (*puse abangbe*), and those called *awaya, amongoni*, and *anzepi* are said to be Mbomu. Others are said to have come from the south: *abedi, abagesangboyo*, and *angoliyonaga*. The variety

[1] Op. cit., 1892, pp. 140-1.
[2] G. Schweinfurth, *The Heart of Africa*, 1873, vol. i, p. 527.
[3] Ibid. p. 251.   [4] W. O. Jones, *Manioc in Africa*, 1959, Chap. 3.

mbara was taken over from the Mangbetu cluster, and a white kind, *aboduru*, was introduced from the west. I have no record of the origin of yet other varieties. De Calonne[1] thought that the Azande must have received the sweet potato from the Abarambo (Amiangba). Its cuttings (*gile abangbe*) are closely associated in Zande minds with traditions of migrations, for they are easily planted and therefore represent, what in fact they may have been, the first food-crop planted in their new homes by the migrants in their displacements.

I was told that, of the cultivated yams, the *gbara nduka* and one of the cocoyams (*manzi*) are old Mbomu plants, the *adumbisikume* is Miangba, the *gbawe* is an introduction from the Uele region, and the aerial yam (*mere*) is a loan from the Abasiri people of the west. The cocoyam just mentioned is the *Colocasia antiquorum* (probably of Asian origin). The other species cultivated by Azande, the *Xanthosoma sagittifolium*, an American plant, was introduced, according to Irvine,[2] to the Gold Coast (now Ghana) from the West Indies by Basel missionaries in 1843. If this was its first introduction into Africa it must have reached the Azande very recently.

Another starchy food-plant cultivated by all Azande is the banana, though Azande of the north-east live on the limits of its distribution. It is doubtful whether the Ambomu knew this plantain before their migrations. Some say that they possessed the kind called *biro*, but others assert that this was taken over from the Amiangba: 'It was the Amiangba who discovered it first, it was the Amiangba who had the *biro* in their homesteads, for it was originally not known to the Ambomu.' I have no doubt that in point of fact this banana came from the Mangbetu, as is shown by its Mangbetu name, *nebiro*.[3] In this case it could scarcely be an old Mbomu plant. De Schlippe says that it is a recent introduction from the Congo into the Sudan.[4] Other bananas now cultivated in Gbudwe's old kingdom (*bagbagawa*, *ngbikpi*—again a Mangbetu word,[5] *lindimbara*, and at least eight other varieties—I need not list all the names) were introduced from the Uele region: 'They all came to the Azande from beyond the Uele, for Azande frequently journeyed there and

---

[1] Op. cit., p. 212.
[2] F. R. Irvine, *A Text-book of West African Agriculture*, 1934, p. 137.
[3] Casati, op. cit., vol. i, p. 177.
[4] Op. cit., p. 71.
[5] Casati, op. cit., vol. i, p. 177.

returned with seeds [and suckers] of plants to their homes here', said a Zande of the Sudan. Some varieties (*bu atara* and *tingi-tingi*) are said to have been introduced much later, probably by the Belgians or their African followers. There can be little doubt, therefore, that the Ambomu learnt to cultivate the banana, at least to any extent, from southern peoples, and most probably from the Mangbetu, from whom their generic name for banana, *bu*, may also have been taken (Mangbetu: *nebugu*). Indeed, de Calonne says[1] that in his time (1905–15) the banana in the eastern districts did not extend, except by chance, to the north of the Kibali–Uele. This is not strictly true, for Schweinfurth remarks that bananas were to be seen among these eastern Azande in 1870, though rarely.[2] From what he had seen he concluded that they were unlikely to be a main support of life at any latitude higher than 4° N. They are also mentioned by Piaggia among Zande food-crops;[3] and he was probably including the most north-easterly of the Azande among whom he chiefly resided. Petherick, speaking of the same region, also says that bananas are indigenous to the country.[4] Nevertheless de Calonne's statement is in the main a correct appreciation, and it is further supported by Junker,[5] who remarks that, though bananas certainly occur in the northern districts, they do so only in small patches; and he says again, when crossing the Uere in September 1882 on his way northwards, 'we were now beyond the limits of the banana zone proper, though a few were still cultivated by the Zandehs of this district'.[6] Farther west the banana was found in greater abundance in northern regions than to the east. Junker found it much cultivated on the Mbomu in Zemio's country, 'in many places forming continuous thickets';[7] and it was found to the west at the end of the last century as far north as 6° Lat. N.[8] Banana culture in the easterly parts of Zandeland must have greatly increased during the present century, for it was cultivated everywhere and by all in my day.

[1] Op. cit., p. 210. [2] G. Schweinfurth, *The Heart of Africa*, 1873, vol. ii, p. 14.
[3] Antinori, op. cit., p. 127.
[4] *Egypt, the Sudan and Central Africa*, 1861, p. 466.
[5] Op. cit., 1891, vol. ii, p. 230. [6] Op. cit., 1892, vol. iii, p. 141.
[7] Ibid., p. 176.
[8] Anon., 'M. M. Nillis and de la Kéthulle on the Borders of Darfur', *The Geographical Journal*, 1896, p. 429.

I have recorded Zande statements about only a few other of their cultivated plants yielding food. The white species (*puse mboya*) of *Hibiscus* or ladies' fingers, possibly an American[1] or Indian[2] plant, comes from Tembura's kingdom to the west. I have no information about the red species, the *zamba mboya*. *Boko*, a pumpkin, is said to have come from the Amiangba and Amadi peoples. The sugar cane is said to have been borrowed from the Mangbetu; Schnell says that it has an Asian origin and was introduced into Negro Africa by the Arabs.[3]

Two interesting cases are the red pepper-plant or chili (*ralia* or *siyata* in Zande) and the cultivated fig-tree (*roko*) from the bark of which Azande manufacture their cloth. The red pepper-plant, of American origin, is a sub-spontaneous growth in cultivations, and I was told that it was not used in old times for culinary purposes. Azande say that they saw Arabs collect the pods and copied them, now using them to give a tang to stews and sometimes adding the leaves to those of manioc, *mbadabu*, and other green vegetables. Old men at first refused to eat it, believing *si ka gbataka bambu awilu*, 'it might destroy their fertility'. That its use may in fact have been copied from the Arabs is further supported by the fact that the word *siyata*, now well established in the language, is the Arabic *shatta*. This conclusion does not conflict with Petherick's statement[4] that in the first Zande village he came to he found growing in the gardens, among other plants, the pepper-plant (Petherick visited the confines of north-eastern Zandeland before any Arab traders are known to have entered that region), for the plant is sown in gardens by birds. When I was in Zandeland, over sixty years later, the plant was not cultivated, though it was sometimes to be found, bird-sown, in cultivations. It may be noted here that Schweinfurth says the Azande will not touch pimento but they season their dishes with the Malaghetta pepper (*Amomum Melegueta*).[5] What I have been discussing is the shrub *Capsicum frutescens*. Schweinfurth says[6] that the Mangbetu use both for seasoning.

[1] De Schlippe, op. cit., p. 70.   [2] Irvine, op. cit., p. 247.
[3] R. Schnell, *Plantes alimentaires et vie agricole de l'Afrique Noire*, 1957, p. 140.
[4] Op. cit., 1861, p. 468.
[5] G. Schweinfurth, *The Heart of Africa*, 1873, vol. i, pp. 462 and 469.
[6] Idem, 'Das Volk der Monbuttu in Central-Afrika', *Zeitschrift für Ethnologie*, 1873, p. 9.

If Schweinfurth's assertion (mentioned above) that the Azande were primarily a hunting people is correct, we might expect that they would have dressed themselves in skins and not in the barkcloth invariably worn by the men in my day, the women wearing bunches of leaves before and behind, for the fig-trees from the bark of which the cloth is made are slow to mature and their culture implies stable settlement. That is precisely what Schweinfurth states[1] was the case in 1870 in the eastern part of Zandeland visited by him. He says—earlier qualifications with regard to his observations have to be borne in mind—

On rare occasions, a piece of material made from the bark of the Urostigma is worn as clothing; but, as a general rule, the entire costume is composed of skins, which are fastened to a girdle and form a picturesque drapery about the loins. The finest and most variegated skins are chosen for this purpose, those of the genet and colobus being held in the highest estimation; the long black tail of the quereza monkey (*Colobus*) is also fastened to the dress. . . . In crossing the dewy steppes in the early morning during the rainy season, the men are accustomed to wear a large antelope hide, which is fastened around the neck, and falling to the knees, effectually protects the body from the cold moisture of the long grass. A covering, which always struck me as very graceful, was formed from the skin of the harness bush-bock (*A. scripta*), of which the dazzling white stripes on a yellowish ground never fail to be very effective.

He says also[2] that the Azande at King Ngangi's court were girded with skins, as became a hunting people; and furthermore that the Zande women wore an apron of hides.[3] On the other hand, he tells us[4] that in Zande homesteads 'Close in the rear of the huts, upon the level ground, were the magazines for corn; behind these would be seen a circle of Rokko fig-trees, which are only found in cultivated spots, and the bark of which is prized, far more than the handsomest of skins, as a material to make into clothing.' (In the English edition the text continues with the statement that further in the background might be noticed an enclosure of paradise figs. This is a translation from the original German edition (p. 176), but it must be pointed out that for the confusing 'paradise figs' we should read 'bananas'.

[1] G. Schweinfurth, *The Heart of Africa*, 1873, vol. ii, p. 6.
[2] Ibid., vol. i, p. 440.   [3] Ibid., vol. ii, p. 104.   [4] Ibid., vol. i, p. 449.

In the last and revised German edition of *Im Herzen von Afrika* the passage reads 'Weiter im Hintergrunde folgt eine vollständige Einfriedigung von Bananen . . .',[1] which is surely what Schweinfurth saw.) However, it is clear from the passage that Schweinfurth intended to convey that, although barkcloth was worn, its use was restricted, and he is quite explicit on this point when speaking of Azande further to the south:[2] 'Throughout the whole of the territory that was subject to Wando, the clothing of all the people consisted of skins, as the fig-tree, of which the bark is so generally used in the south, does not thrive here at all well. For all those who require it, the bark has to be imported from the country of the Monbuttoo [Mangbetu], and is consequently an article of luxury.' He found, as this quotation implies, that the peoples further to the south wore barkcloth and not, like the Azande, skins.

The evidence of other travellers is to some extent conflicting and confusing. Petherick, probably speaking of the Adio Azande, the most easterly Azande, says that 'A thick texture of a dark-brown colour, woven from the bark fibres, was worn by both sexes: by the females round the loins, but the men, generally possessing larger pieces, slung them around the body, leaving the arms in freedom';[3] and again that 'They envelope their loins in a cloth of their own make from the fibres of bark'.[4] Piaggia,[5] speaking of King Tombo in the valley of the Sueh river, says:

I suoi uomini appendono in giro alla cintola simmetricamente disposte e ridotte a forma oblunga ed ovale, variate pelli di quadrupedi, scegliendo quelle fra esse che hanno più ricca la coda per coprirne le reni. Altri invece non hanno al fianco che una sottile e rotonda cintura d'ippopotamo a cui sta appesa una zucchetta gialla tutta incisa a disegni, che contiene grasso per ungersi la persona.

But he also says,[6]

I più erano del tutto scoperti, ma alcuni fasciavano la parte inferiore del corpo con una corteccia d'albero, resa flessibile a guisa d'una striscia di panno grossolano e fermata alla vita per mezzo di cordoni di pelle d'ippopotamo, in modo che una estremità passava sul dietro

---

[1] Idem, *Im Herzen von Afrika*, 1922 ed., 1922, p. 234.
[2] Idem, *The Heart of Africa*, 1873, vol. i, p. 480.   [3] Op. cit., 1861, p. 466.
[4] Mr. and Mrs. Petherick, *Travels in Central Africa*, vol. i, 1869, p. 280.
[5] Antinori, op. cit., p. 122.   [6] Piaggia, op. cit., 1877, p. 7.

della persona, e le due estremità cadendo rovesciate in basso pare-
vano due grembiuli.

In his memoirs he alleges that the young women preferred to
go about naked because they thought that nakedness appealed
to the men.[1] If indeed some were *del tutto scoperte*, and on a matter
of this kind Piaggia's memory could scarcely have played him
false, they cannot, I believe, have been Ambomu or even Azande
in the sense of assimilated foreigners. They could have been
Babukur (Abuguru), a people who probably formed the majority of the population of Tombo's kingdom, about which Piaggia
was speaking, though if this were so he was clearly unaware of
the fact. However, we have no authority for asserting that this
people went about naked. The only other writer who says that
the Azande were naked was Poncet,[2] but he appears never to
have himself visited Zandeland and to have relied on reports
from his Arabo-Nubian followers. He states that the women (of
the Adio Azande) wore leaves before and behind and that the
men were naked. His statement that these Zande men were
naked cannot be correct, for Junker,[3] writing, a few years later
it is true, as an eye-witness of the same Azande (Bombehs or
Makaraka—the Adio), says: 'The men wear a coarse bark cloth
made of the *Urostigma*, the women an apron of foliage, besides
a heavy load of iron rings and other ornaments. . . . As spoils of
the chase the men deck themselves with the skin of *Antilope
scripta*, and of the beautiful Colobus ape, the former hanging
from the shoulder, the latter on the back fastened round the
hips.' He also says, speaking of the same section of the Azande,
that 'The clothes, for the most part limited to loin-cloths, belong
also to the military outfit. They are made of the hides of animals,
the Shirr antelope, the genet, and the beautiful Guereza ape,
and the effect is fantastic and picturesque.'[4] These skins are
worn today only by witch-doctors during their performances,
and perhaps we should regard their professional costume as a
survival of what was once normal dress, as is suggested also by
another of their effects, a belt hung with bells cut out of the
stones of the fruit of the Borassus palm, figured by Schweinfurth

[1] A. Pellegrinetti, *Le memorie di Carlo Piaggia*, 1941, p. 290.
[2] J. Poncet, *Le Fleuve blanc*, 1863, pp. 37–8.
[3] Op. cit., vol. i, 1890, pp. 309–10.
[4] Ibid., p. 435.

and described as 'a favourite ornament with the Niam-niam, worn at dances'.[1]

Marno says that in 1875 the Adio Azande wore *Schürzen von Fellen* whereas the Mangbetu wore *Bekleidung aus Baumrinden-zeug*.[2] Heuglin never reached Zandeland and was relying on hearsay when he wrote that the men wear either aprons or cloth draped round them (*Umhängetücher*), made from foreign cloth or from the bast of a sycamore, while others draw a piece of tanned leather through their legs and this is held in place back and front by a belt. They never go naked. Women's clothing consists of a long body dress (*Leibrock*) made of cotton cloth or barkcloth (*Faser-Stoff*) or leaves tucked into a belt.[3] Cotton clothes might have been worn at this time by an occasional Zande who had been in touch with Arabs to the north and north-west of Zandeland, but their use could not have been common, and they were rarely to be seen even in my day, over sixty years later. Casati[4] says that the Azande make barkcloth from the bark of the Urostigma and that the dresses of the men 'cover from their hips down to the knees, and are made of the bark of trees, pressed and beaten out in imitation of the Mambettu, but in a less perfect manner'.[5] Czekanowski takes this to mean, I suppose rightly, that in Casati's opinion the Azande learnt the use of barkcloth from the Mangbetu and therefore used it only fairly recently, a view which fits in with what Schweinfurth and Marno report of the most easterly of the Azande, and he questions this opinion.[6] He says that in all the territory he covered (the most south-eastern parts of Zandeland) in the years 1907 and 1908 the men wore barkcloth, and he further observes that De la Kéthulle de Ryhove had established that the western Azande also wore barkcloth, and he thinks that Mangbetu influence did not extend that far. Nevertheless he supports Casati in saying that Zande barkcloth is cruder than that of the Mangbetu, and though he doubts whether it was from the Mangbetu that Azande learnt to manufacture it, he seems to take the view that at one time it was unknown to

[1] G. Schweinfurth, *Artes Africanae*, 1875, Tab. XIII, Fig. 18.

[2] E. Marno, *Reise in der egyptischen Aequatorial-Provinz und in Kordofan in den Jahren 1874–1876*, 1879, pp. 103 and 129.

[3] M. Th. v. Heuglin, *Reise in das Gebiet des Weissen Nil und seiner westlichen Zuflüsse in den Jahren 1862–1864*, 1869, p. 206.

[4] Op. cit., vol. i, p. 121.   [5] Ibid., p. 206.   [6] Op. cit., p. 32.

them. Baumann is of the same opinion.[1] I must observe that it does not follow from the fact that Mangbetu influence did not extend to the Azande of the west that the making of barkcloth was not taken over from them in the first instance, for it could then have passed from the Azande of the south-east to those of the west.

My own notes on this issue are, alas, most inadequate, but they are at least sufficient to suggest that it may not be so simple as at first sight it might appear to be, for there may be more than one species of fig-tree from which cloth is manufactured (one appears to be *Ficus Thonningii*, which seems to be found in Africa only in a cultivated state, indicating that it originated elsewhere, probably in Asia; and others may be *F. platyphylla* and *F. glumosa* var. *glaberrima*). While one kind, the *roko kpolo*, was said to be Mbomu, it was acknowledged that the most favoured kind, *bagadi*, was borrowed from the Mangbetu—it is a Mangbetu word, *nebagadi*—and it was suggested that other kinds might have been taken over from the Amiangba. On the evidences presented, I am inclined in this matter to follow Casati, at any rate up to the point of accepting that the universal use of barkcloth among the Azande of the Sudan in my day was the result of outside contacts. I find it difficult to believe that, had barkcloth been the covering habitually worn by the Ambomu, they would not have brought the fig-tree eastwards with them and so continued to dress in their customary manner instead of in the skins Schweinfurth says all but the most privileged were wearing in 1870, for its propagation is simple. The trees in the Sudan must have been introduced from somewhere, for we have the authoritative statement of Schweinfurth that they are only found in a cultivated state in that region and even so do not flourish there as they do further to the south, in the vicinity of the Uele river and to the south of it. De Schlippe's description of them in the Sudan[2] as 'a sub-spontaneous crop often sprouting from fences' would not have made much sense for the Azande of my day, for they did not make fences of *Ficus*. The trees were cultivated round the homesteads and were therefore correctly listed by Schweinfurth among the Zande *Kulturpflanzen*.[3]

[1] H. Baumann, *Die materielle Kultur der Azande und Mangbetu*, 1927, p. 17.
[2] Op. cit., p. 74.
[3] G. Schweinfurth, *Linguistische Ergebnisse einer Reise nach Centralafrika*, 1873, p. 45.

Moreover, since they grow neither wild nor at their best in the Sudan, would it be rash to presume that they do not do so in the Mbomu homeland in the valley of the Mbomu, which is in the same latitude? Taking all the evidence into consideration, I conclude that if one cannot say definitely it was from the Mangbetu that Azande learnt the cultivation of Urostigma (*Ficus*) and the manufacture of its bark into cloth, it may be regarded as highly probable that they acquired these skills from southern peoples, among whom are the Mangbetu, in the course of their southward migrations.

I only touch on a further problem relating to Zande cultivation of plants, for I am unable to contribute information to the solution of it. It is raised by Schweinfurth. He mentions that the Zande name for the tobacco plant *Nicotiana tabacum* is *gundey* and adds that the Azande 'are the only people of the Bahr-al-Ghazal district that have a special designation for the plant'. The other sort, *N. rustica*, which, on the contrary, has a local appellation in nearly every dialect of the neighbouring peoples (apparently denoting that the plant is indigenous to Central Africa), 'is utterly unknown throughout the country'.[1] He says in an earlier passage that there is not another people from the Niger to the Nile which has a native word of their own to denote the Virginian tobacco plant (the *N. tabacum*)—their names for it are all derived from some European form of the American Indian word for tobacco—and that the common tobacco plant (the *N. rustica*) is unknown to the Azande.[2] However, in spite of Schweinfurth's suggestion that the *N. rustica* may be indigenous to Africa, it now seems much more likely that it was introduced from Central America[3] and, if this is so, it could not have reached Africa till the sixteenth century or later. As De Schlippe,[4] in discussing the tobacco plant, does not mention this species, it might be assumed that the Azande do not yet cultivate it, although Schweinfurth says that some of their neighbours did so almost a century ago. Such an assumption would, however, have to be qualified, for otherwise what are we to make of Piaggia's assertion that among Zande cultivated plants he noted *due specie di tabacco*?[5] In matters of this kind

[1] Idem, *The Heart of Africa*, vol. ii, 1873, pp. 14–15.
[2] Ibid., vol. i, p. 254.
[3] E. D. Merrill, *The Botany of Cook's Voyages*, 1954, p. 312.
[4] Op. cit., p. 75.   [5] Op. cit., p. 289.

Piaggia, who had once earned his living as a gardener, is unlikely to have been mistaken. The explanation of this conflict of evidence is probably to be found in the fact that Piaggia mostly resided at the court of King Tombo in the midst of a foreign population, Abuguru and perhaps some Bongo, who, it would appear from Schweinfurth's statements, cultivated both *N. rustica* and *N. tabacum*.

It may be added that two fruit-bearing plants were in process of being introduced by the Belgians and British, and doubtless by the French also, during my residence among the Azande, the pineapple and the mango, though it must be said that the people showed little interest in either and only a few individuals connected with administration or missions cultivated them, and only in a very small way.

Culinary habits are related to the culture of plants. The origin of only one type of preparation of food was inquired into, the brewing of beer. I was told that the brewing of beer from maize (*kpete*), sorghum (*bazagbara*), and one variety of manioc (*bayeko*), is an old Mbomu practice. Beer today is usually brewed from eleusine, and this was said to have been learnt from the Amiangba, a statement which accords with the suggestion earlier advanced that the cultivation of eleusine may have been taken over from that people; and it is also from them that the Azande say they learnt to brew beer from two other varieties of manioc. Brewing from bananas, sometimes practised by Azande of the Sudan, but especially by those in the Congo, was copied from the Mangbetu, from whom, as we have noted, most, if not all, varieties of this plantain were borrowed. From the Congo was also introduced the brewing of *mbira* beer, which I believe to be a brew from the variety of maize of that name. The distillation of spirits from grain, practised sporadically in the Sudan during my time, and the name, *areki*, by which it is known, had been introduced by the Arabs from the north.

Before leaving the domesticated plants I return to a consideration of the question raised earlier, whether the Azande were in past times primarily a hunting people or what they are today, primarily an agricultural people. I will not enter into the complicated problem whether some plants are native to Asia or Africa or both; for, whether they have an Asiatic origin or not, such plants as sesame, banana, and the cultivated millets have long been domiciled in Africa, though there seems to be no way of determining even an approximate date for their introduction or the means of it. We are more fortunate in the case of the plants native to the Americas, constituting about 45 per cent of African cultivated species;[1] for we can say, at any rate in the case of most, if not all, of them that they could not have reached the shores of West Africa before the sixteenth century and that in all probability they did not reach the centre of Africa before the seventeenth and eighteenth centuries or even, in some cases, the nineteenth century, though always ahead of European penetration; and this circumstance has to be weighed together with the high degree of probability that the Mbomu migrations from the valley of the Mbomu towards the south-east took place in the eighteenth century, continuing towards north, east, and south in the nineteenth century. It is likely that when these migrations began the Ambomu lacked, as they certainly did before, some of what are now their main food-crops: ground-nuts, maize, sweet potato, and manioc, and also the tobacco plant. Of other of their chief crops of today they *could* have possessed eleusine, sesame, bananas, and the pulses. But we have noted that banana-culture, either completely or at any rate on any significant scale, was borrowed from the south, and there is also a high probability, if we follow Zande guidance, that the staple crop in Gbudwe's kingdom, eleusine, was ac-quired in the east after the Mbomu left their homeland. It has further been observed that there is reason to suppose that the cultivation of the *Ficus* which provides barkcloth was a loan from a people or peoples to the south.

What is left? Perhaps some millets, sesame, cucurbits, pulses, yams, and a few vegetables (*Hibiscus*, *Solanum*, etc.). But, making due allowance for Zande ignorance, misconceptions, and exag-gerations, though giving due weight to what they say in view of the fact that many of their statements are supported by other evidence, we may accept that at least some of the sorghums, oil-bearing plants, pulses, and yams have probably been intro-duced from foreign peoples during the Mbomu migrations. The details, such as were recorded by me, have already been given. Taking all in all, therefore, there does not remain enough to constitute an agricultural economy such as the Azande have

[1] Schnell, op. cit., p. 114.

today. This is a conclusion of some significance, for it is not con-
jecturing too much to suppose that the political development of
the Azande could scarcely have taken place in the old Mbomu
economy, but took place in the course of their expansion, with
its changes in ways of livelihood, a supposition which is in
accord with their own traditions, slight though they are. Lest
it should be held against me that I have not taken the matter
into consideration, I add, without entering into detailed discussion and in spite of what Junker says,[1] that Zandeland is, or
at any rate was, rich in game and there is also an abundance of
edible insect and wild plant life, so a much less developed agriculture than the present one would by no means have been
incompatible with organized community life and simple
political institutions.

[1] Op. cit., vol. ii, 1891, p. 161.

VIII

ZANDE CULTURE

(continued)

I NOW turn to the borrowing of arts and crafts. I commence with the craft of building. Round huts with conic roofs are, as Schweinfurth[1] and Junker[2] noted, the prevailing style everywhere till the Uele river is approached; at this point, and beyond, they are replaced by square gable-roofed dwellings. According to Czekanowski[3] the Azande of the south had adopted in his day (1907–8) gable-roofs, though their buildings still showed relics of the old round huts. Baumann remarks[4] that conical roofs tend to be typical of a homestead distribution and gable-roofs of village concentrations. Those Azande I questioned on the matter in the Sudan said that the old Mbomu walled dwelling-hut, which is still the most usual habitation in Gbudwe's old kingdom, the *gbuguru* or *gbasendeyo*, is a hut with solid mud walls—the only wood used in them being the lintels—but lacking a clay foundation. My informants added that, compared with today, there were very few of these well-made huts in past times. An elder might have built one for his senior wife, but his other wives had to be content with a *dondoma*, a hut without walls and with very low eaves, or a *basura* (or *barumai*), a simple sleeping-hut, often nowadays erected as a temporary shelter. The first is said to be of Mbomu, and the second of Miangba, origin: '*mbata kina Amiangba na tona dudua basura*', 'it was the Amiangba who were the first to build the *basura*'. Azande regard the *badika*, a hut with clay walls in which stakes are imbedded, as introduced, possibly also from the Amiangba. The wattle-walled huts, sometimes with clay inserted into the interstices, called *nanderugi* and *nakukpe* (or *tame nanderugi*) are a mode of building said to have come from the south, as is the mode of construction called *tatasende*, building on a raised platform of beaten clay to keep vermin out. However, the hut of this

[1] Schweinfurth, *The Heart of Africa*, vol. i, 1873, p. 523.
[2] Op. cit., vol. ii, 1891, pp. 145–6.
[3] Op. cit., p. 41.   [4] Op. cit., p. 32.

type called *kata* was, Azande told me, copied from the Abangbai (the Bombeh of the early travellers) to the east, who now speak Zande but were originally part of a foreign people with their own tongue, the Adio: *Ambomu ki ni di sunge e be yo ka dudua a, si na kodi ti ru na gbuguru ti gu rago re*, 'the Ambomu took the mode of construction from them, and it then joined with the *gbuguru*' (as part of their culture). Junker[1] mentions what is evidently the *kata* among these same Bombeh: 'For the substructure they utilize the hard hillocks of the termites (*Termes mordax*), from which they quarry tolerably uniform blocks about a foot thick, and quite impervious to the rain.' Marno[2] also appears to mention it.

The hut called *basa*, crudely constructed, without walls, and tunnel-shaped and barn-like in appearance, is put up in the bush to shelter boys during initiation by circumcision and for meetings of secret societies (closed associations). It is said together with circumcision, to have been taken over from the Amadi: *Amadi na enge pa basa, mbiko kina yo na tona yera aboro ni ganza*, 'it was the Amadi who originated the *basa*, because it was they who began to circumcise'. On the other hand, a hut without walls or with very low walls, the roof resting on a circle of stakes and reaching almost to the ground, called *yepu* or *bazambe* or *bayepu*, is said to be old Mbomu. It is particularly built by princes for shelter when they sit in court. The *basungo* is much the same type of hut but seems to be mainly distinguished by its floor of clay. King Tombo's hut at court may have been of this type, though it appears to have had some peculiar features, as described by Piaggia,[3] who says that the natives called it *bancaio*, which he translates '*il divano di un Sultano*' (what he heard may have been *ngbanga yo*, meaning 'at court'). The *yapoo* (*yepu*) is mentioned by Schweinfurth.[4] Another type of hut—I am uncertain of the manner of its construction—and the name for it, *toli*, were taken over from the Mangbetu; and a square hut, *gbiliki*, has recently been copied from European rest-houses. It is not clear to which huts Fr. Giorgetti[5] refers when he says that the huts with very high cones, still in use where one finds people of Barambo descent, have been borrowed by Azande from that people.

[1] Op. cit., vol. i, 1890, pp. 308–9.   [2] Op. cit., p. 131.
[3] Antinori, op. cit., p. 112.
[4] Schweinfurth, *Artes Africanae*, 1875, Tab. XI.
[5] F. Giorgetti, 'Il cannibalismo dei Niam Niam', *Africa*, 1957, p. 181.

There have been losses as well as gains. This is evident from Schweinfurth's drawings in his *Artes Africanae*, in which there are a number of features one sees no more; and there is no reason to suppose that their disappearance was in most cases directly connected with the entry of Arab and European elements; though it is possible that European administration was a circumstance which led to the disuse of the 'little huts, with bell-shaped roofs, erected in a goblet-shape upon a sub-structure of clay, and furnished with only one small aperture'.[1] They were called *bamogee* and were sleeping-places for 'the bigger boys of the better class'.[2] On inquiry, I was told that such huts were usually, and in some parts till recently, to be seen at courts, other features of which have slowly vanished after European conquest. I cannot, however, recollect having seen any other reference to them in writings of any other early traveller or in those of the earliest administrators and ethnologists—de Calonne, Hutereau, Czekanowski, etc.[3]—a circumstance which suggests that they may have been of foreign origin. Schweinfurth records that he found similar huts among the Sehre (Basiri).[4] One informant said he thought they belonged to Madi culture but that this was only a surmise on his part.

Every Zande householder today has a granary with a movable roof, called *gbamu*, for storing his eleusine. They are figured by Schweinfurth.[2] This type of granary is said to have been borrowed, though a very long time ago, like the culture of eleusine itself, from the Amiangba: *Azande nga Ambomu a bi e be Amiangba. Ga Ambomu gbamu na ngia kina gburuki na soro. Ono kina Amiangba ki ni tona gu nga gbamu, Ambomu ki ni bi e be yo ka dia a. Dungu ae du be Ambomu nga gu i a bi kina be kura aboro kia.* 'Those Azande who are Ambomu saw it with the Amiangba. The Mbomu granaries were the *gburuki* and the *soro*. But it was the Amiangba who started the *gbamu*, and the Ambomu saw it with them and took it over. Many things the Ambomu possess they took over from other peoples.' The *gburuki* is a grain-store not raised on supports, and the *soro* is an unusually large grain-store with a door instead of a movable roof. The latter is mostly

---

[1] Schweinfurth, *The Heart of Africa*, vol. ii, 1873, pp. 20–1.

[2] Idem, *Artes Africanae*, 1875, Tab. XI.

[3] They are figured in Piaggia's *Memorie*, Pellegrinetti, op. cit., opp. p. 224, but this looks like a composite drawing constructed from Schweinfurth's models.

[4] Schweinfurth, *The Heart of Africa*, vol. ii, 1873, p. 396.

built by wealthier persons, but neither, in my experience, is often to be seen today.

Besides being competent builders in a variety of styles, the Azande have enjoyed a reputation as smiths, potters, and wood-carvers. However, the origin of both smelting and smithery is attributed to various peoples to the south and west of Gbudwe's kingdom, Mangbetu, Amadi, Basiri, and Abandiya: *i na tona ka meka gbigiwi*, 'it was they who started to make kilns'. It is particularly the Basiri, to the west, who are spoken of as the originators of these arts: *ono agu aboro na enge mera gbigiwi, kina Abasiri*, 'but the people who began metal-working and smelting, they are the Basiri'. Curiously enough I have also been told, though it is hard to believe, that the Azande also learnt from them how to make fire by drilling with sticks: *Abasiri na enge pa pakasa sa gayo mara*, 'it was the Basiri who started making fire with sticks on account of their iron-working'; *si ki ni ye ka da ti Azande*, 'and then it came to the Azande'. However, Azande say that it is only a tradition that they learnt to smelt and work iron from others, for they have practised these skills for a very long time. So, even if they learnt them from others, it was so long ago that most of what they now fashion in iron may be said to be part of their indigenous material culture: spears, knives, throwing-knives, hoes, axes, hammers, rings for wrists, arms and ankles, hair-pins, beads, rattles, etc. On the other hand, some iron artifacts are said definitely to be of a more recent foreign origin. Arrows (*aguanza*) used by some of the subject peoples, and harpoons (*akatawa*) belong to the Amadi, the Belanda, and the Abuguru. The Ambomu were spearmen But some of their spears also appear to have been borrowed from their neighbours. Fr. Giorgetti[1] says that the war-spears most spoken of, the *andigbo*, were peculiar to the Amadi and were adopted by the Azande from them. I was told that the Ambomu have borrowed other types of spear from the Mang-betu (*ngbingbi, gbagbaza, mandende*), a large knife (*mawida*), and the ceremonial kind of knife called *nadada*, which has been added to the old Mbomu type, the *badevurambitiyo*. Czekanowski[2] asserts that the Azande use two types of spears, throwing-spears and heavier thrusting-spears, and he says that the first do not differ from those of the Mangbetu. The second (*deli*) are said

[1] Op. cit., p. 181.   [2] Op. ci   p. 36.

to belong to the original Zande weapons. The implication is that the throwing-spears were Mangbetu in origin in contrast to the thrusting-spears, which were Mbomu; but thrusting-spears have never been heard of by me and are not mentioned by any other writer on the Azande and, therefore, one must suppose, were to be found only in the south, where Czekanowski conducted his researches. This would suggest a foreign origin.

Here it must be emphasized that the Ambomu are undoubtedly indebted to the Mangbetu for many improvements in their arts. This is evident, as will be further noted later, in the drawings Schweinfurth made a century ago; and he remarks that in 1870 the two peoples engaged in trade.[1] Furthermore, Junker observed in 1882 that the Azande who lived near the Mangbetu had adopted some of their fashions.[2] Besides those metal objects already mentioned, from the same direction came also the *abeni*, a specially well-worked ceremonial knife (or scimitar) with an ivory handle. Indeed Czekanowski suggests, I think rightly, that the ceremonial knife as such (*mambele* in Zande, *nambele* in Mangbetu), which he calls *Buschmesser*, may well be Mangbetu in origin.[3] A few smiths in Gbudwe's kingdom and during his reign mastered the art of making the more elaborate of these ceremonial knives. One type of axe, called *bamangwa*, which has a little spike so that it can be stuck into the ground and was made not so much for use as for bride-wealth, is also Mangbetu. The throwing-knife is certainly an old Mbomu weapon, but the sort called *kpinga basa*, which lacks the small protuberance between the two front blades, the distinguishing mark of the Mbomu type,[4] came from the Abandiya, though it was in use in Schweinfurth's time.[5] Schweinfurth tells us that the Mangbetu, far more skilful smiths than the Azande, supplied the latter with some of these weapons, receiving in return heavy lances for hunting elephant and buffalo. The Mangbetu, he says, do not themselves use the throwing-knife.[6] Czekanowski cites Emin Pasha in support of the view that the iron hair-pins rarely seen among the Mangbetu are due to Zande influence.[7]

[1] Op. cit., 1875, Tab. XIII.   [2] Op. cit., vol. iii, 1892, p. 38.
[3] Op. cit., p. 144.   [4] See, for example, ibid., p. 37.
[5] Schweinfurth, *Artes Africanae*, 1875, Tab. XII.
[6] Idem, *The Heart of Africa*, vol. ii, 1873, pp. 9–10 and 108.
[7] Czekanowski, op. cit., p. 138; Emin Pasha, op. cit., p. 211. See also Schweinfurth, *The Heart of Africa*, vol. i, p. 472.

One sort of adze (*naba*) is said to be Mbomu; another type to be Miangba. It may be added that Piaggia[1] does not give the impression that he regarded the Azande of a century ago as being more than moderately competent in the manufacture of metal objects.

Smelting of iron[2] was an almost dead technique in my day, trade iron having rendered the exacting labour of working local ores unnecessary, but smithery was still required and was commonly practised. Here again, some fashions have disappeared since the time of the early travellers, e.g. throwing-knives are no longer manufactured nor the spiral iron rings (*maka*, an Mbomu ornament) once worn round arms and legs by women.[3]

Some copper had been introduced from the south. In the first instance this must, I think, have come from the Katanga region to the south of the Congo and, though it is possible that some copper may later have been imported into the Negro countries from the north, from Hofrat al-Nahas and possibly elsewhere, Schweinfurth tells us that it was well known to the Mangbetu before the Arabs first entered their country.[4] Czekanowski remarks in this connection that copper is said to have come from the mines of Hofrat al-Nahas to the Mangbetu before the Belgian occupation.[5] This is a difficult problem, and I have only to add that when Cline in his study of Negro mining and metallurgy says,[6] on the statement of a single authority,[7] that the Azande mined copper I believe him to be in error; and he himself admits that no copper ores occur in the Uele Basin or that, if they do, they are unworkable. Czekanowski[8] states that there seem to be no copper ores in the Uele Basin.

Passing reference may here be made to the introduction of guns: muskets and then rifles. They differ from the other metal objects I have mentioned in that Azande acquired the objects themselves but not the art of making them. It is partly for that

---

[1] Antinori, op. cit., p. 132.

[2] Described in my paper 'Zande Iron-working', *Paideuma*, xiii, 1967, pp. 26–31.

[3] Junker, op. cit., vol. i, 1890, p. 340.

[4] Schweinfurth, *The Heart of Africa*, vol. ii, 1873, p. 19.   [5] Op. cit., p. 133.

[6] W. Cline, *Mining and Metallurgy in Negro Africa*, 1937, pp. 68 and 72.

[7] The source is a few lines reporting a paper by M. Bellucci at the International Congress of Ethnology and Ethnography at Neuchâtel in *L'Anthropologie*, vol. xxv, 1914, p. 373. The place of the copper-working is not mentioned. Certainly the industry does not exist among the Azande of the Sudan.

[8] Op. cit., p. 130.

reason that the reference is only a passing one. The introduction of the rifle, which began before 1870, had profound political as well as tactical consequences. It enabled the Azande to resist more effectively Arab aggression; it gave them superiority in weapons as well as in organization over most of their neighbours; it altered the balance of power between Zande kingdoms, those monarchs who were able to obtain the most guns being able to gain empires for themselves at the expense of their neighbours; and it had other consequences. I discuss some of them later.[1]

Azande men are expert potters, or so it seemed to me, for I attempted, without much success, to master the art under their guidance. This is said to be a craft of the Ambomu, who made certain types of pottery (*duku, gbukudali, kambu, bazangoli, akoro mbida ime, kpongu*) used for carrying water, ablutions, brewing beer, boiling oil, roasting and boiling meat, etc. Some pots are said to be both Mbomu and Miangba (*mele, runge, bayuruyuru,* and others), while yet others are said to be solely of Miangba origin, or to have come from south of the Uele river. On the whole, it was asserted that small-mouthed pots were Mbomu and that designs with larger mouths came from the south, especially from the Mangbetu. The Mangbetu undoubtedly excelled the Azande as potters and their influence on Zande pottery is probably to be noted in the beer-jug with four necks, the property of King Ngangi, which Schweinfurth figures in his *Artes Africanae*.[2] They exerted this influence in spite of the fact that only men are potters among the Azande, whereas among the Mangbetu pots are exclusively made by women.[3] Geyer, writing of the Azande to the west of Gbudwe's old kingdom, says that the best pots come from the Belanda people, from whom the Azande have learnt much.[4] Some of the best pottery in Gbudwe's kingdom came from the same source. The best type of clay used for making pots in that kingdom, *mokanga*, a red clay, appears to be found only in its eastern districts and may therefore be presumed to have been utilized by Ambomu only after they had occupied them.

Of another clay article, the bowl of tobacco-pipes, I was told that a small bowl, into which a long wooden stem is fitted, is

---

[1] See Chap. XIII. [2] Tab. XV.
[3] Czekanowski, op. cit., p. 129. [4] Geyer, op. cit., p. 304.

Mbomu and a large bowl with mouthpiece, stem, and bowl being of one clay piece is Miangba. Schweinfurth figures both types[1] and says that the shape of the small bowl in the first, which he described as 'a chieftain's state-pipe', was copied from the Bongo people. Piaggia[2] says that it was the practice to mould the figure of a human head on the outside of clay pipes. Junker, who also figures both types of pipe, has an illustration of the moulding of the human face.[3] The moulding of human features was probably due to foreign influences, possibly both Mangbetu (to the south) and Bongo (to the north), for it is very seldom that one comes across a Zande who moulds or carves the human figure or any part of it. However, the Mangbetu themselves, Schweinfurth assures us,[4] do not use pipe-bowls, their pipes having for stems the central ribs of banana leaves while a little bag cut out of the same leaves serves in the place of a bowl. This is confirmed by Czekanowski: they smoke tobacco in enormous pipes made from the ribs of banana leaves.[5] I mention this fact because the Azande also make use of the same sort of pipe, called *apokobu*, when they have left their usual pipes at home and have the opportunity to smoke, and they say that they learnt its use from the Mangbetu, from whom they may also have learnt to cultivate the banana, as I have earlier suggested.

The Azande have today something of a reputation as wood-carvers, but they are ready to admit that they learnt their more elaborate modes of carving from peoples beyond the Uele, and more particularly from the Mangbetu, who, as is well known, are skilled carvers—their skill, according to Schweinfurth, being largely due to their knowledge of the use of single-bladed knives which allow control by the index finger.[6] Emin states the contrary when, speaking of Mangbetu carving, he remarks that 'It is true, however, that real artists, who carve heads and figures, &c., are more numerous amongst the A-Zandē'.[7] Emin's knowledge of the Azande was slight—he was only acquainted, and rather superficially, with the Zandeized Adio to the east, and his knowledge of the Mangbetu was also

---

[1] Schweinfurth, *Artes Africanae*, 1875, Tab. XV.
[2] Antinori, op. cit., p. 127.   [3] Op. cit., vol. iii, 1892, p. 287.
[4] Schweinfurth, *The Heart of Africa*, vol. ii, 1873, p. 34.   [5] Op. cit., p. 128.
[6] Schweinfurth, *The Heart of Africa*, vol. ii, 1873, p. 21.   [7] Op. cit., p. 213.

very limited; so I have no hesitation in contradicting him in this matter, and in doing so agreeing with what is implied, with regard to wood-carving, in a remark by Casati, who, though he may not have been so industrious a recorder as Emin, knew very much more about both peoples than he did: 'The Sandeh are greatly admired for their ironwork; the Mambettu are remarkable for the perfection of their wood-carving . . .'.[1] If, however, his remarks are intended also to suggest that the Azande were more skilled smiths than the Mangbetu, the evidence is against him. Czekanowski is surely right when he says that the Mangbetu surpass the Azande in both smithery and wood-carving.[2]

The Azande of Gbudwe's kingdom say that it was their brothers of Wando's kingdom, which bordered Mangbetuland, who first learnt to carve in Mangbetu fashion and that the skill passed from them to those of Malingindo's kingdom and finally, and only lately, reached Gbudwe's territory. They say also that people who journeyed to the south to collect poison for the poison oracle brought home new techniques with them. I have heard further that it was not till a man called Bomoi of the Avumaka clan, a skilled carver, and his kinsmen sought refuge in Gbudwe's kingdom during the wars between Wando's sons Ukwe and Renzi towards the end of last century that the more elaborate carving was established in the north; and even at the end of Gbudwe's reign there were very few specialists. It is still recounted how the first attempts at carving the more elaborate sort of stools began with that known as *barute* and were a crude performance. Nevertheless, Schweinfurth's drawings, made in 1870 and 1871, would indicate that at any rate some of the eastern Azande had already by that time been strongly influenced by Mangbetu styles of carving bowls and stools, and this is particularly noticeable in the carving of human heads on harps and whistles (the latter now no longer to be seen in the Sudan), some of which show the artificially deformed Mangbetu head; but this does not necessarily mean that they were carved by Zande craftsmen, for it was a common practice for those who journeyed to the south to collect oracle-poison to bring back with them also Mangbetu artifacts, carefully bound in leaves, to present to their princes. The objects could therefore have

[1] Op. cit., vol. i, p. 97.   [2] Op. cit., p. 31.

been observed by Schweinfurth in Zande country without the manufacture of them having been practised there. He would have been more likely to have taken note of them than of simpler specimens. Czekanowski says that the carved human heads on harps among the southern Azande are usually interpreted as a caricature of a deformed Mangbetu head.[1] I would suggest that they were a copy rather than a caricature. So little is this an art among the Azande of the Sudan that I can recollect only one craftsman who habitually carved the human figure in Gbudwe's kingdom, and in his figures the head was clearly the elongated Mangbetu head.

Of the wooden bowls now carved by Azande only two are claimed to be Zande, even in the broadest sense of that term: the *baza*, a simple bowl resembling the shell of a tortoise, from which it is said to have been copied, and used for serving porridge, and the *kolongbo ime*, a plainly worked bowl, largely used for bailing out water in fishing. All their other bowls—to mention only a few, *badungu, gada, barungbanduru, sambirambira, sasilikpera*, and *kpasia kolongbo*—are foreign, and most probably Mangbetu, styles. They say also that the wooden stool which is old Mbomu is that called *zagbali*, the simplest of their stools. Schweinfurth gives a drawing of it.[2] The more elaborately worked stools (*barute, kpanga, mbata*, and others) have been either imported from the south or carved by persons who have learnt Mangbetu techniques and designs, as Baumann has observed.[3] The stool called *kitipara*, now very commonly constructed by Gbudwe's Azande, is obviously a copy of the Mangbetu bench, and as it is not figured among Schweinfurth's *artes Azandeae*, it may be presumed to be, as Azande say it is, a recent introduction. Lagae and Vanden Plas give the word *kiti*, 'seat', and say that it is a loan-word,[4] though it is not, apparently, the Mangbetu term, which Czekanowski tells us is *nekalagba*.[5] In his commentary on his drawing for this Mangbetu bench Schweinfurth remarks on its ingenious workmanship, being the only example of joinery he knew of in Central Africa.[6] Over forty years ago, in my time, some of the nobles were using cane chairs modelled on the European deck-chair. Azande

[1] Op. cit., p. 39.
[2] *Artes Africanae*, 1875, Tab. XIV, Fig. 4.
[3] Op. cit., pp. 29–30.
[4] Op. cit., vol. ii, p. 79.
[5] Op. cit., p. 150.
[6] *Artes Africanae*, 1875, Tab. XVII, Fig. 18.

attribute the fine finish of the more elaborately worked handles of their knives to the Mangbetu. Czekanowski remarks of the wooden containers of red dye among the Azande of the south— they are rarely to be seen in the Sudan and only among wealthier persons—that the frequent carved imitations of Mangbetu heads on them is very striking.[1] They would appear to have originated among that people. The wooden trough-like mortar, called *gbakada*, with its accompanying pestle figured by Schweinfurth[2] had become obsolete before my first expedition to Zandeland in 1927. It is said to have been of Miangba origin. Schweinfurth does not mention the upright mortar (*baruaru*) now universally used and said to be the Mbomu one, but it must have been in use in his time, for both types of mortar are mentioned and figured by Junker,[3] and he himself says of the trough-like type that 'This is the ordinary form of the mortar, used for bruising the hard Eleusine corn', which suggests that there was another form in use. I was told that the Ambomu, having adopted the trough-like mortar from the Amiangba, later abandoned it because the women used to squat over it when pounding.

It may be mentioned here that the kind of wooden shrine, called *mbama*, which Schweinfurth speaks of as a conspicuous object in Zande homesteads[4] and which he figures in *The Heart of Africa*[5] is of foreign, probably of Madi or Miangba, origin. It is a dead shrub on the branches of which are hung trophies of the chase and, in Schweinfurth's time, of war also: human skulls and other bones. The ordinary old Mbomu shrine is the *tuka*, a stake split at the top and with the split sections bound to form a receptacle for offerings. This kind of shrine is not mentioned by Schweinfurth, and his failure to do so is further evidence in support of the view, referred to earlier, that he was travelling through country in which the Ambomu were sparsely represented and the foreign elements still unassimilated.

I did not myself make inquiries into the origin of objects worked in ivory and bone. Fr. Giorgetti says that the hair-pins of human fibula belonged to the Madi culture, as did the word for them, *nguma*, a term which later entered into the Zande

[1] Op. cit., p. 67. They are figured in Junker, vol. ii, 1891, p. 191.
[2] *Artes Africanae*, 1875, Tab. XIII, Fig. 23.   [3] Op. cit., vol. ii, 1891, p. 170.
[4] *The Heart of Africa*, vol. i, p. 449.   [5] Vol. i, p. 517.

language and was applied to the fibula of baboons. He also claims that the necklaces of dogs' and baboons' teeth and of worked ivory were all of Barambo-Madi workmanship. He furnishes this information in an attempt to show that Schweinfurth, who mentions the objects referred to, was in the main, as suggested above, writing about only partly assimilated foreigners rather than about Ambomu or true Azande.[1]

The most impressive objects plaited with cane or grass must in the old days have been the shields, figured in drawings and photographs of travellers.[2] There were four varieties, three of the Ambomu (*kube*, *bazakube*, *kpangbada*) and one (*tuango*) borrowed from the Amiangba. Lagae and Vanden Plas also give four types of shield, but instead of the names *bazakube* and *tuango* they mention *gbiliga* and *gbulu*, the last, it would appear, being not of plaited cane, for they say it was *en bois noirci*, adding that it was borrowed from some foreign people to the south,[3] though the Gores, who give the same two names, say that it was a cane shield.[4] The bearing of shields seems to have been forbidden by the British Administration soon after its occupation, so that, except for a few old ones preserved out of sentiment, they were no longer to be seen in the 1920s, though there were craftsmen who could still make them. I have briefly referred earlier to another plaited object, the Zande straw hat, circular at the base and square on top.[5] I said that the hat itself was old Mbomu but that some features of it in its final development, designs worked into the sides and a brim, were taken over from foreigners, the first from the Mangbetu and the second from Europeans. I believe this statement to be correct, but I must record that Czekanowski says that Azande told him that these straw hats are Mangbetu,[6] though they predominate among the Azande to the south of the Bomokandi. It would seem to be on this evidence that Baumann states[7] that the Azande took them over from the Mangbetu and that they then ousted skin caps. He further remarks that the only woven articles of the Azande in the manufacture of which the technique of stepped weaving

[1] Giorgetti, op. cit., p. 181.
[2] See, for example, Schweinfurth, *The Heart of Africa*, vol. ii, 1873, p. 12.
[3] Op. cit., vol. ii, pt. 1, p. 44; pt. 2, p. 50.
[4] Op. cit., pp. 48 and 261.
[5] See, for example, Schweinfurth, *The Heart of Africa*, vol. i, 1873, p. 349.
[6] Op. cit., p. 32.   [7] Op. cit., p. 19.

PLATE II

Prince Gangura and his family

(*Stufengeflechtes*)[1] is employed are these hats of the Mangbetu type.

Of mats, the type called *karakpa* is said to be both Mbomu and Miangba, while those called *nakorogbo* and *bagburu* came from the Abile people to the south of the Bomokandi, a branch of the Azande containing a high proportion of foreign elements; and from the same direction, I was told, were introduced the kinds of basket-strainer (*sanza*), winnowing-basket (*kiaga*), and sieve (*kangira*) in use in the Sudan today. Of open-wove baskets, the one of widest mesh (*mbambamba* or *bangilimbara*) is Mbomu, and the *bangiliadandara* and the *ngindi* are Miangba. The Amiangba are also said to have given the Ambomu the reed-basket called *buma* and the scoop (*kate*) used in collecting termites. The filtering-basket (*kisanguru*) is common to all the peoples of the Zande amalgam. The *kokpo*, a basket on four legs, is Mangbetu. The largest kind of bag (*bamangu*) is Mbomu, though a specially well-worked handle that sometimes adorns it is copied from the Mangbetu. Other types of bags are believed to have come mostly from the Uele region, though I was told that one sort was copied from the Baka people. The funnel-shaped baskets used to trap mice (*ngbatu*) are two kinds, the one Mbomu and the other Miangba. Czekanowski mentions similar traps among the Mangbetu, by whom they are called *gala*.[2] The grass purses one sometimes sees in use today to hold piastres are, like the leather purses one also occasionally sees, copied from trade purses.

Azande are very fond of music. Their great wooden gongs (*gugu*, also called *borua*)[3] are Mbomu. A smaller kind, *karakara*, said to be called *makureki* by the Mangbetu, came from beyond the Uele. The skin-drum (*gaza*, *ndimo*) is Mbomu. It is interesting to note that Schweinfurth says that the Mangbetu have no xylophone,[4] so that here the influence has been in the contrary to the usual direction, Czekanowski saying that in his day they were rare among the Mangbetu and where found were due to

[1] Miss Beatrice Blackwood tells me that the usual technical term for this sort of weaving is 'double twill'.

[2] Op. cit., p. 152. Specimens collected by myself are figured in *Man*, 1932, no. 77, in a paper by Henry Balfour.

[3] Photographs of King Gbudwe's gong were published in *Man*, 1911, no. 8, by C. G. Seligmann.

[4] *The Heart of Africa*, vol. ii, 1873, p. 25.

Zande influence.[1] He believes, contrary to Ankermann's view, that the xylophone is non-African in origin.[2] The Azande have two kinds, the *manza*, made of wood and with a sounding-board of gourds,[3] which is old Mbomu, and the *kpaningba*, made of banana stalks and wood, which probably came from some people to the south. The large bow-harp (*kundi*), sometimes described as a mandolin, is also a true Mbomu instrument—it is particularly favoured by the nobles—though the carved human heads figured on it are, as has already been said, due to Mangbetu influence.[4] Here again the cultural drift seems to have been in the opposite direction from the usual one, for Schweinfurth tells us that the Mangbetu do not have mandolins or indeed any other stringed instruments,[5] while Czekanowski say that the Zande type of mandolin occurs among that people only where Zande influence is strong.[6] He is of the opinion that Ankermann has proved that the instrument came to Central Africa from Asia by way of the Semitic and Egyptian peoples.[7] Casati[8] says that both Azande and Mangbetu have the same stringed instrument which (in translation) is called mandolin and also guitar. There seems to be some confusion in the literature between harp, mandolin, and guitar. An improvised harp (*sekiondi*), made by boys and played in a game, is attributed to the Basiri people. The Sanza, a plucked idiophone (*ngbangbari*), entered Gbudwe's kingdom only after his death (1905). It may have first reached the Azande from the Mangbetu, but it has a very wide distribution in Central Africa, as Dr. Maes has shown.[9] Czekanowski says that it appears to have been brought to the Azande by native soldiers and workers of the Belgian Administration.[10] *Banangbari*, large wooden bells, now obsolete, came from the south. Witch-doctors' hand-bells or rattles may belong to the old Mbomu culture. Certainly they have been part of it for a very long time. Ivory trumpets, now no longer seen, and various hunting-horns may also be Mbomu; I have

[1] Op. cit., p. 147.   [2] Ibid., p. 39.

[3] See, for example, Junker, op. cit., vol. iii, 1892, p. 14.

[4] See, for example, Schweinfurth, *The Heart of Africa*, vol. i, 1873, p. 445.

[5] Idem, *Zeitschrift für Ethnologie*, 1873, p. 25, and *The Heart of Africa*, vol. ii, 1873, p. 117.

[6] Op. cit., p. 146.   [7] Ibid., p. 39.

[8] Op. cit., vol. i, p. 195.

[9] J. Maes, 'La Sanza du Congo belge', *Congo*, t. 1, 1921.

[10] Op. cit., p. 40.

no information about them beyond the statement that one kind of trumpet, composed of a waterbuck horn fitted into a gourd, was copied from the Abuguru people. Wooden whistles sometimes made by boys as playthings are copied from European models and are called by the Arabic name *sufara*. Czekanowski says that Zande rattles do not differ from those of the Mangbetu.[1]

Dances may be diffused together with the musical instruments which accompany them, and they are often readily taken over by one people from another. This has undoubtedly been the case with the Azande, though in most instances I would not be able to describe their dances, some obsolete today, only to name them. The ancient Mbomu dances are said to have been the *bagbere*, a dance to gong and drum, the xylophone-dance (*gbere manza*), and a dance, unknown to me, called *ngbundu*. The usual dance of today, the beer-dance (*gbere buda*), is similar in ground-form to the *bagbere*, which it appears to have replaced, though perhaps as a development rather than an introduction. It is alleged that the beer-dance ousted the older dance in spite of Gbudwe's dislike of it. It was favoured by the younger generation. Since Gbudwe's death the beer-dance has lost something of its form; it has become, Azande say, *gbarakagbaraka*, 'all mixed up'. Probably from the south came another dance, to xylophones (*gbere kpaningba*), together with that sort of instrument; certainly also the circumcision dance (*gbere agangasi*) together with the operation, and dances now, I believe, no longer performed, called *nzangbua*, *akpuka*, accompanied by gong, and *bamara*, by gong and drum. Gbudwe is said to have prohibited the *akpuka* dance in his domains, but I was told that it was at one time popular in the neighbouring kingdom of Wando. The *keli* dance, which also seems to have disappeared, is said by some to have been of Madi, by others of Miangba, origin. The dance *gbere ngbendeli* came from some foreign people in the region of Wau after Gbudwe's death. It is no longer performed. Lagae and Vanden Plas give in their dictionary the names of yet other dances, some of which, they say, have probably been introduced.[2]

A pause may now be made for some general remarks in assessment of what has been said to the present point. It is

---

[1] Ibid.   [2] Op. cit., vol. ii, pt. 1, p. 84.

impossible in most cases to know for certain whether what I was told about the foreign origin of arts and crafts and styles was accurate or not. One can, however, say that this is the way Azande see their culture; that where there are ethnological evidences they tend to support what I was told; and that even if only half the information were correct it tells a remarkable story. In the preceding chapter the conclusion was reached that there was good reason for believing that till recently Zande agriculture was much simpler than it is today. We have now further observed that this is almost certainly true also of their material culture. There have entered into their economy from outside, or through conquest and incorporation of foreign elements, new building techniques; metal weapons and tools have been introduced (possibly even smelting and smithery in a more distant past, though I do not stress this); and the original Avongara–Ambomu stock have learnt from their subject peoples and neighbours new forms, designs, and skills in pot-making, wood-carving and joinery, plaiting with cane and grass, the construction and playing of musical instruments, and dances. When we add these innovations to those noted in our discussion of domesticated plants, we can yet more firmly conclude that since the time the Ambomu began their migrations their culture has undergone considerable changes, becoming greater in content, richer in variety of forms, and more developed and elaborate. These changes must have increased stability, specialization and division of labour, wealth and inequality of wealth, and favoured the growth of a leisured ruling class; in all, bringing about the complex civilization and society of the Azande today.

I should add that any further attempt to investigate the borrowing of culture-traits would probably today be a hopeless task, and also that the situation is even more complicated than I have presented it; for not only is 'Azande' a blanket-term covering a wide variety of groups of different ethnic origins, the composition of which differs from one part of Zandeland to another, but so also are such terms as 'Mangbetu', 'Abandiya', and 'Abile'. To determine the exact provenance of an object or technique would, in these circumstances, require detailed research, and it is probably too late for this to be undertaken. All that can be achieved here is to indicate the scale of borrowing, the heterogeneity of the elements that have gone to make up Zande culture, and the complexity of the problems involved.

I now pay brief attention to a department of culture very different from any so far treated, that which includes such beliefs and practices as I dealt with over thirty years ago in my book *Witchcraft, Oracles and Magic among the Azande*. Of the lesser oracles, one, the *mokama*, worked by twisting a peg in a hollow wooden cone, and most used by witch-doctors, came, like some other practices of witch-doctors, from the east, probably from the Baka people, though the name is Zande (*mo*, 'you', *kama*, 'twist'). Another, the *mapingo*, the placing of two sticks on the ground and a third on top of them and then seeing whether the top one falls or retains its position overnight, has certainly been taken over from the Mangbetu, among whom it has far greater importance, being worked by a specialist with elaborate apparatus and rites. The name is Mangbetu: *na mapingo*. Of the secondary Zande oracles, the termites oracle, the placing of sections of branches of two different trees in the runs of termites and then observing which of them the insects have nibbled more, is said to have been taken over from the Amiangba, though it may have had a wider distribution, for I was told that it was also the chief oracle of the Abuguru before the Ambomu taught them the use of *benge* poison. Another oracle, the rubbing-board, is also said to have originated among the Amiangba. All these oracles are figured in my book.

Easily the most important of all the oracles, *benge*, the poison oracle, the administration of poison to fowls to discover the answers to questions by their reactions to it, presents a special problem. The oracle plays so central a role in the life of the people and is so bound up with the position of their rulers that it is difficult to imagine them without it. But all well-informed and well-travelled Azande have told me that their ancestors did not know it and that it was learnt from some people or peoples to the south of the Uele. What they say is supported by the fact that it is doubtful whether the creeper from which the poison, which has properties akin to strychnine, is extracted grows at all in any part of Zandeland, except perhaps in its extreme southern extensions to the south of the Uele which would have been occupied only fairly recently by the Azande.

Junker notes that the poison plant is not to be found anywhere in Gbudwe's kingdom or in its neighbourhood, but says
that it is found on the Assa stream and that Gbudwe was in
the habit of trading ivory for the poison with the Baka chief
Ansea who resided in that region.[1] Brock may be referring to
the same area when he writes that *benge* 'is rarely found in the
Bahr al-Ghazal and mostly comes from the Belgian Congo'.[2]
But even if it is correct (which I doubt) that the creeper is to be
found in this region as far north as Junker and Brock say, the
Azande could not have used this source till fairly recently
because they had not penetrated so far to the east. I should add
that to the best of my knowledge the Azande of Gbudwe's kingdom do not today go to Baka country to obtain the poison but
in spite of, and ignoring, official regulations, go south of the
Uele, and that this was usual before European conquest too.

Mgr. Lagae,[3] who was better placed to make a judgement on
this matter than I was, says categorically, confirming an earlier
statement by Geyer,[4] that the creeper does not grow to the
north of the Uele–Kibali and that therefore the Azande must
have borrowed it from peoples to the south of that river in the
course of their migrations and conquests. There is no information
on the point, but it seems improbable that, if the creeper does
not grow north of the Uele–Kibali, it is to be found in the valley
of the Mbomu and to the north of that river where the Ambomu
were living when they began to make their migrations. It is a
reasonable surmise therefore that its use must have been learnt
from some foreign people.

From which people they learnt it cannot on our present
knowledge be determined. More requires to be known of the
distribution of the plant and its uses. It would appear that,
though the Mangbetu use it and it grows in their country, it is
of secondary importance among them and its use as an oracle
was probably borrowed by them from the Azande. Its relative
unimportance is indicated or suggested by Schweinfurth,[5] Junker,[6] and more recently by Lelong.[7] Czekanowski says that the
Mangbetu give the poison to people and not to chicken, save

[1] Op. cit., vol. i, 1890, p. 437.
[2] R. G. C. Brock, 'The Zande Tribe', *Sudan Notes and Records*, 1918, p. 259.
[3] Op. cit., p. 84.   [4] Op. cit., pp. 294–5.
[5] *The Heart of Africa*, vol. ii, 1873, p. 27.   [6] Op. cit., vol. ii, 1891, p. 246.
[7] M. H. Lelong, *Mes frères du Congo*, 1946, pp. 252–3.

where there has been Zande influence.[1] It may be inferred from a statement by Junker that the Amadi people use the poison oracle.[2] Fr. Giorgetti thinks that the Ambomu may have learnt its use from the Abire or Ambiri peoples.[3] Craffen and Colombo write: 'The name of *benghe* comes from a small plant which does not grow in the country of the Asande, but which they procure from the Bakango riverains of the U'ele, who themselves purchase it from the Ababua whose forests produce it in abundance.'[4] They add that the Ababua administer the poison to men, mostly slaves, while the Azande administer it to chicken.[5] According to Hutereau,[6] on the contrary, not only does the creeper flourish in the tropical rain-forest in which the Ababua live, but they consult the oracle in much the same way as Azande do, and they call it and the poison by the same name, *benge* (Hutereau's '*benget*').[7] If Hutereau's statements are correct it would seem probable, on the limited evidence available, that both the poison and the procedure of consulting the oracle with chickens—as well as less commonly with men—were borrowed by the Azande from the Ababua or some related Bantu people further to the west and nearer to the Mbomu homeland. Possibly knowledge of the oracle passed from the Ambomu to the Nzakara, who adjoin the Azande to the west and have adopted their political institutions and speak a closely related language, for Von Wiese tells us that this people use '*bengi*', though according to him on humans.[8] The Azande have also passed it on to other peoples who have come under their political and cultural influence, such as the Abuguru. Further discussion of this matter might lead us into very deep waters; and I do not pursue it. I conclude that we can say definitely that the poison oracle must have been borrowed by the Ambomu from foreigners, that possibly these foreigners were the Ababua or related Bantu, and also that the oracle has certainly been in use among the Ambomu and the

---

[1] Op. cit., p. 162. [2] Op. cit., vol. ii, 1891, p. 380.

[3] F. Giorgetti, *La Superstizione Zande*, 1958, p. 106.

[4] E. Craffen and E. Colombo, 'Les Niam-Niam', *Rev. inter. de sociologie*, no. 11, 1906, p. 793.

[5] Ibid., p. 794. [6] Op. cit., 1909, p. 98.

[7] A similar word, *mbenge*, refers to a process of divination among the Momvu people, but the operational procedure in no way resembles that of the Azande and Ababua (H. Van Geluwe, *Mamvu-Mangutu et Balese-Mvuba*, 1957, p. 82, quoting Van de Broele).

[8] Von Wiese in Mecklenburg-Schwerin, op. cit., p. 203.

peoples they have absorbed (the Zande amalgam) for a very long time, though for how long we cannot say. All we can say on historical evidence is that when Schweinfurth visited the Azande in 1870 both the poison oracle and the rubbing-board oracle were well established.[1] Schweinfurth mentions also an oracular usage I have neither seen nor heard of, the ducking of the head of a cock under water until it is senseless and then waiting to see whether it rallies or succumbs.[2] If this was ever a Zande practice, which I doubt—Schweinfurth travelled through a very mixed population and was much indebted for information to Nubians and Arabs, most unreliable informants on Negro customs—it must long ago have fallen into desuetude. It is true that Geyer[3] also records this oracular technique, but it is possible that he took his information from Schweinfurth, of whose account he appears to have made considerable use.

Azande have an enormous number of 'medicines', substances employed in magical rites, and they regard very many of them as being of foreign origin, so much so that they tend to class anyone who uses magic outside a few traditional types as being *ipso facto* a person of foreign origin or at least of foreign habits. So vast is this subject, therefore, that I may be excused for not attempting to treat it in detail, especially as it has often been observed that magic, particularly bad magic or sorcery, is frequently attributed, and perhaps correctly, to foreigners. All I shall do is to give a few examples. Gbudwe was strongly opposed to the introduction of new medicines, but in spite of his opposition some found their way into his realm. The most important of all Zande medicines, *bagbuduma*, used in a long series of rites to avenge deaths caused by witchcraft, had almost certainly been established there before his reign, and it was one of the traditional medicines of which he approved. Nevertheless, it is said not to have originated among the Ambomu but to have been borrowed by them from some people to the west. This may be Schweinfurth's *bongbottomu*[4] which some interpreters gave him, quite wrongly, as a word for divinity and also for a messenger or envoy. He realized, however, that what they were doing was giving him a kind of periphrasis of the Arabic word for prophet, *rasul*. The confusion may have been caused by the

---

[1] *The Heart of Africa*, vol. ii, pp. 32–3.   [2] Ibid., p. 33.
[3] Op. cit., pp. 309–10.   [4] Op. cit., vol. ii, p. 31.

fact that the idea of sending forth the medicine to search for a witch is often expressed in Zande statements about it, as is the idea of sending forth expressed in the Arabic word.

Also present in Gbudwe's day was the most feared of all evil medicines, *menzere*, learnt, I was told, from the Amadi people. From the south, though more recently, came *moti*, a medicine supposed to cause venereal chancres. The magic whistle *fili* came from the Mangbetu. The dropping of the hair of the ant-bear (*garawa*) into a man's beer to kill him is a magical act said to have originated among the Amiangba. One of the protective medicines, *ngua kpoto*, is attributed to the Basiri. Another power-ful protective medicine, *amatangi*, was brought to the Azande from the Bongo people, but it is also found as a sort of fetish among the Nilotic Dinka and Nuer peoples and it probably originated among the Sudanese so-called Jur peoples. Fr. de Graer[1] mentions a number of medicines now used by Azande to treat sickness which have a foreign origin, e.g. a cure for *ima dekurugba*, oedema, obesity, etc., came from the Basiri or the Amadi; a cure for *moti*, the venereal chancres already referred to, came from the Mangbetu; and from the Basiri or Amadi came a cure for *ima batiyo*, convulsions in infants. Fr. Giorgetti mentions a magical substance called *kpoto ngondi*, a dried portion of a crocodile's sexual organs, used to blind people, and says that it came to the Azande from the Bviri (Mberidi) section of the Belanda people.[2] Many other medicines have come, or are believed to have come, from foreign peoples.

If the Ambomu had at one time no poison oracle, and possibly no other oracles, and if they had no magic of vengeance, we may wonder whether at that time they may also have lacked the witchcraft notions so closely connected with the operation of the oracle and the use of the medicine, notions which today dominate their outlook and may be said to constitute their natural and moral philosophy. I have not heard Azande suggest this, and I suppose that it would be impossible for them to entertain the idea. Nevertheless, there is some force in Czeka-nowski's observation that we may think that they may have borrowed their present witchcraft notions on account of the

[1] A. M. De Graer, 'L'Art de guérir chez les Azande', *Congo*, 1929, t. 1, pp. 220–54, 361–408.
[2] Op. cit., 1958, p. 42.

prevalence of similar complexes of beliefs and practices in the south-western part of the Uele Basin and also because of the West African character of the procedure of dissection of the intestines of persons accused of witchcraft.[1] This conjecture is supported by Baumann's map[2] which shows the essentially West African spread of this type of witchcraft complex, the Azande, Logo, Mangbetu, and Abarambo being on the north-eastern limit of its distribution. It is possible that the Ambomu took over both the poison oracle and their present witchcraft beliefs and practices from the Ababua, though this can be no more than conjecture. It is probably true that they have always had witchcraft beliefs of some kind—it would be surprising if they had not. I have noted earlier that it is likely that Browne's statement, in about 1794, that the Gnum Gnum, who hold that all deaths are due to witchcraft, refers to the Azande.[3] More-over, the witch-doctors, if we are to accept tradition, go back to the time of early Vongara rulers, and witch-doctors make little sense without witchcraft. The point under consideration, however, is whether they had their present witchcraft beliefs and practices—an organic phenomenon, autopsies, etc.

[1] Op. cit., p. 73.
[2] H. Baumann, 'Die Sektion der Zauberkraft', *Zeitschrift für Ethnologie*, 1928, p. 83.
[3] Op. cit., p. 310.

IX

ZANDE CULTURE
(*continued*)

IN this section some examples are given of borrowing in areas
of the social life other than those of cultivation of plants and
the arts and crafts.

King Gbudwe, as I said in the last chapter, looked upon new
medicines with suspicion. He was extremely hostile to what
have now (I speak of the nineteen-twenties), in spite of their
prohibition by the Anglo-Egyptian Administration, become a
common feature of the Zande way of life, the closed associations,
usually referred to as secret societies, for the practice of magic.
The other Zande rulers are also said to have opposed them as
undermining their authority.[1] All of them had a foreign origin.
Three entered Gbudwe's realm towards the close of his reign
and were rigorously suppressed by him, though in out-of-the-
way districts they appear to have survived all his efforts to
exterminate them: the *nando*, which originated among the
Mangbetu—the word appears to be Mangbetu[2]—though some
say among the Amege (Amadi); the *siba*, which was taken over
from some foreign people to the south of the Uele; and the *biri*,
which came from either the Mangbetu (*neberi* is the Mangbetu
word for medicine) or the Abangba. Mgr. Lagae[3] states that
it seems to have started among the Mayogo to the south-east.
Czekanowski,[4] speaking of the Mangbetu, says that their *nebeli*
society expresses a need for solidarity among different native
peoples in the face of European conquest; a view I am inclined
to accept if we may include such results of European conquest
as the breakdown of the political institutions of these peoples. He
says that it is generally asserted that it stems from the Mangbetu.

Other societies entered the realm very soon after Gbudwe's
death and the collapse of his kingdom in 1905. The most

[1] Lagae, op. cit., p. 117; Giorgetti, op. cit., 1958, pp. 44–6.
[2] Hutereau, op. cit., 1909, p. 71.
[3] Op. cit., p. 123.　　　　　　　　[4] Op. cit., p. 164.

flourishing of them was *mani*. Azande of the Sudan have
variously placed its origin among the Abarambo, the Amadi,
the Mangbetu, and the Amisiaga. Mgr. Lagae[1] says that those
of the upper Uele declare it to have come from the country
of the Ambili of the lower reaches of that river and also from
even further west. Some of its features betray its foreign origin,
but all we can say for certain is that it came to the Azande
from some foreign people or peoples to the south. The *kpira*
society, on the other hand, was taken over from a northern
people, the Bongo. *Wanga*, the most recent society to enter
Gbudwe's old kingdom, is said by Mgr. Lagae[2] to have originated in a medicine used in the north, the region of Wau. Other
magical associations are little more than names to me: the *wiligi*
came from the Amadi, and the *ruma* from the Bongo. Both have
passed into oblivion, as have other societies, all of them foreign
and ephemeral: *zambi*, *maboro*, *namakpo*, and *tambuakpolo*, all give
a southern origin. Fr. Giorgetti[3] was told that *namakpo* and
nando were the oldest of these associations. He mentions yet
another, the *karu*, which he says came from the Congo more
than half a century ago.

   The earliest of these associations all came from the south. We
have therefore to bear in mind that though Gbudwe's kingdom
was relatively free from outside interference, there was near
chaos in the Zande kingdoms and among other peoples to the
south of it. From about 1870 various types of Arabs were roam-
ing about the region, creating everywhere confusion which was
for a time increased by the arrival of the Belgians with their
native soldiers in 1891. The area to the north of Gbudwe's
kingdom had also been for a long time in a disastrous state, due
chiefly to the ravages of Arab slavers. In both areas it was an
unsettled period, and the magical associations which emerged
in it and later entered Gbudwe's domains can indeed be considered to be a response to a situation in which social life was
seriously disturbed and the ruling classes were losing their
control. They may even be regarded as subversive, having their
own organization of cells not subject to the supervision of the
traditional rulers, kept secret from them and opposed to them.
That this was the view of the Avongara rulers of the Azande is

----

[1] Op. cit., p. 118.   [2] Ibid., p. 131.
[3] Op. cit., 1958, p. 216.

demonstrated by the efforts they made to suppress them. The European administrations also regarded them as subversive and treated membership of them as a criminal offence.

In the previous chapter it was said that very many Zande medicines had been borrowed. We may now add to this observation that all their closed associations for the practice of magic, some still flourishing in my day, entered Zandeland from outside it; and this was not just the taking over of new medicines but also the emergence of new organized social groupings, which had furthermore a political significance in that political conditions different from those obtaining in the past permitted their growth.

I give a few more examples of borrowing before summing up. Circumcision today forms part of an elaborate series of ceremonies, with special adornments, dances, songs, and lodges; and it brings about sets of new social relationships. However, we know that when early travellers from Europe traversed Zandeland, e.g. Schweinfurth[1] and Junker,[2] the Azande did not circumcise at all. Coming from the Islamic north, this was an observation they at once made. When Czekanowski carried out his researches in the years 1907–8 circumcision was in process of being introduced and had indeed become so much the fashion that adults were undergoing the operation, and it became necessary for the Belgians to threaten Zande soldiers and workers with heavy penalties if they underwent it, since it incapacitated them for a time for performing their tasks.[3] All Azande I have questioned in Gbudwe's territory have told me that it was not introduced there in his lifetime, unless clandestinely, except to a very small extent in the province of his eldest son Basongoda, for it was forbidden by Gbudwe and his governors, as it was by rulers in the Congo.[4] It was only after Gbudwe's death that circumcision became established in his territory. It was then performed not only on boys but also on adults who wished to avoid comment among the women, though some of the older men were, I was informed, still uncircumcised in my day. It is remarkable that in so short a time the practice had come to be regarded as so much a Zande custom that *aboro pito*, 'the uncircumcised', had become a scornful epithet used in reference to other peoples.

[1] *The Heart of Africa*, vol. i, 1873, p. 524.   [2] Op. cit., vol. ii, 1891, p. 366.
[3] Op. cit., pp. 35–6.   [4] Lagae, op. cit., p. 180.

Marno[1] says that circumcision, probably introduced by the Mohammedans, was in 1875 quite common near the Arab posts (*seribahs*) in the area lying to the east of Gbudwe's kingdom, but there is no evidence that the Azande took over the practice from the Arabs. They certainly borrowed it from some Negro people, though one cannot be certain from which, for it was practised by several peoples in contact with them when the Azande were still uncircumcised: the Abanga;[2] the Mangbetu;[3] the Amadi;[4] the Abuguru,[5] and perhaps others. My informants said that it came to them from the Amadi. Mgr. Lagae[6] says that the Azande of the south were initiated into the practice by the Mangbetu and the Abarambo, those of the north by the Amadi.

It may be mentioned here, since it is another bodily mutilation, that the practice, so common in Schweinfurth's day,[7] of chipping the incisor teeth to points had been entirely given up fifty years later. Marno[8] says that the Makraka (Adio) Azande sharpened their upper, and many also the lower, incisors, this pointing being done by applying a small knife and tapping on its back. My informants were for the most part agreed that the true Azande (Ambomu) did not mutilate the teeth at all. Then came from some outside source—Fr. Giorgetti[9] suggests both the Madi–Abarambo and Bantu peoples—the practice of cutting into the incisors. I was told that first the incisors were sharpened (*zagbali* or *lindi ango*), then this gave way to *mande*, the boring of a hole pointed towards the gums between the central upper incisors, still occasionally seen during my residence in Zandeland. This in its turn gave way to *masua*, a notch like an inverted V cut between the same teeth, as commonly seen at that time. These mutilations were done *ni ngbanya*, 'for ornamentation'. It may be here remarked upon, as Czekanowski observes,[10] that the Azande, who borrowed so much from the Mangbetu, did not copy their deformation of the head.

[1] Op. cit., p. 129.   [2] Schweinfurth, *The Heart of Africa*, vol. i, 1873, p. 524.
[3] Ibid.; vol. ii, p. 94; Junker, op. cit., vol. ii, 1891, p. 366; Emin Pasha, op. cit., p. 212.
[4] Junker, op. cit., vol. ii, 1891, p. 366.   [5] Emin Pasha, op. cit., p. 384.
[6] Op. cit., p. 180.   [7] Schweinfurth, *The Heart of Africa*, vol. ii, 1873, p. 6.
[8] Op. cit., p. 124.   [9] Op. cit., 1957, p. 181.
[10] Op. cit., p. 36.

Another example of cultural borrowing is the manner of burial and mortuary customs of the Azande. At the present time in the Sudan a corpse is buried under a side niche in a rectangular shaft, and over the grave is erected a low hut with a ridged roof which is eventually replaced at a mortuary ceremony by a high heap of stones. The construction of this heap forms a central part of a complex of rites and festal observances. Now these heaps of stones are a conspicuous feature of the countryside, and early European travellers could not have failed to observe them had they existed at the time of their explorations. So we need not hesitate to accept Zande statements that this is a fairly modern custom, probably introduced towards the end of Gbudwe's reign. It may have been introduced from the north, for it is found there among peoples subject to the Azande, the Mberidi and Mbegumba, who in their turn may have borrowed it from the Bongo. But the movement could have been in the opposite direction, for Schweinfurth does not record it among the Bongo.[1] Also I was told by one old commoner governor (Gami) that the custom originated among the Amadi. The earliest treatment of the surface of the tomb was, according to my information, to beat it hard and cover it with a layer of straw. Then a plain, low hut was erected over it. It then became the fashion to build over the grave a hut of the kind called *kata*, introduced, as has been said earlier, from the east. Such was the custom in Schweinfurth's time.[2] This was replaced by a low, clay structure, called *kanda*, consisting of three tiers of beaten clay, and said to be of Abisanga origin; and this in its turn gave way to the low, ridged hut (*ngongombara*) of today, till at the mortuary ceremony it is replaced by the memorial pile of stones. The shaft of the grave was said to have been originally a more or less circular trench with a side niche, the rectangular form of the trench of today being a recent innovation.

With reference to Zande burial customs, Schweinfurth and Junker make some statements which I have not been able to confirm. The former[3] says that men of rank are interred either sitting on their benches or in a kind of coffin made from a hollow tree. The latter[4] says, speaking of the Adio (Makaraka) section

---

[1] *The Heart of Africa*, vol. ii, 1873, pp. 284–6.   [2] Ibid., p. 35.
[3] Ibid., pp. 34–5.   [4] Op. cit., vol. i, 1890, p. 361.

of Azande, who live separated from the rest to the east, that they smoke the body over a slow fire and when it is desiccated hang it between the branches of a tree or, as he says elsewhere[1] about their chiefs, inter it. Hutereau,[2] on the contrary, says that the Adio bury a corpse in its owner's hut and he gives a drawing of the grave structure.

The introduction of circumcision and mortuary forms are of particular interest because in these instances we do not have to depend on verbal information and ethnological probabilities, the evidence being documentary and beyond question. I make only a passing reference to cannibalism as I have considered this matter at length elsewhere.[3] The conclusions reached there on a comprehensive survey of the evidence were that probably cannibalism was sporadically practised by some men, most of whom were persons of foreign stock. It is likely that cannibalism was not practised by all the original Azande (Ambomu) or their Avongara rulers and that, when some men of Mbomu stock ate human flesh, they were following the example of foreigners in various stages of political and cultural assimilation into the Zande amalgam.

My last example, sparsely illustrated, is taken from the area of language, which can, of course, be very easily influenced from outside. As I explained in Chapter VII, with reference to certain Arabic words incorporated into Zande, owing to the changes a word may undergo in its transmission it can be very difficult to detect that it is not a Zande word. *Bolangiti, neli,* and *bakiti* look and sound very different from the English 'blanket', 'nail', and 'bucket', and *siani* and *geredere* from the Arabic *sahn* ('plate') and *jerdal* ('bucket'); but in these cases the nature of the objects alerts one. Leaving on one side these recent borrowings from Arabic and English, we may ask what influence assimilated or neighbouring peoples, who have in other cultural respects had much influence, have had on the Zande language. As I cannot speak the languages of these peoples I am unable to express a decided opinion on this matter. Fr. Giorgetti, who has made a special and prolonged study of these tongues, is better placed to express an opinion, though, in recording his views, I would

[1] Junker, op. cit., vol. i, 1890, p. 297.   [2] Op. cit., 1909, p. 50.
[3] E. E. Evans-Pritchard, 'Zande Cannibalism', *Journal of the Royal Anthropological Institute*, 90, pt. 2, 1960.

reserve judgement on the evidence for them. According to him[1]
the only words Schweinfurth records as Niam-Niam (Zande)
are really almost all Barambo and not Zande at all. Presumably
he refers only to *The Heart of Africa*, for this would not be true
for the *Linguistiche Ergebnisse*. He is further of the opinion that a
large number of words have been taken over from foreigners and
incorporated into the Zande tongue. The matter is very complicated, and I will content myself here with mentioning a few
examples of common Zande words taken from a list of loan-
words which he has kindly sent me. From Bukuru, Huma, and
Bangbinda have been borrowed *kurungba*, 'canoe' (*mawa* in old
Zande); *gwanza*, 'arrow'; *Kpetekpete*, 'boggy, swampy'; *mangani*,
'catfish'; *kangade*, 'flea'; *dupo*, 'hippopotamus'; *kanga*, 'rhinoceros'; *ngama*, 'green snake'; *zumburu*, 'red pig'; *furo*, 'bat'; *ete*,
'hammerhead stork'; *kpootoro*, 'bulbul'; *turumani*, 'mocking
bird' (in Zande *babibia*), etc. From Madi: *andigbo*, 'small barbed
spear'; *nguma*, 'small bone used in hairdressing', etc. From
Barambo: *biki*, 'granite'; *gadai*, 'chimpanzee', etc. From Bviri
(Bare): *maangiri*, woman's small toilet knife (in Zande *ngbariyo*);
bura, a kind of sesame, etc.

It may also be remarked that there are archaic words, some
of which may be of foreign origin, still heard on the lips of old
people, though others are synonyms, e.g. *pegine*, 'water'; *banda-
vuranikuberu*, 'leopard'; *basilimbia* and *danganingbaru*, 'dog'; *togo*,
'beer'; and *bazaa*, 'subject'. This last was an old word used by
nobles: *mbata agbia a na yemba limo aboro nga kina bazaa; gu limo
re, si na ngia limo aboro ngba agbia*, 'in the past the nobles used
to call people [their subjects] "*bazaa*"; that was the name they
used for them'. Some examples of archaic words which are
probably of foreign origin are *pi*, 'beer' (Madi); *mbomu*, 'maize'
(a word found in the languages of several peoples—Pambia,
Miangba, Huma, Buguru, and others); *gbavura*, 'manioc';
baturu, 'leopard' (Miangba); *timbia*, 'moon' (Miangba); *bara*,
'dog' (Madi); *kpai*, a vegetable oil (probably Mangbetu); *gburu*,
'the rubbing-board oracle' (probably Miangba), etc. It is difficult to trace the origin of some of these archaic words, e.g.
babiti, 'buffalo'; *mianga*, 'colocasia'; and *maba*, 'ceremonial
knife'. I have already shown[2] that, as might be supposed, many
Zande names of clans are in foreign tongues. Words have been

[1] Op. cit., p. 181.   [2] See Chapter IV.

taken over from foreign tongues but, as the archaic words indicate, words are also lost, and it is interesting to read that Junker,
more than eighty years ago, observed: 'The Zandehs told me
that many words current in the time of their forefathers were
now obsolete.'[1]

Some further evidence of ethnic admixture in the Zande
spoken in the Sudan is possibly to be seen in individual variations of pronunciation in the same district, which may be due
to differences of race and culture not yet entirely eliminated
and surviving in the speech of those whose parents or grand-
parents spoke Zande as a second tongue. This was noticeable
in the vowel pronunciation of informants of foreign stock. There
is also a very clear difference of speech between those who
aspirate vowels and those who do not, e.g. between *hareme* and
areme ('today') and *he* and *e* ('thing'). In suggesting that these
individual variations may be due to differences of ethnic background, I am only suggesting what Azande themselves say,
especially what they say about the difficult sounds represented
by Lagae and Vanden Plas by the letters *l* and *r* and by the
Gores by the single letter *r* (now used throughout Sudanese
Zandeland), for they claim that it was at one time regarded at
court as a test, a shibboleth, how a man pronounced these
sounds. If he pronounced the name of the river Lingasi with
the value the Dominican Fathers represent by the symbol *l* he
was considered to be a true Mbomu, whereas if he pronounced
the word Ringasi, giving the value they represent by *r*, then he
was a foreigner.

I have only touched on this matter here, for it is evident that
if the Zande language has been influenced by foreign tongues
it could not have been very strongly influenced by them because,
though Lagae and Vanden Plas list five regional dialects, the
differences between them are, as they recognize, so slight that
it is doubtful whether they should be called dialects at all; as
Schweinfurth[2] also noted, though it is difficult to see on what
his statement could have been based. When we consider how
vast a territory the Avongara-Ambomu conquered and settled
in and how many peoples they have absorbed we may be surprised how slight are the variations which have been developed
in their speech.

---

[1] Op. cit., vol. iii, 1892, p. 280.   [2] *The Heart of Africa*, vol. i, 1873, p. 403.

So, it is not only plants, crafts, medicines, words, etc., what are sometimes called items of culture, that the Avongara-Ambomu have borrowed from foreign peoples, fusing them into the Zande culture of yesterday and today, but also cultural and social complexes—institutions which have become so integrated into their way of life that if we did not have evidence to the contrary we might have supposed that they had always been part of it.

I put forward the following concluding observations:

1. It is necessary to distinguish between relatively static primitive societies and those which are known to have undergone considerable cultural and social transformations. The method of analysis may be rather different in the two cases. This is not simply a matter of historical evidences being lacking in the first case, thereby giving an illusion of stagnation, but of very complex causes such as ecology, type of social structure, and historical circumstances.

2. The developments I have discussed are essentially internal changes in an African society in an African setting. The borrowings have been, save for a few and, if we except the rifle, negligible exceptions, by one African people from other African peoples, whatever their ultimate origins may have been. They mostly took place before Arab or European domination, and even if innovations like secret societies are indirectly a product of a situation brought about by these intruders, they were essentially African in origin, form, and function. I emphasize this point because our evidences show how a people right in the centre of Africa have taken over, used, and developed, long before any contact with higher civilizations, what has appeared to them most valuable in the habits of the peoples they have come into contact with.

3. All the evidence recorded in these three chapters on Zande culture leads us to suppose that culturally the Avongara-Ambomu have undergone much change during the course of their migrations. Can we doubt that with greater cultural complexity social relations have also become more complex and that political institutions have played an increasingly important part in the life of the Azande? The corollary of this supposition is that in the simpler culture of the past, social institutions were simpler and political institutions less developed and dominant.

Such a surmise is supported by Zande tradition, which must not, because it is verbal, be assumed to lack all validity and be ignored. Azande think of their present way of life, as we have seen, as being the result of a long process of development which started when the Avongara consolidated the Mbomu clans and the Avongara-Ambomu began their migrations and conquests, a process shaped by wars, movements into new ecological zones, colonization, ethnic admixture, and cultural borrowings in each new area of dispersal. As they see it, their political system with its ruling class, court etiquette, a regimental organization, an administrative establishment, political control of judicial procedure, and inequality of wealth started from humble beginnings and slowly developed.

4. It was this superior political organization which, it is suggested, developed in the course of wars and settlements and enabled the Avongara-Ambomu to overcome piecemeal the peoples they were to conquer and absorb, peoples not technologically inferior to themselves but lacking the unity and organization which might have enabled them to put up an effective resistance. What held this together (for Africa, a vast empire) was the fact that, although the Avongara-Ambomu may not have numbered a higher percentage of the total population in the conquered territories than the Normans did at the Conquest, they were able through their superior organization to impose their political institutions and their language on a heterogeneous amalgam of peoples with different customs and tongues.

X

THE ORGANIZATION OF A KINGDOM

I

AN attempt is made here to determine some significant features of one of the Zande kingdoms of Central Africa, that of Gbudwe, and to examine, in so far as the literature permits, whether they are general features of Zande political organization.

It must be understood that in every kingdom the king ruled personally over a central province and appointed governors, his eldest sons being the most important of them, to rule over the surrounding provinces of his kingdom. Consequently, when Gbudwe overcame his eldest brother Ngima and took possession of the area his father had kept under his own control, roughly and in the main, between the Hu and the Lingasi (though its most westerly extension was said to have been, to the north, the Azi tributary of the Ya and, to the south, the Mura tributary of the Were), he found other brothers or their sons in possession of neighbouring territories: the sons of Ezo to the west, Wando (roughly to the south of the Yubo basin), Malingindu (roughly east of the Gurba), and Ngoliyo between the last two. These territories had long been virtually independent kingdoms, their rulers making only formal acknowledgement of the suzerain's position, so that they could have been described as nominally provinces of the kingdom of Gbudwe's father Bazingbi centred on his own province or as adjacent kingdoms in each of which the king had a central position and appointed governors to rule outlying districts. Craffen and Colombo[1] call these rulers of provinces '*petits roitelets*'. 'Province' and 'kingdom' are thus terms relative to the degree of political autonomy reached, a matter I discuss more fully later.

In other directions the domains he had acquired were bordered by autonomous kingdoms ruled by other royal families: to the north-west by members of the family of Nunge

[1] Op. cit., p. 790.

(finally Tembura son of Liwa), to the north by Tombo son of Yakpati, and to the east by various brothers, uncles, and cousins —Ndima and Bagilisa, sons of Bazingbi, Zangbaberu and Ngbanzi, sons of Yakpati, Nganzi, son of Muduba, and some brothers and sons of Renzi, son of Yakpati; and a little later by representatives of the Arab trading companies. The western and southern frontiers underwent no appreciable change from the beginning to the end of his reign, whereas large regions to the east and the north came under his control by conquest or peaceful annexation. Except for the territory he kept under his immediate personal supervision, his father's old territories which fell to him had governors appointed to rule them; and all the newly acquired territories were likewise placed under provincial governors, some of whom were commoners and some members of the nobility, the latter being the aristocratic clan of the Avongara and in particular Gbudwe's eldest sons when they were old enough to be planted out. We have to bear in mind that the newly conquered territories contained a number of foreign peoples, some of whom were still only partially assimilated politically; and even then in large tracts of the region his father and grandfather had ruled, the foreign elements, though politically incorporated, were still to a considerable degree ethnically and culturally distinct.[1] It was the duty of the governors to complete the assimilation of these foreigners, spreading among them Zande institutions, language, and ways of life, as well as imposing ever more firmly Vongara rule, and to build up an administration, to ensure peace within their provinces, and to defend the frontiers of the kingdom.

A study of these provincial governorships sheds light on the organization of a Zande kingdom and indicates some of the changes it could undergo in the course of a single reign. However, to make it requires the sifting of a confusing mass of verbal, though none the less historical, detail. I shall not present in full this mass of names of persons and rivers (by reference to which administrative areas were defined), names so common that they add to, rather than diminish, the difficulties of sifting the material. I give from the total information at my disposal only as much detail as is required to provide adequate illustrative evidences for the conclusions advanced.

[1] See Chapter III.

2

It appeared to me that one way of trying to unravel a complicated history of provinces, or at least to appreciate the nature
and complexity of the problem, was to find out as much as I
could about the changes in the governorships of each of the
provinces recognized at the time of my research (1926–30) as
political units by the British Administration in the old kingdom
of Gbudwe, or rather in its western half (Yambio District) for
I was unable to obtain the same information about those in the
eastern part, that ruled till 1914 by Gbudwe's second son Mange
(Meridi district). Most of these units are shown in the sketch-
map on p. 124. It is true that the disposition and extension
of the units were not entirely the same as those of Gbudwe's
provinces at the time of his death, but they were in many
instances approximately so, and therefore an inquiry along
these lines provided useful information about political mobility
and other changes. This in itself was an arduous undertaking,
for it was found that when a province changed hands at the
death, transference, or dismissal of its governor its boundaries
did not always remain the same; or it might be broken up
and its territory shared by neighbouring governors. Governors
sometimes, even though established in a province and retaining
the confidence of the suzerain, asked to be transferred elsewhere
because misfortune had dogged them and the oracles were
unfavourable to their remaining in their present domicile. Then
there was indefiniteness about some of the minor provinces of
the realm in that some of the royal sons and other nobles, and
even commoners, were not formally appointed by Gbudwe but
settled in one or other district, usually more or less remote, and
there, having attracted a following, they were allowed by the
sovereign to retain it, since they acknowledged his overlordship
and paid him tribute. Craffen and Colombo have made the
same observation: royal sons, when they came of age, were
encouraged by their fathers to settle far from court and to found
there what might be called colonies, which slowly spread until
they became small vassal domains.[1] Furthermore, it was often
very difficult to determine at what point in Gbudwe's reign,
especially in its earlier period, a province changed hands and

[1] Op. cit., p. 790.

consequently who at any given time were the governors. It is therefore improbable that this account has altogether avoided minor errors; but in general both the relation of events and the conclusions drawn from it are undoubtedly correct.

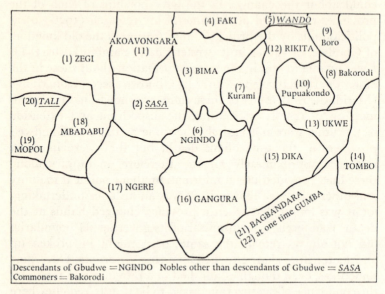

Descendants of Gbudwe = NGINDO　Nobles other than descendants of Gbudwe = *SASA*
Commoners = Bakorodi

SKETCH 3. PROVINCES OF THE OLD KINGDOM OF GBUDWE
IN 1926

Altogether the succession of governors was investigated in twenty-five provinces, twenty-two of which appear on the map, which does not show, as already mentioned, the eastern half of the kingdom; neither does it show its northern extension. Names in capital letters in the map are those of nobles, those underlined not being descendants of Gbudwe; names in small letters are those of commoners. I have selected twelve provinces as representative examples, the numbers in the list below corresponding to those on the map.

(1) Zegi son of Gbudwe ruled an area first given by Gbudwe to his son Binza (also called Gbakoyo) by his wife Nagbakoyo. On his death, Gbudwe gave it to his son Angbele (also called Zaza) by his wife Naduru. On his death, Gbudwe gave it to Angbele's uterine brother Zegi (also called Mbitimo and Zogozogo) who had previously

administered part of the territory of another uterine brother, Gangura, and by his grace, on the southern border of the kingdom.

(2) Sasa was a son of Funa, son of Bazingbi, and consequently Gbudwe's nephew. When Gbudwe's son Kana, who ruled to the east of the Sueh river, was killed by the Bongo people, Gbudwe ordered another son, Bugwa, to take his place, but Bugwa, fearing to be near the route of Egyptian Government expeditions (*gine abolomu*), refused the responsibility. In anger, for this reason and because he suspected Bugwa of going after his wives, Gbudwe drove him from his court without giving him an alternative appointment. He settled in the country where Sasa now is and collected a following there on his own account, for this had earlier been the province of Gbudwe's second son, Mange, on whose translation to the east on the advice of the oracles that he should not stay there, it had been left without a ruler. Before Mange had been appointed to rule there, it is said that the country belonged to one of Bazingbi's sons, Ngbikadi (also called Ngbeka). It appears that Bugwa fell foul of his father again and took refuge in Mange's country to the east. He had a bad reputation among the Azande because he did not settle cases clearly. The country then came into possession of Sasa.

(3) Bima was a son of Gbudwe. His territory is said to have been at one time held partly by Urudimo son of Ngbutuma, son of Bazingbi, and partly by a commoner called Ngbamboli, a man of the Abagua clan and a sister's son of the nobility, whom, it is alleged, Gbudwe executed for witchcraft. Certainly most of it was taken over by Gbudwe as part of his personal domain and remained so till his death. It then came within the sphere of influence of his son Rikita, whose influence and territory were then much greater than in my day, and as shown in the map, both having been curtailed by the British Administration; and he gave it to Bima, who previously had held a very minor position to the north-east on the Sueh river. (It must be borne in mind that after Gbudwe's death there was no longer a king and the various governors acted in their own interests as they thought fit, so long as the Administration acquiesced in, or was ignorant of, their activities.) I was told, however, that Bima chose to make himself directly dependent on the new government station at Yambio. A considerable number of Gbudwe's personal subjects after his death left the neighbourhood of his court because it became the site of this station and they did not wish to be in its immediate vicinity and they settled in Bima's country.

(4) Faki (also called Dekuku), son of Gbudwe, ruled a province to the north of Bima's, between the rivers Yubo, Sueh, and Hu. In Bazingbi's time it seems to have belonged to his brother Kangu son of Yakpati. It was administered for a time, probably after Kangu's

death, by a commoner, the Ngbamboli referred to in the last entry. It later came to form part of Gbudwe's own province and was then occupied by many of his *aboro ngbanga*, his men of the court. When Gbudwe told his son Faki to get out of his court and go and live elsewhere, as is the custom of royalty, he settled in this area and was left there to gather followers around him on his own account. At that time his brothers Gangura and Bima were in the same area, each with a small following.

(5) Wando (also called Muzelenga) is a son of Gamanzu, son of Galimbara, son of Yakpati. He had a uterine connection with Gbudwe in that Mabenge married Dunge, by whom he begat Galimbara, and after his death she was taken in marriage by Yakpati to whom she bore Gbudwe's father Bazingbi, Ukwe, Ngindo, and Mazegbe. Galimbara had a domain to the west, in what became Ezo's country, but his sons Mboli, Madiri, and Gamanzu moved eastwards into Bazingbi's kingdom, and Bazingbi gave Gamanzu the territory where Wando now is. It had previously been ruled by a commoner, Kamundi, said to have been recognized by Bazingbi's brother Renzi as his representative. Gbudwe later confirmed Gamanzu in his possessions, and at his death they passed to his son Wando. The history of this succession is somewhat confused, for I was told that at different times two of Gbudwe's sons, Gangura, till his translation to the south, and Mabenge, till his death, had jurisdiction in a part of the area.

(6) Ngindo (also called Bewadi) was the eldest son of Tikima, eldest son of Basongoda, eldest son of Gbudwe. He was therefore the senior member of the senior line of descent from Gbudwe. His territory came to him in British times, and presumably with the support of the Administration, through his grandfather Basongoda, who survived his father Tikima and at Gbudwe's death acquired this portion of his personal estate.

(7) Kurami, a commoner of the Abakpara clan, administered territory which was part of Gbudwe's personal domain (*boro ga Gbudwe kpolo du*). After Gbudwe's death a man called Asigbara gained for a while the ear of the British Administration and persuaded it to grant possession to a certain Fataki (Abauro clan), but the Administration later deprived him of it and instated in his place Sukutu (also called Gambi), the father of Kurami, who was useful in providing porters and in other ways. Kurami inherited the territory on his father's death. His mother was a daughter of Bakorodi (see below).

(8) Bakorodi (Abakundo clan) was governor of a stretch of country once administered by two commoners, members of the Angbadimo clan, Gunde and Sagara. Gunde died of sickness while

Gbudwe was a prisoner of the Egyptian Government and his son Mange, having control over appointments during his captivity, put his district in charge of Bakorodi, and this was later confirmed by Gbudwe, whose consulter of oracles he had once been. Sagara died after Gbudwe's death, and it was Basongoda who gave him charge of that part of his territory.

(9) Boro (also called Ngbasumba), a commoner of the Agbambi clan, was in charge of country given to Gundusu (Angbadimo clan) by Gbudwe when he removed him from a governorship of one of the southern marches. Gundusu was later executed on a charge of having caused the death of Zabia, a commoner governor of the Akowe clan. Gbudwe then gave it to Tangili (Agbambi clan). He was also executed, probably in 1902, on a charge of disloyalty. Gbudwe did not fill the vacancy before his death, after which Basongoda gave it to Boro's father Busia. He also gave him part of the district of the commoner governor Ngenzi, on that man's death. Boro inherited these lands from his father by direction of the Administration. Part of Ngenzi's territory was given by Basongoda to Gbifi (Avotombo clan), a minor commoner governor not shown on the map.

(10) The district of the commoner governor Pupuakondo formed part of Gbudwe's personal domain, which appears to have stretched unevenly to the river Kisi and in places to the east of that river. Nevertheless at an earlier period he had planted governors there, for I was told that it was once ruled by Gbaro son of Likara, who had been a leader of one of Gbudwe's military companies. He angered Gbudwe in some way and fled to the kingdom of Wando. Gbudwe pardoned him on his return and reinstated him as company leader but not as provincial governor. He was later executed during the Birisi campaign against Renzi son of Wando. Yakpati (also, I believe, called Mosanabamo) son of Gbudwe seems to have taken his place in the governorship but was later driven from it by, according to various versions, Gbudwe himself, Rikita, or the British. As far as I could gather, Pupuakondo was not given charge of the area by Gbudwe, though he was an important deputy and head of a military company in it, but by Ukwe, Gbudwe's grandson, who for a while obtained control of Gbudwe's territory shortly after his death, and its occupation by the British, whose confidence he had won. They are said to have been influenced in Pupuakondo's favour by his kinsman Yango, Mange's most powerful commoner governor, who also seems to have co-operated with the British on their arrival in his master's country.

(11) Akoavongara, son of Yakpati, son of Ngindo, son of Gbudwe occupied a territory once held by Bungi son of Bazingbi. On his death, Gbudwe gave it to his second son Mange together with the

adjacent country which later became Sasa's province (see no. 2), and on Mange's translation to the east he gave it to another son, Borugba. On the death of Bagboro son of Bazingbi, who ruled a province to the south, Borugba was moved to his territory and vacated this northern district, which Gbudwe then gave to his son Ngindo, on whose death, after Gbudwe's reign, it passed to his son Yakpati and on Yakpati's death to his son Akoavongara.

(12) Rikita son of Gbudwe at one time ruled over a very extensive though thinly populated, tract of country to the north of the Sueh river bend, its boundary to the west being the Sueh, beyond which lay the kingdom of Tembura, while to the east its boundaries with the enormous province of Mange were the Maieda and Mago. This country was first ruled by Tombo son of Yakpati and his brothers Gbalia and Ukwe, and then by their sons, Nunge and Ukwe sons of Tombo, Ngbakai and Ima sons of Gbalia, Gambavunu and his brothers Singiya and Mongbi, sons of Ukwe, and others. These were, in one way or another, dispossessed by Rikita. Rikita later moved southwards and occupied the area shown on the map. Eventually, under Government pressure, he had to yield his northern territories (not shown on the map) to his son Banginzegino. His new domain had in part at one time been in charge of a commoner, Zoli of the Angumbi clan, who had died. Part of it also seems to have been controlled by Yakpati son of Gbudwe (see no. 10). Most of the area, however, was the province of Baduagbanga son of Nunge, son of Tombo, whose people left him because he was a bad judge and beat them without cause. Yakpati also lost his people's confidence.

Sketch-map 3 shows most of an administrative district of the Anglo-Egyptian Sudan but it serves also to demonstrate roughly the kind of way in which a Zande kingdom was divided up into provinces and so provides an illustrative basis for a discussion of these provinces. It does not show the full extent of Gbudwe's kingdom, for it does not include the large area ruled by Banginzegino son of Rikita to the north or the vast domain of Gbudwe's son Mange to the east of the Sueh. This eastern extension of the kingdom, occupied by various foreign peoples, had been partly conquered by Renzi son of Yakpati and, on his death in battle, was ruled by some of his brothers (Muduba, Bakiyanda, Zangaberu, etc.) and then by their sons, such as Ngangi son of Muduba and Bagilisa, Ndima, and Fuge, sons of Bazingbi; and during their lifetimes it fell in part under the control of Arab trading companies who began to use routes through it to the Congo forests early in Gbudwe's reign. Gbudwe added it to his domains bit by bit by war, annexation, and taking advantage of Arab difficulties and put it in charge of his sons Mange, Kana, and Sanango and a number of commoner governors—Kulewoka (Abakundo clan), Bagundusu (Avukida clan), Bakekpe (Angumbi clan), and others. I am unable to give an exact account of their disposition and of their duration in office, being little acquainted with the area at first hand. Kana and Sanango were taken captives with Gbudwe by the Egyptian Government in 1882 and both died before his return two years later, leaving Mange and his sons (Ndoruma, Bangbi, Mabenge, etc.) and various commoner governors appointed by him in control of the whole region to the east of the Sueh river south of its eastwards bend, where he ruled as an almost independent monarch as far as the Meridi river. When the British took over the country Mange was living at the sources of the Madeba, tributary of the Sueh. Rikita, as already mentioned, gained control over the country east of the Sueh north of the bend.

Also, the map and notes on provinces only partially show the situation as it was in Gbudwe's time. We have to allow for Gbudwe's substantial personal province which stretched unevenly between the Yubo and the Hu and as far eastwards as the Kisi and in places to the east of that river. To the north it included what became Bima's and Faki's provinces, almost stretching to the Sueh, though later he yielded the northern part to Faki. To the south it extended to the Uze. Moreover, its boundaries changed as he changed his capital; as he moved it in one or other direction, he extended his personal control in that direction and allowed others to take over elsewhere, for example when he took up residence at Belekiwe (Yambio) his son Bafuka had to withdraw his home from the Uze and settle on the Masambu.

We have also to bear in mind that when it is said that after Gbudwe's death Basongoda gave provinces to various people, this was done in British times and presumably with the consent of the British and certainly in some cases under their influence or pressure. Some appointments were definitely described to me by Azande as European appointments, though, with one or two exceptions, they were immediately post-conquest and of short duration—such unimportant persons as Asigbara, Basa, Lebe,

Fataki, and others—for it was found that the Azande would not recognize them and did not readily obey them. But European rule had another and more lasting effect. Apart from destroying royal paramountcy altogether, it froze the political situation more or less as it was at Gbudwe's death so that the normal process which followed the death of a Zande king by which the more powerful of his sons became entirely independent and extended their territories at the expense of the weaker could not operate. It is perhaps idle to speculate what would have happened had Gbudwe died before the arrival of the Belgians and the British, but we can be certain that there would have been strife between some of his sons, and it may be assumed that Mange would have become an entirely independent monarch and probably also Rikita, and possibly also Gangura at the expense of Basongoda in spite of his being the eldest son, for he was a weak character.

3

It will have been noted that the southern provinces of Gbudwe's kingdom were omitted from the list of provinces discussed in the last section. A slightly different line of investigation was pursued in this region, part of which I knew better than the rest of the kingdom since I lived for many months in Gangura's country. These southern marches guarded the frontier of the kingdom against incursions from the followers of Gbudwe's powerful neighbour, his brother Wando, and they formed a co-ordinated line of defence in the sense that if an attack was made on any province all the others, if they were near it, at once mobilized and either went to its assistance or prepared to do so.[1] The statement made before holds here also: it is not possible to determine with certainty the distribution of provinces at any given time. We can, however, present a general picture of the political set-up obtaining at various periods of Gbudwe's reign. In the earliest part of it the southern marches were in charge of persons appointed by his father Bazingbi, and these were slowly replaced by Gbudwe's nominees as they died or were removed from office. I can furnish no reliable information about this period. Round about 1875 to 1880—his reign

[1] See Chapter XVI.

began in 1868 or 1869—three of Gbudwe's eldest sons had governorships on this southern frontier, Basongoda, Mange, and Gumba, the rest being held by five other nobles, Kipa, Gongosi, Ndani (a great hunter), Bagboro, and Rikita, and six commoners, Ongosi, Zengendi, Baipuru, Gundusu, Mai, and Wangu.

Of the sons, Basongoda, the eldest, had first been given a district to the west of the Lingasi in the area ruled by his great-grandfather Yakpati. He was then transferred to the east and given the province roughly corresponding to that of Ngere in the map of provinces, which had before been the domain of Mboli son of Galimbara, son of Yakpati. Mange, as already stated, was in charge of a district to the east of the Sueh river, later to be much enlarged. Gumba had earlier been situated further to the west on the Nagbaka, tributary of the Lingasi. Bagboro, Kipa, Gongosi, Rikita, and Ndani were sons of Bazingbi and brothers of Gbudwe.

The next sketch represents the position as it was some years later. Several governors had been dispossessed on one pretext or another or had been transferred elsewhere or had died in war, and their places had been for the most part taken by Gbudwe's sons. Baipuru (Avukida clan) had been killed in the Egyptian campaign and had been replaced by Bamboti. Ongosi, who had been the most important of King Ngangi's commoner governors and had come to settle in Gbudwe's territory after Gbudwe had conquered his master's kingdom in about 1875, was dismissed on the verdict of the poison oracle that he was unreliable and his province, said to contain large numbers of the foreign clans Abaiwo and Amiteli, was given to Gbudwe's fifth son Bafuka (also called Bokweyo), the frontier between it and Basongoda's province being the Nambia, tributary of Yubo, the Yubo being the boundary between Gbudwe and both sons. Gundusu (Angbadimo clan) was removed to a post in the east of the realm and his country, between the Mbomu and the Uze, went partly to Gbudwe's son Ndukpe and partly to Bazo (Akowe clan), and for a short time Tangili (Agbambi clan) was appointed to administer a section of it, but he was soon translated to office beyond the Yeta. As mentioned earlier, Gundusu was later executed. To Bafuka's province was added that of Gongosi, who appears to have been squeezed out of his domain by Bafuka before he

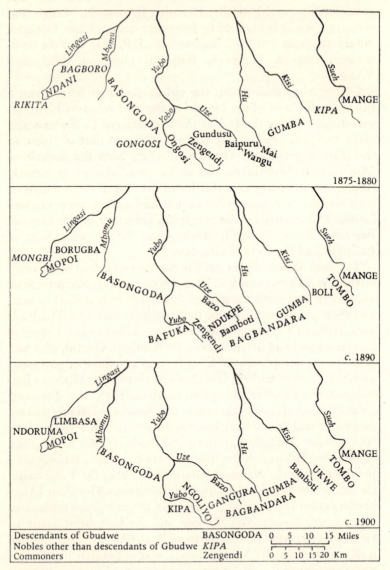

SKETCH 4. THE SOUTHERN PROVINCES OF GBUDWE'S KINGDOM
1875-*c*. 1900.

was killed in the Egyptian campaign. Mai was killed in the campaign of Karikai between Gbudwe and Wando in about 1886, and Gbudwe gave most of his country to his son Bagbandara, the remainder going to his son Gumba (this country is today in the Congo). Wangu (Auboli clan) was suspected of disloyalty and relieved of office, later dying of complications of gonorrhoea, and his province was also given to Bagbandara. Kipa son of Bazingbi had been killed in the Egyptian campaign and he was replaced by two of Gbudwe's sons, Boli and his younger uterine brother Tombo. Bagboro son of Bazingbi was also killed in the Egyptian campaign and was not replaced by his own son Bazamangi but by Gbudwe's son Borugba. The boundary between the territories of Borugba and his elder brother Basongoda was the Mbomu river. Ndani had died and, instead of replacing him by his son Gbate, Gbudwe gave his estate to his own son Mopoi (also called Zimoma and Mbangana). Rikita had been killed in war and had been replaced by his brother Mongbi. It will be observed that the commoner governors had by this time largely been eliminated, that their places had been taken by Gbudwe's sons, and that the collateral descendants of Bazingbi and Yakpati had almost disappeared from the political scene.

Some complications arose from Gbudwe being in Egyptian Government captivity from 1882 to 1884. During his absence his son Mboli, who had been given the eastern part of his province by Bafuka, was expelled by the donor, who placed his own eldest son Kipa in charge of it. Mange, who was then deputizing for Gbudwe, nominally on behalf of the Egyptian Government, dismissed his father's friend Zengendi (Angumbe clan) and gave his country to Bamboti (Auboli clan). On Gbudwe's return he restored his province to him, removing Bamboti to the east of Gumba (his original province going to Ndukpwe); but Zengendi had aroused the jealousy of both Bafuka and Ndukpe, and he was murdered, much to Gbudwe's sorrow, by subjects of Kipa in 1898 or 1899. Gbudwe gave his country to Ngoliyo. He was to prove an unsuccessful ruler who ill-treated his subjects and abused their wives, and after Gbudwe's death he lost his subjects to Gangura. Mange had also removed his brother Boli from office and replaced him by one of his own sons. Boli's province was restored to him by Gbudwe. Then

Bafuka died, probably in 1899, and Kipa took over his province. Ndukpe, whose home at the time was on the Dingbili, tributary of the Duru (in what is now the Congo), died at about the same time and was succeeded by his uterine brother Gangura, who in his turn granted a portion of his territory to his younger uterine brother Zegi, later translated to the north-west (see no. 1), and later still to yet another uterine brother, Ango. Of the commoners, only Bazo and Bamboti seem to have retained their governorships till the end of Gbudwe's reign. When, after Gbudwe's death, they died Bazo's subjects became followers of Bagbandara and Gangura, and Bamboti's went mostly to Gumba for a time but later, drifting from him on account of his taking their women, to Bagbandara (on the death of Gumba, who survived his father, part of his territory was added, presumably by the Belgian authorities, to Bagbandara's domain). Basongoda had placed his son Ngere in charge of the frontier district of his province. Borugba had died, and his son Limbasa had been installed in his seat. Mongbi had died and had been replaced by Gbudwe's son Ndoruma. Boli died, and his place was taken partly by his uterine brother Tombo and partly by his son Ukwe. Ukwe proved unreliable and was driven out of his possessions by Gbudwe at the turn of the century. Gbudwe replaced him by his sons Mboli, Ango, and Kpotogara and two commoners, his former oracle-consulter Kpoyo (Abangbinda people) on the Kisi river and Zai, later shot by the British. However, some four years later came Gbudwe's disastrous attack on the Belgian post at Mayawa and in the following year (1905) his death at the hands of a British patrol. The British restored Ukwe to his territory, and for a time he was put in charge of Gbudwe's province as well. The three sons and Kpoyo thus lost their estates. The final sketch shows the frontier in about 1900, before Ukwe's expulsion. It presents an almost unbroken line of Gbudwe's sons and grandsons.

It remains only to relate the last sketch to the map of provinces as they were in the 1920s. Dika (15) was a son of Mboli, to whom Gbudwe had, as we have noted, given part of Ukwe's territory when he drove him out. When Ukwe was reinstated by the British, Mboli took refuge with Gangura, but he eventually regained his possessions, the British by that time being less well disposed towards Ukwe. Tombo (14), Gangura (16), Ngere (17), and Bagbandara (21) [together with Gumba's estates (22)] have already been accounted for. Kipa, together with his brothers, disappeared from the scene when Gangura, after a fight between their subjects, shortly after British occupation, was authorized by the Administration to take over his country. Ngoliyo had also, as earlier mentioned, lost his subjects to Gangura and hence neither his name nor that of one of his sons appears on the map. Mbadabu (18) was a son of Limbasa, son of Borugba and inherited his province from his father and grandfather. Mopoi (19) has been accounted for. Tali was a son of Binza, son of Malingindo, son of Bazingbi. He originally held some position to the south of the Nile–Congo divide. He fought, and fled from, the Belgians and, having elected to remain in the Anglo-Egyptian Sudan, he was given by the Administration a stretch of country to the west of the Lingasi. Part of this had been unoccupied country between Gbudwe's kingdom and the domains of the sons of Ezo, and part of it had been the territory of Rikita, son of Bazingbi, who was killed in the fighting between Wando's sons in the Congo, and then of Mongbi (or Muengbi), son of Bazingbi and father of Mabenge, on whose death Gbudwe had given it to his own son Ndoruma (also called Pasuda). He appears (I was not well acquainted with this area) to have been dispossessed by the British and, with their consent, Basongoda installed Pelembata son of Ndukpwe, son of Bazingbi, on whose death the Administration gave the territory to Tali.

4

A further approach was to list Gbudwe's sons, those who became adults, and to follow their careers. This provided much additional information and also served as a check on that already obtained.

To record in detail these careers would entail much repetition, and enough information has, I think, already been given to support some general conclusions. I shall therefore merely list the sons in order of seniority and give after each the number of the province he was given charge of (some, as already explained, after Gbudwe's death) or, since the princes were sometimes translated from one province to another, that of the more important appointment. Though, owing to changes in size and

shape of provinces, the numerals can only be a rough indication
of direction they provide a kind of index to persons and places
mentioned in the text. The names at the end of the list may not
be in the right order. Some names of earlier sons have been
omitted because they died too young to have achieved any
prominence, e.g. Rungbakpoto, Keletu, Kurumbise, and Yepu
were mentioned by informants, and there were others who do
not appear in the list.

1. Basongoda	(17)	20. Ndukpwe	(16)
2. Mange		21. Mabenge	(5)
3. Borugba	(18)	22. Bima	(3)
4. Gumba	(22)	23. Gangura	(16)
5. Bafuka	(16)	24. Ngoliyo	(16)
6. Kana		25. Sasa	
7. Sanango		26. Angbele	(1)
8. Boli	(13)	27. Mopoi	(19)
9. Ngoliyo		28. Zemoi	
10. Mopoi		29. Ravura	
11. Faki	(4)	30. Kpotogara	(13)
12. Bavungara		31. Ndoruma	(20)
13. Ngindo	(11)	32. Yakpati	(10)
14. Rikita	(12)	33. Zegi	(1)
15. Bugwa		34. Ango	(13)
16. Binza	(1)	35. Baikpolo	
17. Mboli	(15)	36. Kuruwiso	
18. Bagbandara	(21)	37. Gbandi	
19. Tombo	(14)	38. Limbasa	

Those sons not shown in the table as holding provinces must
now be accounted for. Mange, Kana, and Sanango held provinces in the eastern part of Gbudwe's kingdom, not shown on
the map of provinces. Ngoliyo and Mopoi were killed in the
Egyptian campaign. Bavungara (also called Sungeyo) was not
given a province, but he collected a following on his own
account. Gbudwe deprived him of it for going after his wives and
wounding one of his subjects with a knife. Bugwa also, as already
mentioned, collected a following on his own account but fell
foul of his father and fled to the east. Sasa does not appear to
have been given a province. Gbudwe refused to give Zemoi
any authority in his kingdom because he ill-treated his subjects.
Ravura was taken as a baby to the court of Bafuka son of King

Wando at the time of the Egyptian campaign and stayed there. Baikpolo was killed as a youth in the Derwish campaign. Kuruwiso, Gbandi, and Limbasa (also called Zingbwadu) were too young at the time of their father's death to have been given authority; they were still children.

Given below for easy reference is a genealogy showing the relationship between the nobles recognized as rulers by the Administration of Yambio District in the 1920s. The names of all these rulers appear on the map of provinces except Rikita's son Banginzegino, whose country lay to the north of the map, and Kanimara son of Funa, whose position near the Sueh, where he had attracted a following, mostly of the Abuguru people, also lay to the north. He occupied a stretch of country on the Sueh river which had originally been in the hands of two commoner governors, Ngbandarungba (Agiti clan), who died, and Nagaza (Agbambi clan), who was killed in the Egyptian campaign. Gbudwe then gave it to his brother Bungusue, but he quarrelled with his neighbours and his subjects left him, so Gbudwe told Kanimara to settle there and win over the Abuguru to his allegiance. The genealogy also shows nobles who, though not sons of Gbudwe, are mentioned in the text as having held governorships in the area under discussion.

On page 139 I present a sketch-map of Gbudwe's kingdom as it was in about 1900. My reconstruction has been piecemeal and it has also necessitated an interpenetration of past and present, and this may have made for some obscurity. Also the distribution of provinces loses much of its significance unless it is seen in relation to the central royal province. I have not attempted to demarcate provincial boundaries, only to show the relative positions of the provinces and their proximity to some of the main rivers of the country. Nobles are again shown in capital letters, those other than Gbudwe's sons or grandsons being underlined, and commoners in small letters. On a very rough approximation the distance from the most northern point of the kingdom to the most southern was round about 100 miles, and it was also about 100 miles from the most easterly point to the most westerly. It is impossible to estimate with any degree of accuracy the size of its population. One can only suggest, on the basis of such censuses as we have, that it was somewhere between 50,000 and 100,000.

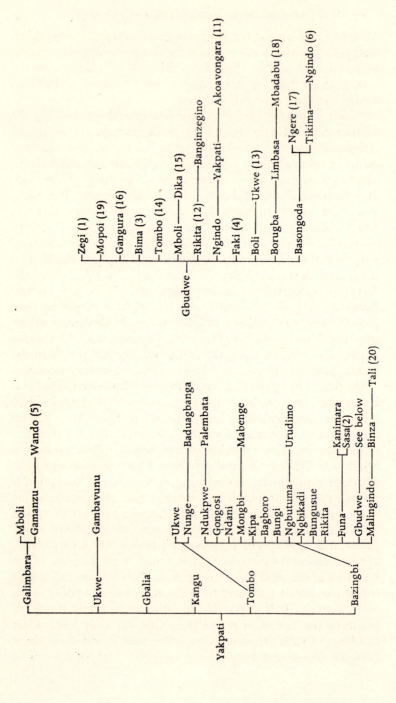

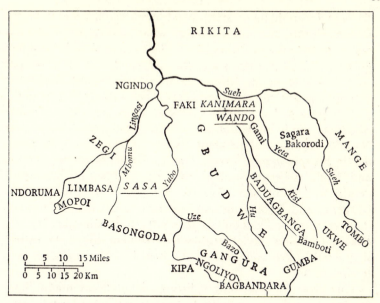

SKETCH 5. GBUDWE'S KINGDOM c. 1900.

5

The details—names of persons and rivers, and movements and successions—form themselves into a picture of a repetitive process. A prince held a province under his father's suzerainty but in varying degrees independent of his control—eldest sons being almost completely independent. Then the king died and the kingdom was not inherited by any one son. Each then became independent ruler of his own territory, formerly one of his father's provinces. However, a vacuum was left at the centre, the portion of a kingdom over which a king had not delegated authority but retained under his personal direction, and this was likely to have been the largest and most thickly populated part of his kingdom and with the highest proportion of Ambomu-Azande (as distinct from foreign elements). This prize did not fall to the eldest son or any other son by right. He took it who could. Bazingbi was a cadet but he gained it for himself. Gbudwe was a fifth son but he wrested it from his eldest brother Ngima; and, as I have said earlier, it is unlikely that his eldest son

Basongoda would have established himself in it if it had not been for British intervention. Therefore what Craffen and Colombo say is correct only in theory: that when a king dies the heritage goes to his sons in such a way that the eldest has the principal part and lives in his father's home while 'les autres doivent s'éloigner et s'établir comme de petits chefs vassaux du premier'.[1]

This process has repeated itself in each generation. When Mabenge died, his senior sons Bugwa, Yakpati, Nunga, and Ngindo became independent monarchs. Then on Yakpati's death, his senior sons Renzi, Tombo, Ukwe, Bazingbi, Pereke, and Muduba became independent rulers. Then on Bazingbi's death, his senior sons Ngima, Ezo, Wando, Maliningido, Gbudwe, and Ngoliyo became in their turn rulers of autonomous territories. Then on Gbudwe's death, Basongoda, Mange, Rikita, Gangura, etc., became independent rulers, or rather they would have done so had the British not taken over their territories.

This process of periodic splitting of kingdoms might have produced smaller and smaller fragments had it not been for two facts. The first is that till the Arabs and Europeans finally obstructed their advance, until, that is, Zande political history may be said to have come to an end, the Azande under their royal houses were still expanding, so it was possible for kingdoms to fragment without necessarily decreasing in size. The second fact is that only the stronger sons maintained their independence and were able to transmit their domains to their sons. The weaker sooner or later had to accept the overlordship of the stronger or they were deprived of their territories. At the beginning of a new reign a king was obliged to give administrative posts to younger brothers and to cousins or to commoner governors because he had as yet few sons of his own old enough to fill them. Thus we saw how in the early part of Gbudwe's reign a number of his brothers—Ngbakadi, Mongbi, Ngbutuma, Bagboro, etc.—ruled provinces, and though some of them may have received these from his father, I think he must have appointed most of them himself because they were all said to be his juniors. In either case, there is no evidence that he wished to oust them from their lands. However, as these brothers died Gbudwe replaced them by his own sons, instead of theirs, as they

[1] Op. cit., p. 790.

became old enough to be planted out, a transference from collaterals to direct descendants facilitated in his case by the massacre of a number of his brothers by Egyptian troops in 1882 (those whose names I have recorded were Ngbimi, Bagboro, Kangu, Gongosi, Bagilisa, Ngbutuma, and Kipa; also several of his sons, Mangu, Kipa, Takapande, and others). I think it is evident that the same procedure was adopted in other Zande kingdoms when the sons of reigning monarchs grew up and could be given political authority. This did not at that time produce a large class of nobles without office, for it must be remembered that almost all the nobles of Gbudwe's kingdom were descended from Yakpati, who was only his grandfather, and also that he vastly increased his domains during his reign, thus providing new provinces for his sons and others to administer. Moreover, in the wars that raged during the reigns of Yakpati, Bazingbi, and Gbudwe a considerable number of princes lost their lives. Nevertheless, as Gbudwe's reign continued, more and more sons had to be provided for, and we have seen that at the end of it the country was mostly in the hands of the royal sons and a few commoner governors, nobles of collateral lines surviving in only one or two places. It may be considered doubtful whether even they would have been able to maintain their estates, on which the sons of Gbudwe were already encroaching, had not the British Administration given its authority to the *status quo*. However, there were other nobles here and there living in the provinces with a small commoner following. Basongoda gave charge of a small district in his province, on a grace and favour basis, to Bavurubele son of Bazingbi (Basongoda was in a rather exceptional position in that he had at the time few sons, and probably only two old enough to rule, Tikima, who predeceased him, and Ngere). Bima likewise gave a small district to Zingbondo son of Pereke, though this must have been in early European times; and even in my day Gbile, a son of Kangu and grandson of Yakpati, though very old and blind, still had a small following in Faki's province. Gangura gave an estate to Mbitimo son of Badiyo, son of Muduba, but his people left him because he demanded too much game from them. Gangura later emasculated him. Two of King Tombo's great-grandsons, Maruka and Agaba, held minor office in Rikita's country. I met other elderly nobles without office of any kind, but they were few. Their homes were maintained by their wives with some aid from themselves and their sons in cultivation and building and from a few neighbouring commoner families who had attached themselves to them. A prince in whose territory they lived did not feel that his authority was challenged by their presence, for they recognized him as master and made him gifts from time to time. Indeed, they were the most frequent visitors to his court where they partook of the meals provided for them in the inner court. Being poor compared to the royal sons, they were unable to acquire so many wives and hence tended to have smaller families. The situation with regard to the younger generation had, however, already begun to be much changed in this respect, for while the sons of the nobility had continued to increase, the means of providing estates for them had correspondingly diminished, a situation which did not exist in Gbudwe's time.

A large number of noble families must, I think, have become extinct, or almost so, through natural causes or through wars. Seldom indeed, other than descendants of Bazingbi, does one meet descendants of the sons of Yakpati: Muduba, Renzi, Manzi, Zangaberu, Maku, Manguru, Pereke, Bagiando, etc.—he must have had at least twenty grown-up sons. They may be more numerous in Ezo's old kingdom and in the kingdoms of the Congo, with which areas I was little acquainted. Seldom also does one meet, other than descendants of Gbudwe and those of his brothers who inherited kingdoms, descendants of the sons of Bazingbi: Ngbikadi, Sisiru, Binikpele, Gbagidi, Dakaya, Bungusue, Ngatua, Rikita, Makisa, Kipa, etc.—he had some forty grown-up sons. Here again, some of these may be living in other parts of Zandeland. In the census taken in Gbudwe's old kingdom in 1929 and 1930[1] it was found that there were about 800 adult or near-adult male Avongara living there. I cannot give exact numbers but I can say that the majority of these were descendants of Gbudwe himself. One need not be surprised at this statement, for Gbudwe had died twenty-five years before, when he was about 70 years of age, and before his death some of his grandsons already had families. Most of his numerous sons were, as we have seen, given provinces and were, by Zande standards, wealthy men who used their wealth

[1] See Chap. I.

and their authority to acquire for themselves many wives, and wives also for their sons, who could therefore marry at an earlier age than most commoners. If each of his sons begat five male children who reached maturity—and many of them begat many more than five—Gbudwe would have had close on 200 male grandsons, many of whom, in their turn, had by 1930 begotten sons old enough to have been included in the census, and even some of these great-grandsons were by that time married men with families.

Others have drawn attention to the size of royal and princely families. Junker[1] says that Bakangai listed 54 of his father Kipa's sons, not including the youngest, whose names were unknown even to Bakangai. Casati[2] says that this same Bakangai possessed more than 500 women, and he also remarks on Kipa's numerous children, stating that his sons alone amounted to 50. Czekanowski[3] comments that the power of a chief (princeling) called Risasi was evidently limited in that he had only 7 wives and 15 living children. Hutereau[4] reports, in noting how rapidly these aristocratic families can increase, that Kipa's son Kana had 46 sons and 33 daughters. Gamu, his fourth son, then aged about 50, had already 24 sons and 11 daughters. Liwa, Gamu's eldest son, aged about 38, had already 6 sons and 5 daughters (there must have been an error in Hutereau's estimates of ages, for even Zande princes do not beget children at the age of 12). Two of the wives of Liwa's eldest son Eliwa, a youth of about 18 years of age, were pregnant at the time the record was made. Akengai, son of the Bakangai mentioned above, had in Hutereau's time already 40 sons and about 40 daughters. Geyer[5] tells us that it was impossible to determine the number of King Tembura's wives and that he himself did not appear to know the exact number. It was stated to be 400. His half-brother Beka, says the same authority, had 15 wives, 16 sons and 10 daughters. Mr. T. A. T. Leitch, at one time a British official in the Sudan, mentions in an unpublished report 39 sons of the same King Tembura, of whom 21 were still alive in 1953. To give a final example: I have myself listed 22 adult sons of a minor princeling, Baduagbanga, in Gbudwe's old kingdom, and 29 adult sons of

[1] Op. cit., vol. iii, 1892, p. 32.   [2] Op. cit., vol. i, pp. 198 and 209.
[3] Op. cit., p. 24.   [4] Op. cit., p. 238.
[5] Op. cit., pp. 284 and 293.

Gbudwe's son Bafuka. The sons of both men were all said to be married and to have families.

6

We have noted that in the early period of Gbudwe's reign there were also among the governors of provinces on his southern frontier a number of commoners. It was at that time the same along his eastern frontier. At the beginning of his reign some of these must have been appointments made by his father, but certainly most of those I have mentioned earlier were his own. There appear to have been several reasons for appointing commoners. Firstly, it was probably necessary to entrust some of the provinces to commoners at the beginning of a reign, the king's sons, except perhaps for the eldest ones, being too young for appointment, even though princelings sometimes received office in their teens, their education in government being entrusted to a wise elder of the court till they gained experience and confidence. Junker, writing in the 1880s, more than once speaks[1] of the authority in provinces exercised by mere striplings and the great deference shown them. They were not to be seen in my day as there was no longer a king with authority to make such appointments. Also there might be too few younger brothers or other nobles suitable for governorates available, for we have to bear in mind that a king like Gbudwe was a rival of the families of his uncles, such as Tombo, Muduba, and Renzi, and also of the families of his elder brothers Ezo, Wando, and Malingindo. They belonged to different and hostile kingdoms which he wished to subdue or against which his attitude was one of jealous opposition. So he was not likely to have appointed, except in very peculiar circumstances, members of these families to governorates in his own domains, and this left available only his younger brothers and such scions of the nobility as belonged to no reigning house. Secondly, commoner governors were more directly dependent on the king than were his own sons, who could become, as we have noted, almost independent rulers even during their father's lifetime, a position a commoner governor could not, in virtue of his class, aspire to. It was therefore good policy to have a sprinkling

[1] For example, op. cit., vol. iii, 1892, pp. 317–18.

of commoners among the governors. Thirdly—and I found that this was the motive Azande stressed—it was the policy of kings to entrust commoners with the difficult task of administering and bringing about the assimilation of foreign peoples (*zoga auro*) or, as they often put it, of pacifying them (*zelesi yo*). This is why, Azande say, in Gbudwe's kingdom we find them ruling provinces on the eastern border, which was populated by various foreign elements, and in the southern marches those to the south-east where the population was at the time of his father's death still only partly assimilated, either politically or culturally. When that task had been accomplished, Azande say, he would either appoint (*fu kpolo*) one of his sons to rule a province in the place of its commoner governor or would let a son settle in the area and, with his greater prestige, win over the population by exercise of generosity and good sense. It is often said of Gbudwe that from time to time he drove his older sons still at court from his home (*do yo*) on the grounds that they went after his wives or stole his subjects' fowls or tormented them (rubbing their skins with seeds of the *abakpa* plant), but this seems also to have been a conventional way of getting them to settle in parts of the country lacking adequate administration or in areas ruled by commoners whom he did not wish to displace directly. A governor accepted the situation. The young man was his master's son. Sometimes, however, Gbudwe just translated a commoner to another area to make way for a son, and a number of commoner governors were, as noted in the records of provinces, for one reason or another, executed. This was for commoners one of the hazards of political office; and, to judge from the number of executions, there can be little doubt that Gbudwe kept a suspicious eye on them. Perhaps this is what Czekanowski meant when he said[1] that the rulers seem to treat important Azande with some mistrust and to look for support against them to the lower strata of the population; though it is difficult to determine for certain the meaning of this observation. The point established, however, is that early in Gbudwe's reign there were a number of commoner governors and that they were bit by bit replaced by his own sons. There were others besides those I have earlier mentioned, but of whose time and duration of office I am uncertain. I can do no more

---

[1] Op. cit., p. 50.

than give some names, clans, and stated provenance: Yangiliya (Akalingo) on the Yubo; Wanangba (Agiti) between the Mbomu and the Singbi (he was at one time a royal consulter of oracles); and Murungba (Agbambi) between the Huru and the Kisi.

This seems to have been a usual process in Zande political history. It was certainly the policy pursued by Gbudwe's father and grandfather, some of whose commoner governors ruled over considerable provinces. Indeed, the only commoner governors holding comparable positions in Gbudwe's realm were Nguasu, to the east, in the earliest period and later his son Mange's general Yango (Abawoyo clan). I am not able to give any exact account of Bazingbi's commoner governors. The best known of them was Nzaniwe (Akowe clan and sister's son to the Apusi). His son Gami told me that he ruled over a wide domain centred in the region of the Hogo (Sudan) and the Manzagara, tributary of the Gurba (Congo). (Gami himself held a territory under Gbudwe near the Yeta, where he still was in my day, though it was a matter of difference between Rikita and the British Administration whether he held it in his own right or under Rikita. This piece of country was before ruled by Rokomboli (Angbadimo clan), who, involved in the death of Gbudwe's son Kana and having speared Gbudwe's brother Duli, took refuge with Gamanzu, son of Galimbara, who executed him. It was afterwards ruled by Gundusu, of the same clan.) Another of Bazingbi's commoner governors was the already mentioned Nguasu (Agbambi clan), who occupied a region in the extreme east of the kingdom which eventually stretched from the Yeta to east of the Sueh. (He was dispossessed by Gbudwe on account of fighting between his sons, and for other irregularities. Also his son Bangumbiyo had speared Gbudwe's brother Mange in the thigh on account of adultery with his wife and, although Gbudwe supported him in this matter and paid him compensation and compelled Mange to do likewise, the incident probably added weight in the scale against Nguasu. His territories were given to Gbudwe's sons Mange and Kana.) Other of Bazingbi's commoner governors were Mbazua, a younger brother of Nzaniwe, on the Mangondi; Sakita (Abangbinda people) beyond that river; Nzunga (Agbambi clan) on the Birisi, in Gangura's present territory;

Kuasi (Abiri people) on the river Moegbu, tributary of the Lingasi; and Bafurumai (Angumbe clan) on the Yubo. Bazing-bi's famous brother, the conquering Renzi, whose domains stretched far to the east also gave large estates to his commoner governors, the best known of whom was Welegine (Agiti clan), to the east of the Sueh. Others were Ngbamboli (the country of Faki and Bima), Kamundi (Wando's country), and Ngbandia of the Avokili clan. One of King Ngangi's commoner governors, Ongosi, has been mentioned earlier.

Probably all Zande kings appointed commoners to govern-orates, such persons being known as *abanyaki*, and it would therefore be curious that early travellers do not mention the fact were it not that the matter is barely mentioned in most writings on the Azande of a later date. Piaggia, it is true, gives the names of certain *fattori* of Kings Tombo and Bazingbi, and some of these may have been commoner governors.[1] The names of others suggest that they were nobles. Schweinfurth[2] knew the word *banyaki* (he writes it as *behnky* and says it is pronounced as a Frenchman would pronounce *bainqui*), but he, and it would appear other travellers, thought that this word meant any chief of a district acting as representative of a king, whereas it is only used by Azande for commoner governors, noble governors being called simply *agbia*, 'nobles'. Schweinfurth, who appears to mention the names of two of Ngangi's commoner governors, was probably unaware that some governors were nobles and others commoners. Junker[3] says that most of the chiefs were of noble blood and that throughout his travels he heard of only one man of political importance who came from foreign stock. Nor, apart from the one exception, Kommunda in Ndoruma's country, does he mention any other commoner governors. Yet at the time of his residence in Zandeland there were certainly some of these in Wando's kingdom, through which he travelled, three of them being on Gbudwe's southern frontier, Bangodiya (Agiti clan), Ndegu (Angbadimo clan), and Ngatuo (Agiti clan), the last of whom was of sufficient importance for his subjects to have defeated an army sent against them by Gbudwe in about 1886; and I consider it certain that there were others

[1] Antinori, op. cit., p. 163. See Chap. XV of this book.
[2] *The Heart of Africa*, vol. i, 1873, p. 436; vol. ii, p. 22.
[3] Op. cit., vol. ii, 1891, p. 193.

in the other Zande kingdoms at that time, e.g. Hutereau[1] mentions one of them in Bakangai's country. Junker tended to travel from the court of one king or prince to that of another and he probably would not have known when he was crossing the territory of a commoner governor if he had not made particular inquiry. Even then, he might simply have been told that it was the country of such and such a king, just as he would not have been told the names of princes' deputies in their provinces unless he asked for them. When he passed through Gbudwe's country he could scarcely have avoided, as his route shows, the territories of commoner governors lining the west bank of the Sueh at that time as they continued to do till the end of his reign; but it must be added that he was in a hurry to reach the Nile and that Gbudwe's kingdom had recently been devastated by troops of the Egyptian Government and was much disorganized. Other writers say much the same, e.g. Craffen and Colombo state that the 'vassal chiefs' are all sons, brothers, or kinsmen of the sovereign.[2] I give further evidence later[3] to show that commoners played an important part in provincial administration.

It should further be mentioned that the more important princely governors sometimes put areas in their provinces under control (*ma kpolo*) of commoner governors of their own and directly dependent on them and not on the king. These did not have the same status as those appointed by the king but, nevertheless, their position appears to have carried more authority than that of an ordinary deputy (*ligbu* or *bakumba*), and the area of their administration was more self-contained than his. Thus Rikita gave jurisdiction to Toi the Bongo, with whom, as the chief of a foreign people, he made blood-brotherhood, after defeating him in war, on condition that he brought his people from the east of the Iba river to the west of it and they became his subjects. Mange gave jurisdiction to Yango, as already mentioned, and also to Pakwiyo (Abawoyo clan) and others; Basongoda to Nganayo (Agbambi clan); Bagbandara to Raliyo (Abafuta clan); etc.

[1] Op. cit., p. 235.   [2] Op. cit., p. 787.
[3] See the following chapter.

7

The organization of Gbudwe's kingdom and the situation obtaining at various periods of his reign are paralleled by the organization of other Zande kingdoms and the phases of their development. There were, of course, many local differences, and in these other kingdoms Arab intervention was an earlier and more disturbing influence, but we may say that much the same pattern emerges from the records of the early travellers and the first ethnological writings. Everywhere the story is the same. A prince inherits part of his father's kingdom; he enlarges it, if he can, at the expense of his brothers and neighbouring foreign peoples; he appoints governors to rule over the provinces of his kingdom, his eldest sons eventually receiving the lion's share; and then on his death his sons, or his brothers if he died young, fight for dominance and the process is repeated. The political circumstances I have described were too obvious to be missed by the early travellers. They are indicated by Piaggia: 'Gli abitatori delle regioni Niam-Niam se ne vivono in piccole tribù governate da capi, molti dei quali sono tra loro stretti in vincoli di parentela, il che non impedisce di trovarsi fra loro in continue guerre per vendicare rapine di robe e di donne, ovvero per non soddisfatti tributi.'[1] Schweinfurth noted in 1870 how Bazingbi's extensive domains had been divided into six small principalities, a heritage which was a perpetual apple of discord among his sons, and how Tombo's kingdom had likewise been cut up after his death into a number of smaller states.[2] He further remarks that whilst the eldest son is considered to be the heir, at the death of a king the firstborn is frequently not acknowledged by all his brothers—some may support him but others insist on becoming independent rulers in their districts: 'contentions of this character are continually giving rise to every kind of aggression and repeated deeds of violence'.[3] Junker speaks of the kingdoms of Ndoruma, Malingindo, and Wando being similarly divided up during the lifetimes of these rulers, and he describes the bitter struggles for power between Wando's sons even while their father was still alive.[4] He relates how in the case of some of the descendants of an earlier

[1] Antinori, op. cit., pp. 121–2. [2] *The Heart of Africa*, vol. i, 1873, pp. 479–80.
[3] Ibid., vol. ii, 1873, p. 22. [4] Op. cit., vol. ii, 1891, pp. 188 and 268.

King Tombo fractionization had led to impotence, and how on the death of Sabiru son of Nunga dynastic wars broke out and his empire was divided among his brothers and sons.[1] Like Schweinfurth, he says, in reference to the inheritance of Bogua, that though according to the traditional Zande right the eldest son succeeds the father 'the dismemberment of the state was a sufficient proof that this legitimate custom had long yielded to the law of might over right'.[2]

De Calonne, the historian of the Azande, has emphasized this repetitive process of fission on the death of a king, especially in connection with the hostility between royal brothers and royal sons; kingdoms again and again being broken up by struggles for power and then being re-established by force of arms, the stronger wrenching their domains from the weaker and making Zande history a monotonous record of murder and rapine.[3] He has also pointed out that the process is contained in the structure of a kingdom, though in normal circumstances it is only on the death of a king that for a time complete disruption ensues. Thus he instances how in the immense kingdom of Sasa, outside the central territory directly controlled by the king himself, the rest of the kingdom was divided into numerous provinces administered by his sons, each being an autonomous whole to such a point that certain of their rulers, for example, Momi and Turugba, between whose provinces there stretched a completely deserted zone, were in a state of open hostility; and he concludes that these provinces 'devaient être considérées comme des états indépendants liés par un engagement féodal de vassalite'. He says further that in each province there is found a particularist spirit, especially when, as is sometimes the case, the provinces are ethnically distinct.[4]

This last point of de Calonne's is of great importance. When a prince had been for some years in charge of a province the people of it came to see themselves as a distinct political community through allegiance to him, and, as the river boundaries of provinces often remained the same when they changed hands, local particularist sentiment was thereby strengthened. The people of Gangura's province or Rikita's province, for example, saw themselves in a broadly patriotic sense as *avuru* Gbudwe,

[1] Op. cit. 1891, p. 194; 1892, pp. 264–5.   [2] Ibid., 1891, p. 200.
[3] Op. cit., p. 235.   [4] Ibid., p. 237.

subjects, or followers, of Gbudwe—political solidarity being expressed by reference to the person, and through the person to the territory, rather than the other way round. But they also saw themselves as a community in a narrower and more intimate sense as *avuru* Gangura and *avuru* Rikita, since their contacts were with, and their affairs were the concern of, Gangura and Rikita and not Gbudwe. Now, all such allegiances imply, even of necessity involve, opposition to similar allegiance, and it had to be on a provincial level and could not be between a provincial attachment and that to the paramount, for that would have meant disloyalty. As we might expect, therefore, there was rivalry between the people of one province and those of one or other of its neighbours, the personal jealousies and ambitions of their rulers combining with the particularist sentiments of their subjects to make a province a kind of proto-state. The struggles which ensued after the death of a king were already latent during his lifetime and sometimes, as has been noted, could in certain circumstances, perhaps chiefly due to Arab interference and intrigue, lead to war between sons even before their father's death. However, in the case of a strong king like Gbudwe, who kept a firm hand on his sons, fighting between one prince and another was not tolerated. Nevertheless, the stage was set for the drama which would inevitably have taken place had he left it before European intervention.

It was the same in all the Zande kingdoms. The facts have been recorded by de Calonne and Hutereau, and I later summarize them.[1] In that summary I barely mention the House of Ndeni, and I therefore take it as my example of the general circumstances occurring in any Zande kingdom to show by a further illustration that, in main features, what has been said about Gbudwe's kingdom is typical. Any other kingdom would have served the purpose equally well.

Ndeni son of Tombo had quarrelled with his brother Ezo. He thereupon departed with his followers to the south, where he founded a domain for himself in the country of the Ababua people beyond the Uele river. He was later murdered by them, and the leadership of his people eventually passed to his son Kipa (or Tikima), who avenged his father's death on the Ababua and then extended his domains, warring right and left

[1] See Chap. XIV.

against other Avongara kings and the Mangbetu and other foreign peoples. In 1868 the great warrior Kipa is said to have died of a snake-bite on an expedition against the Mabode. During his lifetime he had placed his elder sons in various parts of his kingdom to rule over them. At the time of his death the main lines, following de Calonne, of their distribution were: Mange (or Ngura), the favourite son, to the north-east, on the Bomokandi; Kana, the eldest son, to the south-east; Bakangai to the south-west between the Bomokandi, the Poko, and the Makondo; Kamisa to the north-west; Nganzi, Mabura, Zebo, Ngandua, Zakala (on the left bank of the Teli), and Mingemi among foreigners, mostly sections of the Abarambo. Others were in other parts: Gwa, Bangoya (on the right bank of the Poko), Hino, etc. When Kipa died, his sons watched each other with apprehensive hostility.

Kipa was already dead before Schweinfurth's visit, and his eldest son Kana and King Mofio were, according to him, in 1870 the two most powerful Zande kings with the most extensive territories—Kana's territories lying to the west and north-west of the Mangbetu.[1] The domains of some of his brothers were also extensive, for Junker tells us that in 1882 'Bakangai's territory stretches from the Bomokandi three days southwards, and some five days east to west'.[2] Junker's appreciation of the political situation was as follows:

It further appeared that the brothers of Kanna visited by me stood in very loose relationship to him, as did also his other brothers farther east, as well as Kipa's brothers, who also administered various provinces of the old kingdom. In time of war they doubtless rendered him the military service required of vassals; but in other respects they sought to maintain their independence with all the proud arrogance of descendants and heirs of Kipa. Kanna expressed himself frankly enough on these relations, and even harboured the fear that many were plotting against his life. 'Bangoya', he remarked, 'is a chief who holds today with me, tomorrow with Bakangai.'[3]

I think it is clear from this quotation that 'very loose relationship' in fact meant virtual independence and that the word 'vassals' was scarcely applicable to persons in the position of, for example, Bakangai. He makes the further, and important,

---

[1] Op. cit., vol. ii, pp. 22 and 55.   [2] Op. cit., vol. iii, 1892, p. 8.
[3] Ibid., p. 29.

point that 'In the immediate possessions of the suzerain chief, his sons enjoyed more power and governed larger districts than their uncles and Kipa's brothers'.[1] Kana's brother Zebu is an illustration of this sons-versus-brothers situation. He had established himself on the Bomokandi among the Amiaro branch of the Abarambo people 'in order to be independent of Kana, who, as Sebu also complained, took away their power and property from his brothers, and advanced his own sons'. He adds: 'Massumbu was also a son of Kipa, and, actuated by the same motives as Sebu, had migrated hither with his following.'[2] He had settled to the north-east of Zebu. Kamisa resided near the Bomokandi–Uele Confluence.[3] Probably there were more sons of Kipa who ruled provinces than are mentioned by the explorers.

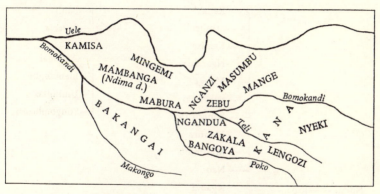

SKETCH 6. KIPA'S SONS *c.* 1882.

The same process was being repeated in each of the domains of Kipa's sons at the time Junker was in the area. The administration of the extensive territory of Bakangai, who died in 1883, 'had been entrusted to ten of his adult sons. They were assigned separate provinces, where they carried out their father's orders by the aid of their Zandeh subjects'[4]—most of the population being foreigners. Akangai, the eldest, resided in the east, on the Poko. Umboiko (I use his spellings) governed the Abarambo tribes of the north-west on the Makongo river. Biemangi and

[1] Ibid., p. 33.   [2] Ibid., p. 34.
[3] Ibid., vol. ii, 1891, p. 336.   [4] Ibid., vol. iii, 1892, pp. 8–9.

Songombosso guarded the southern frontiers, while all the rest were stationed in the interior of the state. 'However, these relations were soon modified, for the very year after my visit Bakangai died, and his death could not fail to be attended by great changes. Although Akengai succeeded his father as paramount chief, civil strife soon broke out among the brothers, as I was later informed.' In the same manner Kana's vassal lords ruled his domains—his brothers or uncles or sons: 'Ten adult sons of Kanna rule as many separate districts.'[1]

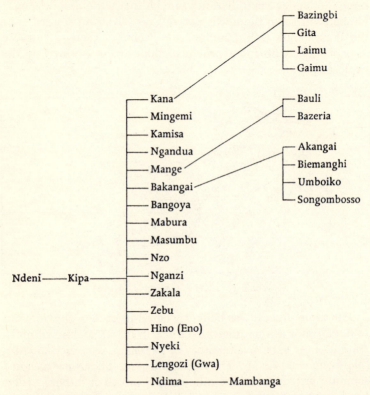

Casati also has something to say about the sons of Kipa and their jealousies and wars. Between the Uele and the Bomokandi he reached the residence of Nganzi, a man 'full of energy, proud but brave', who had fought three of his brothers, Kana, Bakangai, and Mabura.[2] Bakangai, who as a youth had murdered his

[1] Junker, op. cit., vol. iii, 1892, pp. 16 and 30.   [2] Op. cit., vol. i, p. 192.

brother Rufula, extended the small territory to which he was
heir by conquering his brother Ngandua's dominions. Kana,
Bakangai, and Bangue (? Bangoya) were jealous of the predi-
lection their father had shown for Mange, who, however, had
the support of the powerful Mangbetu king Munza and of his
own brother Nganzi. When Munza was killed by the Arabs and
Mange by the Mangbetu ruler Nessugo, a fratricidal war broke
out: 'Nganzi was assailed on the Mambaga and Zungli Mountain, Bakangoi [Bakangai] drove Ngandua from his kingdom,
whilst Kanna fought his three brothers, Mobra [Mabura],
Bangue [Bangoya], and Zaccala [Zakala]'.[1] Kana was the
victor. Before his father's death he was governing a small territory between the Uele and the Bomokandi, which he afterwards
gave to his brother Kamisa, but he enlarged his domains at the
expense of other brothers and made them his tributaries.[2] In
his travels Casati entered that part of Kana's territory governed
by his son Bazingbi, 'a bad and wicked man, at enmity with his
own father, and a rebel against his authority'.[3]

De Calonne adds further information. According to him,
Mange was treacherously assassinated by one of his Abisanga
subjects, and Kana then entered his domain under pretext of
avenging his death, but Mange's son Bauli and Kana's brothers
Gwa and Nzo, believing that he wished to annex Mange's
heritage, compelled him to withdraw. Kana attacked Gwa and
was beaten. Gwa blamed Bazeria, son of Mange, and in the
resulting engagement the sons of Mingemi were killed. Kana
and Bauli joined forces and turned against Gwa, who was killed,
his territory going to Bauli. Then the Ngoya subjects of Zebu
were taken (confisqués) by Nganzi, who was assassinated in 1882
by the Abarambo on the Wara river. Bangoya (de Calonne has
'Bangau') fought Zakala, who sought refuge with Kana. Kana
occupied Zakala's country and made a demonstration against
Bauli, who had succeeded his father Mange in the basin of the
Kilima, and then defeated Bangoya. Bangoya sought help from
the Egyptian post at Tangasi, but they refused to intervene. He
then sought help from Bakangai, who, accompanied by Bangoya
and Bauli, marched against Kana; but, Bauli hesitating, the
two others withdrew. Kana died shortly after his son Laimu,

[1] Ibid., p. 211.   [2] Ibid., p. 215.
[3] Ibid., p. 220.

who had seized upon the territories of Kamisa. Kamisa had fled to his royal cousin Ezo, son of Tombo, and with his support regained his lands, but he was later killed in a revolt of the Abarambo. Gita wished to take possession of his father Kana's domains when Kana died but was defeated by his brother Gaimu.

Hutereau[1] says that at the death of Kipa the provinces of his sons were distributed thus: (1) Kana in the Uele-Bomokandi angle; (2) Mabura (Maboro) to the east of Kana; (3) Mingemi (Mingami) still further to the east, opposite Mount Angba; (4) Nganzi on the right bank of the Bomokandi, between the mouths of the Teli and the Poko, but nearer the first; (5) Bakangai (Bakenge) between the Bomokandi, the Poko, and the Mokongo; (6) Bangoya (Bangoy) at the Mandupa, a mountain on the right bank of the Poko; (7) Ngandua (Gandua) on the Namopali, a tributary of the Poko; (8) Lengosi on the Gani, a tributary of the Teli; (9) Nyeki (Niaki) on the Tago, tributary of the Teli; (10) Kamisa (Kambisa) had fled the country; (11) Boemi was dead and Mingemi had annexed his territory. Hino had long ago been killed by Bakangai. Hutereau[2] tells the same tale of suspicion and enmity between the brothers and their refusal to accept the authority of Kana, the eldest. They had no intention of surrendering their independence. He tells also the same tale of intrigues, fratricidal wars, and assassinations.

Czekanowski,[3] who had access to Hutereau's notebooks as well as his own records, gives a similar account of the distribution of Kipa's sons. He installed Kana (d. 1900) in the eastern part of his kingdom, and yet further to the east, in the Abarambo areas, Mabura and Mingemi (his spellings are different), the latter opposite Mt. Angba. In about 1860 Kipa brought under his rule the area between the Poko, Mokongo, and Bomokandi and there installed Bakangai (d. 1883). Kamisa (Kambisa) was driven out by his father. Ngandua received an estate to the east of the Nemapoli, a right-bank tributary of the Poko. Mange's portion was on the right bank of the Bomokandi, above the mouth of the Teli. Nyeki ruled by the Tago, a tributary of the upper Teli. Eno (? Nzo) was murdered by Bakangai in 1864. Nganzi received the country on the right bank of the

---

[1] Op. cit., p. 237.   [2] Ibid., pp. 238–46.
[3] Op. cit., pp. 90–5.

Bomokandi between the Poko and the mouth of the Teli. Lengozi lived by the Gania, a tributary of the middle section. Bangoya received an area by Mt. Mandupa on the right bank of the Poko. Masumbu and Zebu did not receive estates from their father but settled on their own account north of the Bomokandi, above the mouth of the Teli, shortly before Junker's visit. Ndima had an estate near the present station of Amadi but was driven away on account of a murder, his son Mambanga managing to stay in the country. In the eighties the provinces of Kana and Bakangai were separated by those of Ngandua and Bangoyo, who were situated between the Poko and the Teli, the first in the east and the second in the west. During his father's lifetime, Kana ruled over a small area between the Uele and the Bomokandi, near the mouth of the latter. Towards 1870 he moved to the area to the south of the Bomokandi and east of the mouth of the Poko because of fights with his brother Kamisa (Kambisa) and a rising of the Abarambo caused by them. I have attempted, on the basis of this complicated and not always consistent information, to present a rough sketch-map showing the positions of Kipa's sons about 1882, at the time of Junker's visit.

So the sad story of the death of kings runs on. It is all rather a jigsaw puzzle, but the main features of the story are clear enough. A king divides his domains into provinces over which he sets his sons to rule; he dies and his sons fight for dominance and for control over as large a territory as possible; those who survive in their turn divide their domains among their sons. Poor means of communication over great distances, as Czekanowski justly observes,[1] compelled a king to hand over so much of his authority to his provincial governors that, even in his lifetime, they became practically independent rulers, and at his death autonomous monarchs, each in his own right. The situation appears to have been much the same in the kingdoms of the neighbouring Mangbetu people, as we learn from, among others, Czekanowski.[2]

---

[1] Op. cit., p. 49.   [2] Ibid., p. 154.

PART THREE

XI

THE ETHNIC ORIGINS OF
OFFICE-HOLDERS

As we have seen, the Azande are an ethnic and cultural amalgam to which more than fifty different peoples have contributed. Some of these peoples are peripheral to the Zande kingdoms; others have been subjugated by the original Azande, the Avongara-Ambomu, but still form distinct ethnic and geographical groups speaking their own languages; while yet others, forming the majority of the present-day Azande, even in those areas where the Avongara-Ambomu are best represented, have been entirely assimilated. It was the policy of the ruling Avongara family to recognize some of the chiefs of the conquered peoples, but real power lay in the hands of their own representatives, the noble and commoner governors whom they appointed to rule the provinces of their realms. Now, Junker[1] tells us that in the course of the years during which he travelled widely among the Azande he came across only one man of any political importance who was not either a member of the Avongara aristocracy or of true Zande (i.e. Mbomu) stock. Although Junker does not seem to have been aware that the Azande, both the Ambomu and the peoples assimilated to them, had clans, it has to be borne in mind that in his day (the end of the seventies and the first years of the eighties of last century) it may have been easier than in my day to have spotted men of foreign origin without a knowledge of the ethnic affiliations of the many Zande clans, because the social and cultural absorption of foreign stocks was in a less advanced stage.

[1] Op. cit., vol. ii, 1891, p. 193.

This chapter is written to determine the accuracy of his statement by inquiring into the ethnic provenance of such provincial
governors as were commoners and of persons holding lesser
office. I have in this inquiry to rely on my own information,
which with regard to commoner governors is mainly restricted
to the old kingdom of Gbudwe, for none of our authorities on
the Azande gives any detailed or precise information about the
subject, or even any information at all. One of them, Fr. Geyer,[1]
goes so far as to make the statement that only an aristocrat—a
member of the ruling clan of the Avongara—can become a
chief, and thus he says as a rule only close relatives of a king,
such as his sons and brothers, can become chiefs, a statement
which I would treat with reserve even though it refers to the old
kingdoms of Tembura and Ezo with which I was myself scarcely
acquainted. Much of course, depends on what he means by
'chief' (*Häuptling*). The same ambiguity appears in von Wiese's
statement,[2] speaking of the area near Tembura Post, that 'the
sultans, village chiefs, and under-chiefs are all Asandes'. We do
not know what he meant by 'village chiefs', especially as there
were no villages, nor what he meant by 'under-chiefs', nor,
for the matter of that, precisely what he meant by 'sultans'.
Also, we do not know what he meant by 'Asandes', whether the
Ambomu or 'true' or 'original' Azande as distinct from persons
of foreign origin, or whether he included under the term persons
of foreign origin who had adopted the Mbomu language and
way of life, in contrast to foreigners who had retained their
speech and habits. He may well have been ignorant of the
difference. This is the point which I shall now discuss.

My informants mentioned the names of the following
important commoner governors of provinces in the kingdom
of Bazingbi, Gbudwe's father, who died in about 1868, of his
elder brother Renzi, who predeceased him by many years, and
of Renzi's son Tombo or Bazugba:

Nzaniwe, Akowe clan	Welegine, Agiti clan
Mbazua, Akowe clan	Ngbandia, Avokili clan
Sakita, Abangbinda people	Kuiya, Ameteli clan
Kuasi, Abiri people	Wando, Agbambi clan
Bafurumai, Angumbe clan	Bavungu, Agbambi clan

---

[1] Op. cit., p. 306.   [2] Op. cit., p. 229.

Madu, Agbambi clan	Nzunga, Agbambi clan
Sakondo, Avunduo clan	Ngbamboli, Abagua clan

Now seven out of these fourteen persons belonged to Mbomu clans; while two, those of the Akowe clan, though of Adio stock, had been so early and completely absorbed by the Ambomu that they counted as their social equals. The other five were of foreign stocks.

Gbudwe reigned from about 1868 to 1905. At one time or another during his reign the following commoner governors whose clans have been recorded ruled provinces of his realm or provinces adjacent to it in his elder brother Wando's kingdom or provinces in the vast area administered by his second son Mange, who was an almost independent monarch:

Gunde, Angbadimo clan	Zoli, Angumbe clan
Gundusu, Angbadimo clan	Wangu, Auboli clan
Kulewoka, Abakundo clan	Tangili, Agbambi clan
Zengendi, Angumbe clan	Gami, Akowe clan
Bazo, Akowe clan	Yango, Abawoyo clan
Wanangba, Agiti clan	Bangodiya, Agiti clan
Nguasu, Agbambi clan	Ndegu, Angbadimo clan
Ngbamboli, Abagua clan	Bakorodi, Abakundo clan
Bagundusu, Avokida clan	Nagaza, Agbambi clan
Negenzi, Abananga (Akowe) clan	Yangiliya, Akalingo clan
	Kpoyo, Abangbinda people
Sagara, Angbadimo clan	Pakwiyo, Abawoyo clan
Zabia, Abananga (Akowe) clan	Ngatuo, Agiti clan
Bakekpe, Angumbe clan	Gbaro, Abandogo clan
Baepuru, Avokida clan	Ngbanarungba, Agiti clan
Bamboti, Auboli clan	Dangba, Agbambi clan
Murungba, Agbambi clan	Rhai, Agiti clan
Rokomboli, Angbadimo clan	Rafai, Angbuki clan

Of these thirty-five persons, twenty-seven belonged to Ambomu clans (including the Akowe) and eight to clans of foreign origin.

We may conclude therefore that whilst the Ambomu show numerical preponderancy in the lists of commoner governors it would not be correct to say that only Ambomu held important political office. However, Junker is doubtless right in the sense in which he probably intended his remark to be taken, that, except in newly conquered territories where almost the entire population was foreign, important political offices were seldom held by foreigners, even in areas where foreigners formed the greater part of the population, but were held by Azande, for the persons of foreign origin in the lists must have been completely Zandeized. Without a knowledge of the Mbomu clans and those of the assimilated peoples and an appreciation of the extent to which they were distributed and mixed—and the admixture must have been far advanced by his time—Junker could scarcely have known whether a Zande was of Mbomu or foreign stock.

There can be little doubt, and it is what Azande themselves say, that kings preferred to appoint Ambomu to provincial governorships; and we may suppose that the further back from the present day the more this preference would have operated, for the Ambomu were those who mostly frequented the courts; and it took a long time before a conquered people developed the habit of doing so. It was, in fact, precisely because Avongara and Ambomu represented the king in the provinces of his realm that the foreign peoples learnt the Zande tongue, to take part in affairs at court, and to adopt Zande ways of life.

When we consider the lower forms of political office, leadership of military companies and administrative posts within the provinces, we find that it was service at court and loyalty, ability, and character which counted, regardless of descent, in the making of appointments, though, here again, it stands to reason that the further back we go the more such offices must have been restricted to Ambomu followers of the Avongara. This cannot, however, be demonstrated on account of lack of evidence. The earliest information that I possess is a very short list of deputies and leaders of companies of unmarried warriors in Bazingbi's personal province towards the end of his reign (c.1865). Of the eight persons listed below four belong to Mbomu clans and four to clans of foreign stocks:

Galia, Ambura clan	Yangiliya, Akalingo clan
Sangumboli, Angbapio clan	Batangba, Abandogo clan
Badibwodi, Angbadimo clan	Baepuru, Avukida clan
Bakambara, Angbapio clan	Bidara, Abando clan.

Some of these names appear in the following list of persons holding the same offices in Gbudwe's personal province at one or other period of his long reign, or in the earlier list of governors, for he confirmed them in office, or promoted them, when he took control after his father's death. Of the fifty-four persons listed twenty-five belong to Mbomu clans (including the Akowe) and twenty-nine to clans of foreign origin:

Baepuru, Avukida clan	Bagbaragba, Ambata clan
Gbaro, Abandogo clan	Tikpo, Ambura clan
Ingida, Akalingo clan	Bazambago, Angali clan
Ngbatuyo, Agiti clan	Gbafu, Akpura clan
Dumo, Avunduo clan	Gatanga, Auboli clan
Bombu, Agiti clan	Bangili, Agiti clan
Tule, Abandogo clan	Turugba, Aboro clan
Malimbia, Abandogo clan	Ngbaku, Abaza clan
Gene, Aboro clan	Bangbai, Abandogo clan
Mbikogbudwe, Abaka people	Gibile, Agiti clan
Tupoi, Angbaya clan	Ngbarama, Akudeli clan
Nguma, Abandogo clan	Gbalika, Abandogo clan
Wanangba, Agiti clan	Hiniuru, Abakpara clan
Zengendi, Angumbe clan	Yangiliya, Avunduo clan
Likara, Abandogo clan	Mangbano, Agiti clan
Bambasi, Abangbinda people	Mbilingi, Abangau clan
Ndanya, Abauro clan	Bagudagu, Avunduo clan
Beka, Amisaku clan	Bakura, Abakundo clan
Ngbanzingini, Auboli clan	Basili, Agbambi clan
Busio, Abandogo clan	Banginisue, Ambare clan
Bazilikpi, Akalingo clan	Bambia, Akudeli clan
Nguma, Angumbe clan	Kelendue, Abakundo clan
Yako, Agiti clan	Ndukpezingi, Akurungu clan
Zungbe, Agbambi clan	Yambe, Abangbinda people
Banganzambu, Abakpara clan	Pasua, Agbambi clan
Yawili, Abagbangi clan	Bagaza, Akowe clan
Birale, Akenge clan	Kuki, Akurungu clan.

A further check was made by listing the more important commoners who held similar offices in provinces of Gbudwe's sons Ndukpe, Gangura, and Bafuka during their father's lifetime. Of these thirty-six persons, nineteen are of Ambomu stock (including Akowe and Adio) and seventeen are of foreign origin:

Buze, Abambura clan	Basingbatara, Angbaga clan
Zambu, Avotombo clan	Gbaga, Abawoli clan
Banvunu, Adogo clan	Ziga, Abangbwati clan
Bangugbili, Abangbaga clan	Gbaga, Abaigo clan
Nyakeyo, Avunduo clan	Kpelenge, Abangule clan

Kuagbiaru, Akpura clan
Libiru, Agbambi clan
Bandapai, Abanzuma clan
Uze, Agiti clan
Gbafu, Abuguru people
Gotegbe, Avotombo clan
Boza, Abakpuro clan
Moyego, Abadara clan
Maame, Adio clan
Ndegu, Angbadimo clan
Bakili, Agiti clan
Nambia, Apusi clan
Ngawe, Abadara clan

Kotikoti, Avotombo clan
Kpayaku, Akpura clan
Gorogbe, Avotombo clan
Tungua, Agiti clan
Ganga, Agbutu clan
Gadia, Abatiko clan
Gbanda, Agbambi clan
Ingiwara, Akowe clan
Kusapai, Abadara clan
Bambasi, Abadara clan
Meme, Amengbaya clan
Baro, Ameteli clan
Galipiyo, Agiti clan.

On the evidence cited we may conclude that whilst the Mbomu clans in Gbudwe's kingdom were represented among office-holders in a proportion higher than their membership bore to the total population, it is not much higher and is less than might have been expected, considering the fact that the foreign elements belonged to peoples for the most part conquered by his grandfather Yakpati and by his father Bazingbi and by his uncles, Renzi chief among them.

An attempt was made to test this conclusion against conditions obtaining in 1929-30. At that time the greater part of the Sudanese Azande had been compelled to live in settlements of one sort or another, though some were still in their original dispersed state. However, each settlement was more or less composed of the same people who had lived near each other before, and the headmen were persons who represented the princely rulers in the pre-settlement districts or were the same sort of persons. The Administration did not make the appointments, which were under control of the princes themselves. These appointments therefore not only give some indication of clan, and therefore ethnic, representation among office-holders at the time at which the sample was taken, but also have some bearing on the principles of selection at any time. Quite a number of settlements had been put in charge of princely rulers' sons and brothers and other nobles. This was a new development due to the impossibility of expansion by conquest under European rule and to the equal impossibility of eliminating rivals by traditional methods; and also to the great growth in numbers of the nobility. These appointments are left out of the present inquiry since they are not directly involved in the question at issue. The inquiry covered the whole of that part of Zandeland which lies in what was, at the time it was conducted, the Anglo-Egyptian Sudan or, in Zande terms, what were once the kingdoms of Gbudwe, Ezo, and Tembura. Three hundred and fourteen headmen have been listed and they have been found to be numerically divided among the clans as shown in the table below. In my estimation of what may be regarded as Mbomu and foreign clans, eighty-seven headmen were of Mbomu stock and 227 of various foreign stocks. The Mbomu headmen were thus in 1929–30 about 28 per cent of the total, a percentage corresponding fairly well with the ratio of the Ambomu as a whole to the total population of Sudanese Zandeland. If the Akowe and Adio are included, as before, among the Ambomu, the figures would be ninety-seven Ambomu and 217 men of foreign stocks, making the Ambomu about 31 per cent:

Akowe	9	Abauro	2	Abambaraga	1
Avubanga	3	Abawoli	5	Abaguma	1
Abanya	3	Abadambili	1	Amogba	1
Avonama	1	Avunduo	5	Agbutu	2
Angbaga	7	Abara	1	Ababaimo	3
Avombili	1	Abadangasa	1	Abakango	3
Abagende	1	Abakpa	1	Abananga	9
Abandogo	9	Akangani	1	Abangau	3
Abandiko	2	Avotombo	4	Akpongboro	1
Amemungu	1	Ababadio	1	Apambia	1
Abagiaru	1	Avugiaro	2	Akpura	1
Aremete	1	Ambiro	1	Abakpoto	3
Abagbangi	4	Abaza	3	Aduruwe	2
Abadara	1	Abakangba	2	Abandia	1
Amegburu	1	Abagbaya	1	Abamunga	2
Abaika	1	Abanyere	1	Abagbo	2
Ambata	2	Anguli	2	Abakaya	4
Ameteli	2	Abagbate	2	Abadanga	1
Abanzuma	1	Abagamuna	1	Angbuki	2
Agberenya	2	Abaningo	1	Avando	1
Angbadimo	2	Ametanga	2	Abakuma	1
Andabili	1	Akudere	2	Abakpanda	1
Angumbe	4	Abanzuma	1	Abadigo	3
Abakaya	1	Abaruvuro	3	Avundukuro	1

Awali	1	Amesaka	1	Abiama	1
Avozaba	2	Abalingi	5	Abakupa	1
Abaningba	4	Amorongono	1	Abakpara	1
Avudamara	1	Abangboto	2	Agoro	3
Abangbapere	1	Amizoro	1	Amegbara	1
Avumai	3	Agbambi	9	Amabenge	1
Apambage	1	Abadimo	1	Abuguru	2
Abawoyo	13	Abanguoto	1	Amindamu	1
Abaigo	2	Avuzukpo	1	Avumaka	2
Abayali	2	Aboti	1	Angbapio	2
Abakundo	3	Ababandu	2	Aboro	4
Avokili	1	Abatiko	6	Agiti	9
Avudima	1	Aminguna	2	Adio	1
Abagua	1	Abangbara	2	Amengano	2
Abangbinda	5	Akurungu	5	Abagbuto	2
Abakpuro	5	Akalingo	8	Ambare	5
Aunzo	1	Abangombi	3	Abasapu	1
Auboli	2	Abamage	1	Azuru	1
Amiandi	2	Angali	5	Amadi	1
Abanguli	2	Abadugu	2		
Abatukpo	3	Ababali	1		

The matter which I have been discussing may seem a small one to devote a chapter to, but it is none the less an important one for an understanding of Zande political institutions and mode of administration, and of the remarkable absorption of heterogeneous elements into the single people which we now speak of as the Azande. It has a further and more general interest for the student of African kingdoms, for we often have little information about the social texture of them and, in particular, about the precise manner in which conquest brought about assimilation. This Chapter has some bearing on these questions. Furthermore, it is now or never that such incorrect or ambiguous statements by earlier writers as those which I have mentioned must be challenged. I make no apology therefore for citing some of the evidence which clarifies the statements of these early travellers and possibly, according to the meaning that we attribute to them, contradicts them. A critical examination of sources seems to me to be one of the most useful tasks that can be undertaken by anthropologists at the present time.

XII

THE ROYAL COURT

I

THIS chapter gives a picture of a Zande court and shows, how it was maintained. It is chiefly based on the court of King Gbudwe. I write in the past tense partly for convenience since it is awkward to have constantly to state what courts were like in my day and then again what they were like prior to European rule but also because much of what I describe had vanished between Gbudwe's death in 1905 and my first visit to Zandeland early in 1927. Much indeed had remained because for many years after the conquest of the Bahr al-Ghazal it was administrative policy throughout the province 'to rule the country through the media of the tribal "chiefs" and "sultans" subject to the right of appeal by the natives to a Government official'.[1] It was obviously impossible at that time to administer the Azande in any other way than through their Avongara princes whose authority alone the Azande recognized. Nevertheless, it was equally impossible for a ruling aristocracy to retain its traditional position when real power and authority lay elsewhere. In the early nineteen-twenties new administrative measures led to more direct control by government agencies to the further detriment of the traditional political system.

Gbudwe's sons and other provincial governors still retained courts. The outer and the inner courts and the private quarters were still there, but there were no huts for the warriors and pages. Food was still sent out to the men at court, but not so frequently and in smaller quantities; and there were seldom more than a few men at court at any one time. The companies of warriors had disappeared, and though a prince's deputies still collected the men of their districts to hoe their master's cultivations, they hoed only small areas and for a few days and in

---

[1] *Bahr El Ghazal Province Handbook*, Anglo-Egyptian Handbook Series, I, 1911, p. 37.

small numbers; and even this was kept dark because the Administration held that a prince had no right to demand labour from
his subjects. Government labour on the roads took the place
of labour in the prince's cultivations. Moreover, since they
received little hospitality at court, Azande did not have the
incentive to help their masters in the cultivation of their crops.
For the same reason tribute, though still paid, was not paid on the
scale of earlier days, and payment could not be enforced, at any
rate overtly. The princes still had a number of wives but they
no longer had the same control over them, for if they ran away
it was not easy for their husbands to secure their return, and if
they tried to do so, the wives could complain of ill treatment at
an administrative centre. Above all else, the princes tried to
avoid having to answer to the Government in matters of this
kind. People still came to court to ask the princes to consult the
oracles on their behalf, usually about deaths by witchcraft,
though also about adultery; but since the Administration did
not recognize the validity of the oracles people no longer saw
the point of paying fees for consultations in matters in which
charges could be laid and compensation demanded. The
princes still heard cases, but they were not supposed to do so
except in government courts and under government supervision, and if they gave judgements in their own courts they had
no certain means of enforcing them, and the case could afterwards be taken to a government court, not on appeal but as
though no judgement had been given. There was, of course,
no war. It was largely through war in the past that a prince's
subjects expressed their attachment to him; and there being no
war there was no means by which a prince could provide a
following for his sons except at his own expense. Above all,
there was no longer a king. His place was taken by the British
District Commissioner. So the central feature of the traditional
political system had dropped out.

I want to make it clear that while I had many opportunities
of observing court life it was a court life which had very largely
broken down; and as I found that I was generally treated by
the princes with polite reserve which indicated that I was an
embarrassment to them I frequented courts seldom and only
for short periods. What I describe here is to a large extent a
reconstruction of the past from a combination of what I could

still observe and the many accounts of what I could no longer observe given me by Azande, mostly, though not all, commoners who had lived under the old dispensation. Where there are also descriptions of court life by early travellers, who saw it in full flower, I cite them.

Whilst it is difficult to estimate more than very approximately the size of the Zande kingdoms and of their populations, we can say that for an African people and for primitive peoples in general both were big. Gbudwe's subjects probably numbered between 50,000 and 100,000, and the kingdoms of his brothers Ezo, Wando, and Malingindo probably each contained as large a population, as did the kingdoms of his cousins. All these kingdoms covered large stretches of territory, the distribution of the Azande being as low as perhaps five or six to the square mile,[1] for they lived in scattered homesteads, each with its private estate. Given these circumstances and adding to them the fact that all communication was by foot, it is evident that if a kingdom was to be at all a cohesive and stable political group we might expect to find, as we do find, a fairly highly organized administrative system with a considerable degree of centralization; and Zande kingdoms did in fact display, until disturbed by the Arabs, cohesion and stability for long periods. The conduct of offensive and defensive wars and the maintenance within a kingdom of peace, justice, and security were carried out by the political and economic organization I am about to describe.

2

Zande kingdoms seem to have had always the same layout. In the centre was the province the king himself administered, its people being in an immediate sense his *avuru*, 'subjects', while the people of the other provinces were his subjects only in a very general sense. These other provinces, which on all sides shielded the king's province from attack, were administered by princes, the king's sons or other of his royal kinsmen, and by commoner governors. The princes, who, like the king, were all members of the Avongara clan, and therefore of noble birth, owed

---

[1] I consider Schweinfurth's estimate of about sixty-five to the square mile (*The Heart of Africa*, vol. i, 1873, p. 466) to be far too high.

allegiance to the king and had, with their subjects, to obey his summons to war, to keep the peace among themselves, and, though no exact measure was stipulated, to pay him tribute in kind from time to time, usually at least every year. Otherwise they were independent rulers, especially those with large provinces, and their subjects were directly responsible to them alone and not to the king and were subject to their jurisdiction and not to the king's. The commoner governors were more dependent on the king, who could displace them at pleasure, though he usually found some excuse for doing so, to put one of his own sons in their place. He might displace a kinsman also and with the same end in view, but he only displaced his own sons if they were disloyal or bad rulers. The commoner governors were more strictly bound to him with regard to tribute, and they were obliged to send their subjects to hoe his cultivations. Their position was higher than that of a *ligbu* (to be discussed later), because their subjects were wholly under their jurisdiction and not that of the king, but they did not enjoy the independence of the princes. Nevertheless, when I speak of princes it must be understood that the commoner governors are included unless they are specifically excluded. Indeed, in a discussion of the organization and procedure of a royal court, king, prince, and governor are all more or less interchangeable terms. A king's court was on a larger scale than a prince's but otherwise differed from it in no significant way, and he was governor in his province as they were in theirs. Likewise, a commoner governor's court does not seem to have differed in form and function from that of noble rulers. Therefore, not only does 'prince' in a political context cover 'governor' also, but 'king' and 'prince' are alternative expressions when they are not used expressly to point to the subordinate role of the latter. Put in another way, while the princes were subordinate to the king, *vis-à-vis* their own subjects they were in exactly the same position as was the king *vis-à-vis* his.

Now, the centre of each province was the court of the governor of that province, and the king's court was the centre both of his own province and of the whole kingdom. Paths led from the king's court to the courts of his governors, and it was the responsibility of each governor to see that these arteries were maintained. When the grasses were high they were pressed down on

either side of the paths by means of a pole worked by the feet.[1]
A Zande kingdom thus had this diagrammatic form:

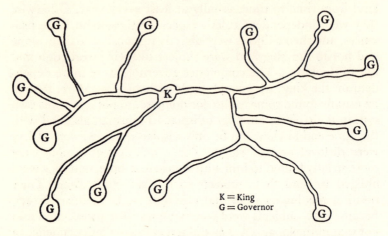

K = King
G = Governor

SKETCH 7. A ZANDE KINGDOM AND ITS PROVINCES.

The layout of each province was on the same pattern as the
layout of the whole kingdom. At the centre was the court of the
ruler, and from that ran the paths, the veins of the kingdom,
which led to the courts of his deputies, the *aligbu*, each of whom
was responsible to the governor for summoning the people of
his district for war and labour and for collecting tribute when
required; and it was his duty to maintain order in that district,
to keep the path leading from it to court open, to settle minor
cases in it on behalf of his master, and to keep him informed of
all that went on in it. These men were constantly at court, at
least for several days each month, where they advised the
governor about matters of justice and policy when called upon
to do so. Without these deputies the king and his governors
would have been helpless, for they could not have maintained
discipline and service except through them. They were the eyes
and ears of the rulers, who seldom moved about their domains
but dwelt in isolation with their wives and small children and
pages, and relied entirely for information on their deputies and
other representatives, but chiefly on the deputies. The diagram

[1] There is a drawing of this in Junker, op. cit., vol. ii, 1891, p. 185.

presented (Sketch 7), therefore, subject to certain qualifications
to be made later, represents a province as well as a kingdom,
the homesteads of the *aligbu* being substituted for the courts of
the governors. Each province, besides being organized under
aligbu for administration, was further organized for war and
collective labour in the ruler's cultivations in military companies, *avura*, which were of two orders, the *abakumba* or married
men, each under a deputy, and the *aparanga* or youths, each
under their own commander, the *bairaaparanga*. More will be
said about these companies later.

3

The arrangement of the court reflected the organization of
a province. The king's court was the largest, though those of
his senior sons might be on much the same scale; but whether
small or large, every court was, as I have said, on the same
pattern, and even a provincial deputy had a court, though
simpler in form. A court (*ngbanga*) consisted of three parts, the
ngbanga proper, a large cleared open space in a spot usually
selected because some shady trees grew there and provided
shelter during the heat of the day, where those who came to
visit the ruler spent the day and where he sat with them to hear
cases and to discuss affairs. Round this court were huts for the
members of the companies of young warriors, and sometimes
one or two huts for married men, though they, being married
and having families, did not usually sleep at court; and if they
did so for a night or two, and there was no special accommoda-
tion for them, they slept in the hut of the companies of youths
to which their sons belonged. Here also, or near by, were the
huts of those of the king's sons who had reached the age of
puberty and were unable to enter their father's private quarters
but, being as yet unmarried and without provinces to administer, had to live at court. The smaller ones lived apart from
the older ones.

Several early travellers have left us interesting descriptions
of these Zande courts. Carlo Piaggia was the first European to
visit a Zande court, that of King Tombo, son of King Yakpati,
in 1864. He says that Azande call it *bancajo* (probably *ngbanga
yo*, 'in the court'), and he further notes that a nearby hut

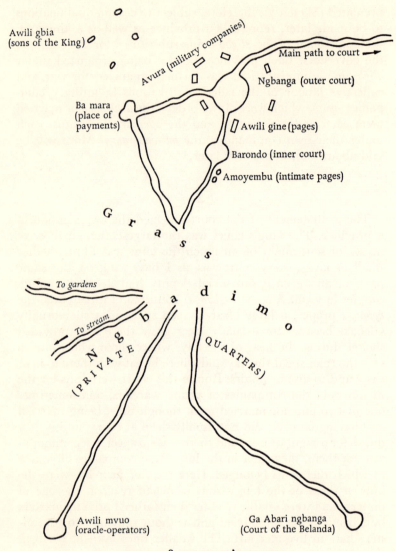

Awili gbia
(sons of the King)

Avura (military companies)

Main path to court →

Ngbanga (outer court)

Ba mara
(place of
payments)

Awili gine (pages)

Barondo (inner court)

Amoyembu (intimate pages)

G r a s s

To gardens

N g b a d i m o

To stream

(PRIVATE QUARTERS)

Awili mvuo
(oracle-operators)

Ga Abari ngbanga
(Court of the Belanda)

SKETCH 8. GBUDWE'S COURT.

(*una cabanna*) occupied by the royal wives was called *bedima* (*ngbad-imo*). He relates that people collected at court to deal with important public affairs such as war, peace, hunting, and tribute—the tribute, he says, was paid in women and boys and products of the soil.[1] Schweinfurth, who visited the court of King Ngangi, son of Muduba, in 1870, says that

His abode consisted of a collection of huts, some larger than others, which he had assigned to his body-guard, and to the wives and children of his closest associates [*sic*]. The mbanga [*ngbanga*] of a prince may be known at once by the numerous shields that are hung upon the trees and posts in its vicinity and by the troop of picked men, fully equipped, who act as sentinels, and are at hand night and day to perform any requisite service. Military expeditions, surprises, conspiracies for murder, are here the order of the day, but frequently other and better employments will arise to engage them—as, for instance, when the discovery is announced that a herd of elephants is in the neighbourhood. Then the signals must be sounded, and everyone without delay must be summoned, the occurrence being recognized as of national importance, for there is a chance of securing many hundredweights of ivory, and perchance ten times the weight of meat. . . . Very modest in its pretensions was the court of this negro prince, and it had little to distinguish it from the huts of the ordinary mortals who had their homes around. The huts were circular and had conical roofs which were usually high and pointed, and were probably constructed to throw off the rain outside, as well as to allow for the dispersion of the smoke which was caused by the fire below. Surrounded by a dozen women, who with some household slaves superintended the tillage of the royal domain, Nganye [Ngangi] had every appearance of enjoying a peaceful—nay, it may be said, an idyllic—existence.[2]

Schweinfurth remarks elsewhere that: 'The residence of a prince differs in no respect from that of ordinary subjects, except in the larger number of huts provided for himself and his wives.'[3] Junker, also, has given us some excellent descriptions of a king's court.

Soon after noon, we reached Ngerria's [Ngoliyo son of Bazingbi] mbanga [*ngbanga*] where the prince with a numerous company awaited me in a spacious gable-roofed open hall. . . . Ngerria's subjects were in the habit of daily assembling at his mbanga, which had

[1] Antinori, op. cit., p. 123.   [2] *The Heart of Africa*, vol. i, 1873, p. 441.
[3] Ibid., vol. ii, 1873, p. 20.

long stood in the same favourable position, undisturbed even by the early trading or plundering expeditions of the Nubians. Hence, unlike the temporary places of assembly of Ndoruma, Wando and Fero [Wando's son, usually known as Renzi], Ngerria's residence presented the stamp of the old traditional usages of the Zandeh nation. A large open space carefully cleared of grass lay a little apart from the huts, and in the centre stood a wide-branching tree, under whose shade the meetings took place. Near it was the hall, which, however, was little used except in bad weather.

Specially noteworthy are the frameworks of timber usually set up on two sides of the mbanga, and consisting of posts connected by horizontal spars, which are disposed at regular intervals one above the other. Thus is formed a kind of large-meshed latticed structure, on which the visitors hang up their shields and rest their spears. As the Zandehs mostly go about with their arms, such places assume a peculiarly characteristic aspect, especially at large gatherings.

The mangbattus [Mangbetu], scorning to sit on the ground, bring their stools and benches with them; but among the Zandehs the Bia [*gbia*, 'prince'] alone sits on a stool, while his subjects squat on the ground round about, the chiefs on their antelope skins or mats, the rest on foliage or a piece of wood from the neighbouring thicket.[1]

Writing of the court of another king, Bakangai, he says:

All that here met my eye was evidently on a scale and in a style that proclaimed the power and greatness of a really formidable African ruler. The number of huts, the size of the well-kept open space, and of the assembly hall, all surpassed my expectations, and even exceeded everything I had yet seen at the headquarters of any native potentate. The mbanga and its surroundings still bore the genuine stamp of the powerful old Zandeh dynasty, which, in the northern territories, had already entered on a period of decadence.

The royal huts spread over a free space of about 1000 yards east and west, with a breadth of perhaps 500 yards, but narrowing somewhat westwards. Probably some 200 huts for the female slaves were disposed in two long rows on the edge of the open space, the broader east end of which, serving for the daily gatherings, was carefully kept free from grass. Here Bakangai usually sat under a large tree, while the assembly took their seats on long tree-stems at distances ranging from forty to seventy-five yards from the prince.

Close by stood the assembly hall, which afforded complete shelter from sun and rain, and which was sixty-five by twenty-five yards, or about the size of our riding-schools. Its roof, artistically constructed

[1] Op. cit., vol. ii, 1891, p. 281.

of foliage, rested on innumerable poles, a central row supporting the ridge, and several side rows the two slopes. The hall was enclosed by mud walls five feet high, so that, despite the doorways on all four sides, the interior was always gloomy. In one corner was an enclosed space, whither the prince withdrew from time to time.

Nor was there any lack of ornamentation, for an accomplished Zandeh artist had covered the walls with all manner of natural and other objects, drawn in rough outline, but perfectly distinct. I noticed that the *pinga* [*kpinga*] or many-bladed Zandeh throwing-knife, was most frequently represented; but simple drawings of tortoises, birds, and snakes also occurred. The building, however, was effective only from its great size, for in the manner of its construction it could bear no comparison with the fine artistic structure of the Mangbattu people.

The Zandehs, in fact, lack the sense of proportion, and the patience for time-consuming details. The mud-floor in the vast hall had not even been levelled, so that the two ends stood considerably lower than the central part, while the roof-ridge described a curved instead of a straight line.

Several other large huts stood round about the assembly hall, all (Zandeh fashion) round with mud walls and conic roof. At the west end of the open space the private dwelling-houses of the prince were visible above a pallisaded enclosure. A similar fence stretched southwards beyond the long rows of huts occupied by the female slaves, and here stood the dwellings of Bakangai's favourite women, in the shade of the trees and neighbouring banana groves.[1]

So did the outer courts of Zande kings appear to early travellers, but it was an outward appearance only, for they were not acquainted with its structural organization, and they were ignorant of the relations of the persons who frequented it. They do not, for example, tell us that at every royal residence a path led from this outer, or main, court to an inner court, the *barondo* or court of secrets or whispers, which was much smaller. Here a prince had a *yepu*, a wall-less hut under which he sat to receive such of his subjects as were qualified to enter the inner court. This hut had two entrances, one facing the outer court for use by his subjects, and the other facing the royal private quarters for the use of the prince himself. Unless especially summoned by the prince, no ordinary person would enter the inner court, only nobles, deputies, company commanders, and certain old men (*aboro mara*) to whom, although they held no office, the prince had given the curved ceremonial knife that deputies bore, as a sign of trust and as a reward for long service. This inner court was called the court of secrets or whispers because there the prince received his councillors away from the crowd at court and could discuss with them matters he did not wish to discuss in public. In the *barondo*, apart from the common people, those who had right of entry ate the food the prince sent out to his followers at court, though the company commanders ate with the men of their companies in the outer court if food was also served there. The place of eating, the *ba liae*, might be a few yards beyond the *barondo*, and that was apparently the arrangement at Gbudwe's court. People only entered the *barondo* to meet the prince or to eat his food. Otherwise they remained in the outer court. In between the outer and inner courts and lining the path connecting them, a distance of some twenty yards, were the huts of the *awili gine*, the ruler's pages, who counted also among the companies of unmarried warriors. The king summoned them, calling them by name, when he had a message to send or for some other errand or commission. Another twenty to thirty yards further on was generally, though seemingly not at Gbudwe's court, a grass screen which shut off from the eyes of the people at court the royal private quarters; and in some cases there appear to have been one or two huts between the inner court and the private quarters where the king's personal and intimate pages slept, so that they were at hand to attend to his requirements by day and night. I gathered that these, or some of them, were small boys who, like his own small sons (*agude ngbadimo*), could enter the private quarters.

If a prince wished to discuss a very secret matter with one or two of his subjects he told a confidential page (*moyembu*) to summon them to meet him at some spot near the grass screen, or in the case of Gbudwe's court at the edge of the patch of high grass which fringed one side of his private quarters, where he could hold converse with them, the page alone being privy to it. Also, men who had private communications to impart to the prince—oracular verdicts, requests for gifts of spears, or gifts to make to their master—tried to attract his attention by coughing so that he might come to meet them on the path to the inner court or at the edge of his private quarters. A prince did not come into either court every day, only every second, third, or fourth day, and those who came with cases or other business had to bide their time in patience. If the oracles were unfavourable or he was sick he might be confined to his private quarters for an even longer period, but in these circumstances one of his sons would deputize for him. However, even on days when he did not appear in court he might grant private interviews to those who had urgent business, if they were men of standing. Such men would listen in the early morning for the sound of his voice, and when they heard it they moved in little spurts, bent from the waist, towards the grass screen, coughing loudly to attract his attention. If he made no response they returned to the court, where they waited till about midday, and if he had not appeared in court by then they went home. If the prince wished to see them he called them to approach and they did so, bent almost to the ground. The pages did not try to interfere with men approaching the grass screen in this manner if they were members of the prince's *gbu*, 'court circle', but if anyone else attempted to do so, they impeded him, asking him where he was going and whether the prince had called him. If the prince did not intervene, they pushed him back into the outer court. At some courts suitors and others who wished for audience crawled on hands and knees to it, but it was more usual to bend low from the waist. Casati remarks on this demeanour: 'They show great respect to their king and to people of rank. In the presence of their chief they bow and advance towards him, stooping low and bending the knee when they stop. On leaving his presence, still bending, they walk backwards for a certain distance and then draw themselves erect.'[1]

The private quarters were also sometimes referred to as *ngbanga*, 'court', and the *ngbanga ade*, 'the court of the wives', but they were normally referred to as the *ngbadimo*, 'the private quarters'. In the case of a monarch like Gbudwe the private quarters, which in his last home lay between the rivers Uze, Nadiagoli, and Asanza, covered several miles. Each wife had her own homestead, consisting of her sleeping-hut, her kitchen, her granaries, with a cleared space, the *vurukpolo*, before her hut, bounded, as in an ordinary commoner's homestead, by a

---

[1] Op. cit., vol. i, p. 207.

nduka, a ridge of earth and sweepings, and her own homestead garden around it. In the midst of his wives the king had his own huts and cleared space and ridge. Here his favourite young wives attended him, and when he wished to sleep with one of them or with another of his wives he sent a child to summon her. It is impossible to say with any assurance how many wives a king or important prince had. Azande are most reticent on this matter, even when it refers to the past, for it is playing with fire to be cognizant of a royal seraglio. In the past, even to mention the name of a prince's wife would have got a man into serious trouble. How dangerous it was to suggest, even innocently, that one might know something about a royal harem is well illustrated by what happened to two youths of Gbudwe's court, as told by Gatanga, one of Gbudwe's company commanders:

There were two youths at Gbudwe's court. One of them went on a journey and he asked his companion, should Gbudwe send out porridge for those at court, to present his little basket so that some porridge might be broken off into it. Porridge was brought before Gbudwe; and then that man who was in charge of the distribution of the porridge to the people came to distribute it. The youth [who had remained at court] took two baskets, one for himself and the other for his friend who was on a journey away from court, and he brought them and put them at the side of the bowl of porridge. They asked him about the two baskets, to whom the second belonged. He replied, 'Master, it belongs to that youth who is on a journey; he said that should there be porridge let his portion be broken off.' Then the older men asked why this youth had spoken in such wise; how did he know that Gbudwe was going to send porridge into court? It looked as though he had been told so by one of Gbudwe's wives. They said that they would seize the youth at hand, because he was in the confidence of his companion who was on a journey. Then they seized this youth and bound him as tightly as they bind bushbuck flesh to carry it from far. They said it would be a good thing to kill him. Others said that since Gbudwe had not been told about the man why did they treat him in this way, especially as it was no affair of his! They spoke about the matter to the nobles [such as were at court], but the nobles kept silence. Those men then said to him, 'Child, you cry aloud so Gbudwe may hear and save you'. The youth cried out very loud to the name of Gbudwe, and Gbudwe in his home heard his cry, and he came and stood at the place where it was the custom to present him with spears. He asked, 'Who is calling me?' They said to him, 'Master, it is a youth they have seized at court for the reason that he brought two baskets to the porridge, saying that one of them was for another youth, who, when about to set out on a journey, said to him that if Gbudwe sent porridge into the court he was to break off his portion and put it aside for him. On account of this the elders asked why he had spoken in this wise unless one of Gbudwe's wives had told him about it [that food would be sent into court on that day] at the time; and so they had seized him and bound him.' Gbudwe then said that they were to bring the youth before him; and then he said, 'Why have they bound him? For this lad has praised me, because he thought that as I always send out food to court, should I do so today he would have his companion's portion put aside for him. Those who seized him, it is they who slight me by suggesting that I do not give food every day to the people at court. Let no one ill-treat him about this matter again in any circumstances.' The youth therefore survived. That affair was to Gbudwe just maliciousness, and he was very indignant with the people about it. He executed many people but he also saved very many people from death. For Azande like to do their fellows ill maliciously as often as they can.

That Azande are unwilling to talk about the wives of princes is not only because they are cautious but also, I think, because they are ignorant; and this was probably all the more so in the past when the number of wives was greater and the penalties for paying them attentions were more severe. They did not know what women a king possessed. They would of course have known if a king took to wife one of their relatives or the daughter of a neighbour, and they would have known the names of the queens in whose names their companies hoed the king's cultivations and their deputies delivered their tribute, and also the names of the mothers of the senior princes; but they would not have known about his other, and junior, wives unless they knew their families; and an inquiry about them would have been tantamount to adultery, with all its grave consequences. Moreover, it was the ancient custom of the nobles to take their kinswomen to wife, including their sisters on the spear-side and their daughters. It was therefore impossible to be certain, at least unless and until they bore children, whether the many princesses who lived in the royal quarters were there as sisters or daughters or as wives or as both. That Azande were largely ignorant of who were Gbudwe's wives is shown by the following story about Ngbatuyo, who figures in it and vouched for its accuracy:

Some five youths of the company of youths of whom Ngbatuyo was the leader went after a man's ripe maize. They began to strip this man's maize, who, however, was Gbudwe's father-in-law; and moreover Gbudwe's wife was in his homestead at the time. The owner of the maize went after these youths and abused them. They continued quarrelling and Gbudwe's mother-in-law said to Gbudwe's wife, her daughter, that she should hasten to come out of her hut and go to the scene, thinking that when the men saw her they would be afraid on account of her being Gbudwe's wife. She arose and went and asked them why they were stripping her family's maize. She made them very angry and they started to beat her, and they took off all the rings on her legs and those on her arms, for she was only a young girl. But the youths did not know she was Gbudwe's wife. They departed with these rings. When Gbudwe heard about it he said he would kill the leader of the youths, who was Ngbatuyo. Gbudwe sent a message to him to tell him to come to court. But Ngbatuyo did not go. He collected spears, some forty of them, and he gave them, together with three baskets of fowls, to Gbudwe in compensation. Gbudwe then at once relented.

Nevertheless, though a great curtain of secrecy hid a king's private quarters from the rest of the world, and woe betide the man who tried to peer behind it, we may say for certain that a monarch such as Gbudwe had dozens of wives, perhaps over a hundred or even, in some cases, more. To indicate the great number of Gbudwe's wives, Azande relate that once when he was walking in his province he saw a pretty girl on the path and wishing to take her to wife he inquired who she was. He was told that she was one of his own wives.

Since no screen hid Gbudwe's private quarters he could be seen approaching when he left them to go to the outer court to receive his subjects there. It was his habit to walk to court along a small path which passed through uncultivated ground—uncultivated so that the homes of his wives would be partially hidden from view—to the *barondo* and the huts of his pages. His favourite wives escorted him a little way and then his pages escorted him as he passed from the inner court to the outer court. As soon as he was seen approaching, all who were in the court, and there were a good number of men at Gbudwe's court, advanced to meet him shouting 'Gbudwe, Gbudwe, Gbudwe'. His trumpeters serenaded him on their ivory trumpets and his courtiers greeted him by waving their ceremonial axes in the air. It was doubtless some such scene which Casati describes when he writes:

At public assemblies the chiefs arrive with their warriors, who, before they take their places, execute martial manoeuvres and sham fights with wonderful speed and accuracy. When the king arrives, those present arise and salute him with shouts of *Bia muie con* ('Good morning king'), whilst the old people in their turn bow and greet him with the words *Bia mipe cotiro* ('King, we salute thee'). The same expressions are used when his Majesty sneezes or coughs.[1]

Azande say that when Gbudwe's subjects rose to meet him the ground resounded from their many feet like *nduu*, the sound of an approaching rain-storm. They closed around him on every side. Gatanga said of Gbudwe's appearances in court:

Gbudwe used to appear in the court in the morning and remain there till midday, when he returned to his private quarters. Early next morning he would come to remain for a long time, till the sun went down, when he would retire to his residence. On another day he would appear in court at midday and stay there till dusk, when they kindled a fire for him in the court itself. Then men made warlike speeches all night, and not till the first cock crowed did Gbudwe rise to retire at dawn. After that he might not come to court on that day, but after a day or two he would appear again at court; because when Gbudwe spent three or four days in his private quarters it was probably on account of witchcraft threatening him at court. When he summoned just the nobles into the inner court and gave food there only to them everyone knew that there was witchcraft threatening him at court; and this gave them cause for reflection, for if a fowl died to the name of one of them [in consultation of the poison oracle] he might be slain without more ado. When Gbudwe intended to give the wing of a fowl [killed by the oracle] to whomsoever was bewitching him he appeared in person and went into the court and summoned that man and gave him the fowl's wing and told him to blow out water on it [to remove his witchcraft] since he was wantonly bewitching him. When he did not want the men at court to kill a man he took an oath by his side, saying that no man should slay him in any circumstances. But with regard to another man whom they

[1] Op. cit., vol. i, p. 207.

wished to kill, he spoke not a word, and when men dragged him
from the court Gbudwe remained silent; and they hacked at him
with their ceremonial knives. If he cried out to Gbudwe by name,
Gbudwe at once rose in the assembly to return to his private
quarters. Then they slew the man, there being no objection. But if
Gbudwe liked a man, and the man cried out to him by name, he
took every oath that no one should in any circumstances slay him.
Then at once they released that man at his orders.

If the people pressed too closely around him, his pages pushed
them back and cleared the way before him to the tree he always
sat under when in court. One of the pages placed his stool there,
and he sat on it while hearing cases, giving instructions, listen-
ing to news, and chatting. It would generally be shortly after
midday when he came into court, and he stayed there till evening. The leading men—deputies, commanders of companies,
visiting governors, and his older sons—formed a semicircle
(*gbu*) in front of him. Lesser people kept in the background. His
eldest sons, on visits from the provinces they ruled in his name,
would be seated on stools, but all commoners sat on animal-
skins, or on a log, or on the ground, as Junker, in the passage
already quoted, says. A few boy pages and some of his little sons
sat on the ground on either side of him, together with his hounds.

All Zande princes were (and still are) accompanied by a
number of these small boys to attend them wherever they went.
Most of them were their own children, some young enough still
to be allowed to live with their mothers, others prohibited from
entering the private quarters, living at court. Junker draws our
attention to them at the court of Bakangai, who was attended
everywhere by quite a number of little boys, who always
squatted in his immediate vicinity: 'Some of these were his own
sons, some those of his brothers, and these lads certainly enjoyed
greater freedom in the atmosphere of royalty than their elder
brothers, who have soon to recognize the unlimited sway of
their paternal rulers, hence prefer to keep at a respectful distance, except when specially summoned to court.'[1] He further
says that these little princelings were admitted into the seraglio,
and also that 'The little fellows were quite spoilt by their
fathers and uncles, who kept stuffing them with porridge, and
even let them have a pull at the beer-jugs'.[2]

[1] Op. cit., vol. iii, 1892, pp. 3-4.   [2] Ibid., p. 8.

Czekanowski, in remarking on the prevalence of homo-sexuality among the Azande, says about this passage from Jun-ker that the boys the German explorer saw being spoilt by King Bakangai and his relatives definitely belonged to the category of homosexuals, and therefore homosexuality could hardly be due, as Europeans in the Belgian Congo told him was the case, to Nubian-Arab influence.[1] It is difficult to see on what grounds Czekanowski makes this assertion with regard to Bakangai, but he is undoubtedly right in his general conclusion that homo-sexuality is indigenous. Azande do not regard it as at all im-proper, indeed as very sensible, for a man to sleep with boys when women are not available or are taboo, and, as we shall see later, in the past this was a regular practice at court. Some princes may even have preferred boys to women, when both were available. This is not a question I can enter into further here beyond saying I was told that some princes sleep with boys before consulting the poison oracle, women being then taboo, and also that they sometimes do so on other occasions, just because they like them.

Some of the commoner pages of a king had a very intimate relationship with their master, so intimate that people called them 'The king's old barkcloth'. These were called *amoyembu* because they could be summoned (*yembu*) by their master at any time of the day or night to perform some service for him; and they were at his side wherever he went into court, to con-sult the poison oracle, to war, on a journey, etc. When small they would even have been summoned by him into his private quarters. Consequently they knew a good deal about his private affairs, both domestic and political, and the first qualities required in a page were therefore ability to keep silence about secret affairs and absolute devotion to his master's interests regardless of any competing loyalties; but, here again, it is better to let a Zande (Kuagbiaru) state what a prince looked for in a page and how hazardous an occupation it might prove to be:

Pages are those boys who are near the private quarters, those whom a prince constantly summons. A prince sees a certain boy who makes a great appeal to him. He sends for him and says to him, 'Boy,

[1] Op. cit., p. 56.

I want you to stay with me as my page. However, when you come to stay with me I do not want you to go to your father's home at all. If I call you in vain and you do not come I will cut off your ear. If you lie to me I will score your back. If I send you with food by night or day to the men at court, do not steal a bit of it, for if you steal it I will score your back so that your companions will be afraid on your account, and they will laugh at you. Do not sit among my subjects to eat food with them, for if I come and see you messing your hand [putting your hand in the bowl] with the hands of my subjects it will be a bad business for you, for that is gluttony. Your hunger is my affair, I am quite capable of giving you food. Do not join with other princes against me, for princes are men of evil disposition.' Then the prince sends for the father of this boy and he tells him that he had better consult well the oracles about his son's fortune since he is going to live with him as his servant; and he says to him, 'You had better admonish him every day about upright conduct'.

The prince also says to the boy that he must not intrude on him in his private quarters: 'If you come with a man you must first stand on the path and cough until I notice you. Anything you may hear anyone say about me, do not hide it from me in any circumstances. You must know the names of everybody who attends court, for if I ask you who is in the court you must be able to name every one of them correctly. Do not steal, for if you steal I will certainly cut off your ear; I will cut off your ear and score your back also.' All this advice, it is how a prince admonishes strongly his pages with regard to himself and about their duties. A prince expects the boy's father to admonish him also. This is the father's advice: 'O my son, since the prince has singled you out among many boys and has taken you alone, do not commit adultery with any of the prince's wives, do not utter even as much as a word to his wives. Do not become too familiar with the prince. Do not join in when others are talking about the prince's affairs. If I had been slack in the service of the princes they would have killed me, or I would now have no lips or hands, for they would altogether have mutilated me, and they would have scored my back also. O my son, you fear all princes and their sons and all their wives; do not be disloyal to them even in the slightest degree, for otherwise they will kill you. If the prince sends you with something do not hide it on the way, for on account of this princes have killed many people so that their kin have been extinguished, for it is shameful. If the prince sends you with porridge, even if it is at night, take it to where you were sent with it and do not sit with it on the path to eat it, for that is a theft which exceeds all other faults, and a prince seizes a person for it and cuts off his ears and scores his back also, for he is a shameless person, a thoroughly shameless one. O my son, all these things, do not do any of them.'

The prince says to the boy that he must not wander far away and that if he calls him in vain he will cut off his ear; for if a prince calls his page in vain and he does not come he cuts off the ear of that boy without more ado, on account of his having wandered far from him. When a prince dies they do not let his pages escape; they kill them after the prince is dead, for they have eaten the prince's oil. People call them 'The prince's old barkcloth' for, because he used to summon them all the time, they are like his old barkcloth.

4

I now mention other parts of the court before returning to the main court, the *ngbanga* in the usual and most comprehensive sense of the word. An earlier quoted text referred to the place where Gbudwe received payments in spears. Gbudwe conducted most official business in the inner or outer courts, unless it was of a very secret nature, but when people paid him spears they did so in a place a little way removed from the outer court called the *ba mara*, 'place of metal'. Here his subjects used to bring him spears (a word which included iron products of various kinds, though usually spears of one sort or another) and also sometimes women. These were mostly fines and fees for oracle consultations. The spears were then taken by small boys into Gbudwe's private quarters where they were deposited, together with others taken in war or sent in tribute by his governors, in a hut built for that purpose. Those who had spears to pay Gbudwe collected in the *ba mara* at sunrise. No one else was permitted to go there. Now, Gbudwe may have used some of these spears for his own marriages—I suppose he did, for otherwise I do not know how he could have obtained so much bridewealth—but by far the greater part of them must have been returned to his subjects in one way or another. He distributed dozens when he went to war, and he is said to have been very generous in giving them to needy suitors, who came to him in numbers, not only from his own province but from the provinces of his governors also. He provided bridewealth for his pages when they grew up and for his young warriors when they had served for some years in one of his junior companies. Indeed, this was why some of the youths came to serve at court.

The king became their father and as such was under obligation
to provide them with the means to marry. It is said that Gbudwe
often gave gifts of spears to his older courtiers also. He never,
if what Azande told me is correct, refused a request for spears.
Those who came to solicit them, his *agino*, 'guests', might have
to wait two or three days at court, but Gbudwe would not let
them depart empty-handed. One day he would come into the
court of secrets and send for them and make gifts of two or three,
or even more, spears to each of them. His sons were not so forth-
coming. Mange is said to have kept suitors waiting several
weeks at court before they received gifts; and others of his sons
might say that they had no spears, though they would try to
obtain them, for it was regarded as shameful to send a suitor
away empty-handed. But a great king like Gbudwe had to live
up to a reputation for liberality, and men came to him for help
in all sorts of difficulties in which they had to meet liabilities,
particularly those concerned with marriage. There was no
shame in asking for aid. A man would ask Gbudwe for spears in
open court and would be told to wait a bit. A man who knew
him well might tease him by saying 'I do not want to go to
Basongoda or to Mange [his sons]', and he would reply 'Of
course not, wait here a little'. The paying of visits to princes in
order to get gifts of spears was a common Zande practice; and
a man might go not only to a prince but also to a deputy or
some other rich commoner, who, if he had any spears at the
time, would give him one or two at new moon. But a commoner
could more easily say that he had no spears. Azande say *agbia
na sarawa nga boro te, kina Azande na sarawa boro*, 'Princes do not
deny a man, it is commoners who refuse a man'. The following
account of the custom of soliciting gifts from princes was given
by Kisanga:

When a man wants to go to a prince to solicit spears from him he
first consults the poison oracle, saying, 'As I am about to go to that
prince, shall I die from sickness or sorcery, or will a wild beast seize
me; shall I die and not return home again?' If the oracle says to him
that if he goes nothing will happen to him he takes another fowl to
the question 'As I am about to go to visit that prince will he give me
spears, will I thank him in my joy?' If the oracle tells him that the
prince will give him plenty of spears he gets up and prepares bread
for his journey. Very early in the morning he rises and calls one of his

sons to travel with him. This boy carries his bag containing his food and he carries also in his hand a gourd containing water. They commence their journey right early in the morning and proceed on their way. If the place is far away they sleep one night on the path, and then they reach the court on the following morning.

They wait there a long time, and if the prince does not intend to appear on that day they sleep in the court. On the following morning they come to court again and wait there. When the prince appears on the path the visitor salutes him politely and then tells him all the news of the country of the prince from whose territory he has come. The prince waits a long time and then he rises to go. His visitor follows him quickly to accompany him on the path to his private quarters and kneels before him and says to him, 'Prince I have not come to be your subject, but I am in great straits. My in-laws refuse to let me have my only wife, I your servant, telling me to bring spears first, some five spears, and then they will let her come to my home. So I considered the matter and said to myself that it is no use just thinking about it, it is better to do something about it. So I have come to you, who are my master, for you to save me in this matter which troubles me. It is about this matter that I have come to visit you, prince.' The prince says to him, 'All right, I will see you later.' This man then waits at court for six weeks. Then on a certain day the prince grants him leave to depart, presenting him with five spears or maybe ten, because he has spent more than a month at court. For if you spend only about five days at court and the prince then gives you leave to depart together with four or five spears you have had a very successful journey, for going to visit a prince to get spears from him can be an arduous business. Each morning you are wearied with waiting. You ask the prince about your departure, and he puts you off till next day, and when you come to depart on the next day he puts you off to yet another day. You tire yourself out in truth with this affair. For a man spends day after day at court until he is utterly bored with it, and he thinks all the time of his wives and children at home. When the prince lets him depart he goes joyfully. However, wealthy princes give people leave to depart after only a few days. They do not have to wait for a long time at court. But those who have nothing ready at hand may keep a man at court for many days while they search for spears from other people, and only when a prince has got enough does he let you depart.

5

At the back of the private quarters at Gbudwe's court were what was called *ga Abari ngbanga*, 'the court of the Belanda', and the *ba benge,* 'the place of the poison oracle'. Gbudwe was perhaps unique among the Zande kings in that, at any rate in the latter part of his reign, there was a small colony of the Belanda people (Mberidi and Mbegumba) to the rear of his private residence, and these Abari, as the Azande call them, had a little court of their own. They were probably refugees who had sought Gbudwe's protection from the Arabs who raided their country to the north. They guarded the rear of the royal home, and they seem also to have acted as his personal craftsmen, for I was told that, besides hunting for him, they beat his barkcloth, constructed his granaries, wove his nets, and made his pots.

At the back of his home and well away from any of its dwellings every prince had his place for consulting the poison oracle, and here were kept the packets of poison and a supply of fowls. Near by were huts in which slept the boys or youths who prepared and administered the poison and looked after the fowls on which the tests were made. They were known as *awilimvuo* or *awimvuo*, children of the bush, on account of their living apart in the bush. Gbudwe or some trusted retainer, more usually a trusted retainer, because it was irksome to observe the taboos which had to be respected if the poison was not to lose its virtue, especially the taboo on sexual congress with women, consulted the oracle almost daily about the king's health, affairs of state, and court cases. I have given a lengthy account of the procedure of consultation in *Witchcraft, Oracles and Magic among the Azande* (1937) and here it is only necessary to say something of the boys who operated the oracle. There were several of these boys or youths at the court of a great king like Gbudwe, though usually only one, or one serving the oracles at a time, at the court of a prince. It will suffice to cite three Zande texts about them. The first was given by Gatanga, who figures in the text:

The *Awilimvuo* used to be in the place of Gbudwe's poison oracle, and their dwelling huts were apart, far away at the back of the royal homestead. He first consulted the poison oracle, and if the oracle told him to gather certain boys in the place of the *Awilimvuo* he did what the oracle said, but he did not take youths except from among the members of the *Audie* company, who were those among whom was Gatanga. It was their task to wander over the countryside to seize chickens for his poison oracle. If it happened that they did not find any chickens they seized one of the youths among the *Awilimvuo* and administered the poison to him in the place of a fowl. But Gbudwe did not often act in this manner, only when his chickens were finished would he then say that they were to seize one of the youths to consult the oracle with him in the place of a fowl. People had only to see this terrible thing and they set off by themselves to catch fowls; and they did not ask a man about them before they took them. For people were afraid, saying that were a man to refuse fowls to Gbudwe they would slay him on the ground. If the *Awilimvuo* did not find fowls Gbudwe would not say anything, but when the time for consulting the oracle arrived he called out the names of those people they should seize to consult the oracle with them. The *Awilimvuo* were handed over to the poison oracle as though they were fowls. That is what Gbudwe used to do. If one of these boys made a single mistake he was at once sent away; he would not take part any more in the consultation of the oracle.

Gatanga was an honest informant and a man well acquainted with Gbudwe's court, and I do not doubt therefore that it happened that the poison was administered to youths if they were not diligent enough in seeking for fowls, though it may have happened only once. Azande, I found, were inclined when speaking of the time before Europeans began to administer them, to suggest that what may have happened only once or twice happened more often. He may have been right also in claiming that at one time youths from his company were selected for operating the oracles, but certainly others were also chosen and, owing to the hazards of the employment, which were even greater than those of the intimate pages, these were often foreign slaves, particularly boy captives of the Baka people, for Azande would not let their sons take the risk of servicing the oracles and told the princes that their own oracles had foretold misfortune should they do so; for apart from the hazard already mentioned there was a further hazard. Lads who consulted the oracles of princes heard about all their most secret affairs and the princes were afraid that when they grew up they might leave their service and spread abroad their secrets. Worse still, a lad might for some reason decide to leave a prince's service and enter into the service of another prince and pass on to his new master the confidences of his old master. Even a foreign slave might take it into his head to run away to his own people and then tell them about his master's affairs. To prevent leakage it seems not to have been uncommon for a prince to have had his consulter of oracles executed on a trumped-up charge, such as adultery with his wives, if the youth was a Zande, or simply to have killed him without advancing any reason if he was a slave in whom nobody except his master had any rights or interest. I quote a text that appeared in my book on Zande witchcraft because it is also relevant here:

When a prince has taken a boy to operate his oracles he continues to operate them till the prince thinks that he has grown up, when he seizes him and slays him. An operator of a king's oracle is not likely to escape death at the king's hands, for the king fears lest he may reveal the secrets of his oracle to some other prince. So he kills him and looks for some other boy to take his place. He kills him for the reason that the oracle always spoke the truth when he operated it.

A king acted in this manner because dead men do not talk. Nevertheless, he gave it out at court that the youth had had relations with one of his wives in order that people might say: 'The king has killed a youth who wronged him', and might not object to one of their own sons taking his place as operator. However, Azande came to understand the king's motives, so that if a boy was called upon by the king to operate his oracles his father would first consult the oracles to find out whether it would result in the boy's death. Consequently princes found difficulty in recruiting sons of Azande, and a man assured by the oracle of future misfortune would decamp with his whole family to another kingdom. So they relied upon captured Baka boys. When one of these was slain there was little comment, for people merely said that the son of a barbarian was slain by the king.[1]

In the same book I have recorded a text describing how when Gbudwe died his son Gangura sent men to slay his father's operator, a Baka youth called Mbikogbudwe, lest he divulge Gbudwe's secrets. He was afterwards cut up and eaten by two of Gangura's subjects.[2] Gangura also slew his own Baka operator of oracles:

Mangiparoni was Gangura's consulter of the poison oracle. He consulted the oracle until he was a grown-up man. Then Gangura said it would be better if he were killed lest he should depart with the secrets of his oracle to some place, for he had grown into a man.

---

[1] Op. cit., 1937, p. 291.   [2] Ibid., p. 292.

He gathered together Mabu, Bamvuru and others of his elders and told them to go and slay that Baka who was Mangiparoni, lest he go away to some other place with the verdicts of his poison oracle. So they went about it and seized Mangiparoni, and they wished to throw him to the earth to bind him and then kill him; but Mangiparoni was too strong for them and they were not at all able to throw him. It was about nine o'clock and the sun was mounting [it was a cloudy day]. As soon as Gangura saw that he was too strong for them he told them to get away from near him so that he could shoot him with his rifle. When he had spoken forcibly thus, Bamvuru took a spear and inserting it between the men trying to hold Mangiparoni stabbed him with it. He continued to stab him till all Mangiparoni's strength had left him and he fell to earth, where they continued to spear him till they killed him. Gangura was delighted.

Many of the Avongara acted in this manner. That person who consulted their oracles, if they suspected disloyalty in him, they would not relent towards him, even ever so little, but they slew him lest otherwise he might go away with the prince's oracle-verdicts to some other place. However, Gangura killed Mangiparoni because he was a man of the Baka people, and he thought he might go away to his own people and that therefore it might be better to slay him.

6

Now, all the people I have mentioned had to be fed: pages and young warriors at court, visiting deputies and elders, visiting provincial governors, the king's sons living at court, the lads who operated the oracles, the king's wives and daughters and small sons in the harem, and possibly sometimes also (I am not certain) the Belanda craftsmen—a considerable body of people. This required organization, both for obtaining the food and for its preparation.

Every day at a prince's court food was cooked by the royal wives and their slaves and then placed in bowls and pots before him. He distributed some to his favourite wives and his small children and then allocated some for his pages, who ate by themselves on the path to the inner court, and some for the youths in the place of oracle-consultation. He then told the pages to take the rest of the food to the men at court. The food might be whatever was seasonable—ground-nuts, beans, maize, etc., but it would normally consist of a kind of porridge (*bakinde*) accompanied by pots of *pasio*, 'meats', to be eaten with the porridge, which by itself is dry and unappetizing: it might be chicken or meat or fish or termites or green vegetables.

A prince at a provincial court who had limited resources but also fewer retainers and visitors might send food into the outer court only every second or third day, but he sent some food into the inner court daily. If he sent out only one bowl of porridge and one pot of 'meats' to this court, the nobles took out of it their share and placed it on leaves and then gave the bowl to the commoners or put the commoners' share on leaves and kept the bowl themselves. The commoner elders then gave part of their share to the company commanders and their seconds-in-command (if the commander was absent, the two men who ranked immediately after him ate in the *barondo*, and if both the commander and his second-in-command were absent, then numbers three and four went into the *barondo*).

About every third day the prince also sent bowls of porridge and pots of meat into the main and outer court. The usual procedure was then for one of the company commanders to break up the porridge, placing some on leaves for the older men, some on leaves for themselves, and then to give the bowls with the remainder of the porridge and the pots with the remainder of the 'meats' to the young warriors. At Prince Gangura's court, in the district where I mostly lived, Kperenge and later Banvuru were responsible for dividing up the food in this way. If there was enough food people could eat till they were satisfied, but they were, especially the older men, careful not to eat too fast or too much, lest others jest about it. If the prince did not send out food to the outer court and only enough to the inner court to feed those privileged to eat there, the people in the outer court returned to their homes or, if they lived far away, sought hospitality at a neighbouring homestead. The young warriors brought food from their homes, which they visited frequently, and shared it with their companions. I was told, however, that a prince never neglected to send food into the inner court, usually about 10 o'clock in the morning and often again in the evening, about 5 o'clock. A prince who did not send food into the inner court daily and into the outer court frequently would soon have found that his subjects ceased to visit his court to pay their respects and to make him gifts. Eventually they would have left his province and become subjects of another and more generous prince.

The time at which food was sent into the courts partly depended on the habits of each prince and partly on the business of the day. If a prince's confidential page told him that there were not many cases to be heard or other business to be transacted, the prince would go to the edge of his private quarters about 6.30 or 7 o'clock in the morning and stand there for an hour or two or even longer, while cases were made and other business executed before him. When a prince did this—and it was still the custom in my time, though princes performed their duties less conscientiously than before—he would send out food about 10 o'clock so that all could partake of it when business was finished. On the other hand, if he learnt that there were many cases to be heard, he told the people to wait and that he would come into court to hear them later. He might then sit in court from about 11 o'clock till between 2 and 3 o'clock and then send out food as soon as he had retired to his private quarters; or he might send out food about 2.30 if he intended, as some princes preferred to do, to sit in court from about 3 o'clock till sunset.

Those who were privileged to eat in the inner court would not permit others to eat there. A man lacking official status or badge who tried to follow the others into the inner court might be humiliated, as an incident related by Gatanga shows:

Gbudwe sent porridge into the inner court for his bearers of the ceremonial knife (*mambele*). When they went there all together a certain man rose who was not a bearer of the ceremonial knife but was just a man of the court to whom Gbudwe had not given the ceremonial knife. This man's name was Batikanzo. A man called Bawali rose and asked Batikanzo why he had entered the inner court since there was no ceremonial knife in his hand. Batikanzo sat down beside the porridge to eat, and Bawali seized his hand in the bowl of porridge and rubbed it in the earth. Now Kanimala [a noble] was present, and Kanimala had a knife at his waist and he drew Batikanzo's attention to it by moving his lips in a sly way. When Batikanzo saw that Kanimala was more or less putting the knife into his hand he jumped up at once, seized the knife from Kanimala's waist, and stabbed Bawali with it and threw him down a corpse; and then he fled. Gbudwe was very angry about this affair. He asked why they should attack his subjects when eating [there was no fault in that]; it was a bad business, and no one was to act in that manner again. And that, master, is the end of the incident.

At the court of a king or of a very important prince, food was sent into the outer, as well as into the inner, court daily. The porridge was brought into the outer court by the pages in an enormous bowl, in which it was heaped some three feet above the top of the bowl, wrapped in *mvue* leaves and bound with *ndokoli* cord. It was followed by a huge pot (a *mele*, such as those used in brewing beer) of meats. These were placed in the outer court and one of the men who habitually attended to the division of it came forward and undid the bundle and called for leaves and open-wove baskets to be brought to him. On the leaves he placed the portions to be distributed to the married men, and into the baskets he placed the portions for the young warriors, a youth from each company being detailed to fetch that company's rations. The portions were broken off the mass by means of leaves held in each hand. Over each portion of porridge the man who was making the distribution heaped a liberal amount of the 'meats'. Then each youth returned to his company with his basketful of porridge covered with 'meats' and placed it in the doorway of his barracks-hut (*yepu*).

The divider sent the portions on leaves to each of the groups into which the married men had gathered. The married men ate their meal first, and the youths stood near by hoping to be invited by their fathers or kinsmen or friends of their fathers to sit down and partake of it. Later the youths ate their meal in their companies, though youths of one company would also eat with youths of another company at their invitation, and some of the married men might be asked to eat with the youths. However, a company commander ate by himself or with another company commander; but if there was a youth present who had recently joined the company, his commander might summon him to share his meal to do him honour. The bowl in which the porridge was brought into court went to each company in turn for three days, and they then got the scrapings in addition to their share. The second-in-command of the company took the head of the table, as it were. He sat opposite the porridge, and the other members of the company sat around him in order of seniority, the most senior member sitting next to him and so on round the circle. The second-in-command ate three or four mouthfuls of the porridge first and then number three joined in, and then number four when number three had eaten three mouthfuls, and so on round the circle. It was considered very bad form for a youth to start eating out of his turn, and if he did so he was fined by the commander. Those who began the eating continued to eat while the junior members came in one by one. Those who began first finished first and got up and left their juniors to finish the porridge. So that not all the 'meats' would be eaten by the senior members and only unpalatable porridge be left for the juniors, they were divided into portions on leaves placed at various positions among the company. They did not so divide the porridge. All ate with the greatest decorum; it was the king's food they ate. I presume that if there were too many warriors to seat themselves within reach of a bowl of porridge, as would be the case at the court of a king, more than one circle would have been formed. Some of the food was given to the boys who served the warriors. All this is, of course, what I have been told, not what I have myself observed.

It was an invariable rule, at any rate in Gbudwe's kingdom, that nobles never ate with commoners. A man of noble birth, no matter how poor or uninfluential, ate with the other nobles. The king's younger sons who had been turned out of the private quarters but were not senior enough to eat in the inner court received their own bowl of porridge and pot of meats. All grown-up nobles ate in the *barondo*. This may have been ancient custom, probably was in fact, but one reason I was given for it is in the story which follows:

This is about why the nobles began to separate off from the Zande commoners in eating meals: about that incident which led to their separating off their place for themselves, which is in the inner court, so that they might eat their food in the inner court. Gbudwe arose and gave a single bowl of porridge to the nobles, together with a fowl, not having yet given the commoners theirs. The nobles collected around this porridge, while the Azande [commoners] just remained seated. They ate this porridge and they gave what was left over to the boys and they finished it. After that Gbudwe gave porridge to the commoners in great quantity; and he sent out another lot with a fowl to the nobles. There was a man present whose name was Nagilinungo, and he began to be angry inside himself with

Yapuyapu, for Yapuyapu was a fat noble, and he might have given him the fowl, because, since they ate the first lot of porridge with a fowl, they might have given the lot which came afterwards to the commoners. Nagilinungo thereupon bewitched Yapuyapu, and he fell sick and died. Gbudwe consulted the poison oracle about him and the oracle gave a verdict against Nagilinungo. Gbudwe sent a messenger after Nagilinungo; and when he had come Gbudwe said to him that he had better go away to live in what had been the kingdom of Ezo, for he was one of Gbudwe's best elders and therefore he did not wish him to be killed in any circumstances. Nagilinungo arose to depart. While he was on his way, Gbudwe's elders were conversing among themselves, saying why should this man get away with the bloodguilt of a son of Gbudwe; it were well that someone should go and slay him on his way. A certain man arose among them and he travelled until he met Nagilinungo on his way when he speared him through his back, and he died. This man returned to tell Gbudwe about it. It grieved Gbudwe in truth; but Gbudwe took no further steps in the matter because this elder was too dear to him for him to kill him on account of Nagilinungo. And that was the end of the affair with Nagilinungo. After that, a man killed a son of Gbudwe with witchcraft. This son of Gbudwe was named Basongo. However, Gbudwe would not put this man to death. It was Gbudwe's elders who killed him secretly without Gbudwe knowing about it. After this affair people began to act savagely. If a man injured another they slew him. However, Gbudwe spared that man [who killed Basongo with witchcraft], saying that he was not to be killed; and it was the Azande themselves who killed him behind Gbudwe's back.

At Gbudwe's court there was always plenty of food for all. He was generous; he had many subjects to hoe his cultivations and to pay him tribute; and he had many wives to prepare the food. Hospitality was on more lavish a scale than at the courts of his sons, even the most senior of them. He sent out food every day; generally at about 7 o'clock in the morning to the boys who prepared his poison oracle; at about 2 o'clock in the afternoon to the inner court; and at about 4 o'clock to the outer court, where there were always a considerable number of men. However, food might be sent out at any time of the day. The food for the *barondo* was placed in bowls and pots at the edge of the private quarters by Gbudwe's wives, who had cooked it, and it was taken from there to the inner court by his pages. One of the pages, a child who could enter the private quarters, was sent by Gbudwe to summon the men who ate in the inner court to their meal. The boy bent low to the senior noble present, and that noble led the way to the inner court. When he was seated, all the food was placed before him and he told the pages to place some of the bowls and pots before the commoner office-bearers. Any provincial governor who might be on a visit to Gbudwe sent a bowl of porridge and a pot of 'meats' to his retainers in the outer court.

The food sent by Gbudwe into the outer court was in an enormous wooden bowl, heaped, Azande told me, some four or five feet above the top of the bowl, and it was carried together with a huge pot of 'meats' in a net (*nanzeli*) which had stakes thrust through the meshes to bear the weight. The porridge was described to me as being *wa go*, 'like a termite-mound'. The bowl was placed between the place of payments (*ba mara*) and the private quarters on the *gine baso*, 'the path of spears', and here Gbudwe's wives came with their contributions and piled them one on another. When it was heaped up and ready to be borne to the outer court some youths were summoned to bear it, for on account of the weight this was a man's job and not a boy's job.

7

Hospitality on this scale was only possible because a ruler's subjects aided him by labour, by gifts of raw foods, and, in the case of a king, by the tribute in kind his provincial governors sent him.

A province was, as I have earlier explained, divided into a number of districts, which were, however, ill defined; and responsible for each district was a *ligbu*, man and office being known by the same name. These commoner deputies were senior men with several wives and large families, but not too old to be active. I return to them later. There were also in each province companies of unmarried warriors, each under command of a *bairaaparanga*, a company commander. The members of such a company lived for the greater part in one district, though there might be some living in adjacent districts. If a man changed his district he was likely to change his company as well, though he had to obtain his prince's permission to do so.

It would not be withheld if the young man's father had received a favourable verdict from the poison oracle for the change. When a youth married he left, on his own initiative, the company of youths to which he had formerly belonged and became a member of the company of married men (*abakumba*) in that district and came under command of the *ligbu*. The contribution to their ruler's resources by the married men was principally in tribute. Unlike the unmarried men, they were owners of property and hence had something in kind to give their master. The contribution of the unmarried youths was in labour. They had no families to maintain by labour on their own estates. Azande say that a youth's labour belonged to his father and that his father gave it to the king, making it a further contribution to the king by the elders beside the tribute they paid him; but undoubtedly it was the youths themselves who insisted on joining the companies, and their fathers could not prevent them from doing so. They performed no more labour for the king than they would have done for their fathers, and they gained prestige and won favour at court by doing it. However, though a man lost part of his son's labour, he was not displeased to have a son at court. It gave him access to the king when he was in trouble or wanted help. When the ruler wanted his cultivations cleared each year he sent for the *abairaaparanga*, the company commanders, and told them to bring their men to the task. He did not give this order through the *aligbu*, the deputies, for the two offices had different functions in civil affairs. They were not, however, of equal status. A deputy was one of the ruler's councillors and was also his representative and therefore more important than a company commander who, Azande say, was *wa wiliko gbua*, 'like his son only'. In war the manpower of each district was mobilized in two sets of companies, that of the younger warriors under their company commander and that of the married men under their deputy, acting as a *livura*, military commander.

Each company of youths had its barracks at court, a rather simple structure resembling a very large hut of the kind called *ba yepu*. It seems to have covered about ten by eight yards. Here some, probably only a few, members of the company were always in residence with their commander, who was never absent from court for more than a few days at a time. Some members, probably a majority of them, were always absent at any one time, visiting their homes and friends. The commander had his bed at one end of this dormitory, and, ranging from his bed, the other beds were occupied by his men in order of seniority. There might be as many as twenty-five beds in one dormitory, ranged along both sides of the hut and sometimes with some in the centre. If a youth was present no one took his bed, but if he were absent another youth might use it. There were more men than beds. If a married man on a visit to court asked for hospitality one of his young kinsmen let him have his bed and took a vacant bed or slept with a companion. Married men who came sometimes to court for two or three weeks at a time, accompanied by one or two of their wives, then built huts of the kind called *dondoma* or a small *yepu* near the court. Though at any given time most of the youths might be absent from court, none stayed away for very long, because prolonged absence was unsatisfactory to their commander, who might, if absence was too long or too frequent, dismiss a man from his company. They returned home to visit their relatives, to obtain provisions, and to get their fathers to consult the poison oracle to make certain that if they continued to reside at court, always something of a hazard, nothing untoward would happen to them there.

Many of the young warriors married boys, and a commander might have more than one boy-wife. When a warrior married a boy he paid spears, though only a few, to the boy's parents, as he would have done had he married their daughter. The warrior in other ways acted towards the parents as though he had married their daughter. He built a hut for his mother-in-law and assisted her in clearing her cultivations; and he used the parents' homestead as a hiding-place for his few possessions. He addressed the parents as *gbiore* and *negbiore*, 'my father-in-law' and 'my mother-in-law'. He gave the boy himself pretty ornaments; and he and the boy addressed one another as *badiare*, 'my love' and 'my lover'. The boy fetched water for his husband, collected firewood and kindled his fire, bore his shield when travelling and also a small bag containing *nzawa* leaves for drying the face and for other toilet purposes, and a small gourd (*lingwa*) containing oil, and a few other odds and ends. The two slept together at nights, the husband satisfying his desires between the boy's thighs. When the boy grew up he joined the company and took a boy-wife in his turn. It was the duty of a husband to give his boy-wife a spear and a shield when he became a warrior. He then took a new boy-wife. Thus one of my chief informants, Kuagbiaru, a member and later a commander of one of Prince Gangura's companies, married three boys in succession. The first, Kpoyo of the Abadara clan, whom he married with six spears, was taken from him by Gangura because, said Kuagbiaru, he was so clear-skinned and good-looking. Kuagbiaru said that his prince took the lad *mbiko ga ko benge*, 'on account of his poison oracle', which in this context meant that he wanted him to share his couch on nights before he consulted his oracle, for women were then taboo to him. Kuagbiaru then married Ngilinga of the Abambura clan; and finally he married Rumoyo of the Avotombo clan. When the last two boys grew up he gave them spears and shields and places in his company, the *Abaza*.

I cannot state with certainty at what age boys joined a company and at what age they told their prince 'I have grown up, I will go and hoe gardens for my sons'; and it probably varied from person to person. From Zande accounts it would appear, however, that a youth would probably have been about 17 or 18 when he joined a company, and marriage in old times being later so all Azande say than today, he would probably have been between 25 and 30 when he left it. If a youth married young he might remain a member for a few years after his marriage. As none of the European travellers, some of whom—Piaggia, Junker, and Casati—lived for years among the Azande, have given us any account of their military organization, we have to rely entirely on verbal information given many years after this organization had disappeared, and therefore we cannot be more precise in answering questions of this kind.

I likewise found it very difficult to compile a certain list of Gbudwe's companies at any one time. He had died twenty-two years before I went to Zandeland and his reign had lasted almost forty years. There were therefore few people still alive who had any very clear recollection of the events of the earlier part of his reign. Also, during it new companies came into being, and men were constantly moving from junior to senior companies. Some of the junior companies had the same name as

some of the senior companies, and furthermore a man was sometimes commander first of a junior company and then of a senior
company, and the two companies might have the same name.
Also a company would sometimes split into two (*kpara gbu*) owing
to internal dissension, a prominent member and those who supported him forming a new company. The split was normally
along territorial lines, the members who came from one part of a
district not getting on with those who came from another part of
it. A prince just accepted the breakaway; it was better to have
a break than to have a company divided against itself. Any man
of influence and with knowledge of the ways of a court might
start a new company by *aparanga* 'recruiting', from an area
where there were not many men who had joined a company,
aboro lingara, 'country bumpkins', who were beginning to feel
that it were better to join a company than to be laughed at and
insulted. *Aboro vura*, 'the king's men', used to object to *aboro
lingara* sitting with them at dances. Nevertheless, in spite of
these difficulties and with the caveat that there may be inaccuracies, I have listed for the court of Bazingbi, Gbudwe's father,
two companies of juniors[1] and six companies of seniors,[2] and
for the court of Gbudwe himself at the end of his reign fourteen
companies of juniors[3] and at least thirteen companies of seniors.[4]
Some informants gave the names of three or four other of
Gbudwe's senior companies, but I am not certain whether these
were fully constituted at the time of his death. It was easier to
obtain the names of the junior than of the senior companies
because most of my informants had been members of the junior
ones at the end of Gbudwe's reign and remembered them better
than the senior ones. I was not able to discover exactly how
many men comprised a company, but on what information I

---

[1] *Abaigo* and *Awilibakungbu*.

[2] *Awiligura, Awilimanziga, Awilisingu, Amusanza, Awiliyambio,* and *Abaigo*.

[3] *Abaigo, Awilingura, Awilibakungbu, Awilitingime, Awililikindi, Awiligine, Alibuanza,
Adego, Audie, Awilimabenge, Agbadie, Awilingbandugu, Afutuo,* and *Aduali*.

[4] *Abaigo, Awilingura, Abaigongbanga, Awilitingime, Awililikindi, Aborolengu, Abo-
rongbarawa, Awilimanziga, Awiligine, Awilisingu, Audie,* and *Awilimabenge*. These
names are a list for only one period of Gbudwe's reign. For other periods there
would be to some extent different lists, though some of the names seem to have persisted from the beginning of Gbudwe's reign to its end. The fact that the same names
often occur among both seniors and juniors is probably to be accounted for by men
having retained the names of their companies when they passed from junior to
senior status.

was able to obtain I estimated, though very roughly, that on an average there might have been some fifty men to a junior company. If that were so, it would mean that Gbudwe could have summoned at least seven hundred youths to hoe his culti- vations; and the work was continued by some hundreds of married men and contingents sent by his commoner governors. If we cannot be precise, we can at least conclude that the labour in his cultivations must have been on an imposing scale, as indeed Azande say it was.

Gbudwe had several eleusine gardens, each at least a mile in length and several hundred yards in breadth. At the end of the month of *Bazinga* (June) he marked the area to be cleared into lanes (*agine*), allotting broad ones to the larger companies and narrow ones to the smaller companies. A company cleared the ground on one of these lanes till they reached the end of the cultivation, a task which took them about five days. They then hoed a second and third lane. Estimates of the time spent in the work varied from ten days to over a month. The companies of a provincial governor did not work for so long, only for some ten days, for his cultivations were smaller. Not all the members of a company worked at the same time. They had only a certain number of hoes, some ten to twenty perhaps in an average company, provided by the ruler. This number of men would hoe for a time and then their places would be taken by another batch. The whole company mustered to hoe their master's eleusine gardens. The eleusine would later be prepared as porridge by the king's wives and slaves for the men at court, among them the members of the *aparanga* companies, and, unless a youth had a good excuse for not having taken part in the hoeing of the cultivations, he would be asked what right he had to eat what he had not cultivated. Other youths of the province who did not belong to any company were persuaded to join in the work with their kinsmen and neighbours, it being understood, however, that if a man had one son in a company he ought not to be deprived of the labour of his other sons. The young men built simple grass huts for themselves and their commander near the cultivations. These gave them shelter, and they slept in them, those who had them, with their boy-wives. They had begun to hoe the cultivations of their fathers before starting on the king's, and when they had done their share of labour for the king they returned home to help their parents finish theirs.

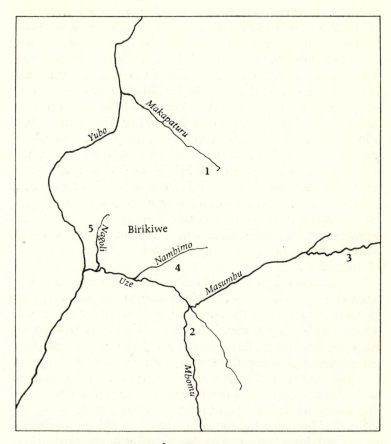

SKETCH 9. GBUDWE'S CULTIVATIONS AT BIRIKIWE.

Note : As the smaller streams are not traced on any printed map no scale can be given. They are outlined here from oral indications.

The site of the eleusine cultivations was changed when it was seen that the soil was becoming exhausted. During Gbudwe's last years, when his home was at Birikiwe (Yambio), the eleusine was said to have been first cultivated at the source of the Maka-paturu and then in the places shown in the sketch-map. It seems to have been in the last of these places, on the Nagoli, tributary of the Uze, that Gbudwe was wounded and captured.

When the *aparanga*, youths, had completed their quota, the *abakumba*, married men, were sent by their *aligbu* to hoe plots at the side of the plots already hoed by the young warriors. Like the younger men, they slept near the cultivations, but only for about ten days. They did not bring their wives with them. Their food was provided by the king's wives, as it was for the unmarried men. When they had finished, contingents were sent by Gbudwe's commoner governors to broaden yet further the area of cultivation by hoeing lanes where the *abakumba* had left off. The main work, however, fell on the youths of the king's province. It is said that the older men and those sent by the commoner governors started off in high spirits but as time went on their lanes became narrower. It seems that, at least generally, only the youths hoed the cultivations of the governors of provinces and the older men were not called upon to assist in the work. As I have earlier explained, it was not possible to check all these statements by observation, only by consulting a number of informants.

The cultivations were hoed in the names of the various queens or chief wives of the king, and these women had food prepared by their slaves and by the king's other wives for the companies which hoed in their names. Men went to fetch it in the evenings from the inner court. Each queen looked after (*mbu ti*) her own companies, this being the only occasion on which bowls of porridge and pots of 'meats' were allocated by the queens to their own companies. The commander of a company of youths also sometimes had food sent from his father's home to supplement that provided by the royal wives. He did this to attract youths into his company. The sketch facing shows the distribution of labour among the different companies.

The married men were told later by their *aligbu* to send their wives, or some of them, to weed the king's eleusine gardens, and finally the men, mostly the youths, harvested it and placed it in huge granaries (*asoro*) erected in or near the cultivations. These granaries were stocked in the names of the queens for whom the cultivations had been hoed by their companies. Besides their main labour in the eleusine cultivations, the youths, mostly the older pages assisted by the youths who operated the oracles,

---

Abanyaki
(commoner governors)

Abakumba
(married men)

Aparanga
(Youths)

Abakumba
(married men)

Abanyaki
(commoner governors)

---

also cleared the king's maize cultivation in wooded country (*bire*). The wives of the seniors weeded it and the young men harvested it. Some of the young warriors also helped the king's pages hoe his ground-nuts plot, and wives of the seniors weeded and harvested it. They also hoed the sesame plot and harvested the crop. The youths prepared the ground for planting sweet potatoes and the wives weeded the mounds. However, it is likely that these subsidiary agricultural tasks were performed by those youths who were habitually at court and that they were not organized on a big scale; for I was also told that those who were called upon to hoe the eleusine cultivation did not do any other agricultural work for the king other than harvesting it. Probably, as the text I am about to cite suggests, some companies mostly cultivated one crop and other companies other crops, and it became a tradition that each should perform the same special tasks each year. The companies of youths also built the king's huts and performed other tasks for him. Some indication of their services is given in the following text, dictated by Gatanga, which speaks of Gbudwe's companies of young warriors:

The *Abaigo* were the leading company which used to begin the fighting before the rest. When Gbudwe used to come into court to declare war he used to distribute war-spears to them first, and then the rest of the warriors contended for the remainder of them at the hand of Gbudwe. The men used to struggle for the spears at the hand of Gbudwe; and if it happened that in the struggling a spear wounded Gbudwe it did not matter, though his subjects always wanted to kill the man who had pulled the spear from Gbudwe which wounded him. It was Gbudwe himself who settled the matter by saying 'Leave him alone, let him die in fighting for me'. Then the men left him alone at once. When Gbudwe used to distribute hoes for his labour he gave them to the leader of the *Abaigo* to distribute to the others. The name of that leader of the *Abaigo* was Baeparu [Avokida clan]. He began his distribution with the *Awilingura*, whose commander was Tikpo. He distributed hoes to all the companies, finishing with the *Aduali*, whose commander was Ngbarama. It was the *Abaigo* who were the first of all the companies. Though there were fourteen companies the first of them was the *Abaigo*. They were the staunchest and they used to do many brave things for Gbudwe. Gbudwe acknowledged their valiant reputation; for should this company be defeated, it meant that Gbudwe was defeated.

The *Awilingura* came after the *Abaigo*; for when the king used to distribute war-spears to the *Abaigo* it was they alone who also took spears from him, because they were next in order in their strength. They came after the *Abaigo* in courage, and Gbudwe acknowledged their strength. Their commander was Tikpo [Ambura clan], who was a man of courage, as Gbudwe well knew.

The *Awilibakungbu* [Gbaro of the Abandogo clan was their leader] came after the *Awilingura* in their strength, for they used to labour greatly; and they were almost as numerous as the *Abaigo*, for they were many. When Gbudwe used to distribute war-spears to the *Abaigo*, and when he had finished the distribution to them, then the *Awilibakungbu* went in front of Gbudwe together with the many other companies who came after them, and they struggled for the spears in front of Gbudwe; and some in tugging at them cut Gbudwe; but he said nothing. Gbudwe used to distribute spears to the *Abaigo* by themselves, but the many other companies struggled for them before him, for they were many.

In numbers the *Awilitingime* came after the *Awilibakungbu*. They were called by this name of *Awilitingime* because when they fought against the Dervishes they were not afraid of their rifles. Although they produced great smoke [*ngime*] they were not at all afraid; they departed right under the smoke of the guns.[1] They used to perform hard work for Gbudwe, for they used to hoe his main cultivations, and they planted his ground-nuts in great quantities. Their commander was Bazambago [Angali clan], one of Gbudwe's best men; and he was also a strong commander of his company, and Gbudwe recognized it.

The *Awililikindi* took the hoes after the *Awilitingime* to hoe Gbudwe's cultivations with them. For it was the custom to distribute hoes to the commanders of companies, one by one, each company receiving some twenty hoes for its use. They called this company the *Awililikindi* because when Gbudwe gave food to them in big quantities he told them to eat it all up as they were going to war; so they called them the *Awililikindi* [*li*, 'to eat'; *kindi*, 'continuously']. Their commander was a man called Ingida [Akalinga clan]. He was one of Gbudwe's best men, for he fought many wars on his behalf. Gbudwe placed him at the head of the *Awililikindi*.

The work of the *Awiligine* came after that of the *Awililikindi* but it was somewhat different, for they were stationed at the entrance to the court path, and when Gbudwe was coming into the court or returning to his private quarters the *Awiligine* drove away the crowd of people following him. This is why they were called the *Awiligine*, for they built huts on the path [*gine*] to Gbudwe's home. Their commander was a man called Gbafu [Akpura clan]. He served Gbudwe very well, and that is why Gbudwe placed him in command of the *Awiligine* to drive away the people surrounding Gbudwe on the path.

The *Alibuanza* used to take their hoes after the *Awiligine*, and their work was to hoe Gbudwe's cultivations for sesame and other oil-bearing plants. Their commander was a man called Kurukaziro. He was so called because when he was a small boy he was afraid of nothing. So when he came to serve Gbudwe at court he called himself Kurukaziro, as though one were to say that that man has escaped death here so often that only after death will he decay [*ziro*]. For he was going to do great things for Gbudwe in war, and if he failed Gbudwe let them kill him. So he called himself Kurukaziro.

The *Adego* came after the *Alibuanza*. They also took their hoes after them for work. However, their chief work was to cut down termite-mounds to make places for huts and to excavate clay from disused

---

[1] As with the case of clan names (see pp. 44–9) these derivations of company-names, or some of them, may well be popular etymology.

termite-mounds for Gbudwẹ. This is why they called them the *Adego* [*de*, 'to dig'; *go*, 'termite-mound'], for whenever Gbudwe saw a mound in his home he summoned them to come and clear it away. Their commander was a man called Ngbatuyo [Agiti clan]. He was a powerful man, for when he was shot with a rifle he survived. This is why he was called Ngbatuyo, because he survived the wound.

The *Audie* took their hoes after the *Adego*, for they came in order after them. Their work was to build Gbudwe's granaries and huts, and to hoe his ground-nuts cultivation. When Gbudwe wanted someone to operate the poison oracle he sent for a youth from among the *Audie* to prepare the oracle for consultation; but they did not resent all these tasks; on the contrary they welcomed them. Even when it came to war they shouted out together in the forefront of the battle. This is why they were called the *Audie* [*a*, plural prefix; *udi*, 'to welcome'; *e*, 'it']. Their commander was Gatanga [also called Mbazingine—Aubali clan]. He was wounded with a rifle in his arm, and the lead is still in it today.

The *Awilimabenge* came after the *Audie*, for when Gbudwe wanted to hunt cane-rats he called on the *Audie* to come and hunt them, but if they were engaged on other work he called on the *Awilimabenge* to come and go with him to hunt cane-rats to kill them. Their commander was a man called Bombu [Agiti clan], a very big man.

Then came the *Agbadie*. Their commander was a man called Turugba [Aboro clan], who was Gbudwe's great talker, for he used to chat away just like the honey bird [*turugba*]. That is why people gave him the name Turugba. His company came after the *Awilimabenge*.

Then came the *Awilingbandugu*. Their leader was a man called Mbikogbudwe [a man of the Baka people]. He called himself by this name because he survived on account of [*mbiko*] Gbudwe; otherwise people would have killed him. His company was the *Awilingbandugu*, so called because they stood before [*ngba*] the rubbish-heap boundary [*ndugu*] of Gbudwe's homestead so that no one might proceed further. Their task was also to hoe the ground-nuts cultivation.

The commander of the *Afutuo* was Batitiroti. Their task was to hoe the main cultivations.

The commander of the *Aduali* was Ngbarama [Akudeli clan]. They bowed [*dua*] their heads [*li*] to their work to do it vigorously.

We need not take the statements in this text too literally. Probably there was a tendency for Gbudwe to tell one or other company to do one or other task, but probably also all hoed his cultivations and those who were at court performed other tasks when occasion arose. One such task that may be specially mentioned is hunting. In hunting game with nets in the wet season (*gbaria* hunting) a prince himself went to the hunting area with his younger sons and his pages, and any men who happened to be at court accompanied him. In this type of hunting a path is trodden round an area of bush and it is observed by searching for spoor whether an animal has entered the square and not left it. Consequently one cannot determine in advance the day of the hunt; and when information is brought that there is an animal in the square, action has to be taken immediately and there is no time to summon men from a distance to take part in it. The prince's nets were woven by the young warriors, assisted by some of the older men, in the court, and in Gbudwe's case by the Belanda in the rear of the private quarters also. In dry season hunting (*tuwa*) the day of the hunt can be fixed in advance, and the prince used to consult his poison oracle as to which of his deputies should take part in it. When the oracle had chosen two or three of them, he summoned them and told them to call on their people to man his hunt. The young men carried his nets. In another sort of hunt, the *tuwa alenvo*, 'cane-rat hunting', the pages, some of the younger members of the companies of youths, and the prince's sons took part. The prince himself did not usually accompany them. It was mainly hunting for young men and boys.

8

In addition to providing labour in the royal cultivations Azande make their princes gifts in kind, a tribute collected by the *aligbu*, prince's deputies. The *aligbu* were the links between the prince or king and his subjects, and they had charge of the various districts in the provinces. It appears, however, that these districts, unlike the provinces, were not territorially well defined. The authority of the ruler of a province extended between certain streams, and anyone who lived between those streams was his *vuru*, subject. The prince ruled (*zoga*) him and he was the man of (*ra fu*) the prince. People who lived outside that area were subjects of other provincial governors, and a man could not live in one province and be the man of a ruler of another province. But though the *aligbu* were responsible for the various parts of a province, these were not exactly defined in terms of rivers; and it seems also that not all who lived in a district necessarily followed the deputy responsible for it, though in the nature of the case the great majority must have done so. When I was in Zandeland most of the Sudan Azande had been moved into settlements along government roads, and their attachment to a prince's deputy was determined by the settlement they lived in, each settlement being in charge of a deputy. In the past, according to the information I was given, when men moved from one district to another they often retained their attachment to the deputy predominant in the district in which they formerly lived, though they presumably did so only if the districts were not very distant from each other. The reason for this seems to have been that the military organization crossed the territorial organization, so that a man who moved from one area to another might still wish to remain a member of his *vura*, 'company', for purposes of fighting, labouring on the royal estates, and paying tribute. The whole following of a *ligbu* would therefore only come together in fighting and hoeing the king's cultivations; and some Azande have told me that, as far as their distribution is concerned, they were *wunzuguwunzugu*, 'all over the place'. This may have been the case, but I believe that in all matters other than war, labour, and tribute a man recognized the authority of the deputy of his district. If this were so, we have to distinguish between the two roles of a deputy, his role as leader of a senior company and his more general role as the prince's representative in a district. The military organization had long disappeared before I first visited the Azande, and I have to admit that I was never quite clear about how it worked in relation to territorial divisions. The information I was given on this question was not always entirely consistent and sometimes appeared to be contradictory, but this I think was due to the fact that the word *ligbu* can be used in a very general sense to mean also *banyaki*, 'commoner governor'. I have heard Gami speak in this sense. He had been a commoner governor of Gbudwe's and was doubtless speaking in terms of his personal relationship to his king, which, he being a commoner, had been closer, in that personal sense, to that obtaining between a king and his deputies than that between a king and his princely governors. Also, Gami's memory took him back to the early period of Gbudwe's reign when his kingdom was smaller than it later became and when his governors were mostly commoners, so that the realm had more the character of a very large province, and its provincial governors that of very influential deputies, than it did later when it became a kingdom of which the provinces were in some respects independent states. The usual view about the matter was stated as follows by an elder called Mvutu:

The *ligbu* men made their homes without any precise order, with their kinsmen near them. Their followers made their homes anywhere, and in the neighbourhood of deputies other than their own. Only when it came to war did companies separate out, each gathering round its commander. As the men mustered each asked where his commander was located. They did not divide the country into territorial areas of influence in the case of deputies. Those who followed one deputy might make their homes near another deputy, but nevertheless they were the men of the first deputy.

Another Zande said:

A prince used to build his home at the side of some stream, with just his own people around him. The deputies built their homes far away from the prince's, along other streams. However, the ordinary Azande lived all over the place. When something important happened at court as, for example, the prince wished to go to war, then the deputies went to court; and when their men arrived they collected where their deputy was. When they came they asked where their leader was. They did not join the men of another leader. Everything had to be in order. The deputies had no boundaries, their following was all over the place. Their men came together only in time of war, together with their leaders.

I have to leave this question with those statements, adding to them only that besides one main deputy in each district there were also lesser ones who acted as his representatives in the district, in the military company and at court.

These deputies were carefully selected by the governor of a province among well-tested men who had served for many years at court. Being a prominent figure and a well-known person at court was always, as I have said earlier, a hazard, but at least in one respect a deputy enjoyed security which a commoner governor of a province lacked. A king who wished to give a province to one of his sons was tempted to find some excuse to remove a commoner governor from office and to hand his province over to his own son or let his son usurp the governor's authority bit by bit, but it would not have been to his advantage to let one of his sons or some other noble gain authority within his own province at the expense of a deputy, for then he might lose labour and tribute, for the Azande would tend to give at any rate part of their labour and tribute to the noble, even though he acknowledged the prince's suzerainty. It is true that a deputy might be removed, but only to be replaced by another commoner representative of the prince. Their master deprived them of their office only for the most serious reasons. Said a Zande:

In the past a prince never took the authority of *ligbu* away from a man for a small matter, only for a big reason, such as witchcraft, disloyalty, theft of tribute, and adultery with the wives of his subjects. It was on account of such matters that a prince used to take *ligbu* from a man and put another in his place. Gangura drove from *ligbu* one of his elders, whose name was Bandapai of the Abanzuma clan. Bandapai had congress with the wife of his own son, because she was pleasing to him. Bandapai also killed with witchcraft another of Gangura's *ligbu* men. On account of these two things Gangura drove him away. Mabu, one of Gangura's *aligbu*, bewitched Gangura's eyes. His eyes closed up altogether so that he could not see with them. The poison oracle said that it was Mabu who had bewitched him. Gangura therefore removed him from the position of *ligbu*.

I was told that a man would have been removed from this position if he displayed cowardice in war or hunting. When a deputy died, his prince would sometimes appoint his son to the position if he were staunch, even if he were quite a young man. Azande told me that in these circumstances some of the elders might grumble, asking, 'Who is this child who is talking to us? We knew your father, but who are you?' If this opposition proved too strong for the man his prince replaced him by an elder; but if he were strong he would face it, replying to his critics, 'If you are going to be unpleasant with me like this I will tell the prince and he will say to you, "You old men killed his father [with witchcraft], why do you want to kill him also? You leave him alone." '

I do not know for certain how many *aligbu* there were in Gbudwe's province, but presumably there were as many principal deputies as there were military companies, which at different times, except at the commencement of his reign, seem to have numbered between thirteen and sixteen. I was given a list of eight deputies for Prince Rikita's present-day province, which is smaller than it was in Gbudwe's time, and a list of fourteen for Prince Gangura's province before the Azande there were removed to roadside settlements, but probably not all these were principal deputies.

The deputies, as has been noted, were responsible in their capacity of leaders of senior companies (*baliabakumbavura*) for some work in the cultivations and for leading their company in war. Other duties were to collect tribute; to visit court frequently to attend their master, acquaint him with the affairs of their district, and advise him on matters of public interest; to settle disputes which did not require royal judgement; and to conduct oracle-tests when any question arising at court requiring them had to be settled. What concerns us here is the collection of tribute. All elephant tusks and leopard skins belonged to the ruler. Also, commoners were expected to give him a portion of animals killed in hunting (only the bushbuck was never presented at court, on account of its timidity) and a portion of their termite harvest, either raw termites or their oil, though no definite amounts of either were required of them. A man who was used to court life and was known to the prince would bring gifts of these and other kinds to court and present them to the prince in person. Such gifts were intended for his personal consumption. Persons not used to court life would make their contributions to a deputy, and all married men made contributions to him in some measure so that the tribute could be paid in the name of the whole company of that district. Since contributions were made by everyone, whether a member of the company or not, the tribute was in fact a levy on the whole district, but it appears to have been presented in the name of the company and to whichever queen the company was attached to. Men who lived at some distance from the deputy's home collected their tribute in the home of the most senior of them, and he sent it to the deputy to be added to the joint contribution of the whole district. Even if a man had already made private gifts of produce to the prince it was still necessary for him to pay tribute to him through a deputy, for otherwise when he was eating at court he might be accused of eating the prince's food without having contributed to it. The only (married) men in a district who did not pay tribute through a deputy in charge of that district were those who paid it to the leader of their company in a different district.

Besides animals and termites Azande presented at court, either privately or through a deputy, many sorts of food, chiefly beans and peas (*abapu, abakpa, abandu*), ground-nuts, sweet potatoes, manioc, malted eleusine, beer, and fowls. Besides these regular seasonal levies, the prince would let his deputies know if his supplies were running short, and they made a general levy on the homesteads of each district of his province. It was said, 'The prince is hungry', a euphemism for saying that he was embarrassed because he was not able to provide liberal hospitality for his subjects when they visited him at court. Every owner of a homestead then brought food to the homesteads of the deputies, whence youths and boys and girls bore it to court. Unmarried men did not make contributions to such a levy, because they had no produce to contribute. However, I was told that if they were members of companies they might sometimes take termites to court and present them to the prince in person. I am here discussing only food, but it may be mentioned that a prince's subjects also made him personal gifts of other things: pots, baskets, barkcloth, knives, spears, etc., and sometimes, I was told, even women, presumably their daughters.

9

Now, it is essential, if the relation between rulers and ruled is to be understood, that it be made clear that the food grown in cultivations worked by a prince's subjects and the tribute in kind paid to him were intended for the people at court and not for the prince or members of his household—they were supposed to look after their own needs. I dare say that in practice what came from tribute in labour and in kind and what came from the labour of the prince's household were not always kept rigidly apart, and that when there was insufficient food for the household it was supplemented from the public store and vice versa. It was only the prince himself and the queens for whom it was taboo (*gila*) to eat of tribute or produce of cultivations worked by the subjects lest by doing so they should cause his following to leave him for another prince. The other wives were not prohibited from using grain and other produce worked by the subjects or their gifts of food, so we may presume that some of it was prepared for the royal household and their own families, and Azande say that this was the case. However, all Azande assured me that, though this might happen, on the whole the produce of their labour and the tribute they paid in kind was reserved for meals sent into court and that it was fully understood on both sides that labour and tribute were for this purpose. *Ru ae*, the giving of things (to a prince), ought to be balanced by *fu ae*, the giving of things (to his subjects). If raw beans went into the royal residence they ought to return to court as cooked beans; if termite oil went into the royal residence it ought to return to court as a relish to flavour porridge; if malted eleusine went into the royal residence it ought to return to the inner court as brewed beer (beer was sent into the outer court only when the prince was present); and if the subjects cultivated their master's eleusine cultivations, the harvest ought to be pounded, ground, and cooked as porridge for these same subjects to eat at court. Consequently, if we use such words as 'tribute' and 'levy' they must be understood in the light of this fact. However, use of the words is permissible, because, although it was held that only he who had made no contribution ought not to eat at court, and although the prince himself would not have attempted to penalize a man who did not make a contribution, the pressure of opinion, the advisability of conforming to general action, and the advantage, if one were later in trouble, of it being known that one had contributed to the common fund must have exercised considerable influence on even those who seldom visited court and kept apart from public affairs; and I believe that, in fact, everybody did make a contribution to the tribute. But if one might use these words, in a rather loose sense, we would not, I think, be justified in speaking of what was presented to a prince as 'tax' in kind; nor can the labour in his cultivations be regarded as a *corvée*. This was not at all the way Azande looked at the matter, in spite of their allegiance to their rulers, the great respect they paid them, and the unquestionably great power they exercised. They saw the matter in a different light. They realized that they themselves were incapable of organizing justice, administration, and defence, and that the nobles could do this; and they saw also that it was, in spite of their rewards, a great responsibility and weariness to the nobles to carry out these functions; and they therefore took the view that their rulers should be helped by them to maintain their services. There is a kind of paradox here, that those who appeared to have not merely an aristocratic position, but autocratic sway, should be regarded by commoners as needing their assistance, but there was an understanding on both sides that this was a mutual exchange of services. If the prince was just, strong, and liberal, they supplied him with the means of maintaining his royal estate by paying him tribute, working his cultivations, and fighting his wars. If the prince was unjust, weak, or mean, his subjects drifted away to serve other princes, a drift which he could not in practice prevent. I do not treat this question in detail now because that would entail a consideration of the whole relationship of ruler to ruled, which would necessitate a discussion of other social activities than those dealt with here, and in particular of the judicial nature of the subject's obligation—which is based on personal allegiance rather than on tenure—to pay dues of one kind or another to his lord. Here I wish only to emphasize that the labour of subjects on their lord's estate and the payment of tribute to him does not mean that the subjects were in any sense serfs or slaves, as clearly some European travellers thought. Petherick, for example, who had only a slight acquaintance with the Azande, was presumably referring to the nobles when he wrote that the labour in the cultivations was 'performed by slaves of which the members of this tribe owned considerable numbers, some individuals owning them by hundreds; and, in case of emergency, they accompanied their masters to battle'.[1] He says also that

The respectability and importance of the chiefs depend on the number of slaves in their possession. These are held to add to their importance as retainers and labourers; and being kidnapped from their neighbours for their own special use, are not bartered either amongst themselves or adjoining tribes. A slave-merchant, therefore, is not known in the country.[2]

[1] Op. cit., p. 468.   [2] Ibid., p. 473.

PLATE III

One of Prince Gangura's sons

It is true that Petherick was writing about Azande on the periphery of their northwards expansion where they were in contact with foreign peoples whom they habitually raided, and that captured or subjugated foreigners had a lower social position than true Zande commoners, but it is probable that Petherick was simply mistaking the free labour of military companies for the forced labour of slaves such as he saw among the Arabs. This misapprehension, it seems to me, in one form or another, also influenced British administration. Sometimes an attempt was made to put an end to these services and dues because they were thought to be oppressive; and at other times it was held that a prince had a right to the labour of his subjects for so many days a year. In fact, there was, in this matter, no oppression, nor was there a right unless a return was made for services rendered. The way Azande regarded it is evident in the two texts which follow, the first by Kuagbiaru, the second by a Zande whose name I omitted to record:

When the season of termites comes and the season of ground-nuts, and of other things like meat and beer, the prince waits and the people make him no gifts of these things; then he summons one of his deputies and says to him that he is very hungry, that he has no food to give to the people at court. This deputy then goes to his home and tells whoever it is comes after him in rank that he had better send messengers to all the people to tell them to bring provisions to the prince because the prince is very hungry. The people begin to collect all sorts of things and bring them to the deputy. When they are sufficient they collect men and small boys in large numbers and they divide the bundles among them, to each his portion, and they take them to the prince. Those who do not give tribute to the prince, their fellows abuse them at meals at the court, so that they cannot partake of them. At the season of oil all present the prince with it; and whoever lacks it so that he does not give oil to the prince is refused oil by his fellows at court, and he just has to eat porridge by itself.

All these things they give to a prince, he does not keep them from the people. If, for example, it is oil, the prince has bowls of porridge cooked, and the relish to go with the porridge will be oil. Those things the subjects of a prince present to him, he must not eat a single one of them, and his chief wife must not eat a single one of them, for if they eat of them the people of his province will all depart and attach themselves to a different prince. It is for this reason that a prince leaves alone that thing his subjects give him. Princes abstain from this food, for that is their custom which long ago originated with their ancestors. Those who are yet growing up learn it from their fellows. However, when an elder stalks a prince with some little gift like meat or some other such thing, the prince eats this thing; but if it is tribute, the prince will not eat it in any circumstances. Such is the custom of paying tribute in provisions to princes. The subjects of all princes pay them tribute.

The second text runs:

Azande like the princes very much, because they are more generous than the Azande [commoners]; they give food to their subjects for nothing. They distribute women to their subjects for nothing also. Anything their subjects present them with they use it for the subjects themselves till it is exhausted. Azande give every kind of thing to the princes. When the season of the *akedo* termites comes they all give oil [squeezed from the termites] to the princes. Who does not give oil, neither shall he eat it at court. If he eats it there his companions seize his hand and rub it in the earth, because he did not give the prince oil. At the season of all things Azande in the same way present them at court to their master; because when they give them to the prince they get them back again when the prince gives them to the people at court. Therefore the paying of tribute is not irksome to Azande, because that same food of theirs which they give to the prince, the prince gives it back to them at court. The princes receive many things from the Azande and in great quantities.

10

Apart from what Gbudwe received from his immediate subjects, those of the province he administered personally, he received tribute of the most varied kinds each year from his provincial governors. This was, in fact, tribute from his subjects in other provinces since it was they who presented it at the courts of their rulers, who then sent part of what they received from their people to their sovereign. When this tribute was from noble governors, the king's own sons for the most part, it was thought of in terms of filial duty, gifts from sons to father, whereas when it was from commoner governors it was rather thought of in terms of subject and ruler, gifts from servant to master. There seems indeed to have been a real difference of emphasis in this matter. The subjects of a noble governor paid tribute to him, and he of his own accord sent whatever part of it he chose to his father, but a commoner governor collected tribute from his people for the king—that was how it was put to me—and had the right to keep half of it for the maintenance of his own court, the other half going to the sovereign's court; and his position in this respect was also contrasted with that of a *ligbu*, who collected at his home tribute for his master, to whom he sent it all, keeping nothing for himself except perhaps a little oil for his immediate retainers. Gbudwe's governors whose names I mention below were those in office in the period round about 1875 to 1885.

The nature of the tribute sent by his governors was to some extent determined by the ecological features of the region from which it was sent; and Gbudwe obtained thereby many articles lacking in his own district or not of such good quality there. From the banks of the Sueh river great gourds were sent by Kana, Nguasu, Gunde, and Sanango: bottle-gourds of every size and shape, large gourd-cups from which to drink beer, cups to draw water and for every household purpose, many with finely cut and decorated handles for the use of his wives. Strung together in bundles at the end of poles, they were borne by a string of porters, black Belanda and chocolate-coloured Bongo and Babukur, subject peoples who had submitted to the Avongara at one time or another. From beyond the Sueh came also, from Kana and Sanango, slaves and ivory. I was told that from the districts of these sons as many as twenty porters at a time bore elephant tusks to Gbudwe's court, and they were followed by a long line of bearers with baskets of dried elephant-flesh and the dried flesh of the hartebeeste, wild boar, buffalo, python, and other beasts; baskets of dried fish; pots of hippopotamus-oil, oil from the *kpakali*, the butter-nut tree, and the *zawa* tree, oil from python's flesh, and sesame oil. From the same region came also fine red pots, and from Mboli's province white *mokanga* pottery. The largest caravan of the year was sent by Mange, who ruled the easternmost part of the kingdom and was in a position to raid and subdue non-Zande peoples and hence to make many foreign captives, some of whom he sent to his father as wives and servants. He sent his father also many elephant tusks, many fine gourd-dishes, dried meats, smoked game (*agoli*), smoked crocodile and hippopotamus, smoked fish, honey (some of the peoples of the area were keen fishermen and

beekeepers), and the kind of durra known as *mbilika*. I was told
that Mange's caravan comprised more than a hundred porters,
many of them men of foreign stocks: Babukur, Avukaya, Moro,
Mundu, Baka, Mittu, and Azande of the Adio stock—a mixture
of races speaking several languages. With the porters came the
slaves. Gbudwe selected the cleverer and more handsome boys
to serve him as confidential pages and to handle his oracles.
The rest hoed his gardens and those of his sons and followers to
whom he gave them. Of the women and girls (some of whom
had babies) he kept the most beautiful in Zande eyes, those
brightest of eye and clearest of skin and with full breasts, for his
couch. Others he gave to his wives to serve them. Some he gave
to his sons and provincial governors, and yet others to his commoner governors and his deputies and company commanders.
But even more welcome than women and boys were the guns
Mange sent his father. He seems to have acquired them—I
am not conversant with affairs in his province—by war and
trade with the Arab trading companies or the Egyptian Government forces which operated in the region bordering his province
to the east. Gbudwe gave these to his followers, increasing, as
he obtained them, his body of gunmen, or to his sons. From
the north and east came also bundles of spears, manufactured
by skilled Mundu and Bongo smelters and smiths.

From the south came tribute collected by his sons Basongoda,
Bafuka, Ndukpe, and Gumba, and his commoner governors
Zengendi of the Angumbi clan, Tangili of the Agbambi clan,
and Mai of the Agiti clan, among whose subjects were many
still only half-assimilated Amiangba and Amadi. Some of this
tribute consisted of goods traded from the Avongara kingdoms
of the south and from peoples to the south of the Uele river,
Mangbetu, Momvu, and Abarambo. The most important of
the southern products were baskets of oracle-poison gathered
in the tropical rain forest to the south of the Uele. From the
south came also pots of red palm-oil (*mbira*), bundles of ceremonial axes—some with ivory handles—from the Mangbetu and
the Abarambo, spears of all shapes and lengths, plates of beaten
iron and iron balls (*ngbeka*) for exchange or for fashioning
into instruments of war, the chase, or agriculture, resin
torches (*baro*), woven hats, mats, utensils for winnowing grain,
and scoops for collecting termites (*kate*), bark-boxes, the red

bark of the *zali* (used for dyeing the hair), and fruits of the *mbianga* tree (used for painting black designs on the skin). From the south also, from soil particularly suited to the culture of the fig-tree, from the bark of which cloth is manufactured, bundles of barkcloth were sent to Gbudwe's court, being borne, like the gourds, on the ends of poles. From the south he received also sabres (*zakuda*), curved knives (*nangongo*), and other knives of foreign workmanship, and beautifully woven ornamental baskets for carrying oil. Slaves were only sent to him from the south when one of his southern governors had conducted a successful raid on the subjects of his brother Wando. Probably no captives came from the west, because Gbudwe remained at peace with, though hostile to, the sons of his brother Ezo, and he was on good terms with Tembura, of the Nunga branch of the royal house, to whom he gave one of his daughters in marriage, a woman still living in Tembura's old kingdom when I was in Zandeland. Tembura used to send him, not of course as tribute but as gifts, bundles of the huge spear known as *zangavoro*, and it was as gifts from him that new species of manioc and ground-nuts and other plants were introduced as novelties into Gbudwe's territory.[1]

In addition to the tribute I have mentioned, his governors also sent Gbudwe baskets of eleusine flour, of malted grain (*toma*), of maize cobs, of beans and peas and ground-nuts, and of termites (especially the varieties *abio*, *akedo*, and *asuo*), and clusters of bananas. All also sent him bundles of spears, knives, bowls, and stools, pots, shields, and other products of craftsmanship.

The procedure when these caravans arrived seems always to have been much the same, so a brief description, as it was given to me, of the arrival of one of Mange's caravans will suffice. Gbudwe sat on a stool, and in a semicircle in front of him sat nobles and commoner courtiers. A man called Kurugine generally had charge of the caravan. He advanced towards Gbudwe and sat on the ground before him with his legs stretched out. He looked silently at the king for some time, holding his hand before his mouth. Then he began to speak, first about matters

---

[1] I was told that Gbudwe sent gifts—not as tribute of course—to friendly monarchs—Malingindo, Binza, Tembura, and Baimi: blue beads (*amanguru*), metal beads (*anzio*), fly-whisks (*amongbara*) of giraffe and wart-hog hair, dogs' teeth and the teeth of crocodiles and ant-bears, ivory mallets for beating barkcloth (*doka*), cup-gourds, bottle-gourds, honey, and boys and girls captured from foreign peoples.

other than those which concerned his mission. Finally he reached the point. Mange would come soon himself to pay his respects in person to his father. Meanwhile he saluted him. Then he gave Gbudwe Mange's report on his province, and finally drew the king's attention to the tribute, telling him that everything Mange entrusted him with was there before him. Gbudwe then inspected the tribute and said that he would see about it in the morning. Everybody knew what that meant, that he would consult the poison oracle about it, to discover whether anyone had made sorcery with it to kill him. The slaves were taken into the private quarters and the rest of the tribute was stacked for the night in one of the large huts in the outer court. Early next morning Gbudwe instructed his chief oracle-consulter, Kpoyo, to ask the oracle about sorcery. Azande told me that if the oracle disclosed that there was bad medicine in the tribute, Gbudwe would at once have sent it all back to his son, and some said that this did once happen, much to Mange's disgust. Gbudwe was more suspicious of Mange than of his other sons. It was only when the oracle declared that the tribute was free of medicines that Gbudwe had it taken into his home. Then, when Kurugine departed, Gbudwe sent him away with messages to his son and a woman or other handsome gift for himself.

Such description as I have been able to give of the tribute sent to Gbudwe by his governors and the manner of sending it is of course what I was told, since it refers to what used to take place before 1905, already twenty-two years before I first made acquaintance with the Azande. But it is the testimony of everyone I knew who was familiar with the court at that period and may therefore, although there may be some exaggeration, be accepted in the main. And even allowing for some exaggeration, it is evident that a great deal of tribute must have poured in from every part of Gbudwe's realm and that, apart from other kinds of tribute, the contribution to the king's food supply must have been substantial. In three respects, therefore, the sovereign's position in the matter of food was different to that of his governors: he received more labour from his subjects, he received tribute from outside his own province, and he received aid in labour from his commoner governors.

In one way or another, therefore, a king such as Gbudwe

procured what was required to maintain his court: by the labour of his immediate subjects and the subjects of his commoner governors; by the tribute of his immediate subjects; and by the tribute of his subjects in provinces other than his own, ruled by his governors, both noble and commoner. All this was food in the raw and had to be prepared for meals at court, and that was done by the king's wives and their servants. Despot though he might in some ways be, his wives had to be the cooks of his subjects. Consequently, apart from other motives, a king or prince had to have a large harem. (I am told that this presents a prince who is a Christian with an embarrassing problem, even though hospitality at court today is expected only on a very moderate scale.) Some organization of the royal household was required to meet the daily needs of the court, and to this I now turn.

II

Zande durable wealth was chiefly in metal, principally spears, but metal was valued most for its use in obtaining wives. The real wealth was in women, and a rich man was one who had many wives, and this was the same whether he was noble or a commoner. The more the wives the more the labour and the more the food; the more the food the greater the hospitality; the greater the hospitality the greater the following; and the greater the following the greater the prestige and authority. But though this was true of commoners as well as of nobles it is only for the princes that we can add, the greater the prestige and authority the greater the wealth—in fines, fees, gifts, tribute, labour, etc.—and the greater the wealth the more the wives. We have come a full circle. Just as in the matter of food there was a reciprocal relation of prince and subject, the subject providing the food by gift and labour and the prince turning the raw foodstuffs by the labour of his womenfolk into meals served at court to his subjects; so there was reciprocity in the matter of spears, paid to the prince chiefly in fines and fees by his subjects and returned to them as gifts or in the labour of his wives obtained by payment of spears. I do not discuss here the psychology of the exchange—what goes to the prince along the path of duty is returned along the path of privilege—for this requires a wider context of discussion. We have now only to consider how a prince's harem was organized in relation to tribute and the labour of the subjects to meet the problem of catering.

The chief categories in a prince's private quarters were the *anegbia*, the *adengbanga*, the *anegili* or *awilizere*, the *negbindi*, and the *akanga*. A *negbia* or *nairakpolo*, as she was called in commoner households and sometimes referred to in princely households also, was a senior wife who had charge of the affairs of the king's home. A king or important prince would have several of these what we may call queens. Gbudwe's varied at different parts of his reign. I was generally given these three names: Nagbakoyo *wili* Bazingbi, his half-sister; Naete *wili* Gbudwe, his daughter; and Nabakatu (Agbambi clan). Naalingi (perhaps the same as Nagbakoyo) was also given by some informants. Nasayo and Naduru (Agbambi clan) were mentioned as having high status in the royal harem, but they do not seem to have been queens. These women were not necessarily the first wives the king married, as is shown by Gbudwe's own daughter being one of his queens. They were women the king trusted and whom he found capable of exercising authority over the other wives and of running his home competently. The queens of his grandson Ngere *wili* Basongoda, to give another example, were Nasayo and Nawilikwoli. We have seen that the companies of warriors were attached to queens and hoed the cultivations in their names, so as the *Abaigo* hoed the gardens of Nasayo, she was spoken of as *naira Abaigo*, 'mistress of the *Abaigo*', and as the *Awiligbudwe* hoed the gardens of Nawilikwoli, she was spoken of as *naira Awiligbudwe*, 'mistress of the *Awiligbudwe*'. Prince Gangura's queens, to give a further example, were Nakidi, Nadekiki, and Nagenebe, and his companies were all attached to one or other of them. I was given the following list of young warrior companies attached to Gbudwe's three queens (their leaders' names are in parentheses by two leaders of his companies, Gatanga and Turugba, for some, presumably fairly late, part of his reign. The list, it will be observed, is somewhat different from that given earlier in this chapter, and I have been given other lists different from either. This may be partly due to the companies being changed both in name and in leadership from time to time, and it may also be partly due to my informants' memories failing them. Such discrepancies cannot be eliminated, but I do not regard them as very important when everybody agreed about the general pattern of the organization of Gbudwe's household and its relations with the court.

Naalingi	Naete	Nabakatu
Abaigo (Dumo)	*Awilibakungbu* (Gbaro)	*Awilisungo* (Ngbatuyo)
Awililikindi (Bangili)	*Awilitingime* (Bazambago)	*Audie* (Gatanga)
		Awilimvuo (Mbiko-
Asongodi (Kpasua)	*Awilimanzigo* (Tule)	gbudwe)
Akenga (Yawili)	*Agbadie* (Turugba)	*Aduali* (Ngbarama)

We have also observed that tribute was paid into court by the senior companies in the names of these queens, but I am not able to supply a list of the companies of married men attached to each queen that has sufficient authority behind it.

Now, most of the other wives had a status in respect to the queens modelled on the pattern of the relationship of subject to ruler, the *adengbanga*, the ordinary wives, being *avuru*, 'subjects', of one or other of them, the expression *zoga*, 'to rule over', and *ra fu*, 'to be subject', being used to describe their relative statuses; and there was said to have been the same competition, with its consequent *sogote*, 'ill-feeling', between the queens with regard to their following as their was between princes with regard to theirs. The subjects of each queen lived around or near her court, as shown in the sketch-map on p. 226, which, I hasten to say, is not intended to be more than a diagram of the relative distribution of the sections of Gbudwe's homestead, as reconstructed from Zande accounts and does not pretend to set out actual distribution or to represent actual numbers of residences.

The queens judged disputes between their subjects as a prince did between his—all Zande relationships tend to be on the prince–subject model. The queens were responsible for the preparation of food for the men at court, and also for the king's favourite wives and his children, his daughters in his private quarters, and his sons who were living at court. This preparation, especially the heavy and monotonous task of pounding and grinding eleusine and the cooking of it, was done partly by the queens' *akanga*, 'slaves'; but part of the work, particularly at the cooking stage, must also have been done by the king's other wives in addition to their daily preparation of meals for themselves and their small children and the preparation, though not every day,

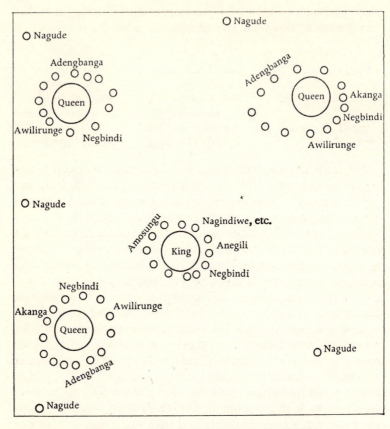

SKETCH 10. THE ZANDE ROYAL QUARTERS.

of food for their master to distribute among members of his
family and household, within and without the private quarters;
and this was organized by the queens, each for her followers. It
was the duty of the queens to see that enough food was prepared
daily for both household and court, and they distributed supplies
to the wives to be cooked by them and then brought before the
king or to the place where the food to be taken to the court was
assembled. Some of these wives, the *awilirunge*, I believe the
most junior of them and for the most part immature girls, seem
to have been attached to each queen as personal servants, with
a status between that of the other wives and that of the slaves;
and it was particularly their duty, together with the slaves and

with the aid of the other *adengbanga*, to hoe their queen's cultivations, her private cultivations as distinct from her public
cultivations hoed by the king's subjects. The queens themselves
did no work beyond the supervision of their slaves and subjects
(the other wives). Their slaves performed all household duties
for them. All this I was told by informants. I was not able to
observe it.

Two sub-categories of wives did not, if I understood the
matter correctly, come directly under the queens. The *amosungu*,
under Gbudwe's wives Nangigbera and Nagbada, were especially privileged wives whose huts were, like those of his favourites
(*anegili*), built around his own court, as distinct from the courts
of the queens. They hoed the king's own eleusine cultivation
for brewing his beer, this cultivation being bordered on each
side by those of his queens. The *anagude* were senior wives with
several children who lived on their own away from the courts
of the king and his queens and who might have slaves given by
their master to assist them in rearing their families.

Carlo Piaggia, our first authority on the Azande, noted that a
king's wives not only cooked for his household but also for the
court, as he had plenty of opportunity to observe during the
many months he was King Tombo's guest. 'Ufficio principale
di queste donne', he remarks, 'è di preparare il cibo per il loro
signore, or per quelli che vivono o si ritrovano nella sua dimora,
e di recarlo alla mensa.'[1] Schweinfurth also recognized that in
spite of the services and tribute Azande rendered to their rulers,
'For their ordinary subsistence they have to turn their attention to the cultivation of the fields; and for this purpose they
endeavour to increase their home establishments by the acquisi-
tion of as many wives and women-slaves as their resources will
allow'.[2] He says further of a prince that: 'For his means of subsistence he depends on his farms, which are worked either by
his slaves or more generally by his numerous wives.'[3]

The ordinary wives had each her own garden and cultivated
it. Each cooked for herself and her children as well as preparing
food for the king to distribute. These wives hoed one large
eleusine cultivation, but each had her own plot in it, allocated to
her by her lord. They hoed these plots in companies, first the plot

---

[1] Antinori, op. cit., p. 125.   [2] *The Heart of Africa*, vol. i, 1873, p. 466.
[3] Ibid., vol. ii, 1873, p. 21.

of one wife and then the plot of another. These companies had names, like those of the men.[1] If, for reasons of age or sickness, some of the wives were backward in the clearing of their cultivations, the king might send his pages and his young sons in the court to help them for two or three days. The ordinary wives were responsible for running their homes, including the building of their huts, for it was only for the queens that the king called on his subjects to build their huts, holding that men should not work for women. Consequently the huts of his wives were simple structures without walls, the kind called *dondoma*. These ordinary wives were, therefore, in much the same position as those of a rich Zande commoner with a number of wives: each ran her own home and also provided for his needs and those of his sons and guests. Hospitality at court was, however, on a much larger scale than in any commoner home and demanded more frequent attention.

The *anegili* or *awilizere*, like the queens, did little work themselves and they ate of the food and drank of the beer put before the king by his other wives. They were the king's favourites, the best-looking of his younger wives, whose main duty was to make themselves attractive to their master, keeping their bodies clean and their hair becomingly coiffured. They attended their master in his homestead, sweeping where he slept and sat, bringing him food, beer, and water, cutting his beard, washing his feet, and in other ways personally attending him. Four of them, I believe four among the youngest, had special names denoting their special tasks: the *nagindiwe*, 'the kindler of the fire' (the girl who placed fire before him in the early morning and evening), the *namoiime*, 'the placer of water' (the girl who placed water before him for his ablutions), the *nakitinzawa*, 'the plucker of *nzawa* leaves' (the girl who brought him these leaves for his toilet), and the *moyembu*, 'the page', who summoned those he wanted to speak to. In the evenings the favourites sat opposite him round his fire, but not too close to it—hence their name *awilizere*, 'children of coldness'. They tended the fire and served their master with beer while he chatted with them. We must remember that Zande kings and princes were lonely persons whose contacts with their subjects were, except in the case of a very few old retainers, formal and of the master-to-servant kind. They were

---

[1] *Abanzoro, Asirikpi, Awilirunge, Awilizere, Abawiya, **Amosungu**, Amopeki.*

therefore very dependent on their wives for easy and light conversation, and, moreover, for two or three days together they stayed in their private quarters and did not appear in court. My two Zande personal servants had been pages at the court of Ngere, son of Basongoda, when they were small boys and therefore had some knowledge of what went on in his private quarters. One of them told me that Ngere had this kind of bantering conversation with his favourite wives as he sat with them round the evening fire:

'That son of mine, you have made a love-bond with him!' 'Oh, no master!' 'Yes you have, you are merely mocking me. That son of mine who is always in the outer court, what is he always waiting for? He has a lover among you.' 'O master how you joke with us.' [Prince Ngere calls one of his small pages and says] 'This boy is your lover!' 'Oh no master, if it were indeed thus how would we escape your anger and live?' 'Hm, come here and draw beer for me.' One of the young women brings him a gourdful of beer from which he drinks, afterwards handing back the gourd to her with a playful tap.

I do not know how typical such a conversation piece would have been. Ngere was regarded as eccentric. A prince slept with whichever of his wives he pleased, and there was not the same need for him to serve all his wives in turn as there was with the commoners. But he chiefly had congress with his favourites. Azande say that a prince sits naked in his hut with his favourites, also naked, playing with them and drinking beer. They say he would have relations with one of them, then drink beer for a time, then have relations with another, then drink more beer. As princes in the past did no work they had nothing much else to do in their private quarters except to drink beer, talk to their wives, and have their pleasure of them. These favourites slept together in a hut or, if there were many of them, in two huts, near their master's hut; but when they had children they became *adengbanga*, wives of the court, and had their own separate homesteads.

The *negbindi* was the king's cook. He was always scared lest one of his wives put medicines in his food, so he consulted the poison oracle to determine which of his wives would be a safe cook for him, and he ate no food other than that prepared by her. She enjoyed great respect in the royal household and had one or two slave-girls placed at her disposal to grind grain and fetch water and firewood for her. A Zande said: 'A prince did not eat food prepared by his many wives, only by that wife about whom he had consulted the poison oracle, saying to it, "If that wife prepares food for me to eat, will she make some trickery with my food?" If the oracle replied "No" the prince stuck to her alone, she always prepared his food; but all the other wives prepared food for the prince's subjects.' In Gbudwe's home each queen also had a *negbindi* whose duty it was to cook the food sent by her mistress into court, and servants and slaves were put at her disposal, for these cooks were *aboro ilisa*, 'esteemed persons'.

Hence three lots of food came to Gbudwe each day: that prepared for his own consumption by his personal cook, that prepared by the personal attendants of the queens (two bowls of porridge with accompanying pots of 'meats' from each queen), and that prepared by the other wives (one bowl of porridge each and a pot of 'meats'). All this food, except his own, was distributed among the various categories of persons, already mentioned, in the royal household and court.

The *akanga*, 'slaves',[1] who worked for the queens and also for some of the other wives to whom their master gave them, were women not married with bridewealth: captives of war sent to the king by his provincial governors and girls paid to the king in fines. Not all the princes had slaves. On the other hand, some commoners had wives whom they treated as though they were slaves. Thus my old friend Ongosi gave a new wife a hut but as she proved to be lazy and let grass grow all round it he degraded her, saying that she was only fit to work *ti yepu*, 'in the kitchen', that is, to grind eleusine. There seem to have been a fair number of slaves in Gbudwe's home. They were generally young girls, for more mature women would usually have been taken to couch by their master. As I have explained, they hoed the gardens, swept, drew water, and collected firewood for their mistresses, but their main labour was pounding eleusine and grinding it under the granaries. When they grew up they were usually taken as wives by the king, and when they bore

---

[1] Czekanowski, op. cit., p. 51 *et passim*, uses the word *Sklave* to correspond more or less to commoner and subject. This is not permissible. The word can only properly be used for servant-girls in large homes (and even here 'domestic servants' might be a more appropriate appellation) and prisoners of war.

him children they became *adengbanga* and were given their own homesteads. When young, they had more work to do than the wives, they were more harshly treated, and they laboured under the direction of others, but when they grew up and bore children they had the same status as wives married with bridewealth. It appears, however, that some, perhaps because they were less favoured or barren, continued to work as slaves until they were old women. Their master then had pity on them and made them into *anangbasoro*, 'women of the granaries'. They lived in huts next to the king's large granaries, built in his cultivations or between court and cultivations to save porterage. There they supervised the grinding of eleusine by girl-slaves; and they were left to lead their own lives in peace if they did not steal the royal grain. If an old slave did not look after a royal granary, then an old wife did so. Boy-slaves could not be kept in the household when they were old enough to work, on account of the royal wives, so they were put among the boys who prepared the oracles or they lived at court and helped in the royal cultivations; but they seem soon to have become absorbed into the ordinary category of commoners, and if they had no relations to assist them their master probably gave them spears to marry with, for one hears nothing about adult male slaves at a Zande court. The following text describes the duties of the slave-girls and the punishments inflicted on them.

Those slaves whom people used to enslave in the days of Gbudwe, their work was as follows. That wife who had several slaves, some four or five, used to tell them to rise and go to the cultivations to hoe them. They all rose and went and hoed the cultivations. Then, evening having come, they returned home to perform many other tasks. In the evening some went to collect firewood and others went to pluck leaves for their mistress to bed on. Some of them went to draw water at a stream for cooking food, while others ground flour. After doing all these jobs they began to cook porridge [a meal] for their mistress to eat. When they had finished preparing their mistress's meal they began to cook their own, everybody by this time being abed. They slept for their part in the kitchen, to rise to get to work very early in the morning. Some of them swept the homestead and some of them went to draw water at a stream. One of them brought out [of the hut] fire for her mistress to sit by and placed water near it so that her mistress could come out to wash her face with it. Some of them had already gone to the cultivations to hoe them, while others remained in the home to perform whatever tasks there their mistress required of them. A wife with many slaves did no work herself. Her work was just to wash herself well and anoint herself with oil; and she took her stool and went to the prince in his court [the women's court in his private quarters] and sat there. If the prince wished her to cook food for the men at court she went and called her young slaves and told them to pound eleusine to prepare it for the people; and one of them did all the cooking of the porridge; and they took it to the king [or prince] so that he could send it out to the men at court. All these many tasks, a queen did not do them herself but her slaves did all her work for her till it was completed.

And this is the way they used to punish slaves. If a slave was a thief her mistress gave her a good flogging. Then she went with her to look for a termite-mound, and she made a hole in the mound and took the arm of this slave and pushed it down among the termites. They covered the whole of the arm and bit her badly. Then the queen asked her whether she had given up her faults, those which people dislike, such as theft and shamelessness and careless preparation of food for people. Then, if she said that she had given up all these faults her mistress let her go. When she took out her arm blood trickled down it, running from the marks of the nibbling of the termites. And if she did something bad her mistress put her among black soldier ants and let them bite her till she said that she would never again steal people's things. It was with these punishments that they punished slaves in the past. But their main punishment was a frequent good whipping.

When these slave-girls grew up into women the king built huts for all of them [let them all build huts] and changed them into his wives, the same as the other wives. They changed themselves into honourable women. Those wives who used to have slaves, they were those wives of a king who had small children. It was them to whom the king gave slaves to help them nurse the children. But that wife called the *nagili*, who was the one the king greatly desired, he gave her a slave to hoe her gardens, since she sat with the king all the time. Her task was to sit near the king and to light the fire by which he sat; and if the king wanted beer she washed her hands well and then poured out beer for him to drink. It was she who used to wash the king's feet before he entered his hut.

12

In conclusion I wish to emphasize the following points: (1) Much of what I have described could no longer be observed when I was in Zandeland and I was therefore dependent on information given me by a number of persons well acquainted with court life. (2) This information was not always in agreement with regard to detail, and which accounts I have followed depended on my assessment of the credibility—I do not mean truthfulness, but age, experience, memory, etc.—of informants and the extent to which a statement was supported by other statements or by known facts. I have not attempted to record every divergence of opinion. (3) I have omitted a good deal of detail either because it was not strictly relevant to the matters being discussed or because it would have clogged the description with an array of names or other items not necessary to bring out the main features of court life. Some of the detail can be presented elsewhere. (4) Some detail which is not strictly relevant has, it is true, been recorded in the text I have cited, but it seemed to me that it was better in this case to record statements that an informant considered to have some bearing on some theme than to act as censor and to omit what from a European's point of view might seem to have little to do with the question at hand. The texts recorded about the royal court were written at my request by my Zande clerk Reuben, son of Prince Rikita. They are therefore to some extent a précis of what informants said and they are sometimes written not in the direct speech of the informants but as what Reuben had been told by the informants. This meant a double selection of the facts, what an informant regarded as significant and what Reuben regarded as significant. There were plenty of ways of checking the accuracy of what has been recorded.

The main points I have tried to bring out may be briefly listed as follows. (1) Given the size of a Zande kingdom or even of a province, sparse distribution of population, and poorness of communications, there had to be both delegation of authority (provincial governors, deputies, and company commanders) and also a central authority in a central position to whom the administrative agents were personally responsible and with whom they maintained personal contact: the king and his governors in their courts. (2) The ruler at the centre controlled, directly or through his delegates, administration, justice, and defence, and he also dispensed largess; and all this brought to his court, and often required the continuous presence of, a fair number of persons—his own sons, the older of them awaiting postings, visiting governors, visiting deputies, members of warrior companies, pages, oracle-operators, suppliants, parties to legal disputes, etc.—and food had to be provided for them; for otherwise they would not, or even could not, have spent many days together at court, and the whole organization would have broken down. (3) The raw material for this hospitality was provided by (*a*) the labour of the king's immediate subjects, (*b*) the labour of the subjects of his commoner governors, (*c*) the tribute of the king's immediate subjects, and (*d*) the tribute of the king's noble and commoner governors. (4) The preparation of this food for consumption was the task of the king's wives and female slaves. It and the maintenance of the royal household required some degree of order and direction (queens, wives' companies, royal cooks, servants and slaves). (5) The king's subjects therefore laboured and paid tribute to provide their own meals at court, the king contributing the labour of his household for the preparation of the food; but although there was this circulation, the king benefited in several respects: (*a*) he was able to maintain his court without expense to himself; (*b*) some of the produce, either because it was a personal gift or through his wives' appropriation, was consumed by his household, which it therefore enabled him to maintain; and (*c*) what came to him as homage was returned to his subjects as largess, he getting the credit for hospitality, liberality, and charity for his distribution of goods to his subjects, goods which they themselves had provided. (6) Nevertheless, the circulation was seen by king and subjects alike as a relationship of reciprocity.

XIII

WARFARE

I

LATER chapters give some account of Zande wars and in particular those fought by King Gbudwe between his taking over his father's kingdom in about 1867 and his death in 1905, and also of the affrays of his provincial governors along a section of its southern border.[1] I propose here to inquire into Zande methods of warfare.

The fighting was of two kinds: a *sungusungu vura*, or campaign, and a *basapu*, or border raid. Raids were conducted by provincial governors on the borders. If the king himself took part in fights, it would mean that the attack was on so large a scale and of such duration that it would constitute a campaign rather than a raid.

Between adjacent kingdoms there were several miles of uninhabited bush. This was remarked on by early travellers, for example, Junker: 'South of Ndoruma's, and separated from it by an extensive uninhabited wilderness, stretches south-west and north-east the land of the aged Prince Malingde (Malingindo).'[2] De Calonne, speaking of the high degree of political centralization in Zandeland, remarked: 'Cette centralisation se marque même objectivement sur le terrain. En pénétrant la périphérie d'une chefferie vers son centre on rencontre généralement une zone de marche presque déserte, surveillée par quelques sentinelles.'[3] By 'sentinelles' he meant the occupants of homesteads situated near the frontier at the orders of a prince. The governor of a border province would walk along the border and select at intervals places where certain of his trusted elders were to build their homesteads. Unless the poison oracle said that such a man would suffer misfortune were he to continue to reside in the place chosen by his prince he remained there,

[1] See Chaps. XV, XVI, and XVII.
[2] Op. cit., vol. ii, 1892, p. 188. Also Schweinfurth, *The Heart of Africa*, vol. ii, pp. 83 and 238.   [3] Op. cit., p. 234; also p. 237.

and his brothers and sons and other retainers would build homesteads near his, and so watch was kept on the border through a string of social agglomerations of this kind. There were not, or at least not usually, similar unoccupied stretches of country between provinces of the same kingdom; and if a prince encouraged an elder to live on the border between his province and another it was not to guard it but to entice people on the other side of it to come and live in his province as his subjects.

Men fought in military companies[1] in campaigns and when making a raid. In putting up a hasty defence against sudden attack it was not possible to fight in company formation, since there was not time to muster the companies. As earlier noted each king and each governor of a province of a kingdom had a number of companies, divided into two classes: the *aparanga*, companies of youths, normally unmarried, and the *abakumba*, companies of married men. I found it very difficult to ascertain the number of men comprising a company. It seems to have varied greatly but not to have been less than 20 or more than 100, except perhaps for Gbudwe's *Abaigo* company, who may have been 200 to 300 strong. The average number seems to have been between 50 to 60 men. Each had its leader, deputy leader, and order of rank or seniority determined by length of service. However, the question of how many men a company comprised is not so important as it might seem to be, because when a kingdom or province was mobilized for war all able-bodied men who belonged to no company, the *aboro lingara*, the people who did not frequent the court, were drafted into one or other company or attached themselves to it for the duration of the fighting. Sometimes married men accompanied companies of youths and youths accompanied their fathers in companies of married men. Members of the nobility also accompanied the force, their pages bearing their shields. Only women, children, the sick, the aged, and those whom the poison oracle had warned not to take part were left at home; and it was the duty of the men among them to prevent panic among the women in the event of defeat and an enemy break-through and to guide the women and children to the refuge of swamps or dense streamside woods. Anyone who failed to report for duty was fined at least ten spears; and each man was expected to bring his own spears and shield. Only

---

[1] See Chap. XII, Section 7.

those who were members of companies had also the *kpinga*, the throwing-knife, as it was *mara ngbanga*, 'court-metal', that is, something which a king or governor distributed to men to fight his battles with. The companies may, therefore, in this respect be regarded as being like a modern army whose regiments are expanded in time of war to receive the entire male population of a country between certain ages. This meant—and here again we cannot be very precise—that a large kingdom, like that of Gbudwe, could probably muster some 20,000 warriors, and one of its provinces between 200 or 300 and 2,000 or 3,000, according to its size.

2

Another point to be borne in mind is that the Azande were essentially a spear and shield people who also used the throwing-knife. True Azande did not use the bow and arrow, and such peoples who used them as were subdued and assimilated by the Azande seem for the most part to have discarded them for the spear and shield. But though the spear continued throughout Zande history to be the main offensive weapon for the vast majority of men, some guns had been acquired before 1870, and in that year and later a fair quantity were obtained from the Arab trading companies by conquest, trade, or gift, and later from the Egyptian Government and the French and Belgians by the same means. Schweinfurth says that King Mofio had 600 riflemen.[1] Ndoruma, son of Ezo, is said to have had more than 600 in 1876,[2] and when the British visited Tembura, son of Liwa, they found that he had about 1,000 rifles.[3] Some of the kings and princes in the Congo, such as Renzi and Bafuka, sons of Wando, and Mbili, son of Malingindo, had also obtained before the end of the century a considerable number of rifles, largely from the defeats they inflicted on Belgian forces. Wando's son Ukwe, who allied himself to the Belgians and therefore did not have this source of supply, brought a hundred riflemen in his forces to assist Delanghe against the Dervishes, and this may have represented only a portion of the guns which had fallen

[1] *The Heart of Africa*, vol. ii, 1873, pp. 417–18.
[2] Romolo Gessi Pasha, *Seven Years in the Sudan (Sette Anni nel Sudan Egiziano)*, 1892, pp. 368–9.
[3] Capt. E. S. Stephenson, *Sudan Intelligence Reports*, 1912, No. 210.

into his hands in resisting Arabs of one sort or another.[1] Later
he offered Baert 2,000 of his warriors, including 150 armed with
percussion-guns, if he would attack the Mahdist fort on the
Akka.[2] Some of the kings in what became French Equatorial
Africa were even better equipped. Zemoi, son of Tikima, who
had obtained rifles in large quantities from Lupton, at one time
Governor of the Bahr al-Ghazal under the Egyptian Government, maintained something like a small standing army—Milz
says it was a guard of 400 men—which included 60 ex-Egyptian
Government troops.[3] Gbudwe, with whom we are mainly concerned, had comparatively few muskets or rifles, for he refused
to have anything to do with the Arab companies and held aloof
from the Egyptian and Belgian Administrations. Such guns as
he possessed were his by capture. It is difficult to estimate how
many he had. I can only say that I doubt, on the general impression I received from informants, whether he had more than
some twenty pieces before he defeated the Dervishes in 1898.
Then a great quantity of firearms and ammunition were captured, and most of his provincial governors started a company
of gunmen (*abanzengeli*). All guns were held in the name of the
king or of one of his governors.

Now, a gun is obviously more effective than a spear, but this
statement has to be qualified by a number of considerations.
The kind of guns the Azande obtained possession of, especially
in earlier years, had neither the range nor the accuracy of the
modern rifle. Azande told me that they possessed four types of
guns. The two oldest were muskets and muzzle-loaders. The
oldest of all was called *biada*. The powder (*ngumbi*) was first
rammed down, then the cotton (*waraga*), then the shot (*bawili*).
The next type, called *orumoturu*, was also loaded from the muzzle
but apparently used percussion caps. These two earliest types
came from the Arabs. The Azande obtained breech-loading
rifles later from the Belgians, first the *abeni*, the kind of rifle
known to the Belgians as Albini, and then the *sipapoi*, the
Remington, which they say was the best of their guns. Moreover, except during the dry season and after the grasses of the
bush had been burnt, guns, and especially those of the more
primitive types, were not necessarily more effective, and could

[1] Lotar, *La Grande Chronique de l'Uele*, 1946, p. 189.   [2] Ibid., p. 202.
[3] Ibid., p. 61.

be less effective, than the spear, for the high grasses of Zandeland allowed for easy concealment and hence ambushes; and
when ambushed at close quarters, troops, however well armed
with guns, even well-trained troops, are at a loss against an
enemy armed with weapons against which they have no protection and at a range at which they are lethal. And even in the
dry season ambuscades could be very effective if laid in streamside forest, where the spearmen were entirely hidden in the
undergrowth. That in either circumstances the spear might be
the decisive weapon was shown by the defeats the Arabs suffered
at the hands of the Azande. They were persuaded by these
defeats to build forts, either of a temporary kind at halts on
expeditions, or of a permanent kind, where they kept their
ammunition, provisions, and stores of ivory and trade goods
under garrison. It was shown also in the defeats the Belgians
suffered on a number of occasions; though it has to be added
that in their attacks on the Belgians and on the Arabs the Azande
had guns as well as spears.

All warriors, except for the few gunmen, carried spears, and
some of them throwing-knives also, and each warrior carried a
wickerwork shield. This shield was very distinctive of the
Azande, who were renowned as much for their shield-play as
for their skill as spearmen; and it is of interest that the word
meaning both 'war' and 'army', *vura*, is also the word for 'shield'.
To discourage fighting, some early British officer prohibited the
bearing of shields, so there were none to be seen in my day, though
some men knew how to fashion them. War having ceased no
one bore the throwing-knife either. The only weapon retained
was the spear, which was used in hunting. We have, however,
a number of descriptions by early travellers of Zande weapons,
of which I will cite two. Petherick, writing in 1858, says:

> Their arms consist of smooth and barbed lances, and a large
> oblong shield, formed of closely-woven matting, composed of several
> patterns, and dyed with many colours. In the centre of the interior
> is a wooden handle, to which are attached two or three singularly-
> formed iron projectiles, resembling a boomerang of rather a circular
> form, bearing on their peripheries several sharp projections.
> Attached to the girdle, a strong leather sheath containing a knife, hilt
> downwards, is worn by every 'Neam Nam'.[1]

[1] Op. cit., 1861, p. 7.

Mr. and Mrs. Petherick say elsewhere that Azande also fought with bows and arrows,[1] but it is probable that these were not true Azande. Writing in 1870, Schweinfurth says:

The principal weapons of the Niam-niam are their lances and their trumbashes. . . . The trumbash of the Niam-niam consists ordinarily of several limbs of iron, with pointed prongs and sharp edges. Iron missiles very similar in their shape are found among the tribes of the Tsad basin. . . . The trumbashes are always attached to the inside of the shields, which are woven from the Spanish reed, and are of a long oval form, covering two-thirds of the body; they are ornamented with black and white crosses or other devices; and are so light that they do not in the least impede the combatants in their wild leaps. An expert Niam-niam, by jumping up for a moment, can protect his feet from the flying missiles of his adversary. Bows and arrows, which, as handled by the Bongo, give them a certain advantage, are not in common use among the Niam-niam, who possess a peculiar weapon of attack in their singular knives, that have blades like sickles.[2]

And in another passage he says that a Zande carries the spear in one hand and the shield and throwing-knife in the other, and has a scimitar in his girdle,[3] and he further comments,

Nowhere, in any part of Africa, have I ever come across a people that in every attitude and every motion exhibited so thorough a mastery over all the circumstances of war or of the chase as these Niam-niam—other nations in comparison seemed to me to fall short in the perfect ease—I might almost say, in the dramatic grace—that characterized their every movement.[4]

3

Bearing the above considerations in mind, we may first give attention to the raid. A *basapu*, 'raid', was normally a surprise attack by night on homesteads near the border of a kingdom, though sometimes the attack was made by daylight, it being then known as a *tame basapu*. Because high grass afforded better concealment, raids were, at least usually, made in the wet season, and the favourite time was just before dawn in the middle of the month; for the full moon lighted the warriors on

---

[1] Op. cit., 1869, pp. 209 and 280. [2] *The Heart of Africa*, vol. ii, 1873, p. 9.
[3] Ibid., p. 11. [4] Ibid., p. 12.

their way to the place of assembly while the moon would have fallen and the world become dark as they moved forward to the attack. A raid was organized by a provincial governor, usually a princeling, a son of the ruler of a kingdom, and it was directed against the subjects of the governor of the province opposite this princeling, who would usually be a son of the king who ruled this adjacent kingdom. However, as I have stated earlier, these governors might be commoners. A prince acted on his own initiative, neither consulting nor informing the king of his intentions.

Before carrying out a raid a prince consulted his poison oracle as to the most suitable place and day for it to take place. He also asked it where he should assemble his warriors and also about each of his military companies, to discover whether they would suffer heavy casualties which might weaken his prestige among his subjects, who would say that he had wantonly sent them to death. If the oracle showed itself to be unfavourable to the venture, it was abandoned. Those companies to which the verdicts of the oracles were favourable were entrusted with the most dangerous duties, and any to which they were unfavourable were either ordered not to take part in the raid or were instructed to remain in the rear with the prince himself or to take up position in the rearmost ambush, where they were unlikely to become engaged with the enemy.

When the objective, time of attack, and place of assembly had been determined by the oracle, the prince sent one of his spies to whom the oracle was favourable to spy out the land. A spy was called *bomoi* or *bamoi*, 'one who prepared the place' (*moi rago*). This spy would, on the excuse of visiting a kinsman, relative-in-law, blood-brother, or on some other excuse such as trading, spend a night or two near the homesteads chosen for assault and would later report on their exact position, their manpower, where their inmates slept, and whether they had had any warning of the planned raid, either from a leakage or through their oracles; for people on the frontier might get information from a kinsman or a blood-brother on the other side, and they frequently consulted their oracles about the possibility of attack, since they were in a vulnerable position. A favourite occasion for a raid was when the people of the homesteads to be attacked were holding a feast, for then they would be both unprepared and defenceless. The men would have laid their spears and shields aside to take part in the drinking and dancing, and they would probably be drunk as well; and there would be large numbers of women present to be seized and taken back captive. A spy would know from the stage of preparation of the beer when it would be ready for consumption, and consequently on which day the feast would be held. It may seem curious that a man from one kingdom could so easily spy on the border homesteads of another, and indeed, the spy ran some risk of being discovered—that is why his prince consulted the oracle about him—though it was probably not great, for there was a good deal of coming and going across the frontiers on one errand or another. I was told that the prince, his principal page (*moyembu*), and his consulter of oracles (*baputabenge*)— who had all been present when the oracle selected the man to act as spy—and possibly one or two of the principal leaders of companies (*alivura*) were the only persons who knew who he was; and this is in spite of the fact that a prince regularly employed the same persons in this capacity. The two chief spies in the province of Gangura, where I spent most of my time, were Kangada of the Abakpoto clan and Ngawe of the Akpura clan.

On the morning before the concentration of the raiding party the spy spent the day watching the path between the place of concentration and the objective, observing all who came and went, but not attempting to obstruct them. When the prince, accompanied by a few attendants, arrived at night at the homestead selected by the oracle for the assembly of his warriors, he instructed the spy that no one was to proceed into enemy country *ka fuga yulu*, to carry warning to the enemy by night, for a man might do so to spare his in-laws or blood-brothers, or relations; and I have heard of cases when this happened. If anyone came along the path the spy seized him and sent him back again.

The prince came to the place of assembly with his page, his consulter of oracles, and a few followers. This place would be the homestead of a man of substance near the frontier and the objective of the raid. From here the prince sent messengers to the leaders of his companies to order them to muster their men. They in turn sent messengers round the homesteads in their vicinity and all hurried in twos and threes to the place of assembly,

where they attached themselves to the various companies.
When all were assembled, the prince summoned the leaders and
explained the tactics of the attack to them and ordered their
dispositions. He also told his page to bring the horn, called
ngbuka, in which he kept his war medicines and rubbed the
medicines with a stick across their mouths. Each of the commanders would also have a medicine horn and would give
medicine to his sons and to men of his company. These medicines, which are said to have been taught to the princes by
commoner elders in olden times, not only gave protection to the
warriors but also helped them to obtain spoil in spears (*baso
vura*) and women (*akanga vura*).

No one attempted to sleep that night, and when the *gulengbe*
bird began to chirp *gulengbe sosoro, gulengbe sosoro*, just before
dawn, the move forwards began. Except for the fires normally
burning in the homestead, neither in the camp nor while waiting to attack were fires allowed, and speech, and above all
coughing, were forbidden. They advanced till they met the
bomoi (spy), and after a short consultation with him the advance
continued. The usual order at this stage seems to have been the
bomoi ahead, followed by the prince's consulter of oracles, the
prince himself accompanied by his page, and then the companies in Indian file, the senior company leading. When they
reached the spot chosen by the spy for the first ambush, the
prince sent forward the attacking party, composed of the riflemen and the companies of youths, and stationed a company of
married men at this point as the first of the ambushes (*anguru*)
to cover the retreat of the assaulting party. He then returned
the way he had come, stationing other companies of married
men at suitable places for the second and third ambushes. The
prince himself waited well to the rear of the last ambush,
together with his small sons, his personal page, his consulter of
oracles, some youths who formed his personal bodyguard (*awili
gine*), a few councillors (*atakpoto*), and such men as had been
warned by the oracle not to take part in the fighting.

The attacking party proceeds in the dimness of dawn under
direction of the spy or spies, for there might be more than
one. At the head of each company was its leader, the *barum-
batayo*, and the company followed him in file and more or less
in order of seniority. Now especially there must be no talking

or coughing: *rago ki onga a onga wa yulu,* 'the place was as silent as night'. When they reached a point some fifty yards from the nearest objective, which was always some frontier group of homesteads along the banks of a stream, they halted and extended. Each company had been allotted its objective by the *bomoi*. Those whose objective was nearest, those in the centre, waited for those with the most distant objectives to attack before attacking themselves, so that the attack could be more or less simultaneous. The senior company (*kuru aparanga*), in Gangura's country the *Awili rungesi*, usually occupied the central position, and those junior to them formed the wings.

If no warning had reached the ears of the inmates of the homesteads selected for attack and if the attackers had been able to reach their homes without being seen or heard, the inmates were likely to be killed as they emerged from their huts. Woken from sleep by calls at the doors of their huts for them to come out, the menfolk gave the alarm (*tatangba*) and then dashed out of the huts, leaving their women and children behind, for if they did not do so the huts were burnt over their heads. As spearmen were ranged on one side of the doors waiting for them to emerge, a man was very lucky if he escaped death; but he might get away with a wound, for he would not be pursued far as the assailants were afraid lest in chasing him they might run into the people who were now making their way towards the attacked homesteads in answer to the warning cries that were heard on every side and were spreading ever wider. If a man was brought down by the spear his ears were at once cut off. Any male over eight years of age was speared, and only females and very small boys who still followed their mothers were spared. They were summoned from the huts and taken captive. However, in an attack on a feast, when men and women were mixed together, women were sometimes killed; and I was told that old women captives were occasionally speared later if they impeded the retreat.

Once the people had been dealt with, there was a hurried search for loot in huts and granaries. Spoil (*ahu vura*), apart from captured women and children, consisted of spears, knives, shields, hoes, axes, drums, and gongs; pots and gourd-vessels; leaf-bundles and pots and gourd-vessels containing ground-nuts, beans, oil, termites, dried meat, and other foodstuffs; eleusine;

hens and chickens. What could not be taken away was destroyed:
dogs were speared; gongs, drums, pots, etc., were smashed; and
the huts and granaries with their contents were burnt. All this
had to be done with the utmost speed, for the enemy might
counter-attack at any moment. The attacking party were not
expected to await an attack but to strike hard and get out quick.
One said, *ngama nide ro, u ga,* 'the viper bites you and makes off'.
Azande also say that they learnt how to make raids by watching
those of the black soldier ants (*apipi*) on termites.

The action had to be as swift as possible, for the alarm, once
given, spread from homestead to homestead, and in every direction was heard the cry *vura o, vura o,* 'war O, war O'; and then
the gongs and drums began tapping out news of the attack, so
that in a very short space of time people living over twenty miles
away knew that there was a war (*vura ti*), though they did not
yet know exactly where it had fallen or for certain whether it
was a raid or a campaign. Now, it was regarded as a most
serious dereliction if all men in the neighbourhood of the
attacked homesteads did not at once take up their spears and
shields and hasten to the scene of action, either singly or in
small parties, and as soon as they were sufficient in number—
some twenty men—they pursued the enemy. Those who arrived
later were told by the women that the pursuit had commenced,
and they ran after the pursuers to play their part. Very soon the
whole province was alerted and men went from every direction
towards the frontier. The prince himself, as soon as the news
reached his court, hastened to the frontier with such warriors as
were sleeping in their barracks at court. Moreover, the subjects
of neighbouring princes, when they heard the alarm, took it up
and passed it down the frontier by mouth and gong; and they
then hastened either to the frontier or to their prince's court,
according to whether their homes were situated on the frontier
side of the court or on the interior side. It was a paramount duty
for at least the neighbouring princes on either side of the threatened province to dispatch as quickly as possible one or two
companies, or rather the men of one or two companies present
at court at the time, while the princes themselves followed with
the rest of their companies. But generally other princes would
also mobilize and prepare to go to the assistance of their peer.
If the action was a raid, the warriors of even the adjacent

provinces might arrive when it was over, but it might prove to be a campaign; and this is why a king was so insistent on his frontier governors at once assisting one another, for otherwise the enemy forces might be large enough to overrun a single frontier province and threaten his own district in the interior. When the subjects of princes whose territories were more distant than those adjacent to the attacked province learnt that the attack was not on a province next to their own and was a raid and not a campaign, they might return home. This was a matter for their master to decide. The king's own district did not mobilize on hearing a frontier alarm. His subjects awaited a messenger from the governor of the attacked province to tell them what sort of attack it was. The older men who frequented the court repaired there to receive news and instructions.

The attackers therefore beat a hasty retreat before the enemy could muster men in sufficient force to attack them. Those bearing spoil and driving captive women before them went ahead and those unencumbered brought up the rear. This rearguard, the senior company of youths, might await the enemy onslaught and exchange a few spears with them for honour's sake, but they made no attempt to hold them. Their retreat was covered by the ambushed companies (*kisi gine ni nguru*). The warriors in ambush trod down the grasses a few yards back from the path, parallel to, and at one side of it, so that they might have both concealment and also room for movement. They crouched in this clearing with about six yards between man and man. The leader of the company was alone exposed. He stood in the middle of the path to observe the approach of the enemy and to give the signal for attack, but on a curve in the path and at the tail of the ambush, so that the pursuers might be well into the ambush before they saw him. We have to remember also that there was still not much light and that there was much confusion. Moreover, the pursuers had in any case to pass through the ambush or give up pursuit altogether, since the grasses were too high and dense to allow a detour; and it was a point of honour to pursue the raiders at any rate up to the first ambush so that it could be told their prince that they had fought.

There were probably always two ambushes and generally three. The first was the most dangerous place in a raid as it had to bear the main onslaught of the enemy. The men who attacked the homesteads were in little danger if they had taken the enemy by surprise and did not linger too long seeking spoils; and the companies forming the second and third ambushes might not be engaged by the enemy at all, for often they would not attempt pursuit beyond the first ambush. The first ambush tended to be placed at or back from the first major path-junction on the attackers' side of the attacked homesteads rather than in advance of it, because it could not be known along which of the paths the enemy would appear. Were it placed in advance of this point the ambush might not serve its purpose and also its occupants might have their own retreat cut off. The first ambush would probably be a few hundred yards back from the raided homesteads, and the second and third ambushes would be spaced at similar distances.

The retreating raiders arrived at a trot at a point where the leader of the first ambush stood on the path and they passed under his raised arms, the last of them maybe running hard with the enemy in close pursuit. They continued through the second and third ambushes to where the prince was waiting. Here they were stopped by a man holding a spear across the path and shouting to them to halt as the prince was present. No one would retreat past him. Meanwhile, when the first of the enemy, in hot pursuit of the raiders, were well into the first ambush its commander hurled a spear at him and gave a shout; and at once the warriors laying in wait began to hurl their spears and, shouting out the names of their king and prince, set about the enemy *wa age*, 'like termites'. The enemy turned immediately, and a fight at close range commenced. Each man carried from two to four spears, one in his right hand and the rest with the shield in his left hand, and he first threw them one by one. If he was a regular member of a company he would also hold in his left hand, pressed against the handle of the shield, up to four throwing-knives, two with their heads up and two with their heads down. When he had exhausted his spears he quickly extracted one of these throwing-knives with his right hand, and after stooping and bending it a little under his foot, threw it, held in a vertical position, against the enemy. I was told that he would throw only one of these knives, and that only after having shouted out that he was about to do so, as it was considered an

offence for a man to throw one of his prince's knives without
this preliminary declaration, for otherwise it might be said that
he had thrown the weapon away in fear. A senior man might
have a large knife of the kind called *mambeli* at his waist as well,
but he would be unlikely to use it on such an occasion as this.
The fighting was accompanied by much shouting—names of
kings and princes and challenges.

What happened next depended on the outcome of this fight.
If the warriors in ambush had the better of it and killed or
wounded several of the pursuers, the latter retreated; and then
the victors, having gleaned their spears and knives and those
of the enemy, retreated through the second and third ambushes
to the prince, leaving the men of these ambushes to hold their
positions for a while to ensure that the enemy did not resume
their pursuit. Spears which had been taken on their shields
belonged to the prince. If they had penetrated the shields they
were pulled out from the inside, otherwise from the outside. If
a man had hurled a spear at one of the enemy and missed him,
he would retrieve it when they retired. This was his own. If he
hit the enemy's shield it would stick in it, and the enemy would
retreat with it and later hand it over to his prince. However, if
the pursuers got the better of the encounter, the men of the first
ambush fled with the enemy after them. They ran through the
second ambush, where the enemy would be held by the men
of that ambush and the action would be repeated, except that
a token exchange of spears might be thought sufficient by the
pursuers. The pursuers would not go beyond this second ambush. They were not numerous enough nor prepared for serious
fighting. Nor had they instructions from their ruler to risk a
larger engagement. Furthermore, they knew that the enemy
had consulted the poison oracle before embarking on their raid
and had learnt from it that they would not be defeated or suffer
heavy casualties. They would say that it was not their day; that
would come later in a return raid. They had fought; honour was
satisfied.

The warriors of the second ambush then retired, having
gleaned the spears and knives, to the prince, leaving the third
ambush in position to await the prince's order to withdraw; or
if the enemy did not pursue as far as the second ambush its
warriors retired after a short wait to where the prince was.

After another short interval the prince ordered the third ambush
to withdraw, and then the whole force went back to the homestead at which they had originally assembled. The raid was of
short duration. The attack took place about dawn. The first
ambush was in action about sunrise or even earlier, the second
returned to their prince about 6.30 to 7, and the third about

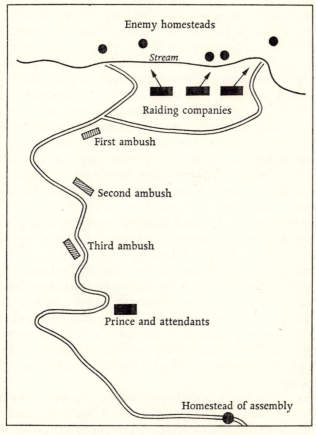

Enemy homesteads

Stream

Raiding companies

First ambush

Second ambush

Third ambush

Prince and attendants

Homestead of assembly

SKETCH II. DIAGRAM OF A RAID.

7.30 to 8. On arrival at the homestead the warrior companies
whirled in circles (*gbidi*) round their prince, singing war-songs.
Then the raiding party escorted the prince back to his court. He

retired to his private quarters while the warriors rested in his court. In the late afternoon he sent out porridge and a seasoning to them; and then in the evening he came into court and sat on a stool or on a skin spread for him on the ground by his page to listen to a detailed account of the raid, hearing of the exploits of each warrior from the company commanders (*sia pa vura*), and asking whether any of them were cowards. Cowardice in the face of the enemy was punished. If a whole company fled, the prince might impose a collective fine of spears on them, and if an individual fled while his company stood their ground he would be fined. Ngawe of the Akpura clan, the spy mentioned earlier, paid ten spears to Prince Ndukpe because he rubbed his shield in earth so that its white centre (*bangili e*) would not be a conspicuous target for spear or rifle. A brave man rubs it with oil to make it shine. Later the same man paid a fine of twenty spears to Prince Gangura for having left the field without permission during the Mayawa campaign fought by King Gbudwe against the Belgians. A worse fate sometimes befell *akaratiru*, 'run-aways'. They were mutilated. A man called Liani, of the Amego clan, ran away in the middle of a fight in Gbudwe's campaign against the Dervishes at Belikiwe and was mutilated by order of Prince Bagbandara. His hands, genitals, and ears were cut off, his lips being spared so that he could tell people the cause of his punishment.

When the company commanders had made their reports, each warrior who had taken a spear on his shield stood up and laid it before the prince and boasted of his prowess and threatened the enemy (*selekpo vura*). Also, each man who had taken spoil, loot from the raided homesteads, and enemy weapons, having first shown them to his company commander in the court, placed them on the ground before the prince, to whom they belonged.

When the prince received captured women and children he asked the women which were their clans, and when each told him the name of her clan someone present would claim her as a sister. If the prince took the woman to wife he would regard this man as standing to him in an in-law relationship; and if he gave her to a commoner, she would visit her kinsman from time to time *in loco parentis* and her husband would perform certain duties of an in-law towards his family, such as burying their dead, helping them in cultivating and building, and even paying bride-spears if she remained long with him. These *akanga vura*, 'slaves of war', were thus not regarded very differently from ordinary wives, their main disability being that they had no family or close kin to turn to in times of trouble. I was told that they very rarely ran away, whereas captured boys often made their way back to their homes when they grew up. The prince sent some, if not all, of the captured women to his father the king. He had the captured weapons tied in bundles (*vodivodi baso*). Some of these he sent with the women to the king, the rest he retained for distribution to his warriors on some future occasion. A prince gives spears and throwing-knives to his followers to fight his wars with them, and what weapons they take from the enemy belong to him because the battle was fought with his spears and knives. Azande emphasize that this is so.

Finally, the prince walked past the ranks of any company which had distinguished itself and gave them the war-song (*sima*), to which they responded. When the warriors departed to their homes they sang these war-songs on the way; and when each returned to his home he spent the rest of the evening boasting to his family of his exploits and telling them all about the fight; and his womenfolk would sympathize with him and say, *nailiwo akumba?*, 'are not men terrible?' and congratulate him on his escape from death or injury.

4

I now turn to a consideration of the campaign. It can be brief, partly because some of the general points which have been made apply to both raids and campaigns, and partly because our information about campaigns is limited. The *sungusungu avura* fought by King Gbudwe during the thirty-seven or so years of his reign will be recounted later.[1] Some accounts of Zande large-scale fighting are also to be found in the writings of travellers and of Belgian officers.

These *sungusungu avura* are so called because they were 'sit-down' or 'waiting' (*sungu*), that is, long-drawn-out affairs, in

---

[1] See Chaps. XV and XVI.

contrast to *basapu*, a word which seems to be derived from the verb *sara*, 'to crack' or 'to burst', which suggests something sudden and quickly over. A campaign differed from a raid not only in duration but, as we shall see, in other respects, particularly in the size of the forces engaged and in tactics.

It was not easy to mobilize a whole kingdom secretly or to surprise the enemy with its army. If it were one Zande kingdom attacking another, news of the mobilization of the aggressor was likely to reach the ears of the other party. What could be kept secret was the point at which the attack would be launched. When a king got news of the mobilization of a neighbouring kingdom and had reason to believe that his territories were to be invaded, he sent messengers to his provincial governors to warn them to be ready to act if necessary and to tell those on the frontier to keep a sharp look-out for signs of enemy activity. Then, as soon as the enemy appeared on the frontier the people on the invaded section of it gave the alarm, and as already described, all the provinces along that frontier mobilized. The king was at once informed that an attack had begun and that there was no doubt but that it was on the scale of a campaign. He then mobilized the warriors of his own central province and sent messengers to his governors of provinces in other parts of his kingdom to order them to mobilize their forces and proceed with them to the area of operations. He then went with his own warriors to support the forces of his marcher lords and to direct the movements of the total manpower of his kingdom.

A king who intended to attack another's kingdom sent messengers to his governors instructing them to mobilize their companies and then to meet him at a certain place and as quickly as possible. This took some time, as some of the provinces were at a considerable distance from the royal court; and those who were most distant arrived later than those who were nearer. There was no attempt at concealment of these preparations. On the contrary, before a war was launched there would be demonstrations at the king's court, and possibly in the courts of provincial governors also, which served to stimulate enthusiasm and hostile intention. This was known as *selekpo vura*, the making of long and boastful speeches threatening the rulers of neighbouring territories or foreign enemies, at Gbudwe's court usually the Arabs. The king himself, such of his sons or

commoner governors who were at court, and Gbudwe's elder
courtiers and leaders of companies made these speeches, which
might continue through the night till Gbudwe retired at dawn.
The scene was described to me thus. Gbudwe is seated and his
subjects are seated in a semicircle around him. One of his men,
such as the commander of a company of unmarried warriors,
steps forward, carefully arranges his barkcloth, and commences
his speech:

Gbudwe, Gbudwe, son of Bazingbi, do not hear cases today; leave
off thinking of smaller matters. Gbudwe, by your limb, by your
limb I will not desert you. If war comes here, I will not survive it;
I will die here in front of your stool. Gbudwe, Roko, son of Bazingbi,
I will never leave you to go and pay service to the cropped-heads
[the Arabs], I will never leave you to serve Wando, to serve Malingindo, to serve the children of Ezo or the children of Nunga. By your
head and your limb, why should I? For they are not greater kings
than you. Why should I leave you for those cropped-heads who have
come here to steal your land? Why should I leave you for the
Avongara? Are there any among them more kingly than you? No,
son of Bazingbi, I will stay here, I will not move from your side. By
the bones of your father Bazingbi, if the sky comes down to fight you,
or if the earth leaps up to wage war on you, I will remain near your
stool. Gbudwe, Gbudwe, Gbudwe, you put me at the head of your
war-company. I did not place myself there. I am here because of
you. You give us spears and we will drive them away. Who says that
I will desert you for another? Who says that I will desert your sons
in their time of trouble? Basongoda is over there [pointing in the
direction of their provinces], Mange is over there, Borugba is there,
Gumba is there, Kana is there, Ndukpe is there; I will not fly from
them in time of trouble, but I will remain with them to face death
just as I would face death for you. When you see the cropped-heads
here in your court you will know they have come, but I will die first.
And what if I die? Gbudwe, by your limb, I will not let these
cropped-headed little barbarians get by. Great king, send me that
we may fight them. You will not see wounds in my back, you will
see them on my chest. I swear by the head of your father Bazingbi,
do not suffer them.

Gbudwe would wait for a pause and would then say:

You speak well. I will not suffer them. By the limb of Bazingbi, by
the limb of Bazingbi, I will not suffer them. Indeed, you speak truly.
The cropped-headed little barbarians will not seize the forearms of

my wives. When I hear the fowls crying out *kio kio* and the dogs barking *gbo gbo* I myself will rush out and fight them on the ridge [*nduka*] of my homestead. You wish to fight, you want me to give you spears to chase these barbarians with them. Very well, I agree. They have guns; so have I. When Bazingbi gave me this country he did not give it to me for me to lose it. I will defend the heritage of my father and of my grandfather Yakpati. They did not conquer their kingdom by sloth but by the strength of their right hands. By my limb, you are right. So you are men! Truly they say that men are good. If someone takes all your wives from you, you may still live, though you are poor in the company of your friends; and then one of your friends will beget a daughter to give you in marriage.

And so forth. Such demonstrations were not held before raids lest the enemy hear about them and the advantage of surprise be lost.

At such demonstrations the king distributed spears, of the kinds called *andigba* and *bagbeagine*, to his warriors, and his governors did likewise to their warriors; and they might distribute throwing-knives (*kpinga*) and curved daggers (*mambele*) also. King Gbudwe had a stock of war spears in his homestead, and he went with his pages to select some bundles of them for distribution, which he made with his own hand, commencing with the senior of his companies, the Abaigo.

Gbudwe used to distribute bundles of some five spears to his leading warriors, calling each forward by name; and later the recipients would give some of them to their relatives. He then began to hand out single spears freely to the other warriors, who, when they saw that the spears were running out, edged in nearer and nearer, and it sometimes happened at Gbudwe's court that they fell on the spears on the ground or tried to seize them from the hands of those who had already received them or of the king's pages or even of the king himself (*i na somia ka de e*). Confusion resulted, and Gbudwe would tell his pages to run with his spears into his private quarters, but the men at court would chase them and take the spears from them. A Zande told me that he had seen Gbudwe on such an occasion take a big stick and start belabouring his warriors with it and that when his pages saw their master beating his subjects they began to beat them too. My informant said that Gbudwe became annoyed if the distribution turned into too much of a riot.

A Zande described the scene thus:

When Gbudwe wanted to make war on anyone he appeared in
court at sunrise, and he gave porridge to the men there; and when
they had eaten the porridge he appeared with tied-up bundles of
spears, about ten of them. He then called up first the Abaigo company, and he threatened war before them, first of all about Ndoruma
[his neighbour to the west] vehemently, saying that if Ndoruma
came to make war they were not in any circumstances to let him be.
Then he broke off his threats about Ndoruma and told them to go
and make war on whatever king it might be. Then he distributed the
war spears, first to the Abaigo, and when they had all received spears
the remaining companies all rushed in towards Gbudwe.[1]

The distributed spears belonged for good to those who received them, but they could be used only for fighting, not for
marriage. The warriors had also their own spears in addition
to those the king gave them.

It need hardly be said that a king did not make war on
another kingdom without first consulting the poison oracle,
which had to determine whether the war would be successful,
where and when the attack should be launched, and which
companies of his own forces had witchcraft hanging over them
that would cause them casualties if exposed in the front of the
battle; and each move in the campaign was submitted to the
oracle for its approval before it was taken. In a sense the war
was between two sets of oracles, each directing the moves of
its army—we are reminded of the part played by the augury in
the tactics of ancient Rome. It is amusing to read in Lotar's
account of the Belgian patrol against Renzi, son of Wando, of
the Belgians' astonishment and irritation when the patrol was
constantly delayed while Ukwe, Renzi's brother and their ally,
consulted his oracle. Delanghe, the leader of the patrol, wrote:

Le 19 [April, 1894], on continuait la marche, pour camper, les
20 et 21, au village de Basugbwa, où Ukwa consultait son 'benge'
pour savoir si Renzi ou lui prendrait l'offensive. . . . On m'annonça
que des colonnes ennemies manifestaient l'intention de nous attaquer
par le N.-O., par le Nord et par l'Est. Je pris des mesures, mais les
sentinelles ne me renseignaient rien. Ukwa, encore une fois, fit
'parler ses poules' pendant plusieurs heures. . . . Le 24, le ciel était
couvert et menaçant. Ukwa prétexta la pluie qui semblait

[1] See also p. 206.

s'approcher pour attendre et il s'en alla dans la brousse 'faire parler ses poules'. . . . [Ukwa] fit répondre qu'il demandait à ses poules de désigner les meilleurs chemins pour partir au combat et pour que nos soldats ne fussent pas blessés. [The question of negotiating with Renzi was discussed with Ukwe, who] réfléchit longuement et alla faire le benge avec le sorcier de Renzi.[1]

Each governor consulted the oracle about the companies of his own forces. Also, any man had a right to consult the poison oracle about his own welfare and that of his brothers and sons during the campaign to discover whether the fate (*pa*) of any one of them was threatened. He first took a fowl to his family as a whole and then, if the fowl died, he took a fowl to each adult male member in turn and consulted the oracle with it. If the fowl died to one of them he told the king or prince, and that man would be permitted to remain with his master in the rear of the fighting. However, it is probable that only important elders did this. I was told that a man had sometimes to restrain by force a son or brother, to whose name a fowl had died, to prevent his going into the fighting, for no one liked to be left behind when his comrades went to fight.

The king's oracle determined the movements of the entire army, and he was commander-in-chief in the field. The army he directed was composed of the force of his own province and the forces of the other provinces of his realm, each of these forces operating as a unit and under command of the provincial governor from whose province they came; and each of these battalions, if we may so call them, was made up of companies of older and younger warriors, each company having a commander and being composed, as I have earlier explained, of a nucleus of 'regulars' to which were attached for military operations men who in ordinary circumstances belonged to no company. The king drew up the order of battle and told his governors what positions they were to take up and in what order they were to attack. Each governor then decided for himself, within the framework of the king's order of battle, the dispositions and tactics of the companies constituting his own force and instructed his commanders accordingly. The governors accompanied their warriors, though usually slightly in the rear of them, and the king's own force took up a supporting position.

[1] Op. cit., 1946, pp. 190–3.

PLATE IV

Warrior with shield

This was the procedure in Gbudwe's army, and I believe that it was the same in the armies of other Zande kings. A Zande text runs:

When Gbudwe wanted to make war he sent his sons in the first place to make it. If it proved too much for them he sent ahead his Abaigo company to take part in it. But it might happen that the Abaigo were defeated by the enemy, and not the enemy by them; and should the Abaigo continue to be unsuccessful it might mean that Gbudwe would lose the war. He never began his part in the fighting in the morning, but only in the evening; for the princes used to start the fighting before the subjects of Gbudwe; and if they were unsuccessful he sent his subjects into it in the evening and they fought till dusk. They withdrew in the morning. But when there was prolonged fighting they continued it in the morning. Such was the war he fought with Renzi in the wood called Karikai. In it Gbudwe's subjects had burnt the huts of a man called Ngatuo, though they did not kill him; and Renzi's subjects killed Mai, one of Gbudwe's commoner governors, which grieved Gbudwe greatly. However, he routed the subjects of Renzi with his many men. Renzi then was afraid of Gbudwe and his warriors. [In fact, Gbudwe's army was defeated at Karikai.]

As a campaign might last for several days, or even weeks, some commissariat arrangements, however crude, were necessary. No one took food on a raid, for it lasted only a few hours, except that a page might carry a small pot of beer for the prince. But when summoned to take part in a campaign, warriors from distant provinces, such as those ruled by Mange and Rikita in the kingdom of Gbudwe, brought enough food, chiefly a kind of bread, to last them for many days. Those whose provinces were nearer to the area of operations brought less food, and when it was exhausted they returned home to collect new supplies. However, it appears that the warriors were always short of food and that they very largely lived on the country. The invading army took away any food they found in captured homesteads. The defenders also, if they were very hungry, helped themselves to anything they found in the homesteads in the vicinity of the fighting, and this caused a good deal of unpleasantness between the men of the province where the fighting was taking place and the companies from other provinces. In the war Gbudwe fought against Renzi, his army ate up everything they could lay their hands on in his son Bafuka's province—ground-nuts, oil, fowls, and even standing crops in the cultivations. They did the same in Bafuka's province in an earlier war, the one Gbudwe fought against King Wando. A campaign could cause a famine in the district in which it took place. In the provision of food each warrior looked after himself. There was no organized commissariat. Some men brought their wives with them to the camp (*limbasa*) to cook for them; and in the camp each warrior erected a temporary hut of the kind called *dondoma*. But though a warrior might have his wife with him and they slept in the same hut, sexual relations were strictly prohibited during a campaign. Princes and commanders of companies wore special girdles signifying that they were in a state of taboo with regard to women. They slept either by themselves or with boys. Piaggia, in the passage I am about to quote, remarks that some women accompanied the warriors to the field; and Junker makes the same observation.[1]

The only European who witnessed a battle between Azande was Carlo Piaggia. His brief description is therefore of some interest.

Si recano alla guerra soltanto gli uomini e quelle poche donne, le più audaci, che non vogliono abbandonare i loro mariti o gli amanti; le altre fuggono a nascondersi per tema di essere preda dei nemici nel caso riuscissero vincitori. I combattenti sono armati di freccie, di lance e di coltelli fatti a mo' di falce; è raro che le battaglie si prolunghino molte ore e che vi sia molta strage; chè appena in uno dei campi si veggono cinque o sei uomini caduti morti, i combattenti presi da sgomento si danno alla fuga e quelli dell'opposta fazione restano vincitori, e così i medesimi, dopo qualche rappresaglia, soddisfatti tornano tranquillamente alle loro abitazioni — Più accanite poi sono le zuffe che avvengono con tribù straniere; e allora spingono la sete di vendetta fino a divorarsi le carni degli uccisi, ed il Piaggia in una di queste guerre ne fu testimonio: d'onde par sia venuto loro la trista celebritá de cannibali.[2]

But if no European other than Piaggia witnessed a Zande battle, we have a number of accounts of fighting between Azande and Arabs and between Azande and Europeans. The tactics employed on these occasions appear to have been the

---

[1] Op. cit., vol. ii, 1892, p. 17.
[2] Antinori, op. cit., p. 124. See also L. Pellegrinetti, op. cit., p. 290.

same as those I was told were invariably used when Azande
fought each other. They were very simple. The companies advanced in file, *abakumba* and riflemen leading, and then extended
company by company when in contact with the enemy, but
though the extension was in company formation, the men of
adjacent companies tended to get mixed up once the fighting
began. Each side had its centre and two wings; and the aim
was to get round or push back the enemy's flanks and then to
assail the centre from all sides. It would seem that the decisive
action was between the wings of the armies, for if a wing gave
ground the centre was enveloped. However, I was told that
since the aim was to get the enemy to withdraw so that victory
might be claimed with as little loss on your side as possible you
usually avoided complete encirclement (*kenge aboro*), for if the
enemy was unable to withdraw they would, seeing that there
was no hope, sell their lives as dearly as they could. You therefore left a gap in the rear. Moreover, there was a further convention, that fighting should begin well into the afternoon so
that those who were getting the worse of it could withdraw under
cover of darkness. This convention was, however, often not
observed.

A battle consisted of individual combats between warriors on
either side all along the line and at short range, usually only a few
yards separating the combatants, for the spear had to pierce a
man's shield before it could pierce the man. The throwing-knife
doubtless carried further, though it may not have been so effective a weapon because it probably met with greater resistance
from the texture of the shield. I fancy that its effect was as much
psychological as physical. I used to practise with it when I was
among the Azande and I learnt to throw it with considerable
force and accuracy. When correctly thrown, one of its several
blades was certain to strike the objective squarely, and the sight
of the blades circling towards one in the air must have been
frightening. The Zande shield, however, protected two-thirds
of the body, and when a man crouched behind it, as he did if a
spear or knife was aimed high, his body was fully covered. If
the missile came at him low, he jumped into the air with
remarkable agility to let it pass under him. I have not, of course,
myself seen a Zande battle, but men have demonstrated to me
with old shields or ones I had made for me, how they moved in

fighting, and it was a most impressive display in the art of self-defence, in the movements of the body to give the fullest protection of the shield, and in the manipulation of the shield to take the spear or throwing-knife obliquely. The hurling of weapons and the taking of them on the shield were accompanied by shouting the names of the kings of the parties involved. When the combatants had exhausted most of their weapons they withdrew to a safe distance where they challenged and insulted each other, as Schweinfurth noted was customary.[1]

I have already quoted Schweinfurth's admiration of the Zande's skill in the use of his weapons. Another writer, Col. C. Chaillé Long, has described how in a fight with the Yanbari (? Nyangbara) he let loose his Azande (Adio or Makaraka Azande) on them:

I confess that I never saw a more perfect ideal of the warrior, not alone in muscular display, but in the bounding élan with which he flew rather than ran—the right hand grasping the huge knife, while with bouclier pressed closely to his side, he met the enemy. Covering his body with it with wonderful quickness from the deadly arrows, that his adversary in vain expended upon the broad shield, he threw himself upon him and cut and stabbed the defenceless Yanbari to death. They burnt at least twenty villages and then ate the enemy dead.[2]

The huge knife referred to is doubtless the scimitar the Azande of this region fought with.

The introduction of rifles (including muskets) led to a change in tactics in campaigns—they did not play so important a part in raids, owing to the time and nature of the fighting. The rifleman was exposed and therefore avoided coming within range of spear or throwing-knife. He crept through grass or undergrowth to within rifle-range of the enemy and then, keeping cover, took careful aim at his man; after firing he ran to the rear or to cover elsewhere to get in another shot. These hit-and-run tactics of the few riflemen probably caused as many deaths and wounds as all the spears and knives. The result was that when rifles began to be used the old more or less hand-to-hand fighting tended, at any rate in the first phase of the action, to

---

[1] *The Heart of Africa*, vol. ii, 1873, pp. 22–3.
[2] Col. C. Chaillé Long, *Central Africa: Naked Truths of Naked People*, 1876, pp. 286–7.

give way to distant exchange of shots, the spearmen keeping out of range or under cover till ammunition was exhausted. Azande had already learnt to be more cautious before Europeans arrived on the scene and they soon became discouraged when they suffered heavy rifle casualties. Belgian accounts of their fights with Azande on the whole confirm the comment of a British writer: 'They will make two or three fierce attacks on a position, and if unsuccessful will abandon the assault.'[1] On the other hand, Burrows, who had opportunities to observe Zande behaviour under fire, speaks highly of it:

Their courage is admirable, their contempt for death supreme. They will stand to a fire that is dropping them by dozens, charging time after time until absolutely compelled to retire. Coming upon seven or eight men armed with rifles, they throw away their own arms and rush their opponents, though they may lose twenty or thirty men in the attempt. They are quite prepared to lose them, knowing that ultimately the guns will be theirs.[2]

The Belgians, who fought a series of battles with Azande, notably against the followers of Mbili son of Malingindo, Ndoruma son of Ezo, and Renzi son of Wando, soon discovered the Zande tactic of encirclement and made their dispositions accordingly. Chaltin wrote in an account of his patrol against Mbili (29 March 1896): 'A ce moment l'avant-garde signale quantité d'Azande armés. On prend la seule position de combat possible en pays zande, où l'ennemi a pour tactique d'envelopper de toutes parts l'adversaire. Un front, deux flancs et mon escorte à l'arrière.' As the patrol continued its advance with the intention of attacking Ndoruma, it was attacked by two to three thousand Zande spearmen: 'Suivent leur invariable tactique, les Azande ont combiné leur attaque de front avec deux attaques de flanc et un mouvement offensif sur nos arrieres.'[3]

Azande in their struggles among themselves and against the Arabs and Belgians endeavoured to deprive the enemy of all food supplies. On the approach of the enemy, women and children took refuge in woods and marshes with as much of their goods and food reserves as they could carry, and a king

---

[1] *The Bahr El Ghazal Province Handbook*, Anglo-Egyptian Sudan Handbook Series, 1, 1911, pp. 35–6.

[2] G. Burrows, 'On the Natives of the Upper Welle District of the Belgian Congo', *Journal of the Royal Anthropological Institute*, 1899, p. 43.

[3] Lotar, op. cit., 1946, pp. 241 and 242–3.

sometimes gave orders for all huts and granaries in the path of the enemy to be burnt.[1] This was particularly effective against Arab caravans and Belgian patrols, for, since they could not live on the country, they had to take their victuals with them as well as their ammunition and, in the case of the Arab traders, their trade goods and ivory. This made them more than ever vulnerable in a strange land whose hostile inhabitants knew every inch of the country; for the porters, being entirely defenceless, naturally dropped their loads if ambushed and sought instant flight, thereby causing panic and disorder among the troops. We learn also from Belgian sources that, to force the enemy to use the paths and hence both to restrict his power of movement and to facilitate the laying of an ambush, Zande kings would prohibit the burning of the bush grasses.[2]

I do not think that Zande armies could ambush each other, and the accounts we have of Zande wars among themselves do not mention that their armies were ever ambushed. Apart from the fact that the wars seem to have been fought, at any rate usually, in the dry season after the grasses had been burnt, it is most unlikely that their scouts could have failed to spot an ambush on the scale required. If this is so, the ambushes they so successfully laid for Arabs and Belgians must have been an adaptation of the *basapu* ambushes. The enemy was armed with rifles and, therefore, to be defeated, had to be surprised at short range. But though better armed, he was both ignorant of the country and impeded by porterage and equipment. Advantage was taken of high grass or forest, the dense streamside forest to which Piaggia gave the name 'gallery forest'. In this way Ndoruma, son of Ezo, and Malingindo and Gbudwe, sons of Bazingbi, waylaid in ambush and defeated Arab columns; and Mbili, son of Malingindo, massacred the Bonvalet–Devos patrol in 1894; and Ndoruma, son of Ezo, massacred the Janssens–Van Holsbeek patrol in 1895. Schweinfurth has described how the Arab columns were ambushed in gallery forests, the Azande concealing themselves in bushes and behind trees, while others lay full length on branches overhanging the path to strike at the enemy from above.[3]

---

[1] Lotar, op. cit., 1946, pp. 185–8 and 190. Also Hutereau, op. cit., 1922, p. 202.
[2] Lotar, op. cit., 1946, p. 238.
[3] *The Heart of Africa*, vol. ii, 1873, pp. 236–7 and 308.

But unless the Arab or European-led troops could be ambushed the Azande were almost certain, at any rate once these enemies had modern rifles, to be defeated by them or at least suffer heavy casualties at their hands. The spear is not an effective weapon at a range of more than some twenty yards, and a rifle bullet has, of course, far greater range and impact, and shields are little protection against it. It is true that the Azande also had rifles, but they were few in comparison, were for the most part of an inferior sort, and were in the hands of men not well trained to make the most effective use of them. The only other feasible tactic, attack by night, seems never to have been practised. Consequently the Azande were in the end, in spite of their numerical superiority and the strenuous resistance of some of their kings, everywhere compelled to submit.

The gun had an even greater advantage over the spear when fired from shelter. Arabs, Egyptian troops, and Belgian patrols therefore added to their superiority of fire by constructing forts. From Zande descriptions of these, they consisted of high palisades of stakes against which earth was heaped. The Arabs called such a fort a *zeriba* and the Azande a *gbata*. Junker describes those erected by Egyptian Government troops in the Azande–Makaraka country: 'All were for the most part defended by strong palisades—two enclosures of stout stakes, the intervening space of about three feet being filled in with logs and thorny scrub.'[1] When Azande attacked these forts they suffered severe casualties, for all they could do was to lop their spears blindly over the palisades, and to do this necessitated coming into full view of the enemy and at close range. A British authority says that they have been known to fire buildings with lighted grass attached to arrows;[2] but no evidence in support of this statement is advanced, and I doubt its accuracy, especially as true Azande did not use bows and arrows, as the same authority recognizes in agreement with all those best acquainted with the Azande. Sometimes Azande simply besieged these forts, attacking the enemy when they attempted forays for food and water, but a strong force well equipped with rifles could always break out to obtain supplies or to lay waste the country

[1] Op. cit., vol. iii, 1892, p. 340.
[2] *The Bahr El Ghazal Province Handbook*, Anglo-Egyptian Handbook Series, 1, 1911, p. 35.

whenever they wished to do so. An enemy fortified and with overwhelming superiority in fire was too much for the Azande.

We may inquire how heavy were the casualties in these wars. It is impossible to give even approximate estimates. King Gbudwe had fought his last war more than twenty years before I began my study of the Azande of his kingdom. But apart from the dimming of detail in the memories of those who took part in his wars, there was the insuperable difficulty that probably few knew the total casualties suffered even at the time of the event. A Zande kingdom covered an extensive tract of territory and a man might be entirely unacquainted with people in provinces other than his own; and during a battle he for the most part observed only what was happening to the warriors of his own province and would know only what casualties they had suffered. I can only say, therefore, that I believe on the basis of what information I was given that, even in the days when there were but few rifles, casualties may have been high in relation to the numbers engaged in conflict, though it is impossible to prove this. Piaggia, in the passage quoted earlier, states the contrary, but he may have witnessed only skirmishes, perhaps of the order of raids. Azande say that very many were killed in their wars, and anyone who has read the books of de Calonne and Hutereau must have remarked on the large number of kings and princes who were killed in battle. I think this can be taken as an indication of high mortality because, though there were notable exceptions, kings and princes remained in the rear of the fighting and were therefore the least exposed to risk. Schweinfurth remarks: 'The chieftains very rarely lead their own people into actual engagement, but are accustomed, in anxious suspense, to linger about the environs of the "mbanga" [court], ready in the event of tidings of defeat, to decamp with their wives and treasures.'[1]

Schweinfurth was here, I think, placing too much trust in his Arab informants or giving way to fancy; but it is nevertheless true that the rulers were less exposed to danger than their followers. When rifles became more numerous, casualties probably increased, though here again, no figures can be given. All Zande accounts of the wars Gbudwe fought against

[1] *The Heart of Africa*, vol. ii, 1873, p. 22.

Wando, Renzi, the Egyptian Government, the Dervishes, and
the Belgians describe the casualties as having been 'like grass'.
They were undoubtedly high also in the fighting between Wando
and Malingindo and in the wars fought by such western Zande
monarchs as Zemoi, Mopoi, and Sasa against neighbouring
kingdoms. However, the only reliable figures we have are in
Belgian records of the victories and defeats they experienced
in fighting Zande armies. When Mbili's men attacked the
Bonvalet–Devos patrol in 1894, both Belgian leaders and almost
all their escort of 50 riflemen were killed.[1] In the same year
Christiaens in a punitive patrol against Mbili killed 150 of his
warriors.[2] Also in the same year Delanghe, aided by Prince
Ukwe, attacked Renzi's camp and killed 100 of his men.[3] In
1895, when Francqui's patrol against Bafuka, consisting of 700
regular native soldiers, assisted by a contingent of King Zemio's,
was ambushed, 54 dead and 40 rifles were left on the field
and many of the troops were wounded.[4] In the same year,
when Ndoruma's men massacred the Janssens–Van Holsbeek
column, both Belgian officers and most of their men were
killed.[5] In Chaltin's expedition against Mbili and Ndoruma in
1896 a fight against Mbili's men caused them at least 400
casualties, dead and wounded, at the cost of 1 dead and a few
wounded on the Belgian side;[6] and in a further fight with
Ndoruma's men the Azande lost between 500 and 600 dead, to
the Belgians' 6 killed and 21 badly wounded.[7]

If possible, Azande carried away their dead and buried them
in their camp. If the enemy (of their own people) reached the
corpses first, they appear frequently to have mutilated them,
cutting off the ears or genitals or both and taking them back to
court as trophies. Whether the bodies of the dead were sometimes eaten or not—Azande had a reputation for cannibalism—
is a doubtful question, the settlement of which would require a
lengthy survey of the evidences. I may refer the reader to Renzo
Carmignani's *Il cannibalismo degli Asandè*, a recent discussion of
this question.[8]

[1] Lotar, op. cit., pp. 177–8.   [2] Ibid., p. 187.
[3] Ibid., p. 192.   [4] Ibid., pp. 209–11.
[5] Ibid., pp. 217–18.   [6] Ibid., p. 243.
[7] Ibid., p. 245.
[8] 1954. The evidences are further given in my paper 'Zande Cannibalism' in
The Journal of the Royal Anthropological Institute, 90, 1960.

5

We may ask in conclusion what was the object of Zande fighting? In the case of the raids it was, if I understood Azande correctly, little more than pride, the desire to display prowess and to have something to boast about. It is true that there was spoil, but the looting was less for the value of the things looted than for the loss their removal caused the enemy. The loot was brought home and displayed at court as a concrete sign of victory. A raid was successful if everything belonging to the enemy in the homesteads attacked was eliminated. When this could not be done by taking booty, as in the case of huts and granaries, these possessions were destroyed, for in the destruction of everything belonging to the subjects of a prince his prestige was lowered and that of his rival raised. The raids were not intended to bring about an occupation of the enemy's country (obviously on so small a scale they could not have achieved this). However, if we are to understand them sociologically we have to look beyond the apparent pointlessness of the border raids to their political action, which was, I would suggest, the expression, by this sort of demonstration, of loyalty to the prince who ruled a province and to the king in whose name he ruled; and hence they served to maintain the political order such as it used to be throughout Zandeland. The same may be said about the campaigns fought against kingdoms. A kingdom might be defined as a territory whose inhabitants fought the inhabitants of a like territory in the name and at the orders of some scion of the royal clan; and it was in war that the unity of a kingdom was best seen and expressed.[1]

[1] See also Chap. XVII.

PART FOUR

XIV

A HISTORICAL SKETCH

THE purpose of this introductory chapter to the fourth part of this book is to emphasize the extraordinary complexity of the facts. In the Preface I have discussed the literary evidences for Zande history and there is, therefore, no need to broach this question again. This chapter is intended to give the reader a general picture of the development of Zande history to enable him to follow more easily the detailed analysis of Gbudwe's kingdom which follows. Anthropological theory often rests on a basis of studies of primitive societies for which there is little recorded history. In the case of African kingdoms, such as those of the Azande, to leave out the historical dimension is to deprive ourselves of knowledge that is both ascertainable and necessary for an understanding of political organizations which have always, to a greater or lesser extent, been transformed by European rule before anthropologists have commenced their study of them, and which, furthermore, have been shaped by events that took place long before Europeans appeared on the scene. That the Azande had been expanding and, under the leadership of their Avongara ruling clan, conquering and assimilating dozens of foreign peoples, as well as taking part in a long series of dynastic wars among themselves, for at least 150 years before Europeans imposed their administrations is surely a fact which cannot be left out of consideration in a study of their institutions and culture.

Azande can give a fairly clear account of the main course of their history from the time of the sons of Tombo and Mabenge. Before that, the information they provide is sparse and has already become mixed with legendary tales that go beyond the credible. Indeed, some legend may have crept into later periods: de Calonne met many men who had known Junker and declared that they had seen him appear simultaneously in different places and cross rivers on small sticks;[1] but Junker was a remarkable phenomenon and certainly one outside Zande experience, and the fact that they credit him with miraculous feats need not weaken our faith in their historical traditions as a whole. I commence this chapter at the point at which these are adequate and, we have good reason to suppose, also reliable, leaving for future consideration what can be reconstructed from interpretation of legend and from ethnological analysis.

In this account I follow de Calonne unless it is stated otherwise. I do this for three reasons. First, because any one account is confusing enough, and to try to piece together every scrap of information in all the different accounts would make for such obscurity that such few general features as I wish to emphasize would be lost in a mass of intractable detail. Second, because de Calonne's account of Zande history, if not as full as Hutereau's, gives all the information required to bring these features into relief. Third, because in all important respects his account is also confirmed by Hutereau and other writers.

The distribution of the various branches of the Zande royal house of the Avongara at the time that French, Belgian, and Anglo-Egyptian forces took over and partitioned Zandeland early in the century is shown in de Calonne's map, a simplified version of which is reproduced on page 269. These branches are all descended from two sons of Ngura: Tombo and Mabenge. Tombo was born on the Fué, tributary of the Shinko, and was assassinated between the sources of the Mbili and the Bitakpo by his rebellious son Banzunguru (de Calonne says on another page that it was his son Yatwa). Mabenge was born on the Sere, tributary of the Shinko, and was assassinated on the Bugutandi, tributary of the Api-Uere, by Mako, his father's brother's son. The genealogy below shows the branches which established themselves as rulers in the areas differentiated in de Calonne's map (to which the numbers refer).

Not all the sons of persons in the genealogy may have been recorded, but certainly all those whose descendants made their mark in Zande history are recorded, and what tradition

[1] Op. cit., p. 9.

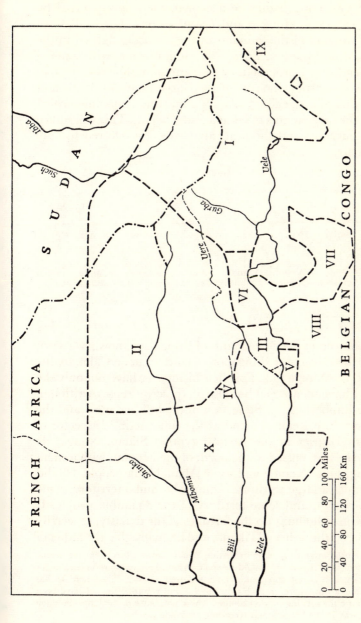

SKETCH 12. DISTRIBUTION OF AVONGARA DYNASTIES.

I. Under Avongara rule—Azande Ambomu
II.   ,,   ,,   ,,   Azande Anunga
III.   ,,   ,,   ,,   Azande Auro
IV.   ,,   ,,   ,,   Azande Apodyo

V. Under Avongara rule—Azande Amokuma
VI.   ,,   ,,   ,,   Azande Embili
VII.   ,,   ,,   ,,   Azande Abele

VIII. Abwameli (earlier invasions)
IX. Azande (not under Avongara rule)
X. Abandya

says of the sons of Tombo and Mabenge and of the descendants of these sons may readily be accepted, for it is supported by literary evidences. Junker and Casati were able to talk with some of the sons of the founders of the dynasties figured in the genealogy, and the first European administrators with some of their grandsons. I propose now to relate in outline the fortunes of the two dynasties who rule the two largest parts of Zandeland —those de Calonne calls the Anunga and the Ambomu—ruled over by the descendants of Nunga and Yakpati. This will suffice for our purpose; and the other dynasties are referred to only very briefly.

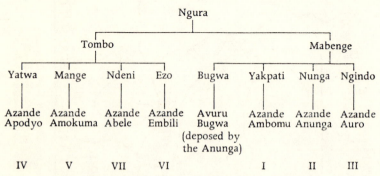

The subjects of the descendants of Nunga are known as Avuru Nunga, the subjects of Nunga, or, according to de Calonne, the Anunga, the Nunga folk. For their history we have not only the sources I have mentioned but also a typescript report written in 1911 by Bimbashi E. S. Stevenson of the 9th Sudanese and the Gloucestershire Regiment and at the time Acting Inspector of Tembura District in the Anglo-Egyptian Sudan. Nunga, de Calonne relates, passed to the north of the Mbomu with a small following, some Azande and some Abangbinda people. He did not conquer a large territory—some Abarambo territory, some Basiri territory, and some territory of the Apambia people. It was his sons who built up the fortunes of the dynasty, especially Zangabero,[1] the father of Tikima, and Bamvurugba, the father of

---

[1] I have used my own spelling in writing Zande names when it appears to me to be evident how the names should be spelt. When the names are unfamiliar or their construction is not apparent, I have followed Vanden Plas where he has recorded them, but where, in such cases, he has not recorded them I have been obliged to use the spellings of de Calonne, whose ignorance of the language often led him astray in the hearing and recording of Zande words.

Sanango (Schweinfurth's Solongoh). When Nunga died, four of his sons divided his kingdom between themselves: Bamvurugba's heritage was to the east, towards the present post of Tembura; Makisa's was between the Gara and a line situated to the west of the Duru (it was bounded to the south-east by the kingdom of Ezo son of Bazingbi); Yengo's was on the Mbomu to the south-west of the last; and Zangabero's was to the west of Yengo's.

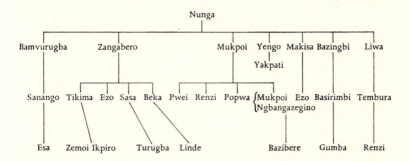

Liwa ruled a domain under the authority of his elder brother Bamvurugba, but on the suzerain's death he refused to recognize the authority of his son Sanango and emigrated with his followers to the east. At this point the Arab slavers and traders, and later the Egyptian Government, began to play a role in this western part of Zandeland. Sanango called in the Arabs to assist him, and Liwa was defeated, captured, and put to death with all but two of his sons, Tembura and Gadi, who were led away captives by the Arabs. After Sanango's death, the Arabs released these two youths, who, with Arab aid, attacked and killed Esa, Sanango's heir; and Tembura took his territories as well as those his father Liwa had conquered during his lifetime. Yengo and Makisa had frequent quarrels, in the course of which Yengo was wounded and taken prisoner. Makisa was also attacked by Sanango. Finally Makisa attacked Ezo son of Bazingbi of the dynasty of Yakpati. The history of the house of Nunga, like that of other Zande royal houses, is a chronicle of internecine warfare and assassinations. These dynastic struggles became fiercer and are more difficult to follow when armed bands of Zubeir's Arabs appeared on the scene as a dominant political influence in the generation of Nunga's grandsons. However, even in the generation of his sons, Junker tells us, intercourse and commercial relations had already been established with itinerant Arab traders from Darfur.[1]

Mukpoi (Mopoi) son of Nunga ruled a district in the territory of his brother Zangabero, on whose death he refused to recognize the authority of his son Tikima, though he accepted that of Tikima's son Zemoi Ikpiro, with whom he made exchange of blood. Shortly afterwards he died, killed, Hutereau reports his sons as declaring, by the treacherous Zemoi's sorcery.[2] Of his sons, Pwei had openly revolted against him and had been killed; and some of the others, led by Renzi, now fled from the Arabs assisting Tikima and took refuge with Makisa. Then the Arabs, led by Rafai, the lieutenant of Zubeir the slaver, installed in the old territory of Mukpoi, turned against Tikima and drove him to the west and continued their advance to the south and attacked Makisa, whose people fled to the country of Ndoruma son of Ezo of the Yakpati dynasty. Later Popwa made his submission to the Arabs and, aided by them, attacked Ndoruma, with whom he had quarrelled, and drove him towards the south-east. At the same time the Arab bands attacked Yengo and killed him. Ezo son of Makisa and Yakpati son of Yengo now followed Popwa's example and submitted to the Arabs and were re-installed in their conquered territories: Yakpati between the Dume and the Mbomu, Ezo in part of the old territories of Makisa, to the north of the Mbomu. Popwa was installed near Yakpati, but, finding his region unfertile, aided by his brother Mukpoi Ngbangazegino, he attacked Ezo, who defeated him. At this point the 'Agadia', Egyptian Government troops, intervened, attacked the partly Arabized Zande princes, put Popwa, Ezo, and Esa to flight, made Ezo prisoner, and killed Esa, replacing him by Tembura son of Liwa. This must have been after 1880, for Gessi records that Esa, whom he calls Tissa, was still reigning in that year, and Junker visited his country (he calls him Yissa) in the same year.[3] Mukpoi Ngbangazegino replaced Popwa and became preponderant in the at-one-time territory of Makisa. We hear no more of Popwa, who was later killed by the Dervishes on the Tangalia, tributary of the Mbomu.

[1] Op. cit., vol. iii, 1892, p. 264.   [2] Op cit., p. 200.
[3] Op. cit., p. 374; Junker, op. cit., vol. ii, 1891, p. 118.

In the meantime another power, Zemoi Ikpiro, was forming towards the north-west. We have seen that on the death of Zangabero, Mukpoi son of Nunga refused to recognize the authority of Tikima. Tikima's own brothers Ezo and Sasa also refused to recognize his authority and revolted against him. Ezo was killed. Sasa took his followers to the south of the Mbomu and installed himself on the Uere, where he was in Junker's time. Tikima, attacked by the Arabs, fled to Yengo; and finally he recrossed the Mbomu and, says de Calonne, probably submitted to the Arabs, though Hutereau says that he was captured and executed by them, his son Zemoi holding his uncle Sasa's sorcery responsible for his father's death.[1] It was this Zemoi who acquired a preponderance in the whole region. He possessed a great number of rifles, most of them given to him by Lupton Bey, then Governor of the Bahr al-Ghazal province, in 1883.[2] Through the power and prestige which accrued to him on account of them he attracted a numerous following. The two powers, Mukpoi Ngbangazegino and Zemoi, clashed, and Zemoi inflicted a bloody defeat on Mukpoi, who then turned south, crossed the Mbomu, and established himself to the south of the Uere.

At this time (round about 1885) the Avuru Nunga, the subjects of (the descendants of) Nunga, were grouped into five kingdoms: those of Tembura, Mukpoi, Yakpati, Sasa, and Zemoi. These were the reigning kings of the house of Nunga at the time Junker was in Zandeland in the early eighteen-eighties, and he has left us interesting descriptions of some of them. I give a short account of their fortunes, following de Calonne. Yakpati was captured somewhere between 1892 and 1896 and put to death on the orders of Sasa, who took his territories and put them under the dominion of his son Turugba. Sasa, who had been brought up by his elder brother Tikima, had, as we have noted, revolted against him and had crossed the Mbomu to install himself on the Uere. Attacked by Tikima and then by the Arabs of Rafai, he appealed for help to the Egyptian Governor of the Bahr al-Ghazal. He later fought many battles, chiefly with the Azande Embili, who followed Mange, son of Tombo, son of Ngura. He was finally overcome by the Belgians in 1911 and 1912, was captured and deported.

[1] Op. cit., p. 201.   [2] Ibid., p. 202; also Junker, op. cit., 1891, p. 98.

When Mukpoi Ngbangazegino was defeated by Zemoi he retired to the south. Zemoi, after his return from the Nile, to which he had accompanied a Belgian force against the Dervishes in 1897, inflicted a second defeat on him. He then abandoned his territories to the north of the Mbomu to one of his sons and asked asylum of Badinde son of Bugwa son of Mabenge who had retained a small territory to the south of the Uere. Mukpoi installed himself in it and then assassinated his host. Then the death of Mbili son of Malingindo son of Bazingbi and dissensions among his successors gave him an opportunity to seize part of Mbili's heritage. He also attacked and defeated Badinde's brother Palambata, who sought refuge with Zemoi. Mukpoi continued to worry all his neighbours till, in 1911, the Belgians forced him to flee to his old territories to the north of the Mbomu, where in 1915 he rebelled against the French, who shot him in a fight.

When Zemoi had driven Mukpoi to the south of the Mbomu he sought to conquer new territories. He crossed the Uere, defeating or subjugating all on his way, and he then continued his march to the south, crossed the Uele and, turning to the east, he subdued the Ababua people. Eventually, on the arrival of the Europeans, he retired to the banks of the Mbomu, leaving two of his sons as governors between the Uele and the Mbomu. He then accompanied Van Kerckhoven's expedition to the Nile and afterwards, as we have noted, again defeated Mukpoi Ngbangazegino, on the right bank of the Mbomu, and took from him the greater part of his northern territories. However, in the end, alarmed by the Belgian advances, he retired to the French Congo in 1910, taking part of his population with him.

Of the five rulers of the five kingdoms of the house of Nunga the only one who seems to have had, after his boyhood adventures, a moderately peaceful life was Tembura. When in February 1896 M. Liotard, representing the French Government, arrived at his court he was welcomed by the king, and a French post was established in his kingdom.[1] When the French withdrew, he equally welcomed Anglo-Egyptian forces. In his old age he drank so heavily as to be considered incapable of

[1] *The Bahr El Ghazal Province Handbook*, Anglo-Egyptian Handbook Series, 1, 1911, p. 58.

ruling, and in 1911 his son Renzi was put in charge of his kingdom.[1] He died in 1914.

The last son of Nunga shown in the genealogy whose fortunes
we have to follow is Bazingbi. Nunga sent him against the Basiri
people on the Kere, by whom he was killed. Zangabero avenged
his death but took his territories between the Kere and the
Mboku and gave them to his own son Beka, who brought up
Bazingbi's son Basirimbi. When this lad grew up he fled to the
Arabs, then to Sasa, then to Tembura, and finally to Zemoi, in
whose prisons he finished a life of intrigue.

If I have recorded so much detail as to make the brief account
I have given of the fortunes of the house of Nunga stodgy and
unpalatable I have left out much of the detail given by our
authorities; and such detail as has been recorded has been presented partly so that the reader can appreciate the complexity
of Zande history. Each kingdom has its own history, and it is a
tangled one. Kings and princes pursued their ways amid long
successions of wars, revolts, and assassinations. Hardly a prominent person died a natural death. Liwa and all his sons but two
were put to death by his nephew Sanango. Esa was killed by
Tembura. Yengo was killed by the Arab slavers, Popwa by the
Dervishes, Tikima by the slavers. Ezo was killed in fighting his
brother Tikima. Yakpati was executed by Sasa. Sasa was deported by the Belgians, Mukpoi Ngbangazegino assassinated
his host Badinde and was himself later shot by the French.
Bazingbi was killed by the Basiri people and his son Basirimbi
died in Zemoi's prisons. And while these dynastic wars and wars
with Arabs and Europeans were going on, new territories were
being conquered and their inhabitants dispersed or brought
into subjection, each new conquest adding to the ethnic confusion. Only a few of these peoples have been mentioned:
Abangbinda, Abarambo, Basiri, Apambia, and Ababua. There
were many more, even in the restricted area of Zandeland ruled
over by the house of Nunga: Akare, Mbegumba, Mberidi,
Huma, Basiri, Golo, etc. The ethnic and cultural complexity
resulting in the Zande kingdoms has been earlier recorded.[2]
And while kings battled with each other and murdered their
rivals and conquered and subjugated foreign neighbours there

[1] *Sudan Intelligence Report*, No. 210, 1912.
[2] See Chap. III and Part 2.

appeared on the scene, especially in the western kingdoms of the house of Nunga, the Arabs. They brought some of the Zande kingdoms into dependence on themselves and were drawn into Zande dynastic quarrels, turning them to their own advantage; and not one lot of Arabs but three, the slavers and traders, the forces of the Egyptian Government, and the Dervishes, all struggling among themselves as well; and in the south even a fourth lot, the Zanzibar Arab slavers. Finally the Europeans appear on the scene; and here again not one lot but three, French, Belgians, and British (Anglo-Egyptian); and they, whilst fighting the Dervishes and Zanzibar Arabs, as well as keeping a watchful, jealous eye on one another, also sought to subdue the Azande and to exploit dynastic rivalries to this end; and the Zande kings tried to use both them and the Arabs to advance their own interests. This, whilst being part of Zande history, is also part of the history of colonial expansion and of international history of the nineteenth and twentieth centuries.

A similar situation existed in varying degrees and forms in the kingdoms to the east of those I have been discussing, and a second example is sketched to show that this is the case. Most of the Ambomu followed the fortunes of Yakpati and his descendants,[1] and it is only in territories ruled over by Yakpati's heirs today that they are found in any numbers; and it is presumably for this reason that the inhabitants of these territories are known among Azande of other regions, as would appear from de Calonne's account to be the case, as Ambomu. In the area itself, however, the word does not refer to the entire population but only to those of true Ambomu stock in contrast to assimilated elements. This distinction between true Ambomu and assimilated foreigners may not be made in other parts of Zandeland. The details of the history of the dynasty of Yakpati are as complicated as those of the house of Nunga, and I have again omitted much of what de Calonne and Hutereau have recorded and, in this case, much of the considerable detail I recorded myself.

Yakpati was first installed on the Dume, tributary of the Uere, and he died on the Sueh. My own information is that his last court was at the junction of the Birasi and the Sueh and that he died on his way to repress a rebellion on the part of his son

[1] See Chap. I.

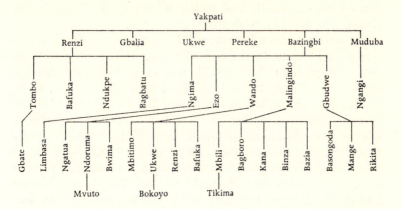

Ngindo and was buried on a small hill near the Magibitiki, tributary of the Ngomo, tributary of the Sueh. He and his sons conquered vast territories. His son Renzi, especially, was a famous warrior, who with his brothers and sons fought the Amadi, the Abangbinda, the Amiangba, the Abuguru, the Abaka, the Adio, and the Kakwa. He was killed—Azande say as a consequence of his father's curse on account of an insult—fighting the Amadi on the Mazugburu, tributary of the Sueh. His son Tombo or Bazugba sought to avenge his father but was also killed, on the Roi, tributary of the Sueh. Another son, Ndukpe, led his followers as far to the south-east as the Gangu, tributary of the Dungu, where he and very many of them died of plague (I was told, of famine). Azande told me that two other of Renzi's sons, Bafuka and Bagbatu, were killed in the fighting, which must have been very fierce, between Renzi's Azande and these foreign peoples especially the Amadi and their allies the Amiangba. The enormous territory conquered by Renzi, which stretched far to the east of the Ibba, passed, I was told, at his death and the deaths of his older sons to Ngangi, the son of his brother Muduba (also, de Calonne says, killed in fighting the Amadi), and to several of his brothers, Gbalia, Ukwe, Pereke, and others. All of these princes were eventually ousted either by Bazingbi's sons Gbudwe and Wando or by the Arab traders. The last of Renzi's line to have retained any authority seems to have been Gbate son of Tombo, who, Azande told me, allied himself to some Arab band to overcome the resistance of the

Amadi but eventually had to flee for refuge to Wando's son Renzi, who put him to death.

Bazingbi's position became much stronger after the death of Renzi, and eventually the entire heritage of Yakpati and of his other sons passed to his heirs. He was on the Salanga, tributary of the Uere to the east of the Hoko. His neighbour Bugwa son of Mabenge quarrelled with him and killed two sons of his son Wando and the mother of Wando's eldest son Mbitimo. Bazingbi attacked him, put him to flight, and killed his son Bali. Dynastic fights were rampant. Bazingbi also fought Kipa son of Ndeni, and his son Wando was constantly at war with princes of the house of Nunga. Bazingbi recalled Wando and placed him on the Dungu, tributary of the Gurba, and put another son, Malingindo to the west of the Gurba (where he fought with Wando), and he placed his son Ezo near the present post of Doruma.

As I record in the following chapter much of the more recent history of Bazingbi's descendants I give here only a brief summary of de Calonne's account. Bazingbi died on the Naguse, tributary of the Sueh, killed, it is believed, by the medicines of his eldest son Ngima, whom he had disinherited. Ngima sought to take his father's kingdom but was captured and mutilated by his brother Ezo. His son Limbasa avenged the indignity he had suffered by slaying Ezo. Gbudwe (Sukangi) overcame and killed Limbasa—I was told that Limbasa was murdered by Renzi son of Wando and Ngima by Ndoruma son of Ezo—whose people then submitted. Bazingbi had in his lifetime divided his kingdom between Ezo, Wando, and Malingindo; and Gbudwe now took over the country his father had retained in his own possession.

Ezo extended his domains by seizing part of the territories of Makisa of the house of Nunga. On his death Ndoruma became predominant among his sons. I was told that his territory was to the west of the Beki and that his brother Ngatua ruled to the east of that river and down to the Uere. Ndoruma defeated the Arab traders but was finally compelled to submit to the Egyptian Government. In 1896 he overwhelmed a Belgian column but was severely defeated by another column in the same year. His son Mvuto got Bazia son of Malingindo to assassinate his uncle Bwima and placed his own son Zemoi in

Bwima's territory. In 1910 the Belgians deported Zemoi. Mvuto murdered three other uncles besides Bwima.[1]

Wando subjugated the Amiangba of the Kapili and the Duru, the Abuguru on the tributaries of the same rivers, the Amadi on the Nambia (Mayawa), the Abaka of the Aka and the Garamba, and he then attacked the Bangba. I may add that he fought wars with his brothers Malingindo and Gbudwe and, I believe, the sons of Ezo also. Wando divided his kingdom during his lifetime among his sons Mbitimo, Ukwe, and Renzi. Mbitimo made an agreement with an Egyptian force to punish the Mabisanga people to the south of the Uele for the destruction of an Arab column, and he installed himself in their territory as their ruler in 1883. Renzi and Ukwe in the northern part of Wando's territory were at daggers drawn, and Ukwe was in addition in rebellion against his father, as we know from the writings of Junker, who tried to heal the breach between them in 1880.[2] Renzi allied himself to the Egyptians and later to the Mahdists; so Ukwe allied himself to the Belgians soon after they appeared on the scene in 1891. Renzi's brother Bafuka, to whom he had delegated the administration of his northern provinces, destroyed in 1894 a Belgian column but shortly afterwards both brothers submitted to the Belgians and Bafuka accompanied Chaltin in his march against the Mahdists at Rejaf in 1897, while Renzi aided Gérard to suppress the revolt of his nephew Bokoyo in 1898.

Malingindo in his lifetime divided his kingdom among his sons: Mbili on the Gurba, Bagboro on the Bwembi–Gurba, Binza on the Bafuka–Doruma route, Limbasa on the Buere, Tikima on the Dundu, Gbudwe on the Mangbwaru, tributary of the Buere. On his death Mbili took precedence and fought his nephews. In 1894 he massacred a Belgian column but was defeated by another two years later. On his death his son Tikima succeeded him, but he and his nephew, Migida, were attacked and killed by the people of Mukpoi Ngbangazegino of the house of Nunga. Mbili's brother Bazia then attempted to obtain predominance and harassed Kana, another brother. In the end the Belgians deported him.

When Gbudwe (son of Bazingbi) gained control over his

[1] Hutereau, op. cit., p. 167.
[2] Op. cit., vol. ii, 1891, p. 276.

father's personal domains to the west of the Yubo he set about subjecting the country to the east of the Sueh river at the expense of the last remaining descendants of Renzi, of Ngangi son of Muduba, and of the sons of Tombo son of Yakpati. This is recounted in the following chapter, as are also his fighting with foreign peoples, his kinsmen, and Arabs, Belgians, and British. He was shot by a British patrol in 1905 and died of wounds.

Some of the facts concerning the house of Yakpati have been presented in a highly condensed form as further illustration of the appalling confusion of the times. Whole peoples were raided and uprooted or passed under the Zande yoke: Amadi, Amiangba, Abuguru, Abaka, Adio, Bangba, Kakua, Mabisanga, Moro, Bongo, Jur, etc., a score of different peoples. There were the same ceaseless struggles between kings and princes, who stopped at nothing to attain their ends. Gbudwe, Ngangi, Malingindo, Wando, Ndoruma, the scions of the house of Nunga, etc. fought one another. Yakpati's son Ngindo rebelled against him and his son Renzi was in almost open revolt too. Bazingbi disinherited his son Ngima. Ukwe was in revolt against his father Wando. And there is the same history of murder and violent death. Renzi and his sons and nephews were killed by the Amadi. Bugwa killed two sons of Wando. Bazingbi killed one of Bugwa's sons. Renzi executed Gbate. Ngima was mutilated by Ezo and later murdered by Ndoruma. Limbasa slew Ezo. It is an endless story of bloodshed, of slayings and treachery. Well may Mgr. Lagae ask 'of how many murders of their kin have not the Avongara been responsible?'[1] Added to these rivalries and wars and murders among the Azande themselves were, as in the case of the house of Nunga, the intervention of the Arab traders, each company jealous of the others and all opposed to the Egyptian Government, which also sought to impose its rule over the Zande kingdoms, until it was itself overthrown by the Mahdists, whose columns also entered the Zande countries seeking to subjugate the inhabitants and adding further confusion. Then finally the Belgians from the south and the British from the north entered the domains of the dynasty of Yakpati both to destroy the Mahdists and to impose their rule on the Azande, each striving to get as much of the country as they

[1] Op. cit., 1926, p. 16.

could, and as quickly as possible, into their possession; and they added their quota of destruction—war, killings, executions, and deportations. The history of the other Zande dynasties is much the same story, so I shall do scarcely more than mention them.

Bugwa son of Mabenge installed himself to the south of the Uere at the expense of the Amiangba people. His descendants were replaced by the house of Nunga. Both his son Badinde and his grand-nephew Palembata 'had been more or less brought into subjection by Zemio [Zemoi]' by 1880,[1] and Badinde, as we have earlier noted, was later assassinated by Mukpoi Ngbanga-zegino, who took his remaining territories. The heirs of Ngindo son of Mabenge rule the Azande called Auro, who live in the triangle Uele–Uere, with a fraction of them to the south of the Uele. The term 'Auro' has the sense of 'easterner' and therefore of 'foreigner' and in a later sense of 'Azande not of true Ambomu stock'; but it seems to have become the name for this political conglomeration, probably because it consisted almost entirely of people originally of foreign stock. When Ngindo died, his son Bazigba refused to accept the authority of his elder brother Nzongo but was defeated by him in war.

We have so far been following the fortunes of the sons of Mabenge who conquered to the north and east. It remains to say a few words about the line of Tombo, Mabenge's brother,

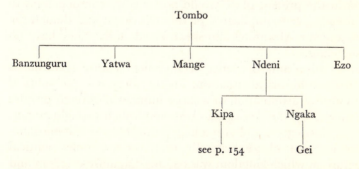

see p. 154

whose wars were with the Abandya on the western frontier of Zandeland and with the descendants of Ngindo son of Mabenge, and whose conquests were to the south and south-east and also later than those of the descendants of Mabenge. Tombo, as we have earlier noted, was assassinated by one of his sons near the

---

[1] Junker, op. cit., vol. ii, 1891, pp. 199–200.

sources of the Mbili. His son Ezo led his people across the Api–Uere on their march towards the east. They were for a time on the Mbili, where they acquired the sobriquet 'Embili' ('Ambili'). Another small group ruled over by Tombo's descendants are the Amokuma, at the confluence of the Uele and the Uere and between the left bank of the Uele and the Bima. Their royal family is the line of Tombo's son Mange. Another small group, the Apodyo, were ruled by the line of Tombo's son Yatwa until they lost almost all their possessions to Sasa of the house of Nunga. The final political group ruled by descendants of Tombo are the Abele or Avuru Kipa, those of the forest or the subjects of Kipa. A dissident group of Embili (Ambili) took the name Abele when they followed Ndeni, who had quarrelled with his brother Ezo, and departed for the south, attacking the Ababua people and carving out a domain in their country. The story of this man and his remarkable son Kipa, who died in 1868,[1] and Kipa's children runs true to type. It is a story of bitter quarrels and violence.[2]

It is not necessary here to say anything of the three final groups shown in de Calonne's map, the Abandya, Adio, and Abwameli, for though the Abandya have taken over Zande speech and institutions, they appear to be ruled over by an aristocracy other than that of the Avongara, and a discussion of them in the present place would add further complications to an already over-complicated picture of events; and though the Adio and the Abwameli also speak Zande today they have no ruling clans.

From this résumé of events certain salient features stand out in the politico-historical situation. Firstly, there was the political and cultural assimilation of a large number of foreign peoples conquered by the Avongara–Ambomu which brought about, but only by degrees and over a long period of time, a homogeneous society and culture. Secondly, there was a complex political structure in which kingdom was balanced against kingdom and within each kingdom there were provincial rivalries which on the death of a king, or even before his death, led invariably to the disintegration of the kingdom until one or other of the princes gained mastery, or it became divided among two or more princes who then fought each other for dominance and

---

[1] Schweinfurth, *The Heart of Africa*, vol. ii, 1873, p. 56.   [2] See Chap. X.

survival.[1] Thirdly, there was the part played within this political pattern by intrusive elements, Arabs and Europeans, with a more powerful organization and superior equipment which more than compensated for their having to operate from distant bases. All that is intended in this chapter is to give the reader a picture of events sufficient to enable him to appreciate their complexity and to understand how the study of an African kingdom, and all the more of several kingdoms, is a much more difficult and complicated task than the study of politically less developed societies in which there is little historical tradition and for the history of which there are only scanty documentary evidences. The complexity, indeed confusion, in the case of the Azande was not of short span or duration. It was spread over a vast area, and in different parts of it different circumstances prevailed, so that it is well-nigh impossible to write a history of the Azande, but only separate histories of each kingdom. If we take 1905 to be the year in which European rule was finally established in Zandeland, there had been European contacts for 47 years before that date. It is today over 100 years since the first European contact with the Azande. Arab contacts began at about the same time as European contacts, probably somewhat earlier in parts of Zandeland; and they influenced the Azande far more, since the Arabs who entered Zande country were far more numerous and were more firmly rooted in it than the handful of transient European travellers who penetrated it. But before even Arab or European arrived in Central Africa the Avongara–Ambomu had been moving for a century east, south, and north, conquering great territories and subjugating their inhabitants. It is against this background that their institutions and culture have to be examined if they are to be well understood.

[1] See Chap. X.

XV
THE KINGDOM OF GBUDWE

I

THIS chapter is not an examination of the Zande migrations and conquests, but a study of one only of the Zande
kingdoms, that of Gbudwe (Yambio). Events in other
kingdoms are mentioned only when they are relevant. Literary
records from travellers and administrators go back to 1858 and
cover, though with gaps and with varying degrees of sufficiency,
the period from that date to Gbudwe's death in 1905. I have
tried to relate these records to Zande traditions.

Gbudwe's kingdom was the most easterly of the Zande kingdoms in what was till recently the Anglo-Egyptian Sudan,
though part of it lay on what used to be the Belgian Congo side
of the frontier. To the west of it was the kingdom of Gbudwe's
deceased brother Ezo (ruled by his sons), and to the north-west
of that, in the latter part of his reign, the kingdom of Tembura,
who belonged to a different branch of the Zande royal family.
The branch with which we are concerned is that of Yakpati son
of Mabenge, who with his sons conquered vast territories to the
east. His sons, among whom was Bazingbi, Gbudwe's father,
continued these conquests in various directions, and at Bazingbi's death the territories over which he ruled broke up into
independent kingdoms ruled by his elder sons, of whom Gbudwe
occupied an area which had been directly administered by his
father between the rivers Lingasi and Hu.[1]

It is said that Gbudwe, when he was a young man, was inclined
to be morose, and that he seldom smiled or joked; and I have
sometimes been told that this was due to the troubles of his early
youth, the greatest of them being the manner of his mother's
death. The story, as I relate it here, was told me by his nephew
Kanimara son of Funa, son of Bazingbi.

Gbudwe's mother was not of true Zande stock (Mbomu) but
belonged to a conquered people called Akalinga, who were
probably of Pambia stock and are not to be confused with the

---

[1] See sketch-map in Chap. I.

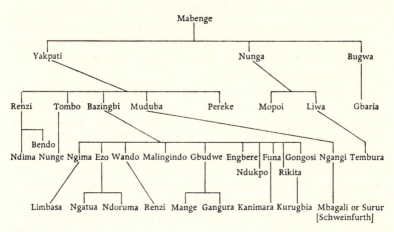

Mabenge

Yakpati — Nunga — Bugwa

Renzi   Tombo   Bazingbi   Muduba   Pereke   Mopoi   Liwa   Gbaria

Bendo
Ndima Nunge Ngima Ezo Wando Malingindo Gbudwe Engbere Funa Gongosi Ngangi Tembura
                                        Ndukpo Rikita

Limbasa Ngatua Ndoruma Renzi Mange Gangura Kanimara Kurugbia Mbagali or Surur
                                                                    [Schweinfurth]

(The genealogy gives most of the names mentioned in this Chapter, but only such
as can be identified with a high degree of probability.)

well-known Zande clan of the same name, who, nevertheless,
sometimes claim Gbudwe as a sister's son.[1] Bazingbi was constantly extending the boundaries of his kingdom and subjugating foreign peoples, among them being these Akalinga who
lived on hills far to the west. Gbudwe's mother, Ngbiara, was
a captive of these wars. Bazingbi gave her as a servant to
Namanza, the mother of his son Ezo. Namanza seems to have
become greatly attached to her servant, and when Bazingbi
took her away to give her to one of his deputies who governed a
border march of his kingdom Namanza pleaded with him to
change his mind. But her pleadings were in vain, and the deputy
departed from court with his new wife. However, Namanza
was a persistent and impulsive woman. She journeyed after her
servant, and when, weary, she reached the home of the deputy
on the third day, this Zande received her with the respect due
to a wife of Bazingbi and the mother of one of his sons. He sent
out to her, as she sat in his court, oil and spears and other gifts.
When he came to greet her she said to him that Bazingbi had
indeed been good to her and had given her many things, but
the one thing that she most desired, her servant and the nurse

[1] Czekanowski makes the extraordinary statement: 'Nur aus endogamen Ehen
geborene Kinder sind vollberechtigte Avunguru.' This is quite wrong. Most kings
and princes had commoner mothers. Op. cit., p. 49.

of her baby, he had taken from her. On hearing this the deputy went back to his private enclosure and told Ngbiara to come out. When she came out and saw her mistress sitting in the court she ran into her arms and beseeched her mistress not to leave her again but to take her home.

On the following morning they started for home, and after sleeping two nights on their way they reached on the third day that province of his kingdom which Bazingbi administered directly himself.[1] Here Namanza was seen by some of her husband's subjects who ran to meet her and said to her: 'O mother of princes do not return here; flee away quickly for Bazingbi threatens you with death and he has decreed to all his subjects that if anyone see you he shall slay you.' Tired and hungry, they turned back in the direction from which they had come; for among Azande he who has incurred another's wrath does not approach him empty-handed but with a present in his hand. As was customary, and still is today, when a man has incurred the disfavour of his prince he seeks help from his father or brother, his relations-in-law, his sisters' sons, and his blood-brothers; but when the daughter or wife of a prince is in like trouble she will often flee to her father's or husband's relatives and implore their mediation. Thus Namanza fled with Ngbiara to the homes of two neighbouring nobles, cousins of Bazingbi who lived in his kingdom, and asked their assistance. These two men collected a large number of spears and went with them and the two women before Bazingbi and told him they had brought a number of spears to appease him and to wipe out his shame. Bazingbi replied nothing but just sat with his face resting on his hand as though deep in thought. This silence meant that he accepted the spears and forgave his wife her rashness.

Ngbiara returned to the daily routine of the household: cooking, gathering firewood for her mistress, bringing her warm water to wash with in the early mornings, hoeing her gardens, and attending the baby Ezo. The baby grew into a child, and Ngbiara grew also and her breasts developed—it is in this way that Azande reckon the age of a girl. One day Bazingbi went in after her and she conceived Gbudwe; and when she had borne him she was given a hut of her own and the status of a king's wife and a prince's mother.

[1] See Chap. X for an account of the organization of a kingdom.

It is not, of course, possible to date these events accurately, but as Gbudwe according to all accounts was an elderly man, probably over seventy years of age, when he died in 1905, we may hazard a guess that he may have been born round about 1835. Ezo, Bazingbi's second son, was, as the story relates, born some years earlier.

I have recorded nothing more of Gbudwe's mother save the circumstances of her death. Gbudwe was at this time a boy living at his father's court, and his father and the men at court are said to have already been impressed by his bearing. Some qualities of his character appear in this further story related to me by Kanimara.

One of Bazingbi's children died of sickness and the poison oracle accused Gbudwe's mother of having bewitched him. Bazingbi gave orders for her execution, and it was carried out. Grieved and hurt, Gbudwe swore that it was the lying tongues and the jealousy of his father's other wives which had caused the death of his mother and that she was no witch; and he gave a pledge to a courtier of the Abakundo clan, requiring him to cut open his mother's corpse and see whether there was really witchcraft-substance in it or not. This man cut open Ngbiara's abdomen and found witchcraft-substance in it. So Gbudwe was not only the child of a servant but also of a witch.

Gbudwe bought back his pledge, as custom required of him, from the man to whom he had given it; and he then fled from his father's court and vengeance. Bazingbi was outraged at the verdict of his oracle having been questioned and the abdomen of his wife having been cut open—his orders treated as nothing by a mere boy. He swore by his limb, by the head of his father Yakpati, and by the graves of his ancestors that just as Ngbiara's abdomen had been cut open so would he cut open Gbudwe's abdomen also. But Gbudwe fled before the storm, to let it exhaust itself; for every Zande knows that, though a man swear by the limbs of his ancestors that he will never see son or father again, he will see him, even though it be when the mourners are bearing him to the grave. For anger gives way in the heart of a boy to longing for home, and the heart of an old man yearns after the sight of his son once more. This is the sense of a well-known proverb: *bakuuroyo aya u abinga bakudiyo te, i abi ti yo abi,* 'the man in the east said that he would not see the man in the west, but they will see each other for sure'. So Gbudwe fled to the courts of two other nobles and abided with them.

After a time these nobles collected some sixty spears and several women, and took them as gifts to Bazingbi. They placed Gbudwe between them, and one of them said to his father, 'Bazingbi, prince, see, we have brought your son so that you may slay him. It would be well that you slay him while we are here so that we may bury him, for he is noble and our kinsman.' Since Bazingbi said nothing but sat looking at the ground with his cheek on his hand they knew that it would be well with Gbudwe, for such is the custom of princes, they pardon when they are silent. All knew well that Gbudwe would be pardoned by his father, for he could not dishonour those nobles who had brought him gifts, for it would have shamed his kinsmen had he done otherwise.

Another incident in Gbudwe's early life is recorded in the text which follows. As the text relates, Gbudwe was at the time a youth at his father's court while his elder brother Wando had already been given a province to administer.

While Gbudwe was still at court at his father's home dangers began to beset him. He departed and joined with [his brother] Engbere, and when they had arrived they entered the homestead of a certain man. Gbudwe's dog whose name was Biriade followed him. While they were staying in the home of this man, who was a subject of Wando, Gbudwe began to call his dog by its name, which was Biriade; and the man said to himself that he was not just calling the name of the dog but was calling it by a word which had a double meaning. The man hastened to his master Wando, and when he told him about it Wando said that Gbudwe and Ngbere had insulted his subjects; and he went to fight them. Gbudwe took his shield, and Ngbere took his, and Wando took his, and they began to fight among themselves. Wando wounded Gbudwe between his fingers. When Bazingbi heard about it he was very angry on account of Gbudwe, and he wanted to make war on Wando; but people calmed him, and he turned back on the way to war. Then, when Wando heard that Bazingbi was angry on account of Gbudwe, he paid twenty spears and sent them with a woman to Bazingbi. Then Bazingbi dropped the matter.

One more story about Gbudwe at this period of his life shows us how he is believed to have already made a deep impression on old and experienced princes. Gbudwe and one of his elder brothers, whose name was not given, were sent by Bazingbi to pay their respects to their old grandfather Yakpati, Bazingbi's father. They were both boys in their teens. It is customary when such visits are made to an important prince for the visitors to remain for about a month at his court, daily paying him their respects, forming part of the semicircle of nobles and commoner courtiers who sit in front of him when he hears cases and discusses affairs. When he desires to depart the visitor asks leave to do so; and he is told to wait a day or two longer. The prince in the meanwhile selects presents for his departing guest, for it would never do for a man, even were he a man of no social importance, to say that he had gone empty-handed from the court of a prince. The prince would feel that to be a blot on his name; and it might also encourage his subjects to leave his dominion for that of a more generous kinsman. So, when Gbudwe and his elder brother were about to depart, he called them to the edge of his gardens, where they adjoined his court, and there gave them a parting message for his son Bazingbi and gifts for themselves. To Gbudwe's brother he gave twenty spears and a wife, but to Gbudwe he gave only a broken adze and a broken axe.

When the boys reached home, Gbudwe showed the broken adze and axe to his father, who laughed when he saw them; and he asked his son whether he felt hurt at receiving so poor a gift. Gbudwe replied that it was not because he felt hurt that he had come to show his father the gifts but because Bazingbi was his father and it was seemly for a son to show to his parent any gift he might receive. Bazingbi then explained to him the symbolism of the gifts. Yakpati had given the other boy twenty spears and a wife because he knew that the lad would never be rich and powerful and would need all the spears and women his relatives could give him, whereas he gave the broken adze and axe to Gbudwe to signify that he would become a great king who would possess spears and women in abundance.

2

Gbudwe was much concerned during his long reign with powerful intruders from far-off countries: Arab ivory- and slave-traders, Egyptian Government officials, the Dervishes, and

finally the British and Belgians, all of whom Azande speak of
as *abalomu* or *abalemu*. These *wasiwasi wili auro, kpekpe li aboro*,
'Dirty little barbarians, cropped-heads', as the Azande of
Gbudwe's time used to call them, one after the other threatened
his kingdom from all sides.

According to Azande, relations with the Arab traders from
the north were at first cordial, if cautious, and what they say
accords with what we learn from the reports of early travellers
about the policy of the Arabs. The Zande kings were powerful,
and their peoples could not be enslaved or pillaged as many less
organized peoples were; and their kingdoms were distant from
the rivers from which the Arabs operated, the Bahr al-Ghazal
and the Nile. All the first traders asked for was that the Zande
kings should grant them hospitality and allow them to purchase
ivory and provisions, and grant immunity for their caravans
transporting ivory and slaves from Mangbetu and Abarambo
country and other regions of the south to their northern stations.
With these ends in view, they sought to win the favour of the
kings by gifts. However, this situation could not have lasted,
considering the suspicion and hostility of the Zande rulers
towards any possible rivals and that the leaders of the trading
companies were brigands and their followers a rapacious
rabble; and it did not last.

According to the Zande story these traders were at first on
good terms with Bazingbi, gave him presents, and treated him
with respect. It is said that Bazingbi called them *abadiaru*, his
friends, and some say that he made blood-brotherhood with
them. All went well till one of the Arabs, a certain Adarisi
(Idris), asked for the hand of a daughter of Bazingbi in marriage.
Bazingbi agreed to the match, and Adarisi began to return
home with his bride. The girl soon became homesick and fled
back to her father's court by night. Adarisi followed her and
entered his father-in-law's court loudly claiming back his
marriage-spears, an unpardonable insult among the Azande.
When Bazingbi appeared he further insulted him by mentioning
marriage-spears in his presence and by pointing a stick at him;
some say that he even struck his leg with it. Dissembling his
anger, Bazingbi went into his private quarters and there collected some twenty spears of poor quality which he placed
before Adarisi, who, not perceiving that they were of bad

quality, counted them and departed with them. Smarting from the insults he had suffered, Bazingbi told his son Gbudwe to follow after Adarisi and lay an ambush for him. The Arab was attacked by Gbudwe on his way home and, though he defended himself bravely with his back to a tree, six of his men were killed and their rifles captured and taken back to Bazingbi. Adarisi returned in anger to the court of Bazingbi and complained of treachery. Bazingbi disclaimed all knowledge of the affair and spoke of the disobedience of his sons, who were fools and unruly and did not listen to his words. He said also that Gbudwe was not a son of his at all but his sister's son, a light-headed young man over whom he had no control. He then called for the six captured rifles to be brought out and he gave them to Adarisi, who returned home. But Bazingbi's rancour continued, and he encouraged his sons to waylay and kill Adarisi's men without involving himself in responsibility and retaliation.

Another version of this story, which is different in particulars, was given by a Zande thus:

At the beginning Bazingbi made friendship with the Arabs, and they married one of his daughters also. They came to his home here frequently. On one occasion in the past they came and stayed with him a long time, and after he had got to know them well they began to ask him about a wife and he agreed to give them one. At that time Gbudwe alone was at the court of Bazingbi his father; all his [elder] brothers who had been with him had been given provinces by Bazingbi. Only Gbudwe was at court because he had not been given a province on account of his being a hot-tempered young man. But while he resided at court he made followers among those youths who were living at court. Then it happened that the Arabs began to ask for the daughter of Bazingbi in marriage, and he gladly agreed to their proposal. They paid him bridewealth for her but they did not take her away with them. They left her with her father and returned to their own home. They remained there once more for a time, and then they came to visit their friend; and they collected all sorts of presents and brought them to him, for he was their relative-in-law. They arrived and entered his court, and the place was dirty. They sent a messenger to Bazingbi to tell him to come. For in the old days a king's court was not kept tidy as it is today. Ashes were strewn all over the place. They sent a boy to Bazingbi to ask him where they were to reside. The boy they sent returned on his way because he was afraid. So they waited in vain and did not see him, and then

they entered his private quarters, since he was their good friend
and they wished to tell him that they had sent boys to him in vain and
they brought back no answer. They entered his private quarters and
wandered all around them, asking his wives about him. He remained
where he was watching what they did. A boy went and appeared
before Bazingbi and said to him, 'Master, the Arabs are asking
about you persistently, saying that they are quite worn out with
sending messengers to you and yet they have not seen you at all'.
Bazingbi then appeared before them, because he had been in another
small homestead of his. He came and shook hands with them warmly
and he went with them and showed them a good place to reside in.
When they had well rested he visited them and they gave him many
fine presents. He then called their wife and she came to where they
were. They told him that they would spend four nights and afterwards return home. He gave his assent to what they said. He then
returned to his home and sent a messenger to Gbudwe to tell him
to come. Gbudwe came and appeared before him, and Bazingbi said
to him, 'O my son I am truly tired of these men, because they summon me as though I were a dog. You had better go with the Abaigo
company [of warriors] to lie in wait for them, because if they persist
in coming to my home here all the time I shall be put to shame by
them, because they are not honourable men. All those sons of mine
who have provinces are afraid of them, so you had better go with
your Abaigo company to waylay them. If you fight them do not come
back here to court, because then they will say that it was I myself
who arranged deceit with you. If they ask me I shall say that you
are a sister's son and an idiot and that you do not pay any attention
to my orders.' He told Gbudwe that he was not to attack them near
his home in any circumstances. Gbudwe went and waited for them
on their route. When they came to depart Bazingbi gave to all of
them fine presents of Zande craftsmanship. He said to them deceit-
fully, 'alas! My kinsmen-in-law, my friends, your wife is away from
home just now; I have not seen her at all. But it is of no consequence;
you go on your way and when I see her here I will send her after
you, since she has wandered from you.' He said this to deceive them,
because he was keeping her away from them lest she should be killed
in the fighting with them later.

   They proceeded on their way, and when they were far from
Bazingbi's home Gbudwe set his company of warriors across their
path, and when they were all in the middle of the ambush they
appeared before them to fight them; and they captured all their
rifles and all their goods, and they killed many of them. However,
part of them fled back to Bazingbi. They said to him, 'Your sons
attacked us on our way and they have killed indeed many and

captured all our rifles.' He said to them, 'O my friends I cannot understand this attack on you. You see that all my sons are administering
provinces, that is, those who make war on my behalf. If I had wanted
to fight you I would have told it to one of my sons who has many
followers. As for this youth, he is just a sister's son and an idiot; he
never listens to what I have to say to him. He came to reside near my
court and began to gather followers around him. I have admonished
him in vain, he pays no attention to what I say. He even wants to
fight with me!' The Arabs then returned to their home; and while
they were there Bazingbi died. While he was dying he urged
Gbudwe against the Arabs, saying to him that he must never leave
them in peace. It was Gbudwe to whom Bazingbi gave his blessing,
saying that he alone was to take his inheritance, because he had
obeyed his words well, more than his brothers who had been given
provinces.

The Arabs remained where they were for a long time and then
they began to think of their wife and of their many goods they had
given Bazingbi for his daughter. They began again to collect another
lot of presents to take them to ask about their wife. They made a
long journey and when they reached Gbudwe's territory he attacked
them at once, because it was he who occupied the place of his father.
He fought them for a long time and overcame them. After that the
Arabs began to rouse themselves against Gbudwe to make war on
him, and they altogether overcame him.[1]

For the princes of old did not at all wish to make war with the
Arabs. It was Bazingbi who began fighting with the Arabs. When he
died it was Gbudwe who stayed in his place to make war with the
Arabs often and for days together. The cause and origin of the wars
with the Arabs was the affair of the daughter of Bazingbi. It was
that with which the fighting with the Arabs started and continued
about.

One or other version of the story of the Arabs and Bazingbi's
daughter has been told me by a number of Azande, and there
is no reason to doubt that such incidents as the story relates took
place. We know from Petherick's account that it was the custom
at the time for the traders to make blood-brotherhood with the
Zande rulers and to take their daughters in marriage.[2] We
cannot give a certain date to 'the war of Bazingbi's daughter'

---

[1] This refers to the action of the Egyptian Government against him in 1881–2.
See pp. 332–4.

[2] Op. cit., 1861, p. 472. Also Mr. and Mrs. Petherick, op. cit., vol. 1, 1869,
pp. 62 and 141.

but an approximate date can be determined from various evidences.

It was a Welshman, John Petherick, who first opened the door through which later every sort of blackguard from the Northern Sudan was to enter the region of the Bahr al-Ghazal, spreading misery and desolation everywhere. Schweinfurth tells us that the first boat which entered the Bahr al-Ghazal was that of a Khartoum merchant called Habeschi in the year 1851 and that Petherick followed two years later.[1] Petherick himself also says that he went up that river in 1853. Petherick had been a mining engineer in the service of the Khedive Mehemet Ali. On the death of his patron he first established himself as a trader in gum arabic in Kordofan, and later in 1853, he became engaged in ivory trade in the Southern Sudan. At the close of that year he sailed up the Bahr al-Ghazal to open up trade from that river with the peoples living to the south of it. For several years he returned each year for the same purpose, penetrating ever further to the south, reaching first the Dinka, then the Luo (Jur), then the Bongo, and finally, in 1858, the confines of Zandeland—the first European to meet Azande in their own homeland.[2] Reports of his success in the ivory trade began to circulate in Khartoum and various Arabs of that town equipped expeditions to compete with him; and even as early as 1855 there was fighting between these traders and the Dinka of the Bahr al-Ghazal. Soon they were to spread rapine and terror far and wide. All we have to note here, however, is that when Petherick returned to England in 1859, Arab traders had not, except for those employed by himself, reached the eastern Zande kingdoms. In 1861 Petherick returned to the Southern Sudan,

---

[1] *Im Herzen von Afrika*, 1922 edn., p. 65. In the 1878 edn. and in the English translation, op. cit., vol. i, p. 127, the year of Habeschi's entry is wrongly given as 1854.

[2] These Azande, who appear to have been living between the Sueh and Ibba rivers, had been carried there by the conquests of Renzi, Tombo, and Muduba, sons of Yakpati. Petherick mentions the following nobles in this area: Dimoo, Urumbo and his brother Djungee and his father Hookooa, Bashima and his brothers Basia and Ringa and his father Gorea or Goria, shaikh of Beringi, and his grandfather Harquati, and Pereka son of Yaquatti. Ringa became Petherick's agent and he was later installed by the Arab traders as ruler of the Adio (Makaraka) section of the Azande to the east. He continued to act in this capacity under the Egyptian Government till he was brutally murdered by his employers. He is mentioned by Schweinfurth, Junker, and Casati. Schweinfurth says that he was a brother of Indimma and a son of Renzi (op. cit., vol. ii, p. 36).

accompanied by Mrs. Petherick, to meet and provide for the explorers Speke and Grant on behalf of the Royal Geographical Society, an undertaking which led to many disasters and re-criminations. He does not seem to have visited his station on the confines of Zandeland again, but he received reports from his agents in that region. It is scarcely possible for these not to have known had other merchants entered into commercial or hostile relations with the eastern Zande kings; nor does there appear to have been any reason why, had they known of any such relations, they should have concealed them from Petherick or why he should not have recorded them. He records only a skirmish between some Azande and one of his agents, a certain Mussaad.[1] We may assume therefore that the Arab merchants could not have had any dealings with Bazingbi before 1861. On the other hand, when Schweinfurth visited parts of Zandeland in 1870, Bazingbi was dead, and his death must have taken place some years previously, because the struggle between his sons for his inheritance had already occurred, leaving Gbudwe firmly established in his father's domain. We may state with some assurance therefore that 'the war of Bazingbi's daughter' took place in the middle sixties.

We may further conclude that it took place after 1865 and probably round about 1867 because, while we know from Schweinfurth's account that the trading company of Muham-mad (referred to later) did not open up a route to the south, running to the east of Bazingbi's territory, till 1866, and that he was the first to do so, we also know from Piaggia's account that the other company operating in these parts, that of Ghattas, are unlikely to have penetrated on a direct southern route (the Sueh river) before that date; and therefore, till Muhammad reached an agreement to work in co-operation with them it is also unlikely that they could have entered Bazingbi's kingdom at all before 1866; for this company did not operate to the west of Bazingbi's domains and could not therefore have entered them from that direction. We conclude that Ghattas's company could not have penetrated down the Sueh from the fact that the eighty riflemen belonging to this company, which had earlier entered into trading relations with King Tombo, who escorted Piaggia, were so scared when they met the king, whose kingdom

[1] Mr. and Mrs. Petherick, op. cit., p. 209.

lay across this route,[1] and his warriors that they asked Piaggia's permission to return to the north. This he gave them; and then this remarkable man remained entirely by himself among the Azande for 26 months. The company whose route to the south lay to the west, through the territory of King Ezo, was that of Aboo Guroon, who, according to Schweinfurth,[2] was already trading as far south as the kingdom of Kipa as early as 1866; but we have no evidence that he encroached on Bazingbi's kingdom as early as that. It is indeed unlikely that he had opened up a route through Ezo's country before 1865, for Piaggia, whose travels covered the area through which the route lay, does not in Antinori's account give any indication of the presence of Arab caravans or posts in it.[3]

Carlo Piaggia was born at Cantignano, near Lucca, in 1821 and died at Sennar in 1882.[4] After having earned his living as a gardener in Tunis and then in various jobs in Egypt he became a hunter and merchant in the Sudan, where eventually, in 1863, he found his way to the Zande kingdom of Tombo on the upper Sueh. Though Petherick may have been the first European to have seen Azande in their homeland, he barely reached the confines of their country, and to Piaggia must go the credit of having been the first to penetrate it.[5] He must indeed have got to know the Azande well, probably better than any other traveller of the last century; but he was, alas, no scholar. All that we have by his own hand (apart from the publication many years later of his perhaps not very reliable Memoirs) about the Azande is a paper that he read to the Academy of Lucca in 1877, but what he says there of his travels is almost nothing. However, there is no reason to doubt his statement that during the years 1863 to 1865 he resided among the Azande,

---

[1] F. Giorgetti, *Our African Missions*, vol. vii, no. 6, 1952, p. 82, claims to have established that Tombo's court in 1863 was at the source of the Manvuga river, a tributary of the Menze, in Lat. 5° 28′ North and 28° 38′ Long. East.

[2] Op. cit., vol. ii, 1873, p. 95.

[3] In his Memoirs he gives (p. 217) an account of a battle between Imbio (Gbudwe) and Arabs in 1862, but not much reliance can be put on such details in that book.

[4] Dates according to R. Hill, *A Biographical Dictionary of the Anglo-Egyptian Sudan*, 1951, p. 306.

[5] Though Heuglin's account would suggest that Johann Kleincznick, an Austrian hunter from Carniola, may have been in touch with Azande to the west as early as 1862 ('Travels in the Sudan in the Sixties', trans. M. Mare, *Sudan Notes and Records*, 24, 1941, 157–8).

for by far the greater part of the time at the court of Tombo,[1] who housed and fed him; and even though the information he gives us is negligible he could hardly have failed to tell us had any Arab expeditions passed through Tombo's territory or had there been hostilities between Arabs and Tombo's subjects during his residence at his court.[2]

Fortunately Piaggia's friend and fellow hunter and trader the Perugian Marchese O. Antinori put together what Piaggia told him of his travels in Zandeland,[3] and from this account we learn that in 1864 to 1865 he visited the territories of a number of kings and princes, reaching as far south as the kingdom of Kipa (Chipa).[4] There is nothing in Antinori's record to suggest that Ghattas's company, or any other, had as yet penetrated to Bazingbi's country; on the contrary, the evidence implicit in it makes this seem highly improbable. In 1865 Bazingbi was still alive. In January of that year Piaggia attempted another journey to the south from Tombo's court: 'Ma arrivato alle vicinanze di Perchie [Pereke] gli fu d'uopo retrocedere, avendo appreso che il capo Perchie, sebbene fosse uno dei figli di Tombo, fatta alleanza con Basimbei [Bazingbi], avea mosso guerra alla propria famiglia.'[5]

Antinori's account and the map accompanying it place Bazingbi's home to the west of the River Dio. This is probably

---

[1] De Calonne says that Tombo was a son of Renzi and grandson of Yakpati (op. cit., pp. 59 and 63); so does Hutereau (op. cit., p. 159), but as both say that he was killed shortly after the death of Renzi, which Hutereau says occurred before 1840, the Tombo they speak of as a son of Renzi could not have been Piaggia's host of 1863. Vanden Plas also gives Tombo as a son of Renzi (Lagae and Vanden Plas, op. cit., vol. i, p. 49). Schweinfurth, on the other hand, says that Tombo, who was dead by the time of his visit, was a brother of Renzi, and he tells us that his sons were still independent and hostile to the Arab companies (op. cit., vol. i, p. 480). Piaggia and Antinori also make Tombo to be a son of Yakpati, listing him as will be seen later, as brother to Bazingbi. There appear to have been two men of the name Tombo, one a son of Yakpati and the other a son of Renzi. This Tombo was, I believe, the former. The only other prince mentioned by Piaggia in his paper was Sati, a brother of Tombo. This name has not been identified, and in Antinori's account (see his list) he is given as one of Tombo's deputies.

[2] Piaggia, op. cit., 1877. See also Lotar, 'Souvenirs de l'Uele', *Congo*, 1930, t. i, pp. 1–8.   [3] Antinori, op. cit., 1868.

[4] Schweinfurth (op. cit., vol. ii, 1873, pp. 56–7) refused to accept that Piaggia reached Kipa's country and accused him of fabricating his routes, largely on the ground of the speed with which he travelled; but Schweinfurth did not take into account the fact that Piaggia travelled only with a Zande escort and was not impeded, as he was, by a caravan of a thousand people: troops, porters, and slaves of Muhammad.   [5] Op. cit., p. 121.

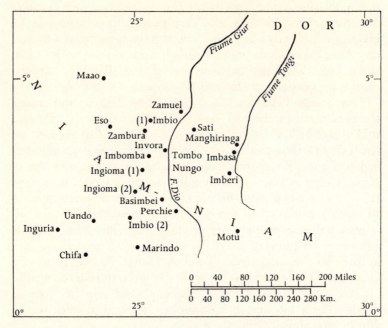

SKETCH 13. THE POSITIONS OF ZANDE PRINCES
After Antinori and Piaggia.

the Sueh—*dio* means in Zande either 'at the river' or 'towards
the west'. His second son Ezo is marked to the north-west of his
home, his eldest son Ngima to the west of it, his sons Wando and
Malingindo to the south-west and south of it, and his brother
Pereke[1] to the south-east of it. It is true that Antinori's account
of Piaggia's travels contains some inaccuracies and raises some
difficulties, but considering the circumstances in which Piaggia
travelled and that the report of them has come to us at second
hand, it is remarkable how accurate it is. One difficulty, which
particularly concerns us, is that two persons of the name of Imbio
are mentioned, the one living to the north-west of Tombo and
listed among his *fattori*, and the other living to the south-west

---

[1] The Perchie marked on Antinori's map and referred to in the quotation above
could scarcely have been a son of Tombo, as Antinori says he was, if his position
on the map is even approximately accurate. The position is probably not approximately accurate, but in any case, I think he must have been the son of Yakpati
mentioned by Petherick.

of Bazingbi and listed among his sons. This second Imbio can hardly be other than Gbudwe (Yambio, Mbio). If this is so, he must at that time have been living at some distance from his father's court. All Azande I knew said that he was not given a province of his own to administer during his father's lifetime— Piaggia does not say that he was a ruler in his own right—but he was by this time a man of about thirty years of age and he must have had a home and family of his own and have kept up a princely state in it, though in a minor way. It has often happened that a young prince has gathered a following around him and become ruler of a small district without having been formally invested with authority in it by the ruler of the kingdom.

	GRAN CAPI		
Tombo	e suo fratello	Basimbei	
Figli		*Figli*	
Zamuel	Nunga	Ingioma (1)	Ingioma (2)
Perchie	Invora	Marindo	Imbomba
		Imbio (2)	
Fattori		*Fattori*	
Imbio	Manghiringa		
Imbasa	Sati	Zambura	Eso

PICCOLO CAPI INDIPENDENTI

Kifa figlio di Inguria – Uando – Maao – Motù (ciasuno di questi cinque capi, compresa Inguria, si reggono da sè).

ZANDE PRINCES LISTED BY PIAGGIA AND ANTINORI.

It cannot be said with certainty who the Arabs were whom Gbudwe attacked both during his father's lifetime and afterwards, but since their leader in all Zande versions is given as Adarisi (Idris) there is a strong probability that they belonged to the trading company of the Copt Ghattas, whose troops had escorted Piaggia to the court of Tombo, and that the Idris was the agent of that name who was in charge of Ghattas's chief station in the northern Bahr al-Ghazal at the time of Schweinfurth's visit in 1869 (the station had been founded thirteen years before). Schweinfurth says that he was a negro by birth and had been a slave.[1] Lotar, writing in 1930, remarks that he was 'Célèbre par ses randonnées dans l'Uélé, dont parlent

[1] Op. cit., vol. i, 1873, p. 178.

encore aujourd'hui les très vieux indigènes.'[1] Some of the fighting at this time between Gbudwe and the Arabs was, however,
with a company formed by a Nubian called by Schweinfurth
both Abd es Sammat and Aboo Sammat ('Abd al-Sammad is
probably the correct transliteration), and whom I will refer to
by his first name Muhammad. Schweinfurth made his explorations as a member of his caravan. In 1870, leaving Schweinfurth
in camp, this man, as I shall relate later, advanced into the
kingdom of Gbudwe (then called by an earlier name Yambio, and by Schweinfurth Mbio or Mbeeoh) with the purpose
of attacking him. Schweinfurth does not tell us the reason for
this hostile act, and we can only suppose that it must have been
preceded by some show of hostility towards Muhammad's
company by either Gbudwe or his father Bazingbi. It is unlikely
that he would have attacked him without provocation for there
was nothing to have been gained, and much to have been lost,
by doing so. At this time Ghattas's company and Muhammad's
company were acting in concert, which may explain how
Muhammad became involved in a quarrel associated in the
Zande story with Idris.[2]

We learn also from a casual remark by Schweinfurth that
the merchant Aboo Guroon had also engaged in fighting with
Gbudwe. This one-time agent of Petherick, perhaps the first of
the merchants to establish commercial relations with the Zande
kings of the south, operated, according to the information he
gave Schweinfurth, on a route well to the west of Gbudwe's
kingdom.[3] One of his garrisons had been, probably in 1869 or
1870, massacred by the sons of Ezo, and their hostility to the
merchant 'had an indirect connection with the proceedings

[1] Op. cit., 1930, t. ii, p. 149.
[2] Schweinfurth tells us that Muhammad was known to the Azande by the name
of Mbahly, 'the little one'. No Zande I have met had any recollection of the name,
and Schweinfurth's etymology is in any case unacceptable. On the other hand, I
have heard Azande speak of a certain Angbali, 'termite', and there is evidence
which suggests that he may be identified with Muhammad. In spelling other Zande
words Schweinfurth uses the letter *m* when he should have written *ng*. I may add
also that I never met a Zande who had any recollection of the name by which
Schweinfurth assures us he was known to Azande, Mbarikpa, 'leaf-eater', on
account of his botanical interests. The correct transliteration would be Barikpe.
I have heard it said that the first European they heard of was a certain Amani, who
attempted to enter Zandeland but was compelled to withdraw. Could this be a
memory of Miani? News of him may have spread to the Azande of the Sudan.
[3] Op. cit., vol. ii, 1873, pp. 496–7 (omitted in the German editions).

taken against Muhammad by Mbeeoh [Gbudwe], who had surprised Aboo Guroon's company in the same way as the combined companies of Ghattas and Aboo Sammat.[1] The scene of war had merely been transferred from Mbeeoh's territory to that of the sons of Tombo and Ezo.' It is not clear, how, when, or where Gbudwe surprised Aboo Guroon, but Schweinfurth's account suggests that it was prior to Ndoruma's attack on the merchant's post and therefore before 1870, and we must presume that he entered Gbudwe's kingdom from the west. Thus we may conclude, thanks to Schweinfurth, that shortly before 1870 and in that year Gbudwe had fought the troops of three trading companies: those of Muhammad, Ghattas, and Aboo Guroon. To him they were probably all one, and he doubtless regarded their attacks on him as sequels to the incident of Bazingbi's daughter. I return later to a discussion of the situation at the time of Schweinfurth's visit. We have first, if we are to follow the sequence of events, to record the struggle for power among Bazingbi's sons after their father's death.

3

The story of this struggle is one of the best known of Zande historical traditions, and de Calonne, Hutereau, and others have recounted it. I have heard it from several Azande. The version given here was told me by Kanimara, whose father Funa was a participant in the events it relates.

As is customary among the ruling Avongara, Bazingbi had divided up his kingdom during his lifetime among his elder sons Ngima, Ezo, Wando, and Malingindo,[2] he himself taking a central position.[3] On his death his eldest son Ngima, who appears to have been ruling a province near the source of the Guruba (Gurba) river, between the provinces of Ezo and Malingindo, intended to take his domain. His second son Ezo

[1] Schweinfurth, op. cit., vol. ii, p. 286. The English translation says that Gbudwe was surprised by Aboo Guroon, but see *Im Herzen von Afrika*, 1922, p. 440. Also cf. 1878 edn., p. 397.   [2] See Chap. X.

[3] His last residence is marked on Schweinfurth's map just west of the Yubo and to the south of its junction with the Yabongo. Azande told me, however, that it was further to the north-west, between the rivers Ya and Nagasi; and de Calonne says that he died on the Nagusi (Nagasi), tributary of the Sueh (op. cit., p. 60). Hutereau says that he died on the Lingasi, probably in 1865 (op. cit., 1922, p. 163).

was ruling an area to the west in the neighbourhood of the Biki river. Neither Ngima nor Ezo thrived in their kingdoms and both consulted the poison oracle about the advisability of their remaining in them. The oracle told both of them that if they stayed where they were misfortune would overtake them, so Ngima journeyed to the court of Ezo to suggest that they exchanged kingdoms, to which proposal Ezo agreed. When the news of this exchange spread, Ezo's followers at court showed great indignation, for Ngima had a bad reputation among the Azande, and he was also considered to have been disobedient to his father. Ezo's followers supported one of his courtiers of the Abakundo clan who told his king that they would never serve Ngima and upbraided him for letting his brother depart in peace. This courtier called upon the young warriors at court to follow him, and they ran after Ngima and beat him with sticks. They tied a stick to his member and twisted it round and round until it was in a terrible state, and so they left him. Ezo said nothing when he was told what had happened.

Ngima returned to his court and appeared in it naked before his subjects that they might see the shame that had been done to him. His subjects shouted for war and vengeance, while his eldest son Limbasa came forward and urged his father to hide his nakedness, which Ngima refused to do till vengeance had been sworn. Limbasa swore by the limb of his father that he would not rest till he had taken vengeance on his uncle Ezo for the treatment his father had received. After he had heard his son's oath, Ngima went into his private quarters and covered his nakedness with a tiny piece of barkcloth and then he returned to sit in court and listen to his followers threatening war.

Limbasa summoned his young warriors and advanced with them in haste and secrecy to Ezo's court, where he surprised the king carousing with his subjects. When Ezo saw men approaching he asked who they were. His answer was Limbasa's assault on his unprepared subjects. Ezo leaped up and ran to his private quarters, where one of his wives handed him his shield. He reappeared in court armed for the fight, but he was driven back with his followers by the superior numbers of the attackers. Limbasa, like Achilles seeking Hector, sought Ezo alone to avenge his father's humiliation, asking everyone whether they had seen him and calling upon him to come forward. First one, then another, of Limbasa's warriors saw Ezo but passed him by in silence, not wishing to shed the blood of a king. But one man who saw him in flight shouted out that he had found Ezo. As he was surrounded, Ezo cried out, 'O subjects of Bazingbi, what do you want with me? What have I done? It was you, and not I, who mutilated Ngima. I knew nothing of the affair.' When he had spoken thus, a certain Nduka of the Abandogo clan speared him, and he died. Meanwhile news of the attack had spread in all directions as the warning cry was carried from mouth to mouth from one end to the other of Ezo's domains, and his warriors came pouring in till Limbasa's force was outnumbered and driven back.

Now when Gbudwe heard of these events he swore that he would not rest till the best of his brothers had been avenged; for Ezo was to him as his mother's son, since his mother had borne him on the hearth of the mother of Ezo and had carried the baby Ezo on her hips. So Gbudwe sent messages to his brothers, calling upon them to assist him against Ngima and his sons. To this call some of his younger brothers, such as Funa, responded, but his elder brothers Wando and Malingindo, who already possessed domains of their own, regarded the affair as no concern of theirs. Aided by his younger brothers, Gbudwe advanced into Ngima's country, plundering the homesteads of his subjects. Limbasa gathered his warriors and went out to meet him. In the engagement Ngima's warriors were defeated and Limbasa was wounded in the mouth by a spear. It went into his mouth and through his cheek, and when he drew it out it left a large gaping wound.

The success of Gbudwe in this war is partly attributed to his possession of a magic whistle called *ngbuka anya*, over which he had uttered a spell and which he then blew before the fighting commenced. This whistle had been a cherished possession of Bazingbi, who on his deathbed had charged Kilima of the Angumbi clan to hand it over to Gbudwe. For some reason this man did not give the whistle to Gbudwe, and no one knew what had happened to it till an old wife of Bazingbi came forward and told Gbudwe that it was in the possession of Kilima. This whistle remained with Gbudwe for the rest of his life, and on his death it was removed from his hut by one of his chief wives, Nanduru, who gave it to her son Gangura, who had it till his recent death.

Defeated in battle, Limbasa fled to the court of his cousin Renzi son of Wando. He requested Renzi to consult the poison oracle on his behalf to find out what the future had in store for him. Renzi consented to do so and next morning the two princes, accompanied by several courtiers, went to a place a short way away in the bush, where they were to consult the oracle. There was no hint of foul play in the arrangements for the consultation. Limbasa sat facing the man who administered the poison and Renzi and his courtiers sat behind this man, so everyone present was before him and at a safe distance. After poison had been administered to several fowls about a variety of questions, Renzi told one of the attendant courtiers to go and cut a few short sticks to tie to the feet of the chicken which had survived the tests (this is done so that the fowls can easily be caught when the oracular seance is finished). This courtier, following a pre-arranged plan, strolled casually past Limbasa, who sat with his curved ceremonial knife across his knees, and when he was just behind the prince he flung his arms round him, pinioning him so that he could not use his hands. Limbasa struggled but was immediately pierced by a spear. He was buried in a grave near that of his grandfather Bazingbi and that of his uncle Funa, who had been killed while assisting Gbudwe against Ngima, and one or two women had their arms and legs broken and were buried alive with him, for Renzi said that he was a prince and a kinsman and it were meet that he be honoured in his death. It seems that Limbasa had gone to Renzi to ask his help against Gbudwe. Renzi's motives for this cold-blooded assassination appear to have been a desire to avenge the death of his uncle Ezo coupled with the usual jealousy of one prince towards another.

When news of his son's assassination was brought to the mutilated Ngima, he took his harp and bag of sweet potatoes and ground-nuts and went into the bush to mourn his son. Now Ndoruma son of Ezo sent men to follow him, and after a long search they discovered him sitting alone outside a simple grass hut and playing on his harp. When Ndoruma's men approached he greeted them and asked them who they were and whence they had come. They replied that they were subjects of Gbaria son of Bugwa and that they had come from his court. When Ngima heard their reply he entered his hut and took down his rubbing-board oracle and asked it, 'Are these men subjects of

Gbaria?' The oracle said they were not. He asked the oracle again, 'If these men are not what they claim to be, subjects of Gbaria, are they then subjects of Ndoruma?' The oracle said that they were subjects of Ndoruma. He then asked the oracle a final question, saying, 'Now oracle listen and tell me the truth, is this my death?' The oracle said that it was. When he heard he was to die Ngima came out of his hut and said to the men, 'My children you have come to kill me.' Taking a hide he spread it on the ground and lay face downwards on it and requested the men to kill him. They speared him and he said, 'Bravo my child.' They speared him a second time and again he said, 'Bravo my child.' When he was dead they cut off his head and carried it and the headless trunk to the court of their master. Ndoruma had the corpse placed on the top of a hut in the sight of all and he held a dance to celebrate the event. The body was then taken down and buried near the graves of Ezo, Funa, and Limbasa at the side of the River Ya.

A different version of this story, though varying from the other only in particulars, was told me by Gami, the important old commoner governor in Gbudwe's kingdom who has been quoted before:

When Bazingbi died, Ngima was the eldest son, and Ezo came next. When Bazingbi was dead Ezo appeared first to seize his kingdom. Ngima rose up to come, and Ezo gave orders to his followers to seize Ngima and twist his member. They seized Ngima and twisted his member. He fled to his home to summon his subjects to war. Ngima fled till he reached his home. He told his son Limbasa to rise up with his followers, who were the Abangburo people, and they came against Ezo and slew him. A man cut off Ezo's genitals and ran with them to Ngima. Meanwhile Gbudwe had already come to Zaniwe [Gami's father], who hid him lest the sons of Bazingbi should slay him, because Gbudwe had said he had come to take Bazingbi's kingdom, but one of his father's subjects, Zaniwe, hid him. After Ngima had slain Ezo Gbudwe came and stayed at the home of a man called Bandukpo on the banks of the river Dunde. Gbudwe resided there and he made war against Ngima at that river which is called Manguoko. Gbudwe prevailed against Ngima, who fled to the kingdom of Malingindo; but the sons of Malingindo slew him. Gbudwe thereupon took the kingdom of Bazingbi and he kept it. In that war which Gbudwe fought against Ngima the followers of Ngima killed Funa son of Bazingbi. They speared another son of

Bazingbi whose name was Gongosi. Funa begat Kanimara. Gongosi begat Kurugbia. But though they speared Gongosi he recovered.

De Calonne, in his account of these events, says that Ngima was a sorcerer who had been disinherited by his father and was later believed to have killed his father with magic.[1] Hutereau says that Ngima was killed, by men sent for that purpose, at the home of Mazinda son of Bugwa son of Mabenge, where he had sought peace and refuge.[2]

There emerge from Zande comments on this story some points which are, I think, of significance for a study of their political institutions. Azande took it for granted that when a king died his senior sons would fight for his inheritance. These already had provinces to administer during their father's lifetime and consequently were able to mobilize their subjects against their rivals. It follows, and Azande themselves make the point, that the issue was decided by the amount of support each prince received from his subjects and those of his father; that, however autocratic the rule of the Avongara may appear to have been, ultimately it must have rested on the consent of their subjects. This is evident from the story I have just related; for Gbudwe, who eventually took his father's kingdom (that part of it which Bazingbi himself administered), at the time of his father's death did not even have a province of his own, as his elder brothers had. It is said that his father Bazingbi and his grandfather Yakpati had both consulted the poison oracle about his future and had been told by it that as he was destined to be a great king there was no need to give him a province. He was able to succeed only because he was the favourite of his father's subjects, and especially of his father's military companies. It is often said that it was Bazingbi's senior company, the Abaigo, who gave Gbudwe his kingdom. On the other hand, the Zande story and Zande comments on it make it clear that Bazingbi's eldest son Ngima failed because he did not have the support of his father's subjects. Azande also say that his fall was attributed to ill feeling between him and his father, for he committed adultery with his father's wives, and some say that he killed his father with sorcery. It is said likewise that Renzi, the eldest son of Yakpati, was killed when fighting against the Amadi on

---

[1] Op. cit., p. 60. [2] Op. cit., p. 167.

account of his father having cursed him; and some of Gbudwe's sons, especially Mange, are said to have met with bad ends on account of their father's ill will. Azande regard it as a usual circumstance that there should be suspicion and animosity between a king and his senior sons.

It is not possible to date exactly the events I have just recorded. Ezo is shown as dead in Schweinfurth's genealogy, and Gbudwe, as already mentioned, was in occupation of Bazingbi's territory (that part of his kingdom he personally administered) when Schweinfurth was making his explorations, so Ezo must have been killed and Ngima must already have been defeated by Gbudwe before 1870. However, Schweinfurth's genealogy shows Ngima as still alive and therefore, unless this is a mistake, Ngima's death at the hands of Ndoruma, which in the Zande story took place not very long after Gbudwe had ravaged his country, must have occurred after 1870. The fighting between Ezo, Ngima, and Gbudwe may therefore be assumed to have taken place somewhere round about 1868–9. We have now reached a point where we begin to have historical records of value.

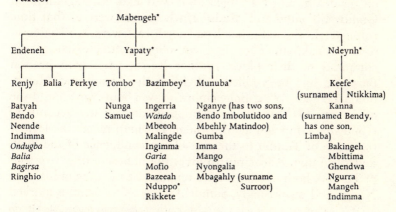

Of doubtful relationship with the line of Mabengeh:

Ezo*
|
Ngettoh
Nderuma
Ngettue

ZANDE PRINCES LISTED BY SCHWEINFURTH.

(The names of ruling princes are printed in italics. The names of deceased princes are marked thus *.)

4

Georg Schweinfurth, an eminent Russo-German botanist, was the son of a merchant and was born in Riga in 1836. He had already considerable experience in Africa when in 1868 he began his famous exploration of Central Africa. He arrived in Zandeland shortly after the events I have just recorded had taken place, and his account of his travels and his map tell us what was the position in 1870. Gbudwe (Mbio, Mbeeoh) was ruling a region between the upper courses of the Hu and the Yubo (the western boundary was almost certainly the Lingasi and not the Yubo—Schweinfurth had no opportunity to visit the area). His kingdom was bounded to the south and south-west by the domains of his elder brothers Wando and Malingindo. To the west of it the country was ruled by the sons of his brother Ezo (Ngatua and Ndoruma). To the north and north-east were the sons of Tombo and Ngangi son of Muduba. The kingdoms of Wando, Malingindo, and the sons of Ezo, as well as his own, had all been part of the domains of his father Bazingbi. Ngima's territory ceased to be a separate domain on his death, and his subjects followed Ezo, Malingindo, and Gbudwe. Tombo and Muduba, whose sons were at that time ruling territories to the north and north-east, were, like Bazingbi, sons of Yakpati. They had consolidated and extended the conquests of their oldest brother Renzi, who, with his son Bazugba, had been killed in fighting the Amadi and Abangbinda peoples. What Schweinfurth says about Ngangi and the other sons of Muduba is mentioned later in my account of Gbudwe's campaign against them. His map places the former residence of Tombo to the east of the confluence of the Sueh and the Yubo. Schweinfurth gives the names of only two sons of Tombo, both of whom were reigning at the time of his visit, Nunga and, surprisingly, Samuel.[1] Nunga's residence is marked

[1] It is difficult to accept this as a Zande name and we must suppose that it was incorrectly heard or faultily recorded, for it could scarcely be a Christian name. The first and only Christian mission in the Southern Sudan, nowhere in this vicinity, was that opened by the Catholic Church at Gondoroko on the White Nile in 1851 and abandoned in 1862 owing to the appalling mortality among the community (S. Santandrea, *Bibliografia di Studi Africani della Missione dell'Africa Centrale*, 1948, pp. x–xi). Whatever the explanation may be, it is amusing to note that Antinori drew attention to the resemblance between three Zande names of persons recorded by Piaggia—Intogno, Zamuel, and Zeresi—and the Italian Antonio, Samuele, and Teresa (op. cit., p. 163).

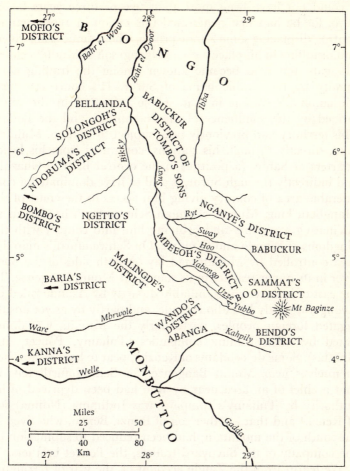

SKETCH I4 THE POSITIONS OF ZANDE PRINCES
After Schweinfurth.

on the east bank of the Yubo near its confluence with the Sueh, and Samuel's much further to the north and well to the west of the Sueh, between that river and the Biki (Schweinfurth had not himself visited this area and his pointing of the seats of these princes must have been by verbal indication or, more likely, taken from Antinori's map).

To the south-east of Gbudwe was an area over which Schweinfurth's Arab trader friend Muhammad had recently—

it could not have been more than two or three years before 1870, for he had first penetrated this region in 1866—gained control, displacing some Zande prince, whose name is not given, and installing in his place a son of Ngangi son of Muduba called Mbagali, but who became known among the trading community by the Arabic name of Surur. His court was near Muhammad's station in Lat. 4° 50′, situated in the angle formed by the confluence of the Nabambiso and the Boddo. This territory had previously been subject to Wando. Muhammad, directly through his stations, controlled from his headquarters at Sabby (a position in the central Bahr al-Ghazal), and indirectly through Surur, is said to have dominated a considerable area of country giving him access to the court of the Mangbetu king, Munza, of whom Schweinfurth has left us so fascinating a picture, and bringing him into contact with the kingdoms of Wando and Gbudwe. On Schweinfurth's map this area controlled by Muhammad lay on both sides of the Sueh river in its upper reaches to its sources at Mount Bangenze. To the east of it the country, inhabited partly by Azande ruled by Avongara, partly by Adio Azande, and partly by as yet unsubjugated foreign peoples, particularly the Mundu, was dominated by other trading companies (Tuhamy, Poncet, and Ghattas). Some descendants of Renzi appear to have established themselves near Mount Bangenze, for Schweinfurth tells us that a chief of an area near by who had been deprived of his authority by Tuhamy's company was Indimma (Ndima) son of Renzi,[1] and that another son of Renzi, Bendo, who lived to the south of the mountain, had been reduced to submission by the company of the Savoyard traders, the Poncet brothers.[2]

We learnt from the Zande account of 'the war of Bazingbi's daughter' that relations between Bazingbi and the Arab traders were at first amicable; and we shall see later that Ngangi son of Muduba was on excellent terms with them; and so at first were Wando and Ndoruma son of Ezo. Only Gbudwe from the beginning and continuously refused to have anything to do with them.[3] However, soon the behaviour of the traders in one way

---

[1] Op. cit., vol. ii, 1873, p. 210.　　　　　　　[2] Ibid., p. 217.
[3] I do not discuss the situation in the western Zande kingdoms, mostly in what used to be French Equatorial Africa, where relations with the Arabs were earlier, closer, and on a larger scale.

or another outraged Zande feelings. The kings were threatened
or in some other way humiliated before their subjects; and their
subjects were plundered, as indeed can be seen to have been
inevitable when we realize the great distances which had to be
covered by the caravans and their size—some hundreds of
persons, for human porterage had to be used (the caravan
Schweinfurth accompanied was just short of a thousand souls
with a marching column of not much less than four miles in
length—and their need to live, at least to a large extent, on
the resources of the country they had to traverse; and also that
they were composed of adventurers of low class and character.
The princes were quite prepared to receive gifts of iron and
copper, which they, at any rate at first, regarded as being more
in the nature of tribute or as payment for security of transit than
as trade, a form of exchange they were unacquainted with.
What they were asked to give in return was ivory, a commodity
of no great value to themselves, for Azande made little use of it
—for ornaments, knife-handles and trumpets. Elephants were
slaughtered for their flesh rather than for their tusks. To ensure
a regular supply of ivory, however, and also of provisions, the
traders began to depart from what they thought of as purchase
or exchange and to take hostages, to help themselves to the
produce of gardens and cultivations, to enslave captives, and in
various other ways to provoke retaliation; so that by 1870 their
relation with the princes, who saw their own authority, and
even their security, threatened by these intruders, had deteri-
orated. The princes were thinking in terms of their social
position—in the Zande accounts I have never even heard ivory
mentioned—and the Arabs in terms of commercial profit; and
this divergence of interests soon led to clashes between them.[1]

Ngangi, it is true, was still on good terms with Muhammad.
The latter's relations with Wando were at this time far from
cordial. On crossing the Yubo, the combined caravans of
Muhammad and Ghattas, accompanied by Schweinfurth, met
Nduppo (Ndukpe), a brother of Wando and subject to him but

[1] Schweinfruth (op. cit., vol. ii, 1873, p. 287) expresses the opinion that one
of the main reasons why the most northerly princes turned against the traders
was that, when their own supplies of ivory began to fail, they did not wish to see
trade opened up with their rivals further south. This may have been a consideration,
but it has to be borne in mind that Schweinfurth knew nothing of the feeling of these
princes and was merely recording what the traders told him.

at the time on very bad terms with him and in terror of being
assassinated by him, a fate which befell him a few days after the
departure of the caravan from his home. The next move was
to the home of Rikkete (Rikita), another brother of Wando and
also subject to him but in his case a loyal subject: his reception
of the caravan was regarded as a test of Wando's intentions.
Two years previously Wando and Muhammad had been
friends and Muhammad had married Wando's daughter; but
during Muhammad's absence in Khartoum his brother, whom
he had left in charge, fell foul of Wando, and there had been
recriminations and plundering on both sides. However, in the
event, Wando let the caravan proceed. On arrival in Wando's
own country, he received Muhammad in a manner which both
Muhammad and Schweinfurth considered equivocal, and both
threatened him. It is therefore not surprising that when a caravan of another merchant company, that of Tuhamy, which was
on its way southwards and which shortly afterwards joined
Muhammad's caravan, entered Wando's territory almost
immediately after Muhammad had left it, it was so violently
attacked that its members were compelled to defend themselves
for two days behind an extemporized abattis and suffered some
loss of life.[1] The people of Muhammad's caravan, on their return
journey northwards from Munza's court, expected to be
attacked also, and they made this the more likely in that, although
they kept as far away as possible from Wando, they ravaged his
country. An incident occurred in the country of the Abanga,
a people who recognized Wando's suzerainty, and Muhammad
was wounded. He thereupon ordered the country to be given
over to pillage; and the porters went off to steal the people's
food supplies and to burn their homesteads, and the Nubians to
slaughter and to make slaves, torturing their child victims. The
fighting which ensued was, however, with the Abanga, and
neither Wando nor his Zande followers were involved; Wando,
it was said, having been warned by his oracles not to take part
in the fighting.[2]

If Wando's attitude had been regarded as uncertain, Gbudwe
was held to be an avowed enemy, on account, we must presume,
of earlier events. Schweinfurth tells us:

---

[1] Schweinfurth, op. cit., vol. i, 1873, pp. 542–3.
[2] Ibid., vol. i, Chaps. XI and XII; vol. ii, Chap. XVII.

Besides Wando on the south, he [Muhammad] had another enemy on the west, viz. Wando's brother Mbeeoh [Gbudwe], who, as an independent chieftain, ruled the district on the lower Yubbo [Yubo], before its union with the Sway [Sueh]; and the combined attacks of these two placed his possessions at times in considerable jeopardy. To escape this difficulty Mohammed now resolved to undertake a campaign against Mbeeoh first, and, as soon as this was accomplished, to proceed with his measures of reprisal against Wando.[1]

This was in May 1870. The campaign was not a success. Only a portion of the missing ivory in Wando's country was recovered. Wando himself, having been warned by his oracles, remained concealed in inaccessible places. Consequently the operation was mainly directed against his brother Gbudwe.

Contrary to the general practice of the Niam-niam [Zande] princes, Mbeeoh [Gbudwe] had been personally engaged in the conflict and had exhibited remarkable bravery. On one occasion it had been with the greatest difficulty that Muhammad had held his own against the hordes of his opponent, and in a raging storm had been obliged to erect a kind of rampart, made of straw, to afford a shelter from which anything like a steady fire might be opened upon the assailants.[2]

Shortly after Muhammad's return from this campaign and while he was starting to make for the north, a messenger brought a report from the commander of his corps that had been sent towards the west, a certain Badri, stating that, when crossing a gallery forest in Malingde's [Malingindo's] territory, the force had been ambushed by the combined strength of three chieftains (we are not told who they were, but Schweinfurth's remarks suggest that Gbudwe's forces were engaged). Three of their number had been killed and, out of their ninety-five soldiers, thirty-two had been severely wounded. They had been closely besieged for six days, and they asked for speedy relief. However, before Muhammad reached them they managed to extricate themselves, but at the cost of all their ivory. Many of the bearers (mostly Bongo) had also been killed or wounded.[3]

At the end of the same year (1870) the Arab traders suffered an even heavier defeat at the hands of the Azande, this time the

---

[1] Ibid., vol. ii, 1873, p. 193.   [2] Ibid., pp. 219–20.
[3] Ibid., pp. 229–30.

subjects of Ndoruma son of Ezo. This king's territories were
nearer than the kingdoms of the south to the main trading
stations in the northern Bahr al-Ghazal. Like the other Zande
kings, he had at first welcomed the traders, who brought him
copper and other commodities useful to him in exchange for the
ivory which he did not greatly value; but, as in the other kingdoms, the behaviour of the companies turned him into a foe,
and, among other incidents, a trading station in his territory
had been destroyed and its garrison massacred, the arms and
ammunition falling into the hands of the Azande, who then
used them effectively against the Arabs. Ndoruma had some
fugitive Zande slaves at his court who were acquainted with
firearms and instructed his men in their use. The station belonged to the former servant of Petherick, Abderahman Aboo
Guroon, and he persuaded the leaders of other companies to
combine with him in exacting vengeance. The operation, in
December 1870, was a disaster for the Arabs. Their caravan,
consisting of soldiers from the three companies of Aboo Guroon,
Hassaballa, and Kurshook Ali, the entire party numbering
close on 2,250 men, of whom not less than 300 bore arms was
ambushed and totally defeated. The attack, led by Ndoruma in
person, was by rifle as well as by spear; and, besides a number
of bearers, 150 Muhammadans were reported to have been
killed, including Aboo Guroon himself and another leader,
Ahmed Awat. All the baggage, including a hundred loads of
powder and ammunition, fell into the hands of Ndoruma. The
Arab mercenaries who served the trading companies, Schweinfurth tells us, dreaded bullets; and it was going beyond what
they had bargained for when they met an enemy possessing
firearms and a knowledge of their use, for their own superiority
lay not in their courage but in their weapons. It was also a
surprise to them, after their easy subjection of the peoples of the
northern Bahr al-Ghazal, to find themselves up against powerful, populous, and well-organized kingdoms; for the strength of
the Azande consisted, as Schweinfurth observed, 'in their con-
stitutional unity'.[1] Eager though they were to acquire ivory and
slaves, the campaigns of 1870 taught the Arabs that it was not
profitable to make war on the Zande kingdoms nor easy to
persuade their soldiers to escort caravans into them. Up to

[1] Op. cit., vol. ii, 1873, p. 309.

PLATE V

Bitarangba (showing mutilation of wrists)

1870, therefore, we find that these kingdoms, if not inviolate, were able to hold their own and inspire respect.

There now were added further complications to the already complicated picture. Their cupidity excited by the easily gained wealth in ivory, and the still more easily gained wealth in slaves, two more sorts of vultures descended in numbers on the hard-pressed natives of the Bahr al-Ghazal. The merchants, as the name 'Khartoomers' often applied to them in the literature suggests, were mostly Khartoum merchants, and their soldiers seem to have been for the most part Nubians driven by poverty and taxation from their homes, supported by irregulars who might be from any of the peoples of the Bahr al-Ghazal. The Egyptian Government now, in 1870, proceeded to establish posts in the province. Kurshook Ali, an Osmanli and one of the ivory merchants of Khartoum, who owned a station near what is now its capital, Wau, was invested with the title of *sandjak* and placed at the head of two companies of government troops, one of Turkish regulars (*bashibazouks*) and the other of Negroes (*nizzam*). This caused consternation among the traders, whose position was jeopardized and who had to submit to taxes and imposts threatening them with bankruptcy and ruin, and there was much hostility between them and the troops. If they demanded supplies and services from the natives, so did the troops demand supplies and services from them. Confusion was worse confounded; and far from the presence of government forces making for order, they only increased the disorder. 'For the suppression of the slave-trade they did absolutely nothing.'[1] Indeed, they were perhaps the worst offenders. The commanders of the troops, which in course of time increased and formed new garrisons, took every opportunity to acquire slaves for themselves and, furthermore, committed every sort of atrocity on the long-suffering Negroes. All our authorities are in agreement in this matter. The other sort of vultures which now descended on the Bahr al-Ghazal are referred to in the literature as *Gellaba* (*Jelabba*). They were a riff-raff of poor but avaricious Arabs, chiefly from Kordofan and Darfur, who engaged in various religious practices, in peddling, and in the Bahr al-Ghazal invariably also in the purchase and sale of slaves. These bigots arrived in hordes—there must have been several thousand of

---

[1] Ibid., p. 305.

them—and attached themselves to the garrisons and trading stations, from where they carried on their nefarious activities. At one trading station alone there were early in 1871, Schweinfurth estimated, 2,700 of them.[1] There is no means of calculating how many thousands of Negroes must have been enslaved and sold in the markets of the Northern Sudan through their agency.[2]

By this time, however, reports of what was happening reached England, and humanitarian bodies there and elsewhere brought such pressure on their governments that they, in their turn, were forced to put pressure on the Khedive Isma'il to do something to stop the trade in slaves. He appointed Sir Samuel Baker in 1869 to be Governor-General of the Equatorial Provinces; and in 1874 Baker was succeeded in this position by Col. Charles Gordon, who in 1877 became Governor-General of the whole of the Sudan. Gordon recruited a handful of Europeans, and a serious effort was made to put down the trade. But their Turkish and Arab officials were for the most part hopelessly corrupt as well as being in one way or another participants in the slave trade themselves. On the Nile some control over the trade could indeed be exercised, but this only increased the traffic in the interior, and especially in the Bahr al-Ghazal, where Gessi was to make an attempt, as heroic as it was hopeless, to eradicate it.

5

The gap between two of our main sources, the Russo-Germans Schweinfurth and Junker, is bridged by an Italian, Romolo Gessi, born at Constantinople in 1831, the son of a lawyer of Ravenna who was a political exile. He had an adventurous early life, in the course of which he twice met Gordon and as a result was invited to serve under him in the Egyptian Sudan. In 1874 he visited the region of the Bahr al-Ghazal, and again between the years 1878 and 1880, when he was entrusted by Gordon with the task of crushing the revolt of Suliman Ziber Bey, the chief of the slavers who were decimating the peoples of the Bahr al-Ghazal. He died of his exertions at Suez in 1881.

[1] Op. cit., vol. ii, 1873, p. 357 (*Im Herzen von Africa*, 1922, p. 475; but the footnote giving this number is omitted).

[2] These various Arab elements were often divided by tribal animosities (see Holt, *The Mahdist State in the Sudan, 1881–1898*, 1958, p. 36).

On his first visit to the Bahr al-Ghazal he found that the situation was as bad, if not worse, than at the time of Schweinfurth's visit a few years earlier. A large part of the region was controlled by traders in ivory and slaves, the principal of whom were Catasc, Kutshuk Ali, Agat, Hassabella, Abu Muri, Magajub, Biselli, and Zibehr Bey, the *mudir* (Governor) of Shakka.[1] The Egyptian officials turned a blind eye to the depredations of these trading companies, and they committed further atrocities of their own. Gessi did not himself visit the Zande kingdoms. For us the most valuable part of his account of them is confirmation that the traders had discovered that they were too powerful to be raided with impunity and, at any rate so far as those in what is now the Sudan were concerned, both they and government troops kept away from the Zande kingdoms. Writing in March 1880 to the Editor of the *Esploratore*, after he had destroyed Suliman Ziber's forces, he said that he had recently established cordial relations with King Mdarama (Ndoruma, son of Ezo) and that Mdarama, Mbio (Gbudwe), and Mofio (Mopoi):

command a vast still unexplored territory which remained closed both to the united enterprise of the Dongolese [Nubians], and to the slavers' settlements. Scarcely had the campaign against Suleiman ended—I could dispose of about four thousand soldiers—than all the chiefs expressed a wish to attack Mdarama, to revenge themselves for his having killed in various combats some thousand Arabs and perhaps five times as many Besingers[2] and porters. But I did not listen to their desires. I felt more inclined to fight those who had revolted than Mdarama, who, by killing so many Arabs, had rendered a great service to humanity.

By means of a faithful negro Sangiak,[3] named Raffai, I opened up secret negotiations with Mdarama, assuring him that I would not molest him. All news in Africa, in spite of the want of post and telegraph, is swiftly propagated to the most distant regions. Mdarama was aware of all that had happened in the district under my jurisdiction, and he sent me salutations through Raffai, with a gift of sixty large elephant tusks, asking me to send him a seal, that he might seal and forward some letters which he had got a friend of

[1] Gessi, op. cit., p. 50.

[2] Irregular troops. The word is probably formed from *bezingra*, a word in a Nubian, probably the Dongolawi, dialect.

[3] This is a Turkish word referring to a province; in the Sudan it had the sense, not, I believe, found elsewhere, of a senior official or officer.

Raffai to write. I did what he wished, sending besides a sword and some cloth and beads.

When Mdarama received these presents, he let me know that he meant to come in person to make my acquaintance and see the man who had annihilated Suleiman and his troops, and had done so much good to the persecuted natives.[1]

Ndoruma, then a man of about thirty-five years of age, paid Gessi this visit, apparently at Dem Bekir, presented him with forty large elephant tusks, and offered to hand over about seven hundred guns which he had taken from the Arabs. Gessi told him to keep the guns in case he needed them for use against the Arabs on some future occasion.

What Gessi says about Gbudwe is somewhat ambiguous, and we have to remember that he was both ignorant and confused about the relations existing between the Zande kings, and also that he was making as strong a case as he could for the success of his administration. He says that Ndoruma let him know that he had sent 1,300 of Gbudwe's men to Dem Suliman laden with ivory as a present to the Government, a statement which makes no sense at all.[2] He says further, that Ndoruma told him that Gbudwe wished to visit him, and on the strength of this questionable information he advanced the claim that Gbudwe was about to submit or even had submitted.[3] Elsewhere he says that he placed little faith in Gbudwe, and that Gbudwe and Ndoruma were hostile to one another, while Gbudwe and Wando were allied against Ndoruma and the government troops.[4] Speaking of Ndoruma and Gbudwe in a letter written in January 1880 he says,

These two kings have massacred all the Arab expeditions that entered their district. Four years ago the natives of the settlements of Kutshuk Ali, Wau, and Jur Gattas made an alliance and marched against Mdarama with more than two thousand soldiers armed with guns and three thousand native spearmen. Mdarama, who possessed more than six hundred guns, defended the passes, fell upon the Arabs, and massacred them all. The poor spearmen suffered the same fate, and since then the terrible Mdarama was never again attacked. His district is very rich in ivory and other products. Suleiman Ziber, after some unfortunate enterprises against

---

[1] Gessi, op. cit., pp. 347–8.   [2] Ibid., p. 349.
[3] Ibid., p. 368.   [4] Ibid., p. 375.

Mdarama, had tried to bribe him to be a friend, but the cunning emperor refused his gifts and repulsed all treaties.

He adds: 'Almost all the secondary Niam-Niam chiefs depend on Mdarama or Mbio [Gbudwe].'[1] The six hundred guns mentioned in the quotation above were presumably, most of them, booty taken in the earlier fight between Ndoruma and the Arabs, mentioned by Schweinfurth as having taken place in 1870.

The map accompanying Gessi Pasha's book (a posthumous collection of letters and reports) is of no ethnographic value, but his statement of the distribution of the Zande kingdoms with which we are concerned is of some interest in that it shows us that nothing very much had changed since Schweinfurth's visit:

To the south of Mdarama [Ndoruma] lives King Jettua [Ngatua], the brother of the former, and still farther south lives King Malingde [Malingindo], where the governor of the Bahr-el-Ghazal has a seriba for storing ivory. To the east of the kings Mdarama and Jettua lives King Mbio [Gbudwe], and south of Malingde, across the river Blima, is the powerful tribe of Uanda [Wando]. Continuing towards the south the Welle is met with, after crossing which one is in the midst of Monbuttu [Mangbetu].[2]

In general we learn from his account that the Zande kingdoms with which we are concerned were still independent up to 1880, and in particular that Gbudwe was displaying the same hostility to the Egyptian Government as he had towards the trading companies.

Gessi's confidence that Ndoruma was willing to submit to the Egyptian Government, and possibly also Gbudwe, was soon shown to have been misplaced; though had Gessi retained the governorship it is conceivable that the situation might have developed differently. Before the year 1880 closed, both Gordon and Gessi had gone, and corruption and disorder became everywhere once again prevalent, if indeed it can be said that they had ever ceased to be, for even when Gessi was governor of the Bahr al-Ghazal, 'Administration was practically non-existent and the slave-traders held sway.'[3] Lupton Bey, who had been the captain of a Red Sea merchantman and had succeeded Gessi

---

[1] Ibid., pp. 368–9. [2] Ibid., p. 375.
[3] Sir Harold MacMichael, *The Sudan*, 1954, p. 34.

as governor of the province, was soon up to his ears in troubles. The Mahdi had begun his revolt in 1881, and the provinces to the north (Kordofan and Darfur) were in his hands by 1883; in which year also the Dinka of the northern Bahr al-Ghazal rose against the Government. In April 1884 the Bahr al-Ghazal garrisons surrendered to Mahdist forces and Lupton was taken captive. As will later be related, it was during Lupton's period of office as governor that Gbudwe was overcome by government forces, in the year 1882. However, Zande accounts place before these events a campaign they call 'the war of Ngangi'.

XVI

THE KINGDOM OF GBUDWE (*continued*)

6

WHEN Bazingbi died and Gbudwe inherited his personal kingdom (as distinct from those parts of it which were governed during his lifetime by his sons) its eastern boundary was the upper course of the Hu river. To the east of the Hu and the Sueh there were at the beginning of his reign a number of sons of Yakpati: Ngindo, Ukwe, Gbalia, Muduba (or his son Ngangi), Tombo, and others. Some of these, it would seem, Gbudwe early displaced (their territories going to his sons Mange, Kana, and Sanango); and some were displaced by the Arab trading companies. The history of the area is entangled and cannot altogether be unravelled; nor will I make in the present place an attempt to trace the history of all these princelings. I speak here only of Piaggia's friend Tombo, and very briefly of him, and of Schweinfurth's acquaintance Ngangi. Tombo was already dead in 1870, and his kingdom to the east of the Sueh river had been inherited by his son Nunge. It appears that on Nunge's death his son Mbatu never succeeded in establishing himself in his father's domains; he died at Hill Zengu on his return from west of the Sueh, where he had for some reason fled. The reason for his flight was probably incursion into his territory by the Egyptian Government. Tombo's subjects eventually transferred their allegiance to Gbudwe (his son Rikita). I have a note that one of his grandsons, Baduagbanga, son of Nunge, collected a following between the rivers Hu and Kisi and was left undisturbed in this district by Gbudwe, who liked him because of his loyalty. Another of his grandsons, Kana (Kanna) son of Ukwe (Hokua), and his brothers were living in 1883 near the head-waters of the Yeta.[1]

Ngangi, a son of Muduba[2] and grandson of Yakpati, was ruler of a territory between the Sueh and the Iba; the boundary

---

[1] Junker, op. cit., vol. iii, 1892, p. 324.
[2] According to Czekanowski he was murdered by Pereke and other of his brothers (op. cit. p. 82).

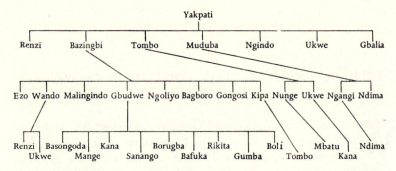

(The genealogy gives most of the names of Zande princes mentioned in the text.)

between his country and that of Tombo being roughly the Mawa, tributary of the Menze, to the junction of the Menze and the Iba. His kingdom was on both sides of the Menze and the Maida and along the Rasi, tributary of the Iba. Muhammad had built a fort (*zeriba*) for him on the Mapuse, a western tributary of the Iba. Schweinfurth, as related earlier, met him in 1870; he was at that time on good terms with Schweinfurth's friend and protector, the Nubian trader Muhammad 'abd al-Sammad. Schweinfurth tells us little about him. He says that he was a tolerably rich chieftain. His court was modest, and he himself was naked except for a little apron. He regarded Muhammad as a friendly neighbour who paid him an annual tribute of copper, beads, and stuffs, in return for which he stored up ivory for Muhammad's purchase. The name of his most northerly 'behnky' (*banyaki*, 'commoner governor') was Peneeo. When Schweinfurth passed southwards from Ngangi's court he came first to a district ruled by one of his brothers, called Gumba. Continuing to the south, he arrived at the court of another brother, Bendo, who had been put in charge of a district near hill Gumango and the River Rye (Rei), a tributary of the Sueh. Besides Gumba and Bendo, Ngangi had five other brothers: Imma, Mango, Nyongalia, Mbeli, and Mbagahli. The first four of these acted as his representatives in charge of various districts; while Mbagahli, as said before, acted (under his Arabic name Surur) as a direct subordinate of Muhammad, who had established him in command of the country he had subjugated, which was bounded by the territories of Ngangi,

Wando, and Gbudwe. Continuing southwards, and just before reaching the Sueh, Schweinfurth passed the hamlets of Marra, one of Ngangi's commoner governors. He then reached the River Hu, a tributary of the Sueh. A little further, across a stream called Manzilly (Manzari), he reached the farmsteads of Kulenjo, which were the first Zande settlements subject to the immediate control of Muhammad. On his return, some four months later, Schweinfurth again crossed Ngangi's domains.[1]

Gbudwe's campaign against Ngangi could not, therefore, have been before 1870;[2] and it seems unlikely that it could have taken place before 1875, since Muhammad was still alive at the end of the previous year and his people would undoubtedly have become involved in it. On the other hand, if it preceded Gbudwe's war with the Egyptian Government, as Azande say it did, and as is clear from other evidences, it must have taken place before 1881. We can say therefore that it probably took place between the years 1875 and 1880 and more likely closer to the earlier than the later date.[3] My informants, who in 1927–30 were elderly men, remembered the campaign taking place when they were boys. Gbudwe was then over forty years of age, and his eldest sons, who took part in the campaign, were already governing provinces of his kingdom.

The following account was given me by Basingbatara, an elderly man. At the time Gbudwe's court was on the Dunde, a tributary of the Lingasi (in the country which was ruled by his son Zegi when I was in Zandeland). An Arab force, which must have belonged to some trading company or to the Egyptian Government, led by a man called Gawaga,[4] had attacked Gbudwe's second son, Mange, who had been given a district to rule on the eastern frontier of his kingdom, and Mange had sent a messenger to his father to ask for assistance. Gbudwe and

---

[1] Op. cit., vol. i, pp. 453–60; vol. ii, p. 243.

[2] See Chronology of Events, p. 458.

[3] That Ngangi's kingdom is still marked on the map of Junker's exploration in the years 1877–8 and 1880–5 signifies little. Junker did not visit the area, and the entry was copied from Schweinfurth's map.

[4] There is no means of knowing who this person might be. The name Gawaga is presumably the Zande pronunciation of the Arabic *khawaga*, and, if so, it would suggest that he might have been a European; but it does not seem possible that any European could have been in this region at that time. The word might, however, be used in reference to a Copt, and it is possible that one of the Ghattas family is referred to.

his senior sons advanced to Mange's aid, but by the time they had reached the Sueh, Mange had repulsed the Arabs. Nevertheless, Gbudwe felt that, as he had had the trouble of going so far, it would be a pity to return home without a fight; so he decided to make war on Ngangi, saying that Ngangi was responsible for bringing the Arabs to his territories. He advanced to the Bambu, a tributary of the Iba, and there he made camp. That evening Ndima, one of Ngangi's brothers (not mentioned by Schweinfurth), made a surprise attack, what Azande call a *basapu*, sending, by way of ironical greeting, a rain of spears into Gbudwe's camp, one of which pierced a certain prince called Gamanzu just above his buttock. Gbudwe was advised to retreat but determined rather to press forward. He took with his own warriors a central position and sent his sons Basongoda, Bafuka, and Borugba with their companies out to one wing and Mange and his companies to the other wing. The opposed forces advanced with only a few paces between each man and those to the right and left of him; and animals surprised between them ran first to one side where, greeted with spears, they turned and fled towards the other side. Ngangi's force, whose main company was the *Awili Bai*, had an advantage in that they were far better equipped with guns than were Gbudwe's men, since, as we have noted, they had been long in friendly contact with trading stations; and at first his wing opposite Mange put his men to flight. But on the other wing Basongoda and his brothers drove back the enemy, a certain Nambia of the Apusi clan killing Ndima. Meanwhile Gbudwe's men twisted round to attack in the rear the force pursuing Mange, a manœuvre which proved so successful that soon the whole of Ngangi's line gave way. Gbudwe decided not to pursue the enemy in person but sent Basongoda and his brothers after them. They captured Ngangi's homestead and took all his wives prisoners.[1] A few days later Ngangi came in to surrender himself with his sons and brothers.[2] In making submission to Gbudwe, he asked for a piece of land where he could settle in peace. Gbudwe said that

---

[1] One of them was the mother of one of my Zande friends, Tembura. She became Gbudwe's wife.

[2] Schweinfurth says that Ngangi had only two sons recognized as legitimate (whatever that may mean): Imbolutidoo and Mattindoo. The names of those recorded in my notebooks are Ndima, Tumusa, Mabenge, Basilingbi, Bazia, and Tembura.

he would think the matter over, and on the following morning he consulted the poison oracle about it. The oracle said that Ngangi must depart with his sons and brothers into Malingindo's territory, which they afterwards did. The Azande of Ngangi then subjected themselves to Gbudwe, some coming westwards to join him and others remaining as subjects of Gbudwe's sons Mange, Kana, and Sanango, to whom their father entrusted the administration of his new domains. These, if they did not at once include the whole of Ngangi's territory, embraced after this campaign all the western part of it, subjugation of the eastern part being completed by Mange later. Gbudwe's realm was thereby much increased in both numbers and renown, for Ngangi had been ruler of a populous territory and one in which were living many true Mbomu families who had followed his father Muduba when he had been sent to complete the conquests of his elder brother Renzi by their father Yakpati. Gbudwe declared that now he had got possession of Yakpati's domains he would not allow them to pass out of his possession.

A text about this campaign, taken down from Ongosi, one of Gbudwe's courtiers with whom I had the privilege of friendly acquaintance and who witnessed at any rate some of its events, describes it thus.

That *bolomu* [Arab] Gawaga came to fight Mange, and Mange fought against him for a long time and overcame him. When Gbudwe heard about the fighting he started to go and take part in it, but while he was still on the way Mange overcame that *bolomu*; but Gbudwe said that he was going to see the site of the fighting. He continued on his way, and when he arrived at the site of the fighting he said he was going up against Ngangi because he was always hostile. Gbudwe continued to advance, and Ngangi brought out his force and disposed it for fighting, and there was a mild engagement in which five men were killed. Gbudwe then left off fighting him and went on beyond to fight another man. He defeated this man and occupied his deserted homestead. Ngangi went home and brought out his army on the banks of the river Bambu. When Gbudwe heard of his movements he prepared his warriors for an engagement. He ordered Basongoda to the right and Mange to the left, while his commoner governors were in the centre, and his own companies also. Thus, while fighting began ahead, Gbudwe came up in the rear. Basongoda started it, and they were engaged in fighting.

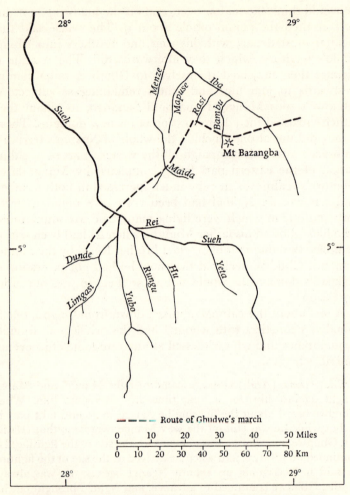

SKETCH 15. MAP OF THE CAMPAIGN AGAINST NGANGI.

Gbudwe ordered his followers to move towards the west. Mange then engaged the enemy. Gbudwe continued his advance. His two sons crumpled on the wings and fighting was concentrated in the centre. His men rushed into the fighting and they fought for a long time. Many of Gbudwe's men were wounded, and many of Ngangi's men were slain. The fighting became very fierce, and Ngangi gathered his riflemen and fled with them. They came and told Gbudwe 'Ngangi has already fled.' Gbudwe replied, 'Not at all, onward to the fighting.' They advanced in vain, for Ngangi fled to the Iba river. So Gbudwe ordered an advance on his home, and he went to stay there and he burnt all his huts. Gbudwe spent a long time there, and while he was there his men went off to seize the women of the country. Gbudwe ordered beer to be brewed that they might drink it and return home; and when they had finished drinking beer Gbudwe distributed women among his followers; and then they all arose to return home. Such is this history. It began with Bazingbi, who fought against the father of Ngangi, Muduba, and scattered his sons. Therefore Gbudwe had said that his father's campaign was incomplete and that it would be well for him to finish it. Hence he went up against Ngangi.

Another short text, given by Gbudwe's old commoner gover-nor Gami, also a witness of some events in the war, and likewise one of my acquaintances, runs:

After Gbudwe had been for a time in his father's stead he went up against Ngangi son of Muduba, because Muduba had taken part of the kingdom of Yakpati. So Gbudwe said that it were well that he should make war against Ngangi to drive him out of the country. Gbudwe arrived near the confluence of the Sueh and the Yubo. He continued and crossed to the other side of the Menze and halted at the Maida. He arose again there and halted at Kpazigi on the river Rasi [Rashi]. He remained there in the morning and went to fight at the Bambu river. Gbudwe overcame the followers of Ngangi on this side of the Bambu and pursued them to the other side and left off pursuing them at the foot of Mount Barangba [Baramba]. Gbudwe arose at Mount Barangba and went ahead and stayed at the homestead of a man called Banzere. Gbudwe then pursued Ngangi across the Iba river, and when he was in headlong flight Gbudwe began to stay at the homestead of Sangumaru. When he arose from there he went to stay at the home of one of his commoner governors, Nguasu. He remained there till he returned to the west.

Gbudwe's march, as will be noted from the sketch opposite, covered extensive stretches of country, and the campaign must have been a lengthy affair.

Ngangi's son Tembura told me that before this campaign took place his father had become involved in disputes with the Arab trader Angbali, whom we may identify with a high degree of probability as Schweinfurth's friend Muhammad, and Gbudwe had encouraged him to attack his posts, promising to help him, but in the event not doing so. According to his son, Ngangi was responsible for Angbali's death and was himself later slain by Angbali's relatives. This does not appear improbable, for though one informant said that he surrendered to Gbudwe, this was not borne out by others, and those the most likely to have known the facts; and if Tembura's information is correct, we can relate it to what Schweinfurth tells us of Muhammad's troubles and death. Schweinfurth, having returned to Europe, obtained for this Nubian adventurer a German decoration to reward him for his services, which had undoubtedly been generous, and on 6 September 1873 Muhammad wrote to thank him, and in the same letter told him of the difficulties he had recently encountered.[1]

We have already noted that the Arab traders had suffered severe set-backs at the hands of Wando, Gbudwe, Malingindo, and Ndoruma. Now Muhammad had to face a revolt of his Zande mercenaries (*Landsknechte*). It is true that in his letter to Schweinfurth Muhammad does not say that Ngangi had anything to do with the revolt, but he was too hard pressed at the time to have had more than a meagre intelligence of the situation, as is indeed clear from his letter; and in view of what Tembura told me, and of his proximity to Muhammad's assaulted stations, we may suppose that it is not unlikely that he was involved in the affair. The mutineers seized three of these stations, captured a large number of rifles with stocks of ammunition, and plundered his stores of goods and ivory. Muhammad found himself on the defensive and in dire straits for some weeks and, although with the aid of men of the trading company of Muhammad Ahmad al-Akkad he defeated the rebels in an engagement, he was attacked and killed by them on 10 November 1874.[2]

The circumstances of his death are recounted somewhat differently by another famous traveller in the Sudan, the Austrian Ernst Marno, who in 1875, in the company of the American Col. Chaillé-Long, explored the Makaraka (Azande) country of the Nile–Congo divide. He says:

Eine Concubine Abd el Samat's soll mit einem seiner angenommenen und aufgezogenen Jungen, Namens Machbub, umgang gepflogen haben, war, um den Züchtigungen zu entgehen, zu dem schon früher geflohenen Machbub entlaufen und hatte diesen angeeifert,

[1] *Im Herzen von Africa*, 1922, pp. 529–41.   [2] Ibid., p. 541.

Abd el Samat umzubringen. Machbub wiegelte die zahlreichen Niamniam Makalil oder Basinger[1] auf und wollte auch Surrur, einen anderen Pflegling und Wequil auf einer der Seriben, für dieses Complott gewinnen. Dieser ging jedoch hierauf nicht ein, sondern warnte vielmehr Abd el Samat, jener aber gewann auch die umwohnenden Neger für sich und bereitete alles zu einem Ueberfalle vor. Es war im Ramadthan des Jahres 1874, als Abd el Samat den grössten Theil seiner Leute mit dem Elfenbeine absandte, er aber mit seiner Familie und wenigen Leuten in der kleinen Seribah am Chor el Canna zurückblieb. Troz öfterer Warnungen Surrur's und der ihm ergebenen Schiuch, dass Machbub mit grosser Macht demnächst einen Ueberfall beabsichtige, machte Abd el Samat nicht die geringsten Vorbereitungen zur Vertheidigung, sondern überliess sich während der drei Festtage am Ende des Ramadthan reichem Genusse geistiger Getränke. In der Nacht des dritten Festtages, als in der Seribah Alles berauscht im Schlafe lag, überfiel Machbub mit seinem Anhange dieselbe, setzte sich vor allem in Besitz der Tukul, in welchen die Pulver- und Munitions-Vorräthe lagen und machte die Meisten der Bewohner im Schlafe nieder, welche kaum zum Gebrauche ihrer Waffen gekommen sein sollen. Abd el Samat sollen die Arme und Füsse und hierauf der Kopf abgeschnitten worden sein. Nur Wenigen gelang es, zu entrinnen, auf die nächsten Seriben zu fliehen und diese Nachricht zu überbringen.[2]

The death of Muhammad and the destruction of his stations in 1873 and 1874 would explain why his forces were not involved in the campaign Gbudwe fought against Ngangi, and also how Gbudwe was able to take over his new territories without being involved in further hostilities with them; for after Muhammad's death his company seems to have restricted its activities to the more docile peoples of the north, who had been broken and reduced to serfdom, and to have avoided any further commercial operations through Zandeland to the south. The company was not dissolved. Junker tells us that in 1877, three years after Muhammad's death, of his seventeen stations only six (Ungua, Boiko, Ngama, Kero, Qana, and Manduggu) remained in the hands of his heirs, nephews, and stepsons, and that they were all unimportant, being small and garrisoned with only a few Dongolan soldiers. These were all outside Zande

---

[1] *Makalil oder Basinger werden die zum Waffenhandwerk in den Seriben aufgezogenen Eingebornen genannt und hatten diese erst ein Jahr früher eine Revolte in Scene gesetzt.* (Marno's note.)

[2] Op. cit., 1879, pp. 94–5.

country, mostly in Mittuland. Nothing remained of the past prosperity of these stations, largely because their garrisons 'had so ruthlessly plundered the poor negroes [Mittu] that whole villages fled, some to seek protection with the powerful A-Zandeh Sultan, Mbio [Gbudwe], others to the Loobus or the Abaka chief, Ansea'. The Babukurs or Mabuquru (as Junker calls them) were also on the road to complete destitution and they also took refuge with Gbudwe and established themselves in his kingdom. Later when Gbudwe 'after a long and brave resistance was overpowered by the Egyptians, the Babukurs fled to the territory between Mount Baginse and the Abaka'. The Azande (Bombeh-Adio) of the Baginse district had, since the death of Muhammad, been at open warfare with the Egyptian Government forces which had replaced those of Muhammad in that area, and it could no longer be traversed, even in strong convoy, without grave risk of disaster.[1] Casati also speaks of 'the people of Abd-el-Samath' as still active in Mittuland as late as August 1884.[2] But, apart from the revolt of the Zande mercenaries and the impoverishment of the countryside, another development must have made for the decline of the company. Some years before the time at which Casati wrote, government forces had occupied King Munza's Mangbetu territory, where they murdered him, committed many atrocities, and spread chaos all around them. They had presumably by this time brought all independent trading activities in the region to an end, ivory having been declared a government monopoly and the trading stations in the south having been taken over by government troops. These troops maintained contact with the north through the country somewhat vaguely called Makaraka, to the east of the Meridi river, leaving Gbudwe's domains in peace. In 1880 Mangbetu territory was transferred from the administration of the Bahr al-Ghazal (Gessi Pasha) to that of Equatorial Province, centred on Lado on the Nile (Emin Pasha), which further obviated any need for government troops to enter Gbudwe's domains, Mangbetuland being reached by an eastern route which did not necessitate traversing them.

At this time therefore Gbudwe had not only preserved his entire independence but had also expanded his kingdom to

[1] Junker, op. cit., vol. i, 1890, pp. 304–5, 420, 428, 432, and 440.
[2] Op. cit., vol. i, p. 294.

embrace large tracts of country to the east. The territories added to his kingdom were very extensive, for, it may be remembered, in Schweinfurth's time Ngangi ruled over an area which stretched from the Iba river to west of the Hu. It was about this time, and possibly to mark his victory, that Gbudwe changed his name from Yambio (generally given by early travellers as 'Mbio') to Gbudwe. The name 'Yambio' then fell into disuse among the Azande themselves, and during my sojourn in what had been his kingdom I rarely heard the name Yambio spoken, even by old men, but only the name Gbudwe; his erstwhile subjects were also almost invariably spoken of as *avuru* Gbudwe, 'the subjects of Gbudwe', and not as *avuru* Yambio, 'the subjects of Yambio'. I do not know what was the meaning of the sounds *yambio*; *mbio* means a yellow-backed duiker. The word *gbudwe* means to tear from the inside, as a lion tears out the inside of its prey. A Zande said,

This name of Gbudwe, he took it from an ordinary Zande; his real name was Yambio. A man came and stood before Yambio and said to him, 'By your limb, son of Bazingbi, I swear in (an earth-shaking roar), if you hear it said of me that I have run away in fighting do not believe it. I am Gbudwe who tears (*gbudwe*) the intestines from a man's side.' When Yambio heard the name of this man he adopted it, and he said that his name was Gbudwe; by his limb, let no man address him again by the name of Yambio; let people use the name of Gbudwe alone. From this time everyone took up the name of Gbudwe.

As Gbudwe was soon to suffer defeat and humiliation, it is at this point, at which he had both consolidated and greatly expanded his father's kingdom and had also successfully resisted all encroachments by the well-armed Arab companies from the north who had reduced so many peoples to serfdom or slavery, that we may fittingly insert into the narrative another text. In it a Zande extols his virtues and prowess, as no doubt, other Azande in other kingdoms extolled the virtues and prowess of their ruler.

Those princes, like Bazingbi, who lived in past times used to have cooked only one large bowl of porridge for the people at court, and the people divided it into portions and ate it all. But this was not at all to the liking of the men at court. Gbudwe was just a member of his father's court. All his brothers had been given provinces to rule, and he was just at court, where his subjects were such members of

the Abaigo military company who were at court. When Bazingbi
died Gbudwe took his place and ruled over his father's subjects. He
took the inheritance of his father on account of his strength, for he
was the man who first made war on the Arabs. After the death of
Bazingbi he made himself master of all his father's territory. When he
heard it said of a prince that he had many followers he made war
against him, and he set one of his sons in his place to reside there and
to rule over all who used to be his subjects. Thus Gbudwe prospered
and became a great king, for he made war against any prince who
opposed him. He only was a great king and continued as such.
Gbudwe was a powerful and a daring man, for he overcame all
princes, and for him alone they all became meek. After he had overcome them all he rested in peace; and he distributed provinces to
all his sons, and he left it to them to make war against many peoples.

7

I now relate a series of incidents known to all senior Azande
of my time who when younger had taken part in affairs. They
are known to Azande as 'the war of Rafai'. This war took place
when my informants were youths, so they had a good memory
of it; and we are fortunately able to fix exactly the date it
occurred from literary evidences at 1881–2. The version I give
here was told me by Basingbatara.

Gbudwe's court at the time was on the Rasi river, a tributary
of the Rungu, in its turn a tributary of the Sueh (between what
in the nineteen-twenties were the districts of Bima and Faki,
sons of Gbudwe). Ndoruma son of Ezo had been attacked by an
Arab force (Rafai representing the Egyptian Government) and
had sought refuge at Gbudwe's court. While he was a guest
there he took offence at what he considered to be a slight done
to him by a certain Baipuru, one of Gbudwe's courtiers.[1] He
was sitting facing Gbudwe, and when he rose to speak, Baipuru
noticed that the waist-cord which held up his barkcloth covering
was loose and he respectfully tightened it for him. This act
was in accordance with court etiquette, but Ndoruma persuaded himself that he had been shamed with Gbudwe's
acquiescence and would not forgive him. When he returned to
his own country he entered into relations with his erstwhile
enemy Rafai and incited him to invade Gbudwe's territory,

---

[1] A version of this incident is recorded by Hutereau, op. cit., 1922, p. 171.

promising his aid. The two men advanced with their forces into his kingdom,[1] where they were resisted, Baipuru being killed in the fighting. Ndoruma, his honour satisfied, now backed out of the engagement, and hostilities ceased for that year.

In the following year they were resumed by Rafai, assisted by a contingent of Ndoruma's men, during the season of the *abio* termites (April–June), and Rafai built a fort near the frontier between Ndoruma's and Gbudwe's kingdoms on the Nagasi, tributary of the Sueh. Gbudwe summoned his sons to attack it. For about two months the opposed forces watched each other, each waiting for the other to take the initiative. Then Gbudwe made an assault which lasted, on and off, for two days; his men suffering heavy casualties. On the third day Rafai made a sortie, and Gbudwe's men, already dispirited by their losses and their failure to make any impression on the fort, broke and fled. Rafai advanced further eastwards and built another fort close to Gbudwe's court. This time Gbudwe did not attempt to assault it but decided to besiege it, detailing a company under Bamboti of the Auboli clan to cut off any of the besieged who left the fort to forage, hunt, or draw water. Eventually, after a hunting party had been killed, Rafai lost patience and began to pillage and terrorize the countryside, his soldiers burning, raping, thieving, slave-making, and murdering. They threw some of their captives, even children, into the Sueh to drown.

Gbudwe retreated eastwards, seeking protection in the domains of his son Mange, but at last, perceiving that further resistance was useless against a force so well supplied with arms and ammunition, he returned to the west to negotiate. He and his sons brought to Rafai many elephant tusks in sign of submission, it being thought by the Azande, in view of their previous relations with Arabs, and not without good reason, that it was ivory the aggressors were seeking. On his first meeting with Rafai, Gbudwe was well received and was given to understand that his person would not be touched. Emboldened by this assurance, he paid Rafai's camp a second visit and was treacherously seized and bound (this was, according to another informant, Kuagbiaru, who was, however, at the time only about six years of age, at the season of the *asua* termites:

[1] This was towards the end of the year, for Junker (op. cit., vol. ii, 1891, p. 417) tells us that by the end of September operations had not yet commenced.

August–October). When Gbudwe had been bound he asked
that his younger brother Bagboro might come and speak with
him. When Bagboro saw Gbudwe in bonds he said he would
not survive the sight and, drawing his knife, he plunged it into
one of the Arabs standing near by and killed him—some say he
killed two of the soldiers. This action initiated a general mêlée
in which a number of nobles were shot and killed: among them
Bagboro himself, his brothers Gongosi, Ngbimi, Kangu, Bagilisa, Ngbutuma, and Kipa, and Gbudwe's sons Mangu and
Kipa. Another of his sons, Bugwa, was wounded. Mange, who
was also present or near by, was captured, but Gbudwe obtained his release by promising that he himself would not resist
his captors. So Gbudwe was taken into captivity by Rafai. In
telling the story, Azande say that Gbudwe's bitterness was increased by the knowledge that he was being led into captivity
in the sight of Ndoruma's men, who were mostly what Azande
think of as barbarians (*auro*), foreign peoples such as the Abari
(Belanda). Mange was left in charge of Gbudwe's kingdom,
with three or four of Rafai's lieutenants to supervise him. Some
other of Gbudwe's sons fled the country, Rikita, Ngindo, and
Ndukpwe seeking refuge with Ongoliyo. Gbudwe was taken to
the north and held prisoner at Dem Zubeir or Dem Suliman,
or both. He said afterwards that humiliations were heaped on
him by his captors, and he never spoke, I was told, of this period
of his life without bitterness, swearing that he would rather die
than suffer like treatment a second time. Nor did he ever forgive
Ndoruma for his part in the attack on him. Said a Zande:

> In that war between Gbudwe and Rafai they captured Gbudwe
> and took him to the Arabs. Ndoruma accompanied the force against
> Gbudwe; and they made war against Gbudwe and captured him
> and took him away. When Gbudwe returned from captivity he gave
> orders that no one was to have any dealings with Ndoruma. When
> he used to appear in court to threaten war, he threatened war to the
> name of Ndoruma first, before he threatened war against other
> people. Whenever he threatened war, he threatened Ndoruma the
> first of men, because Ndoruma had accompanied the attack on him.
> This is why Gbudwe was always threatening him; but he never
> actually made war against him.

Such is the Zande version of these events. We have a European account of this war in the writings of Wilhelm Junker.

Just before Gessi left the Bahr al-Ghazal to endure his mortal sufferings he met three men famous in the annals of the Sudan: Junker, Casati, and Marno. Here we are concerned only with Junker's account of 'the war of Rafai'.

It will be remembered that Gessi, after his defeat of Suliman, congratulated himself on having established friendly relations with King Ndoruma and had hopes of winning over Gbudwe as well; and Junker therefore decided to enter the southern Zande kingdoms through Ndoruma's territory. He tells us a rather different story of Ndoruma's relations with the Egyptian Government from that told by Gessi. Writing in May 1880, when he had just met Ndoruma for the first time, he says that the king had in recent years been brought into frequent contact with the Arabs and spoke a fair amount of Arabic. Indeed, some eighteen months earlier, his independence had been broken in war by Rafai Agha. This Rafa'i (Rafai)[1] was a negroid Muslim adventurer who had once been in charge of one of Ziber's trading stations in part of western Zandeland. He deserted Ziber's son Suliman and joined Gessi's forces against him. He was in consequence entrusted by Gessi with control, on behalf of the Government, of the country to the west of Ndoruma's domains; and it is he who is referred to in the passage earlier quoted from Gessi about his 'faithfull negro Sangiak, named Raffai'. Junker further says, writing of 1880, that the relations between Gbudwe and Ndoruma had by this time become so bad that they were threatening to break into open war, and that they were probably further exacerbated by his own visit to Ndoruma. This could hardly have failed to arouse Gbudwe's distrust, for he could not abide the Arabs or anyone who had anything to do with them.

But the hostile feelings of the two most powerful Zandeh rulers at that time had broken into open feud, especially since Ndo-ruma, vanquished and hard pressed by Rafai's forces, had been fain to show himself more obsequient to the Egyptian Administration. In their sore distress during this war with Rafai, Ndoruma and his people had received neither aid nor protection from Mbio's [Gbudwe's] subjects. Hence Ndoruma's deadly hatred of Mbio, a

[1] Not to be confused with another Rafai, known as Rafai-Mbomu, a Bandia who played an important role in the history of events at this time (Junker, op. cit., vol. iii, 1892, pp. 230 and 238). The R.P. Lotar tells us (*Congo*, t. ii, 1931, p. 505) that this other Rafai was the eighth son of Banyangi, descendant of Gobenge the Bandia.

feeling which had since been fostered by sanguinary conflicts along the frontiers, so that it now threatened again to burst into open hostilities. Characteristic of the present situation was a bundle of twenty sticks which were brought to me, and which were intended to indicate the number of Ndoruma's people who had in recent times been killed by Mbio's subjects in the border lands.[1]

Junker wrote:

There were certainly substantial reasons for Ndoruma's hatred of Mbio. During the struggle with Rafai, Ndoruma had escaped to Mbio's territory, whence, however, he had been expelled, and thus obliged to come to terms with Rafai. But many of his subjects had at that time remained in Mbio's, and here they were afterwards joined by others, especially women, eager to escape from Rafai's exactions, and for other motives. Mbio's thus became in course of time a land of refuge for various broken tribes and family groups, refugees not only from Zandeh Land, but also from other native oppressors and from the Nubians.[2]

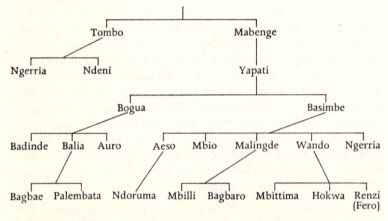

GENEALOGICAL TABLE OF THE ZANDE DYNASTIES
after Junker.

But Gbudwe was about to fall and his country to be wasted by a sanguinary war. In December 1883 Junker traversed his desolated territory. Writing in August 1882, he says that he had received news that the government troops operating against Gbudwe had suffered heavy losses, so that Rafai had to be

[1] Op. cit., vol. ii, 1891, p. 129.   [2] Ibid., pp. 152–3.

summoned with his men to their aid. 'Thereupon followed, quite recently, the reduction of the last independent Zandeh ruler north of the Welle.'[1] About the war itself Junker speaks thus.

The reader will remember that this war broke out in 1881, when the troops marched against Mbio about the time of my departure from Ndoruma's. Gessi Pasha had already left the Bahr el-Ghazal province, and was represented first by Saati Bey and then by Ibrahim Bey Shauki.[2] The war was conducted by Osman Bedawi and Hassan Mussat, who had at their disposal a few regulars with their officers. Jointly with Ndoruma's people they invaded Mbio's western territory, where a sanguinary struggle was maintained for several months, with heavy loss on both sides. Hassan Mussat was wounded, the officers of the regulars killed, and the whole expedition compelled, by the arrival of the rainy season, to march back to the Bahr el-Ghazal province. But the war was resumed early in 1882, this time with the co-operation of Rafai Aga, and after a severe struggle Mbio had at last to succumb.[3] He was banished with his two sons to Dem Soliman,[4] and the country placed under the indirect administration of Osman Bedawi and Hassan Mussat, the former in the west, the latter in the east, the river Yubbo [tributary of the Sueh] forming the boundary between the two. Some of Mbio's sons had fallen in the war, others had escaped and again returned, while others again took refuge with Wando, or in the wilderness.

But after the outbreak of the disturbances in the north, Osman and Hassan were summoned to the Dinka war, so that only a few dragomans remained in the conquered territory. Hence fresh troubles in the eastern province, where Tahir Aga took the place of Hassan Mussat, who had fallen in the Dinka war.

In Osman Bedawi's province there remained only the dragoman Taïb with a few basingers, who, by conciliatory measures, had gradually restored order.[5]

[1] Ibid., vol. iii, 1892, p. 139.
[2] If Lupton had not yet taken over the province he could not have ordered the attack on Gbudwe. It is possible, but improbable, that Gessi did so. It would have been quite contrary to his policy. It would seem likely that it was planned and carried out by these two Arabs who had charge of the administration between governorates of Gessi and Lupton, and Junker (op. cit., vol. ii, 1891, p. 304) more or less states that this was the case. Lupton was, however, in office by 1882 when Gbudwe's country was invaded for the second time and he himself was captured.
[3] *The Bahr El Ghazal Province Handbook*, 1911, p. 56, sums up the war thus: 'Sultan Yambio, who in the previous year (1881) had totally defeated a mixed force of N'doruma's followers and a few regulars under the command of Osman Bedawi, was captured and his territory annexed by Lupton's lieutenant, Rafai Aga.'
[4] Where Junker says he sent him messengers and little presents (op. cit., vol. iii, 1892, p. 302).   [5] Ibid., pp. 319–20.

In the east, Junker found the situation one of acute disorder. At a place called Morjan near the Yeta river

> I found the thirty basingers stationed here playing such high jinks that some of Mbio's old chiefs and sons, who had returned to their homes after the conclusion of the war, had since for the most part again taken to flight. Amongst them was Bassangadda [Basongoda], Mbio's eldest son, who now sent me secret envoys, asking whether he might visit me. He dreaded to come to the stations, but met me on the way to Morjan. He was a genuine Zandeh, already advanced in years, and betraying little princely dignity.[1]
>
> The object of his visit was soon apparent. Spreading out so many bundles of rods before me, he explained that a part of them indicated the number of loads of corn, other provisions, and ivory, which he had previously consigned to the Morjan station; another part stood for the number of women kidnapped from him and of his adherents killed by the basingers. Now he claimed my protection, and although I pointed out that I could make no delay, nor interfere in their affairs, Bassangadda still wanted to come with me to the station.

When they approached the station, Basongoda panicked and fled into the bush.[2] Junker was an eye-witness of the frightful devastation by the government troops in Gbudwe's kingdom.[3]

The situation at the end of 1883, when Junker crossed Gbudwe's territory, was chaotic. The Egyptian Government was on its last legs. Before its collapse it had, however, succeeded in breaking the independence of not only Gbudwe's kingdom but also, and earlier, the neighbouring Zande kingdoms, in all of which posts had been established, from which Arab garrisons acted independently and in their own interests. I will not discuss the position in the other kingdoms in detail, as we are chiefly concerned with the fortunes of that of Gbudwe. The one-time agent of Ziber Pasha and his son Suliman, and now of the Government, Rafa'i Agha, had established himself as over-lord of the area to the west of Gbudwe's domains and had brought Ndoruma into a dependent position, and the sons of his brother Ngatua (who had died between 1880 and 1883)[4]

---

[1] That Basongoda was a weakling is true—'the bee begat a fly', as Azande say— but he could hardly have been 'advanced in years', for his father did not die till twenty-two years later, and then by violence.

[2] Junker, op. cit., vol. iii, 1892, pp. 322–3.   [3] Ibid., p. 316.

[4] Ibid., p. 316.

also. It would seem that Malingindo and Ngoliyo (Ngerria) had both, at any rate nominally, recognized the Egyptian Government and paid tribute to its representatives. Ngoliyo, a son of Bazingbi, ruled over a kingdom to the west of Renzi son of Wando, the boundary between them being the parting-line between the tributaries of the Yubbo and the streams flowing south-west to the Mbruole. Wando's kingdom had been disrupted by the rebellion of his son Ukwe, who allied himself with the Arabs against his father.[1] A test of whether a king had submitted, or had ceased to be openly hostile, to the Egyptian Government was provided by Junker himself, who travelled under shelter of its prestige. It was Gbudwe alone who forbade him entry into his country and prevented it till his defeat in 1882. The situation at this time was therefore both complex and fluid, and the sketch taken from Junker's map, which leaves out all details, is intended to give only a general idea of the state of affairs obtaining.

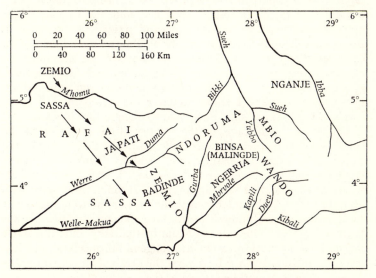

SKETCH 16. MAP AFTER JUNKER 1877–85.

[1] Ibid., vol. ii, 1891, p. 160. This began in 1880. The Arab leader was Abdu 'lallhi, a nephew of Muhammad 'abd al-Sammad, Schweinfurth's friend. He was now a government agent. He and Ukwe had taken Wando's eldest son Mbitimo captive. Wando was a fugitive in the bush, and soldiers had been stationed in his country.

Hutereau says that Gbudwe was in captivity for only one or two months,[1] but Azande say that he was away in the north for about two years; their estimate is confirmed by the statement of *The Bahr El Ghazal Province Handbook* that he was released by the Dervish Amir Karamalla Kirkesawi, a Dongolawi ex-slaver, after the Amir had gained control over the northern part of the province in April 1884.[2] His captivity was shared by two of his sons, Kana and Sanango. Sanango died in captivity, it being sometimes said that he was killed by his captors. Kana, as the text below describes, was sent by his father on a mission to Mange and was killed by the Bongo people on his journey back to the north.

In the old days disloyalty was a serious matter, for it was deception. That man who was disloyal in the past, his name was Tangili. Mange, Gbudwe's son, gave him a district to administer as his representative; though this was after Gbudwe had been taken away into captivity by the Arabs. Gbudwe, while he was among the Arabs, sent his son Kana [who was confined with him] to come here [Gbudwe's kingdom] to collect provisions to bring to him for him to hand over to the Arabs, for they had told him that he might return to his home. So Kana came and resided at the home of Mange; and he told these instructions of Gbudwe to all his subjects. They assembled a mass of things at Kana's residence, and they impressed very many bearers. Mange summoned his provincial governor Tangili and told him to consult the poison oracle about the fortune of Kana with regard to that route he was about to go by to return to Gbudwe. The oracle said to Tangili that if Kana went by that route which traversed the country of the Bongo people he would be killed by them. It were well that he should journey by the route which traversed the kingdom of Tembura. Tangili reported to Mange everything the oracle had revealed. Mange considered the matter further, and he said to himself, 'Ai! Since Kana went with Gbudwe to the Arabs, it looks as though it were he who might take the inheritance on Gbudwe's death, for he knows the language the Arabs speak.' So he despatched Kana by that very route the oracle had told him he must not go by it. Mange hid the declaration of the oracle from Kana because he desired the death of Kana. Kana proceeded on his way, and he arrived at the country of the Bongo, and they attacked him and killed him right away. They plundered all those things which Kana was taking to Gbudwe.

[1] Op. cit., p. 170. Hutereau appears to be further at fault here, for he suggests that Gbudwe and Ndoruma were made prisoners at the same time.
[2] Op. cit., p. 35.

So when Gbudwe arrived home and appeared, he was told all about this affair from beginning to end. Gbudwe said that it was not the fault of anyone except Tangili, for though Mange had deceived Kana in this way, it was, after all, Tangili who had consulted the poison oracle; he ought to have told Kana that Mange was deceiving him. It would seem that Tangili was disloyal; he and Mange had plotted together against his son, so that he died. Gbudwe sent a war party to go and slay Tangili and all his kin of the Agbambi clan. When the others [of his kin] heard about it they fled to Gangura's territory, and some of them fled to Bagbandara's territory [the mothers of these two princes were women of the Agbambi clan]. They killed Tangili on account of disloyalty. In the past people were in no way agreeable to disloyal persons; they always killed them, because disloyalty was a most serious offence. People used to deceive their fellows to bring about their deaths. Such a person stood no chance of survival.

I have heard this story from more than one Zande, but, if it is true, Gbudwe must have kept his grievance secret, because Tangili does not seem to have been put to death, together with other members of his kin, or even deprived of his office, till some twenty years later, when a further offence was charged against him. He was held responsible for the death of one of Gbudwe's sons, Baikpolo, who was killed by the Dervishes. This youth had gone on a visit to Tangili who, when he heard of the approach of the Dervish force, instead of keeping him with him, sent him back to his father's court where he was shot by the enemy. Nevertheless, Gbudwe does not appear to have ordered his execution till even long after this event, perhaps not till 1904. Azande say that princes who bore a grudge against a man were sometimes known to harbour it for many years and then to execute him on a charge other than that which moved them to vengeance.

An account of these events was given to the late Major J. W. G. Wyld round about 1935[1] by an old[2] noble, Tombo son of Kipa[3] son of Bazingbi. Though I regard the story it relates of the manner of Kana's death with some reserve, I record it as a

---

[1] Copied from *Yambio District Records* and circulated by A. T. T. Leich.

[2] The record says that he was probably over eighty, but as Gbudwe was captured in 1882 and Tombo was a child at the time he could not have been much over sixty in 1935.

[3] Presumably the Kipa killed by Rafai's troops.

different version to that I heard myself. Tombo's first memories of Gbudwe were of him when he was a man of about fifty years of age and living on the River Musukue. He said that Gbudwe was very greatly feared by his people, who dared not approach him unless summoned, and then on their hands and knees. But though feared, he was held in high esteem for his generosity and wisdom, and he inspired devotion. He did not mutilate people, as some of the princes did. In appearance at this time he resembled his eldest son Basongoda most and of those of his sons who are still living (in 1935), Rikita. He had Rikita's eyes and figure, though he was taller and lighter-skinned.

Gbudwe's capture took place when Tombo was a small child. A heavy action took place on the River Munya, tributary of the Nagasi, between Gbudwe's men and Rafai's troops aided by Ndoruma; and after it Gbudwe was forced to retreat eastwards, first to the Lingasi and finally as far east as the Yeta, where he capitulated with a number of his sons and followers. His younger brother Bagboro was so enraged when he saw Gbudwe in chains that he drew his knife and killed two of the guards. In revenge Rafai had the prisoners surrounded and shot down. All the captured princes and the eighteen members of Gbudwe's body-guard were killed, with the exception of three men, two of the princes and one member of the bodyguard. Rafai then took Gbudwe and the two surviving princes, Kana and Sanango, to captivity at Dem Zubeir, leaving Mange in charge of Gbudwe's country. He also had a fort (*zeriba*) constructed on the Yeta river and left three detribalized Azande (Sadi, Ngbatiyo, and Kuboi) in charge of it. As soon as Rafai had departed, Mange attacked and overcame the fort. Mange also fought several indecisive engagements with Wando, and he conducted successful campaigns against the Bukuru and Baka peoples and occupied the country east of Meridi as far as the River Iro (Naam) near Mvolo.

After three years Kana returned from Dem Zubeir to tell Mange that Gbudwe was to be released (Sanango had died in captivity). Mange collected a party of young men and girls to escort Gbudwe home and dispatched them with Kana, but the parents thought their children were being led away into slavery and they went after Kana and killed him on the River Sueh. Gbudwe returned with only three men: a Zande called Rafiri, a Bongo called Nyoko, and another man. On his return he lived first on the River Manzari, then on the Magaga, tributary of the Hu, then on the Bazumburu, and finally at Birikiwe.

I was told by many Azande, and the information is undoubtedly correct, that when Gbudwe returned he found Mange not only occupying his kingdom but also apparently not prepared to leave it and depart to his own domain in the east. This episode, which Azande considered most shameful, was described by a Zande as follows.

This is about that great wrong Mange did to Gbudwe. Gbudwe returned [from captivity], and when he was near his home he rested. He sent a messenger to Mange, for he had left him in his stead when the Arabs took him away. Gbudwe said by the mouth of the messenger that he was returning; let him [Mange] get out of his country and return to his home on the other side [to the east] of the Sueh river. But this was not at all according to Mange's ideas, and he just stayed where he was. Gbudwe sent further and many messages, but Mange would not move an inch. Gbudwe told Basongoda [his eldest son] to come and make war on Mange to get him out of his country. The messenger having arrived at Basongoda's home, he sent a commoner governor, called Bamboti, to Mange, telling him to go and speak to him [Mange] very firmly—that if he continued to stay where he was, then early next morning he himself [Basongoda] would come to fight him. Bamboti went to Mange and said to him that it were well that he should honour his father by departing to his own country on the other side of the Sueh river. Mange thereupon departed. Early next morning Basongoda arrived with his warriors. Gbudwe told him to return home because Mange had departed. This was that remarkable affair which happened when Gbudwe returned from the Arabs. It was frightful in the eyes of all that Mange had set himself up against his father in his father's kingdom. Mange was, it seemed, in rebellion, for he had not once come to greet Gbudwe. This is a frightful and shameful thing among great princes.[1]

A further trouble met Gbudwe on his return. He found that certain persons, called Teri, Bogu, and Denegi, whose names

[1] Mange had done various acts contrary to his father's wishes during his absence. He had, among other things, removed from his governorate Zengendi, Gbudwe's favourite courtier, and replaced him by Bamboti; and he had removed Boli, his brother, from his province and put his own son in his place. On the other hand, Gbudwe later confirmed the appointment of the commoner Bakoradi, whom Mange had put in the governorate left vacant through the death of the commoner Gunde.

suggest that they were Negro troops, had been left by Rafai with instructions to keep watch on him, and that they had built a small post near his court.[1] The details of what happened to these men are obscure. The country was still much disturbed, and many families had sought refuge in neighbouring kingdoms; and these included some of my best informants, who were consequently at that time no longer witnesses of events in Gbudwe's kingdom. It seems that it was an unusually dry year and that Gbudwe, who had presumably come to the conclusion that it was better to fight the Arabs than to submit to them, summoned his sons to blockade the post. The besieged men dug deep for water, but in vain, and when their water-carriers went to near-by streams they were killed. It would seem that eventually, of the three leaders, Teri and Bogu were killed and Denegi fought his way out.

Gbudwe had thus regained not only his liberty but also his independence, and he kept both till his death twenty-one years later. That he was able so easily to throw off the yoke was due to a change in the wider situation: the overthrow of the Egyptian Government and the establishment of Mahdist rule. The victory of the Dervishes was a stroke of good fortune for Gbudwe. The Amir Karamalla had released him, hoping for a return in slaves and support, neither of which he got. What he got instead, as will be related, was a severe mauling of his troops at the hands of Gbudwe's subjects. In the meanwhile he was too occupied with trying to induce the Egyptian Government posts still holding out in Equatorial Province (Emin Pasha) to come over to the Mahdist side, or to reduce them by force of arms, to concern himself with Gbudwe. Moreover, not only had Rafai had to withdraw most of his garrisons from Zande country for service against the Mahdists but he had himself been killed in serving against them. Consequently, after his return home, Gbudwe was able to re-establish the autonomy of his kingdom free from Arab interference of any kind for the time being. The order of his residences from now till his death is given by a Zande as follows (this account is fuller, and probably more accurate than that given by Tombo to Major Wyld).

---

[1] Most of the garrisons of the posts established in his kingdom by Rafai had been withdrawn to deal with the Dinka rising in the north. Only a skeletal force remained in occupation.

When Gbudwe returned from captivity among the Arabs he made his home on a tributary of the Hu river, the Magaga. When he left that place he moved to a new home on the Bandiokpo, a tributary of the Bazumburu. When he left that place he moved to the Bazumburu. When he left there he removed his home to the head of the Yabongo. When he gave that up he came to make his home on the little stream Maka, tributary of the Namama. After he had resided there he moved to where the government fort is today [Yambio]. This place of the fort was the last of his homes. Having established himself at the place of the fort, he made war with many peoples. However, at that time the Europeans had not built their fort; they were still in their own country.[1]

During the period from 1884 to 1905, a period of somewhat over twenty years, Gbudwe seems to have held court in six different places, giving an average of between three and four years' residence at each place.

8

Not long after Gbudwe's return from captivity he began to threaten war against his elder brother Wando, whose kingdom adjoined his own to the south. He felt that his defeat had lost him face in the eyes of his brothers, and he was further shamed by having to carry out Karamalla's instructions on his release that not only was he to make war no more, but he was also to send messengers to the courts of his brothers and kinsmen to tell them to come to him to hear the new government's orders, for they replied in humiliating language that they would come *zegino te!*, 'in no circumstances whatsoever!' At this Gbudwe's old fire burnt in him again. He declared that the Arabs had humiliated him in captivity—he had even been forced to dig his own grave—and now they caused him to be insulted by his brothers; and he said that he would stand it no longer. If he wished to fight his neighbours he would do so, and if the Arabs invaded his country again he would fight them also.

Gbudwe, already nettled by Wando for the reason given above, was incited by a border incident to make war on him, a

[1] His home on the Magaga was in what in 1928 was Kurami's country. The Bazumburu is a tributary of the Bodo and in what in 1928 was Ngindo's country. In another account the second and third sites are given in reverse order. When he resided in his final home at Birikiwe (Yambio), the River Uze was the boundary between his territory and that of his son Bafuka.

war the subjects of Gbudwe call 'the war of Wando'. As we have noted, on his return he made his court on the Magaga. His son Bafuka had made a levy of beer on his subjects to greet his father's return with a feast. Gbudwe was happy to be home again and among his own people and was gaily taking part in the drinking and dancing when a messenger arrived from his son Basongoda to tell him that he had been attacked by Renzi son of Wando, whose people had killed two nobles in the fighting. Renzi was said to have declared ironically that he had come to give Gbudwe a greeting on his return home. Gbudwe sprang from his stool and announced war against his nephew Renzi.

Gbudwe would not take part in the campaign himself, as it was not fitting that he, an independent ruler, should engage in hostilities in person with Renzi, who did not rule in his own right but as representing his father and subject to him. He entrusted direction of the campaign to his sons Basongoda, Bafuka, Gumba, Borugba, and Boli, who were aided by contingents provided by his commoner governors Wangu, Tangili, Zengendi, and Mai, and by his own senior company, the Abaigo. The force was divided into two columns. One of these, under command of Basongoda, never entered into action. By the time they had arrived in Bafuka's country, through which they were to proceed to attack Renzi's domains after they had joined the other column, their supplies had run out and they began to help themselves from the homesteads of Bafuka's subjects, stripping the country bare of victuals (*ka gbu e*). They stole every pot of oil and every basket of ground-nuts they could lay their hands on, and some of them even went so far as to tear metal ornaments (*maka*) off the women. Those of Bafuka's subjects who had warning of what was taking place fled with their possessions into the bush to hide there till the column had departed. Bafuka was enraged at the treatment of his subjects, declaring that one might suppose the campaign to be directed against him and not against Renzi. He was soon to be avenged. In the hunt for food a basket was found and taken back to camp, it being assumed that it contained food, and when it was opened there were disclosed some kittens of the kind Azande call *adandala*, witch-kittens born of a woman by a cat. The sight of these cats caused the column to lose its way so that it never came up with the second column. This second column, consisting of Gbudwe's Abaigo and contingents of some of his commoner governors, traversed Bafuka's country to attack the border governorships of Renzi's principality. Its leaders had been told by the poison oracle to sleep only one night in Bafuka's country, but, as there was very heavy rain, they remained there for two nights. On the third day they marched into the district of Ndegu of the Angbadimo clan, one of Renzi's rulers of the border marches, and they laid his country waste. They then passed over, still pillaging and burning, into the district of Ngatuo of the Agiti clan.

A very rough sketch drawn for me on the ground—not to be regarded as an exact representation—indicates the relative disposition of provinces or districts under various princes and commoner governors (the names of the latter italicized) on either side of the frontier:

		E		
	Gumba			
	Wangu			
	Mai		Suma	
N	*Bazo*		Yakpati	S
	Gundusu		*Ngatuo*	
	Bamboti		Ndegu	
	Zengendi		Malingindo	
	Bafuka		Bafuka	
	Basongoda			
		W		

(left margin: GBUDWE'S KINGDOM; right margin: WANDO'S KINGDOM (RENZI))

While Gbudwe's men were pillaging Ngatuo's country, which they found deserted and defenceless because non-combatants had withdrawn, the warriors, as they were soon to discover, had gone by a circuitous route to burn their camp (*limbasa*) and lie in ambush (*nguru*) for them in a dense wood called Karikai, which is said to be at the junction of the Bomoi-yega and the Digbili streams, tributaries of the Duru. When returning to their camp, Gbudwe's men fell into this ambush, suffered severe losses, and fled in disarray. Among several important persons killed was Gbudwe's commoner governor Mai. A certain Nakpi of the Agbutu clan tore off his barkcloth to make hastier flight and was captured naked. He was not, however, handed over by Ngatuo to Renzi as he was Ngatuo's blood-brother, and when the poison oracle was consulted it said that he should be allowed to escape.

After the retreat of Gbudwe's men Ngatuo had the spears, knives, and throwing-knives, which strewed the ground, gathered into baskets and sent to Renzi, saying that he had driven back Gbudwe's invasion, in proof of which he sent him the spoils. Renzi sent them on to his father Wando, saying that Gbudwe had been defeated and that it had not even been necessary for him to proceed to his frontier to protect it; it had been sufficient to leave its defence to a Zande (a commoner)—a proud and wounding comment. Wando was delighted with the news and praised his son, though, Basingbatara told me, he reproved him for allowing the heads of the dead enemy to be cut off and sent in baskets to his court as well. He said that this was an improper thing to do.

Gbudwe was humiliated. Coming so soon after his defeat at the hands of the Arabs, we may suppose the blow to have been a heavy one for him. It is said that several men were driven from his country on charges of their witchcraft having caused the casualties. He also reprimanded Basongoda for having allowed his men to plunder Bafuka's country instead of engaging the enemy. Azande attribute the defeat to three causes: sight of the *adandala* cats, which was due to the plundering of Bafuka's subjects and occasioned loss of route; failure to carry out the instructions of the poison oracle with regard to timing; and the fact that Bazingbi, the father of Wando and Gbudwe, had threatened his sons with the vengeance of his ghost should they fight among themselves, so that, in spite of provocation, Gbudwe ought not to have attacked Wando's people. Gbudwe did not invade his brother's territory again during the lifetime of Wando.

The account of 'the war of Wando' I have just recorded was compiled from the statements of several informants. A text given by a different informant relates the history of it as follows.

This is about Ngatuo of the Agiti clan, how he made war with Gbudwe. Bazingbi had told Gbudwe that he must never make war against Wando, for they had been good friends to each other, and when Bazingbi saw this love between them he spoke to them in this wise, that they should not make war on one another. Should they

do so, they would not receive his blessing. Then a certain time came
in a certain year, and Gbudwe summoned all his men and his
commoner governors also, and when they had arrived at court
Gbudwe told them all to go to Basongoda that he might make war
on Wando and let him see their shanks in it [what they were worth
as fighters]; for the sons of Wando had constantly raided the sons
of Gbudwe [in border fights]. It was true that Bazingbi had said
that he was not to make war on Wando, but he was wearied of
Wando.

The army moved off together, and they advanced till they reached
Bafuka's territory, and there they lost their way so that they did not
know in which direction to go against Wando. They remained in
Bafuka's country, where they plundered his subjects of all their
possessions. Then the army broke off and turned in an easterly
direction, thus going astray; because the ghost of Bazingbi did not
consent to fighting between Gbudwe and Wando. This is why
Basongoda went astray and got lost on the way to Wando's country,
so that he did not know where to take his army. This army of his
turned to the east to advance, for they thought that it was in that
direction that they must face to attack Wando's country; whereas
they were mistaken.

They continued to advance and arrived against Renzi's commoner
governor whose name was Ngatuo. He had many subjects. They
arrived opposite Ngatuo at midday; and they said that they might
as well burn Ngatuo's home. They turned their attention to Ngatuo's
huts and burnt them all. The subjects of Ngatuo then began to
collect and they hurled themselves against Gbudwe's army, and
they overcame it first on one wing and then on the other wing, and
they entirely crumpled it and completely routed it as far as Karikai.
They killed many of Gbudwe's subjects. The survivors scattered all
over Renzi's country; and they practised deception, saying that they
were subjects of Renzi. When some of them were found out they were
slain with the spear. The army remained for six days in the bush
slaughtering Gbudwe's subjects. They killed Gbudwe's commoner
governor whose name was Mai. A man called Wandi, one of
Gbudwe's married subjects, went astray. He continued to wander
till he arrived at Renzi's court. He continued on his way till he
arrived at the bottom of Renzi's private quarters. He then drew a
knife at his waist and threw himself on the wives of Renzi, Renzi
himself not being present. He was at the home of his father Wando.
This man assaulted Renzi's wives, and when one of them thought to
flee he stabbed her with his knife and she died at once; and when
another tried to flee he stabbed her also, and she died. When Bangara heard the cries of Renzi's wives he snatched up his shield and

went after Wandi as he was assaulting Renzi's wives. Bangara speared him with his spear, and he died.

The rest of Gbudwe's men had already returned home, to where Gbudwe was, and they told Gbudwe what had happened, and it was indeed bad news. Gbudwe said, 'By the limb of Bazingbi, by the limb of Bazingbi, it does not please me, it does not please me. What is this? When I began the war I said that Basongoda was a capable man for it, and then he goes and causes my subjects to go astray, so that an army comes and destroys them like this. By the limb of Bazingbi, it does not please me, it does not please me.'

Ngatuo collected all the spoils of war he had taken from the subjects of Gbudwe, and he took them to Renzi. Renzi bound all these spears into bundles for his father Wando. Wando said, 'Musanabamo, Wando, Bafiro,[1] yes indeed, by Wando's limb, by Wando's limb, I will not let it rest there, I will not let it rest there; Musanabamo oo, by Wando's limb, my friend said let us fight with him; no matter, it was one of my commoner elders who chased him away; it was the ghost of my father which favoured me.' Wando waited for a time, and then he said, 'All right, since it was like this, that Gbudwe made war on me first, it looks as though he was making a weakling of me.' He gathered together all his younger brothers and all his commoner governors also, and he said to them that it were well that he should go to make war on Malingindo son of Bazingbi, since Gbudwe had attacked him [Wando]. Wando collected all his men, not a single adult male remaining at home, only the women remaining at home by themselves. Malingindo, when he heard of it, drew up all his leaders of companies and said, 'By the limb of Bazingbi, this war, do not leave it off whatever happens. If you see Wando, do not spare him; attack him with the spear. I want it to be to the death. However, since I speak thus, you plait palm-tree bast, each to his upper arm, so that you will recognize each other by it. By the limb of Bazingbi, by the limb of Bazingbi, we are going to have a fight with Wando the fame of which will not be forgotten. Know-your-foot o, know-your-foot, know-your-foot is Wando. He who comes on his feet will be carried back on people's heads. Let them tell him, he comes for me to cook him a mash; let him wait, I will cook it; but when I come to open the leaves in which it has been cooked in front of him, will he eat it to finish it?' The mash means the Azande; it is a metaphor.

Wando advanced and he arrived in Malingindo's territory and he captured the camp of his army just as it was. When Malingindo had intelligence of him he arose with his entire army and appeared

---

[1] His various names. Konabiro was his first name.

before him. They fought for a long time, till the sun went down, for they began it very early in the morning. They continued fighting till evening and Malingindo, having defeated Wando's army, first on one wing and then on the other, drove all his men back. His people captured Wando's son Renzi, but he deceived them, telling them that he was a subject of Malingindo, so that they released him and he survived. Only Ukwe continued to fight, fighting till his head was almost on fire; then he was overcome also. Wando's big bag in which he used to keep his bread when he went to war, this bag of his was captured and taken away with them by Malingindo's subjects.

Wando then returned home in haste. They killed many of Wando's subjects. When Wando arrived home, those women whose husbands had been killed wailed all over the countryside on account of their husbands. Wando then said to the Azande that they should consult the poison oracle about their kinsmen who had died in the war, and if the oracle declared a man [witch] to be responsible they should put him to death. The people then consulted the oracle about all those who had been killed. Those whose names the oracle disclosed were not spared. Wando told the people to kill them, for they were witches who had attacked his subjects at war; that is why they were to be put to death. But he said that some of them should pay indemnity in spears, twenty and another ten in addition. Some of them paid a woman and twenty spears. Even if it was a woman to whose name a chicken died, saying that it was she who had caused a certain man to be killed in the fighting. Wando said that she was not to be spared in any circumstances, let her be slain. But she whom he did not wish to die, he ordered her to pay compensation to the relatives of the man who had died in the fighting. On account of this affair many persons indeed died at the hand of their fellows. If a man met on the path the man on whom he wished to be avenged he asked no questions, he just stuck him at once with his spear.[1]

When did these events take place? We have no means of knowing for sure. The European travellers on whom we have hitherto relied for dating events had been compelled to withdraw from the region of the Nile–Congo divide before Ghudwe's return from captivity on account of the Mahdist rising. If we are to accept the Zande account, they happened within a year or two of his return and therefore probably between 1885 and 1887. This would accord with the statement of an informant Bage, who told me in 1928 that he was at the time an infant of

[1] An account of this war is given by Hutereau, op. cit., pp. 179–82.

about three years of age, he being in 1928 a man of about forty-five years of age.

This was the only occasion that Gbudwe and Wando are recorded as having fought each other; for though Wando was not personally involved, nor even was his son Renzi, Gbudwe's attack was on a sufficiently large scale to be spoken of as a war against Wando. However, after Wando's death there was one major war between his son Renzi and Gbudwe, and Renzi later aided the Belgians against his uncle. There were also frequent border skirmishes between the lords of the marches on both sides. We may indeed note here that the subjects of Gbudwe especially expressed their sense of unity in their loyalty to him in feelings of rivalry and hostility towards the kingdom of Wando, and later of Renzi, to the south. To the north, the old kingdom of Tombo probably by this time either had disintegrated or was in process of doing so, for one hears nothing about it; and the scattered communities of the Bongo and Belanda peoples of the north seem either to have been subjugated by the Arabs or, together with the Azande of Tombo's kingdom, to have sought refuge in Gbudwe's domains. To the east, the descendants of the brothers of Bazingbi (Renzi, Muduba, and others) had been ousted or, if any remained, they acknowledged the suzerainty of Gbudwe's son Mange, who here held sway as an almost independent monarch, though he continued to give formal recognition to his father and to pay him tribute and to obey his summons to war till his (Gbudwe's) death. Beyond Mange, further to the east, were various foreign peoples (chiefly Mundu, Babukur, Abukaya, and Baka) and the Adio branch of the Azande (who were not subject to the ruling Avongara family), in whose lands were a number of Egyptian Government posts, threatened by Mahdist forces and propaganda from the north. To the west was the kingdom of Ndoruma son of Ezo, between whose subjects and those of Gbudwe there may have been, as Junker asserts, border affrays, but nothing on the scale Azande call a campaign or war, between the two kingdoms.

9

The collapse of the Egyptian Government saved Gbudwe and preserved for more than twenty years the independence of his kingdom; for not only was he released by the Dervish Amir Karamalla but the turn of events was such that, though the Government and its forces were eliminated in the Bahr al-Ghazal province, the Amir was unable to establish Dervish rule over more than the most northerly parts of it. We need not follow these events in detail, but a sketch of them must be given.

Lupton had been forced, by the desertion of his officers, to hand over the Bahr al-Ghazal to the Amir without striking a blow in its defence. The Amir had then in mind to reduce also the last remaining province of the Sudan still under control of the Egyptian Government, represented in the person of Dr. Emin Bey. This extraordinary man became, in consequence of the position in which he found himself, a world-famous figure. His real name was Eduard Schnitzer, and he was born, of Jewish race but of Protestant parents, at Oppeln in the Prussian province of Silesia. He studied medicine, first at Breslau and then in Berlin, and in 1864 he went to Turkey to practise it. He returned to Europe in 1875 but in the following year he entered the Egyptian service under the Muslim name of Dr. Emin Effendi, claiming to be a Muslim (it is uncertain to what extent he was acting a part in so doing). He eventually became the chief medical officer in the Equatorial Province of the Egyptian Sudan at the time when Gordon was its Governor; and later, in 1878, Gordon, who was then Governor of the whole of the Sudan, entrusted him with charge of the province. Emin was a most learned man, a brilliant naturalist, and a meticulous observer and recorder whose researches added greatly to European knowledge of the peoples, animals, insects, and plants of the Southern Sudan and Uganda.

It is much to be regretted, therefore, that he did not have an opportunity to visit Zandeland proper—only the Adio or Makaraka section of it—especially as he was intending to pay Gbudwe a visit shortly before his capture. In a letter to Herr Hansal, the Austro-Hungarian Consul at Khartoum, dated 28 November 1880, Emin says,

I have received a friendly invitation from Chief Mbio [Gbudwe], who has been considered unapproachable for the last eighteen years, and I intend to avail myself of it, for the wealth of this Nyam-Nyam ruler in ivory has become almost proverbial, and I have always had at heart the opening up of friendly communications with the native chiefs.[1]

We may note in passing that this remark of Emin's shows how right Junker was in thinking that Gbudwe's refusal to receive

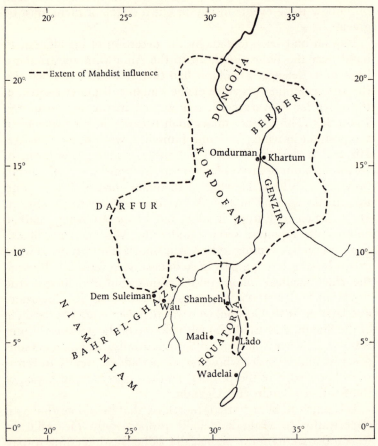

SKETCH 17. MAP SHOWING EXTENT OF MAHDIST INFLUENCE IN 1895 (after Rudolf C. Slatin Pasha).

him was at least partly due to his desiring to visit him from a hostile quarter, the quarter of Ndoruma, Rafai, and the Bahr al-Ghazal Administration. He was not at this time, it would appear, averse to relations with the Governor of Equatorial

[1] Emin Pasha, op. cit., p. 259.

Province, who approached him from a direction in which lay no hostile Zande kingdoms and no powerful Arab rulers like Rafai. It shows us also that, as Junker so often found was the case, those Zande kings who had had no close dealings with the Egyptian Government were unaware that the different officials they came into contact with, or heard about, owed allegiance to a single government. They thought, not without some justification (Gessi and Emin detested each other), that each served his own interests and was opposed to those of the others. Gbudwe must have known that an invasion of his kingdom from the Bahr al-Ghazal was not improbable, and it is therefore understandable that he attempted to come to some agreement with the rival Governorate of Equatorial Province. But Gbudwe and Emin were not to meet. Writing in 1882, Emin says,

> According to the latest intelligence, Mbio himself, after a six months' war, and after he had destroyed all his ivory, has been captured by Rafai-Aga and Hassan-Aga's soldiers, and taken to the Bahr-el-Ghazal, where he is now in captivity. I was going to visit him, but now my journey will be considerably shortened. I am sorry for this brave warrior.[1]

Emin, however, met Gbudwe's elder brother Wando who, he says in the same place, had sought refuge with many of his people at Kabayendi post (in his province) from the oppression of Rafai Agha. Emin, who offered him an area of land on which to settle his people, describes him as 'a well-built, athletic fellow': Junker, who met him two years earlier, says he was aged and obese![2]

Emin's main force and his headquarters were at Lado on the Nile. He had a number of smaller military posts in that part of his province which lay to the west of the Nile, and after the collapse of the Government in the Bahr al-Ghazal these were threatened by the forces of the Amir Karamalla or were enticed into revolt by his agents. Emin was compelled to withdraw his garrisons from some of these posts, since he could not defend them all with the troops at his disposal, for they were widely distributed and communications were by foot; and he was consequently able to reinforce his garrison at Amadi on the Yei (Ayi) river. If that post fell, withdrawal from Lado to the south

---

[1] Ibid., p. 374.   [2] Op. cit., vol. ii, 1891, pp. 274 and 276.

would become a military necessity. The situation in this area was so confused that not even Emin rightly knew what was happening. A sort of civil war had developed between those who favoured the Egyptian Government and those who favoured the Mahdi, and it added greatly to the confusion that in the government stations it was no easy matter to say who were government troops and who were Nubians and other Arabs living on slave labour and trade in slaves. Pay was no distinction between them, because government troops seldom, if ever, received wages other than in kind (including slaves); nor was engagement in traffic in slaves, for officials and non-officials were equally involved in that.[1]

Amadi fell in March 1885, and to all appearances Equatorial Province was lost; and it certainly would have been if the Amir had not been summoned to the north to deal with a revolt in Darfur against the Khalifa Abdallah (the Mahdi had died in that year). He took with him the greater part of the 'Nubian' rabble, like an outgoing tide that takes with it all the filth on the shore. Consequently Emin was able to write in a letter dated 2 October 1886:

> Since the retreat of Keremallah and the destruction of himself and of all his people on the borders of Kordofan, everything has remained in perfect peace, and indeed the war has in some respects done good, for the whole of the Bahr-el-Ghazal district has been totally freed from the slave-dealers. . . . In the whole of the Bahr-el-Ghazal, I repeat, there is today no single Khartoumer remaining. It is true that a few of Lupton's old Negro soldiers are still there, but they are living peaceably with the natives. In my province I have only sixty-two Danagla left, and I am quite able to prevent them committing any excesses.[2]

In a subsequent letter, written to Dr. R. W. Felkin in April 1887, he said proudly:

[1] For the situation at this time, besides the Letters and Journals of Emin and the volumes of Junker's travels, Major Gaetano Casati's *Ten Years in Equatoria and the Return with Emin Pasha* (two vols., 1891) may be consulted. Casati (1838–1902) was born near Milan. After a career as a regular soldier he devoted himself to cartography. He went to the Southern Sudan early in 1880, in answer to Gessi's plea for someone to be sent from Italy to explore the lower course of the Welle river. His explorations were brought to a close by the Mahdist rising. What he has to say about the Azande refers almost entirely to those of kingdoms well to the south of the region with which we are concerned.

[2] Op. cit., p. 505.

I have been obliged to evacuate Lado, as it was impossible for me to supply the garrison there with corn; but, as a set-off to the loss of this station, I have been able to reoccupy the district of Makraka. At present, therefore, we occupy the whole of my former stations in Makraka: Rejaf, Beden, Kiri, Muggi, Labore, Khor Ayu, Dufile, Fatiko, Fadibek, Wadelai, Songa, and Mahagi, nearly all the stations which were originally entrusted to me by General Gordon; and I intend and expect to keep them all. I should like here again to mention that if a relief expedition [the Stanley expedition] comes to us, I will on no account leave my people. We have passed through troublous times together, and I consider it would be a shameful act on my part were I to desert them. They are, notwithstanding all their hardships, brave and good, with the exception of the Egyptians. We have known each other many years, and I do not think that it would be easy at present for a stranger to take up my work and to win at once the confidence of the people. It is therefore out of the question for me to leave, so I shall remain. All we would ask England to do, is to bring about a better understanding with Uganda, and to provide us with a free and safe way to the coast. This is all we want. Evacuate our territory? Certainly not![1]

Nevertheless, for reasons we need not here enter into, Emin soon afterwards did withdraw; and eventually, with Stanley, to the coast of East Africa.

As far as Gbudwe was concerned, after 1884 both Egyptian Government and Mahdists might not have existed. On his return from captivity he eliminated, as we have noted, such Arabs as remained in his kingdom, an action presumably referred to by Emin when he wrote on 2 January 1885 that it was stated by prisoners captured by the government garrison at Amadi that Abdullahi's [the Dervish commander besieging Amadi] 'rear is endangered, Mbio's Nyam-Nyam having risen and burnt his *zeribas* [fortified posts]'.[2] It was not till thirteen years after this date, in 1898 and just before the collapse of Mahdist rule in the Sudan, that a Dervish force was dispatched under command of Arabi Dafalla, to subdue Gbudwe. Official accounts record that Gbudwe totally defeated this force at his home at Birikiwe—now called Yambio.[3] Azande themselves do not claim so much; only that they drove the Dervishes out of

[1] Ibid., pp. 510–11.   [2] Ibid., p. 475.
[3] Bimbashi A. B. Bethell, *Sudan Intelligence Reports*, 1904, no. 122; *The Bahr El Ghazal Province Handbook*, 1911, p. 35.

their country. The campaign is known to them as *vura anzara*, 'the war of the Dervishes'.

It was told that at that time Gbudwe had already established his court at Birikiwe (hoeing his cultivations where in 1928 his grandson Renzi son of Gangura had his settlement). People were harvesting their millet when news came from the east of the approach of the Dervish force. Gbudwe thereupon sent a man called Rafai with three other men to discover their intentions. This Rafai is said to have been an 'Arab' who, added some of my informants, might have been a relative of the Rafai who took Gbudwe captive many years before. He was probably some Arabized Negro, left behind in Gbudwe's territory after the withdrawal of government forces, who had attached himself to Gbudwe. This man was instructed by Gbudwe to meet the Dervishes and to tell them that if they came as friends they should remain to the east of the Hu river. Meanwhile Gbudwe prepared for war. He created three new companies of bachelor warriors (*aparanga*): the *Audie* under Gatanga of the Auboli clan, the *Awili Singu* under Ngbatuiyo, and the *Awili Manziga* under Tule.

When Rafai returned with the intelligence that the Dervishes were no friends, Gbudwe ordered the mobilization of his own companies, and he dispatched his sons Ndukpe, Bafuka, and Mboli, who happened to be at his court at the time, to their districts to mobilize their men with all speed. The Dervishes crossed the Hu and advanced on Birikiwe (through what in the 1920s was Bima's country); and Gbudwe withdrew before them with his wives and children to south of the Uze river, leaving a company, the *Awili Gine*, to drive his herd of goats after him. It seems that he had at some time acquired some of these animals, otherwise unknown to the Azande. The Dervishes were conducted by a man called Birale, one of those who had been sent to ascertain their intentions and had been captured and compelled to act as guide to Gbudwe's court. Before they reached it they were ambushed by the *Awili Gine*, who captured a number of their rifles. However, they reached the court after this skirmish and at once proceeded to build a fort in Gbudwe's vacated private quarters. For close on a month sporadic fighting took place around this fort, both sides suffering a number of casualties. When Basongoda and other of Gbudwe's sons arrived to support their father, the attack was strongly pressed and continued fiercely for three days; the Dervish dead being, with Gbudwe's encouragement, eaten by the Azande. On the fourth day the Dervishes, leaving five men behind to blow trumpets to make Gbudwe's men think that they still occupied the fort, stole away under cover of night. When their flight was discovered at dawn, scouts (*abomoi*) were sent to report on their movements. Gbudwe's men followed their retreat to the Bodo river, where they were encamped for the night within a thornwood enclosure. The Azande were tired, hot, and thirsty after their pursuit in dry season temperature and they ran down to the Bodo to drink water. Some Dervishes, hidden in near-by bush, opened fire on them, killing a number of them at the side of the stream as they made for cover. The water was tinged with their blood.

When Gbudwe heard what had happened he said that he had lost enough men and he sent Nduga of the Andebili clan to order the pursuit to be discontinued. Other messengers were sent to governors of the eastern provinces of his kingdom to instruct them to follow and harass the retreating Dervishes till they had departed from his domains, but though Mange and the other eastern governors hovered about the column, no more fighting took place, and the Dervishes never returned. The campaign had been a victorious one for Gbudwe, but it is said that he had lost so many men that he could not bear to sit in his court, where they had been killed in attacking the fort. He therefore changed the site of the court and no longer sat in his accustomed place under the large *bakekpe* tree which stood near where in my day was the District Commissioner's (Major P. M. Larken's) house at Yambio, but always under the shade of the *abanza* trees which were near what was to become the store of the honest and obliging trader Ibrahim Muhammadain.

10

More than ten years before Gbudwe defeated the Dervishes, Azande of the west and south-west of his kingdom had come into contact with European forces, and by the year of their defeat the French and Belgians had already established posts in adjacent kingdoms. Gbudwe was not, however, owing to the easterly position of his territory, at all involved with the French and only later with the Belgians. We can therefore postpone discussion of his relations with the latter, bearing in mind for the present only that Renzi son of Wando was already in contact with them at the time he attacked Gbudwe, for this may have some bearing on his motives. It also explains his superiority in rifle-fire.

According to Azande who took part in it, the attack took place between the defeat of the Dervishes and an attack by Rikita son of Gbudwe on a British patrol, that is, between 1898 and 1904. It is not possible to date it more precisely from literary sources, but there is no reason for not accepting Zande statements that Gbudwe's attacks on the Belgian Post on the Mayawa river in the dry season of 1904 took place four harvests after it; and this would date the war with Renzi as the dry season of 1899. It is known to Gbudwe's Azande as 'the campaign (*sungusungu vura*) of Birisi', after a hill of this name near the Yubo river, in the proximity of which the fighting took place in the Zande months of *wenza* and *tamvuo*, roughly between September and November. Its cause is said to have been Renzi's desire to make his name famous after the death of his father by attacking Gbudwe, as one king in his own right attacks another.

Renzi's army advanced on Bokwiyo son of Bafuka, son of Gbudwe, who lived to the south of the Yubo river, and burnt his court and homestead. His father Bafuka then came against Renzi and fought him in his (Bafuka's) cultivations, where he had a large granary (*soro*), on the northern side of the river. Gangura then appeared on the scene and made his camp (*limbasa*) in Bafuka's cultivations opposite Renzi's headquarters, which he had established in Bokwiyo's court; and various other sons of Gbudwe ranged their companies alongside him. Renzi drew up his companies in order and crossed the Yubo (*Renzi ki sapu gako vura ki si yubo*). He declared that he wanted to fight Gbudwe, not his sons. Gangura's scouts now brought him intelligence that the enemy had crossed the river and was preparing to attack on the morrow, so he told his men, through his military leader Boza, not to sleep; and he withdrew his companies so that when Renzi's men attacked they would find the eastern part of Bafuka's cultivations undefended and occupy it, for his poison oracle had revealed that this would be the most suitable place to advance on them. Renzi attacked at dawn. His first attack was repulsed by Boza, who drove Renzi's companies of spearmen out of the cultivations into the bush, but when Renzi's riflemen came up, Boza gave ground. The enemy riflemen drove back the companies of Ngoliyo, Angbele, Baduagbanga, Bagbandara, and other of Gbudwe's provincial governors who were also in the field. Gangura's men maintained their position, and so also did those of Yakpati (son of Bafuka), whose companies had not yet, however, become engaged in the fighting.

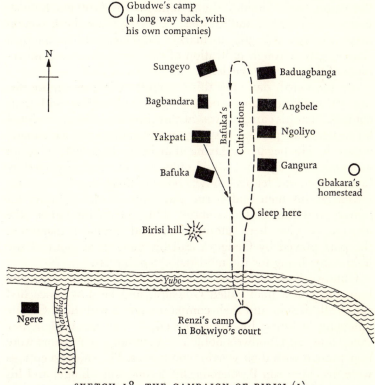

SKETCH 18. THE CAMPAIGN OF BIRISI (1).

Fighting began before daybreak and went on till midday, when Renzi's men ran out of ammunition. They carried their rifles, nevertheless, as though they had plenty of ammunition left, and they shouted to Gangura's men that they had a good supply, although it was in fact exhausted. Gangura's companies pressed the enemy back towards the Yubo river, both sides losing a number of men. On Gangura's side the casualties included his general, Boza, and a number of other well-known men: Rungeziboro, Narungeparanga, Sara, and others. All these were rifle casualties. Gangura's men captured a rifle and sent it to Gbudwe together with bundles of enemy spears gleaned from the ground. As Renzi's men were returning to the Yubo, Yakpati's men assailed them and, being fresh, hastened their retirement to their camp on the other side of the river. In the camp were, besides Renzi himself, his brothers Bafuka, Kana, and Tombo, and his sons, led by Ngilima. Both sketch-maps, (see pp. 361, 364) as marked on the ground for me by a Zande, give a rough indication of the dispositions and movement of this opening battle.

On the fourth day after this encounter Gbudwe's more distantly situated sons and commoner governors arrived with their companies at his camp. It was at this time that Gangura visited his father and, placing a spear and a shaft at his feet, made a speech. He began by saying that he had come to give an account of the fight but would only recount the part played by his own men and let his brothers boast of their own deeds themselves. As his men had borne the brunt of the fighting, his remark was intended to impress that fact on his father (the account I give here emphasizes, and perhaps magnifies, the part played by Gangura and his men on account of my informants being for the most part his subjects).

Gbudwe had been told by the poison oracle to go to the homestead of a man called Gbakara, and he now proceeded there, all his sons and their companies going with him. On the following morning his grandson Ukwe arrived. With a few exceptions, all Gbudwe's noble and commoner governors were now present with their warrior companies. The chief exceptions were his eldest son Basongoda, his second son Mange, and his grandson Ngere. His poison oracle had told him that if Basongoda took part in the fight Renzi would be killed, so he told him to remain at home; for unless there was personal enmity between rulers of two kingdoms at war, neither wished to see the other killed, for they were kinsmen. They desired only that their names might become more famous by everyone speaking afterwards of the events of the war in their names. Mange was not present because I was told, there was embarrassment amounting to estrangement and suspicion between father and son, and Mange regarded himself as being almost independent of his father. Nevertheless, Mange's son Ndoruma was there to represent him. Ngere remained at the junction of the Yubo and the Nambia to guard the approaches to his province.

Renzi did not again attempt to cross the Yubo, but while Gbudwe was consulting his poison oracle to determine his movements and order of battle, he was busy building near his camp, in imitation of the Arabs, a stockade of tree stems surrounded by a trench (*kanda*) said to have been some ten feet deep and six feet wide. Here he lived, and in the event of attack it could hold a proportion of his men, who slept in huts in the camp around the fort.

Gbudwe pressed the attack on this fort, for he wished to harvest his eleusine which, if left ungarnered much longer, would rot in the cultivations. He waited till the first days of the new moon (*ngbangbwa*) had passed and then attempted to take the fort. Early in the morning he ordered his grandson Ukwe and his commoner governors to assault it. Ukwe withdrew at the last moment, and the commoner governors scarcely engaged the enemy. Gbudwe spent the afternoon railing against Ukwe. On the following morning he drew up his forces for a further attempt at taking the fort. His sons and commoner governors were ordered to advance across the river, and his own companies to support them in the rear. His grandson, Ndoruma son of Mange, who had only recently arrived with some of Mange's companies, was told to rest. Renzi struck the first blow. At dawn riflemen crossed the Yubo and climbed Birisi hill from where they opened fire on Gbudwe's troops, who retreated as Renzi's first companies of spearmen crossed the Yubo to attack. By the time the rest of his detachments were crossing the river it was already midday. These companies of spearmen were supported by riflemen (*asinzili*). Gangura's followers then closed with them, and fighting went on till evening, first one side driving the other back and then vice versa (*dururu ko no dururu ko yo ni bakamikami*). Eventually Renzi drove back Gbudwe's sons and commoner governors, leaving Gbudwe's own companies to face the enemy alone, except for Gangura, who refused to retreat, with the consequence that Gbudwe's first company, the Abaigo, led by Basili, who were supporting him in the rear, did not take part in the fighting. By nightfall Gbudwe's men had driven Renzi's forces back to their camp. The sketch-map showing the positions of the various noble and commoner governors was drawn for me in the earth (I do not suppose that those facing Renzi's fort are in the right order, but probably the sketch as a whole correctly indicates who were present and their relative dispositions). Ngoliyo, Bagbandara, Gangura, and Ukwe were on the east flank to protect their territories, and Ngere and Bugwa were on the west flank to protect theirs.

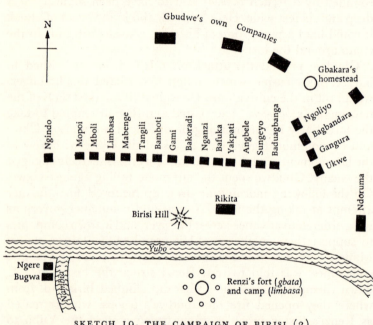

SKETCH 19. THE CAMPAIGN OF BIRISI (2).

Next day Gbudwe moved forward with all his forces. He then distributed to his warriors war-spears of the kind called *andigbo*. Two nights passed without further action. After this lull Gbudwe and his son Gangura consulted the poison oracle about what move to make next. Kuagbiaru, my main informant about this campaign, and Gbafu were present at this seance; and the first two fowls were given poison to their names to discover whether they could be relied upon to keep silence about the revelations of the oracle. Next day Gbudwe sent for his grandsons Ngere son of Basongoda and Ndoruma son of Mange and he instructed Ngere with all the commoner governors to close in on the fort on the western side and Ndoruma with Mange's troops to close in on it on the eastern side (in view of Mange's somewhat ambiguous position, his men kept apart from those of Gbudwe). Both attacked at midday. Their men were told not to fire till they had established contact, lest they should inflict casualties on one another. This pincer movement (*gangi*) was successful. There were heavy casualties on both sides, one being Basili, the commander of Gbudwe's senior company, the Abaigo. Gbudwe's men burnt Renzi's camp and fort and, Renzi's men having withdrawn, retired along the bed of the Yubo. Gbudwe ordered his people not to pursue them but to let them depart unmolested. As Azande reckon victory and defeat, the victory was Gbudwe's.

A rather horrible story recounts the manner in which Basili was buried.

Renzi made an attack on Gbudwe, and Gbudwe's men all went to take part in the fighting. They fought for a long time; and the subjects of Renzi shot one of Gbudwe's elders, whose name was Basili, in his thigh, and it was broken completely. When the campaign was over and the people had returned to their homes, Basili died. They then took his wife and broke the joints of her legs and the joints of her arms, and they buried her in the grave with him. She kept on jerking herself till she made a little hole and she scraped away at it till it became a larger hole. She then started on this larger hole and scraped away at it till it was pierced through to the surface, when she pushed her head through the top of the grave. People saw her and ran to tell what they had seen to others in their homes. Many people came and saw her in this situation; and they speared her and pushed her back into the grave to her husband, and they replaced the earth on top of her. This man Basili was one of Gbudwe's commoner governors. He was senior to all commoners, and he was very highly esteemed by Gbudwe.

This 'campaign of Birisi' is often spoken about by Azande. The account I have given has been put together from a number of informants. My chief informant about the affair, Kuagbiaru, may now speak for himself in a text dictated by him and which I have translated freely and with some cuts.

Now, Renzi went to the Belgians and said to them, let them give him rifles to fight Gbudwe and drive him out, but let them go along with him. To this the Belgians said, 'Renzi, you princes are cheats, and how do we know that you will not tell our plans to Gbudwe so that we fall into an ambush? You go and fight your father by yourself.' Renzi agreed to this proposal; let them give him ammunition and he would go to war with Gbudwe, and they would beyond a doubt hear report of it. So the Belgians gave him many rifles of the kind called *basuka* or *ngburungburu* [percussion-gun] and plenty of ammunition also; and they told him that he had the means to go and wage this war.

So Renzi departed, and when he arrived at his home he had his gong beaten and it sounded the summons to arms, and his men appeared in great numbers, as numerous as grass, at his home on the watershed of the Duru river, near the fort called Yakuruku [Yakaluku], where the Belgians had built it, at the wood Bandani. Gbudwe knew nothing of what Renzi had done. Now it happened that a man came from there to Gbudwe's kingdom, and he told Gangura on the frontier here that Renzi had brought out a large army, but he did not know against which province it was to be directed. When Gangura heard this he went to consult his poison oracle, and he took a fowl and said to the oracle, 'That army of which I have heard, it is my territory it will first fall on, oracle kill the fowl; it is not so, I will hear about it falling somewhere else and we will take part in the fighting there, oracle spare the fowl.' The oracle told him that the war would not first break on the frontier of his province. He said, 'Put your hands in the basket and take out another fowl and pour poison in its beak.' They did so. He said to the oracle, 'Bagbandara, will I join forces with him in his country? Then oracle kill the fowl.' The oracle said that the attack would not fall there first. He said, 'Put your hands in the basket and take another fowl', and he said to the oracle, 'What about Ukwe's country? If Renzi will attack there first, oracle kill the fowl.' The oracle spared it, and he took another fowl and he said to the oracle, 'It will be outside my province and somewhere in Bafuka's province? Oracle kill the fowl.' Hardly had his words been heard than the fowl collapsed at the nape. Then he began to consult the oracle about the leaders of his companies to know which of them would die in the fighting. Then he came out of the bush and he took one of the fowls' wings and he summoned one of his men, Mabu, and he said to him 'Take this fowl's wing and place it before the son of Bazingbi [Gbudwe] and say to him that it is said that Renzi has marshalled a big army and that nobody knows against whom it is intended, so he [Gangura said] would keep watch on his frontier to see what Renzi intended to do with regard to him, whether he clashed with him first or he clashed first with the other sons of Gbudwe before clashing with him. You pay attention to what bumps into you; and when he [Gangura] would see him [Renzi] face to face he would know him, for he is his cousin.' When the matter had been fully reported to Gbudwe, he sent out news of it in all directions to his sons—Rikita and the rest of them—and to his commoner governors to whom he had given provinces: that Renzi had taken the field and was advancing with his men and his arms in a big attack; all had been warned; Gangura had already put out his forces; and Gbudwe was waiting to see where the attack might fall so that he might proceed there, and he had sent forward his young warriors to protect his granaries.

Now, Gangura came out to the men gathered in his court in the evening, and while his subjects were making war-speeches to him, Mabu came back from Gbudwe's court and said to Gangura, 'Gbudwe says, Gangura, you keep your ears open, and where the attack commences, you go there in full strength.' While he was still speaking the alarm was heard, a man called Mbira was giving the alarm as he ran towards them, crying, '*Ra ra ra*, war o, war, war o, war.' When he saw Gangura he placed his shield on the ground and with sweat running down him, he moistened his lips and stood before Gangura and said to him, 'Prince, the attack has begun. It is located in Bokwiyo's territory, on the boundary between him and Basongoda. Bafuka told me to come to you and say to you that if you are not quick Gbudwe's granary will be in flames. The enemy are in great strength, and it seems that they are the joint forces of Renzi and Bafuka son of Wando, and that there are also Europeans in the army. He [Bafuka] is too far off, and Kipa is insufficient to take care of them. It will not be like wars he had fought before, for it appears that Renzi has come with foreigners, Europeans.' Gangura said, 'How is it that they did not give the alarm? Man, you get up and go to Bagbandara and say to him, "That snake we have stalked seems to have entered Bafuka's hut." Let him come and join me ahead, for Gbudwe has said that he [Bagbandara] is my friend.'

So Gangura had his gong beaten and it sounded the summons to arms, and when his men had assembled he arose and took up his abode at the home of Kpayaku [the speaker's father] to wait for Bagbandara. But when Bagbandara arrived he sent a messenger to Gangura to tell him that he was going ahead. Gangura said that he was not to go ahead. He himself would lead. So he drew up his men in the afternoon, and then went to sleep at the home of a man called Nambia. Bagbandara slept at the homestead of Revura. Then at cockcrow Renzi said that Gangura's companies worried him, and he ranged his forces to fall on Bafuka at daybreak. There were many reports of guns, and Bafuka's men were overcome on all sides and driven into the bush. Gangura cried aloud, 'Who has heard the sounds of battle with Bafuka and sleeps, doing nothing? Take me forwards.' Now, when Gangura had reached Bafuka's granary, Bafuka had been defeated and he was fleeing to Gbudwe to tell him that the fighting had scattered his men; but Gangura told people to summon him, for he would not get beyond his spear-shaft to go to Gbudwe. Let Bafuka come and tell him what had happened in the fighting. Renzi would not eat the millet of his granary, he [Gangura] would stand by it. When Bafuka came, Gangura took a spear with its shaft and barred the way with it before him, saying to him, 'Bafuka, by your limb, by your limb, your granary will not be burnt today. Should the battle go against me, I myself would set it alight.' His subjects all said the same. Bagbandara took a spear with its shaft and barred Bafuka's way with it, and he said to him, 'By your limb, by your limb, your granary will not be burnt today. I have come here, I, Bagbandara, I, Bandiama, I, Baakayakpe.'[1] Another prince, Baduagbanga, came forward and said to him, 'I have come, who am Baduagbanga.' Then they drew up their companies. Gangura drew up his and arranged their order, and he told his subjects to make little paths, beginning at the cultivations and treading the paths into the bush, and to leave the cultivations so that should the enemy burst into them they would have an ambush prepared to fight them from it. Let no one throw away his war-spears, let them use them to spear the enemy.

Now people came to Renzi and told him that while he delayed the sons of Gbudwe had arrived nearby with large forces. Smoke rises above men's heads. So Renzi and Bafuka [son of Wando] divided up their forces, and on the following morning at daybreak Renzi arose and came against the sons of Gbudwe. A single man arose and at daybreak went to draw water near the camp of the sons of Gbudwe, and when he had drawn water, some armed men came, without his seeing them on account of the early morning mist, and went alongside him till they reached the camp of the sons of Gbudwe, where they shot him. Everyone was awakened from sleep by the report and at once took up formation. Gangura then came forward to fight this fight. Bagbandara and the other princes fled from the sound of Renzi's approach, he and Baduagbanga and Sungeyo. Only Yakpati and Angbele joined Gangura, and they fought hard. Gangura captured a rifle and sent it to Gbudwe at the Masumbu here, saying to Mabu, 'Take it, and say to Gbudwe, "That snake which keeps on putting out its head, Gangura has cut off its head." '

---

[1] Like many princes he had several names.

Rikita now arrived and the place resounded with the [foreign] speech of the Abare people. Toi was with the Abare, and he had many riflemen among his followers. Toi swore to Gbudwe that with regard to that son of his, Rikita, should he initiate anything they would not depart from it; he [Rikita] would not be ashamed while his [Toi's] men were present; his people were men. When he had moved away, Ukwe came forward and stood before Gbudwe and said to him, 'By your limb, by your limb, I have brought Boli's [my father's] spear.' Gbudwe told Ukwe to approach, and when he approached, Gbudwe told him to take his [Gbudwe's] commoner governors and stir up Renzi with them. But Ukwe, as he went on his way, said he would not fight, he would merely be breaking his bill-hook in his friend's forest [a common Zande proverb]; and he turned back. When they related this to Gbudwe he said, 'Oh, what a rotter Ukwe is, he is my grandson and he speaks to me thus! Who gave this billhook? It was I who gave it to his father.' And then, as they looked towards the east they saw that Mange was coming, although not Mange in person, for he had sent his son Ndoruma with his men and Yangu [Mange's chief commoner governor], who came with his [Mange's] own men; they came together, Yangu and Ndoruma, and Mange returned to his home. When people saw Ndoruma coming, they said that now Renzi would depart in the night; but in the mean-while Renzi and Bafuka [son of Wando] were digging their trench, to fight Gbudwe from the protection of their fort. Now, when Ndoruma had arrived, Gbudwe said to him, 'Now that you have come, rest awhile, for you have journeyed hard. Your fathers have fought much; and now that you have come to your father's place, rest awhile while I discover what Renzi is about.' So it happened, and then, on a certain day at sunrise, Gbudwe arose at the home of Gbakara, where he was staying, and he went to look at Bafuka's granary, where the fighting began; and when all his sons had come he began to arrange the disposition of his army. He told his sons to start the battle and he placed his own companies behind those of his sons, so that if the battle went against his sons his own men could take it over, to help them with it. He gave orders that no one was to start fighting before Rikita had done so. When Rikita had attacked, the others could join in. He himself would go to his eleusine, which was about to rot in the cultivations.

The men arose and went forward till they met Renzi's sentries and they pelted them with shot. When Renzi's men fled to the shelter of their fort Gbudwe's men did not pursue them but relaxed at the side of the Yubo river, and there they spent the day. It was already late in the afternoon, past the time when Gbudwe had told Rikita to attack; and when Gangura saw that it was approaching sunset, he said, as he was leaning on the arm of Kuagbiaru, 'Alas, Rikita has left the fighting for Gbudwe. How is this men? Let us go and fight for the King, for Rikita has given it up.' So they directed their steps to the west to the Yubo, and there they met Renzi's troops, who suddenly came against the men of the sons of Gbudwe to engage with them in a big fight. Renzi overcame the sons of Gbudwe on every side and scattered them into the bush. The onset held up Rikita at a cave, he and his page Bawaku, and it held up Gangura with his pages Kuagbiaru, Mangiparoni, and Otoka. Only those of his men who were called the Abangadu held their ground by the side of Gangura. Then, the companies near Gangura having retreated, Basili seized Gangura's arm to flee with him, to send him back to his home. While they were in this situation the sun sank and the warriors began to move away in the dusk. They went and saw Gbudwe sitting with his shield and his spear in his hand. He burst into speech, saying, 'By my limb, what is all this? I told Basili to drive Renzi away and they let him go again. By my limb, it does not please me. Truly by the limb of Bazingbi, it does not please me. But the Belgians are behind him. However, at daybreak tomorrow I will give him something to remember me by.'

Now Ngere [son of Basongoda] stood before him and said, 'Gbudwe, master, the man who started this affair, was it not Bagbandara who began running away before anyone else?' Gbudwe said that he did not want to hear anything more about it. Let them stop talking about it. He took beer and gave it to the princes. Then he slept. At daybreak he arose and went to his warriors; and when he had seated himself under a *banga* tree and his men were assembled, he cut the cords binding bundles of spears, to distribute them to them, telling them to shape the shafts as quickly as possible, for he and they were going to fight Renzi till eventide. A war leader stood up and in a resounding voice sang the opening stanza of a war song, and the refrain resounded back; and the trumpets sounded a blast, sounding, 'It is Gbudwe o, it is Gbudwe'; and the drums were beaten by the drummer. Gbudwe took porridge in a huge bowl and gave it to his men, together with the flesh of an animal cooked in a large pot; it took three men to carry the porridge into the court. When they had eaten this meal, he said that as the sun had set they would not fight on that day, but he had something to show Renzi on the following day. They then went to sleep.

Gbudwe said that Bagbandara and Kpoyo and Wanangba and Bakorodi were to come to consult the poison oracle. Bagbandara took with him his page Gbafu, and Gangura took Kuagbiaru. They went to the place of consultation, and they began to consult the oracle about Renzi. The oracle told them that they must not attack Renzi on that day, but on the following day. Then Gbudwe, having noticed the pages, Kuagbiaru and Gbafu, asked Gangura, by the limb of Bazingbi, whose children they were. Gangura stood up in the place of oracular consultation and replied to him, 'Master, that one is Kuagbiaru son of Kpayaku. Gumba used to send him on errands to you.' Gbudwe said, 'Let him drink poison [let a fowl be given poison in his name]; let him give a test to Wanangba [ask Wanangba to consult the oracle about him]; and let Wanangba say to the oracle that if he is going about with Gangura to hear my affairs and will then spread them abroad, oracle kill the fowl—if he will not spread them abroad let the fowl survive.' Kuagbiaru gave the test, and the fowl survived. Gbudwe then asked about Gbafu, and Gbafu gave a test to Kpoyo. They consulted the oracle about both lads, and the fowls survived.

Then they all left the bush, and when they got back Gbudwe sent messengers to Ngere and Ndoruma to summon them. When they had come, he said, 'You, Ngere, you take over my Abaigo company and all my other companies. You, Ndoruma, take charge of all your father's companies and cross the Yubo from the east side while Ngere comes up it from the west.' So Ndoruma collected his father's subjects and went with them as Gbudwe had directed, and Ngere collected his men and went with them as Gbudwe had directed. Now when the subjects of Renzi looked into the water they saw mud there [disturbed by Gbudwe's men in the river] and by this they knew that they would fight the subjects of Gbudwe on that day. Then, after Gbudwe's men had gone and closed the route by which Renzi had come, fierce fighting began and Renzi was overcome on all sides and his forces driven into the bush. Men died like dust in numbers; the subjects of Renzi died like grass, and the subjects of Gbudwe died like grass. Renzi started with all speed to flee. Then, when full daylight came, Gbudwe said that, as Renzi had insulted him, he would continue to fight him. So his men pursued Renzi for some time, and it was Gbudwe himself who threw down the hand-bells and told people to summon back with them the warriors who were pursuing Renzi, for he gave him up, so let him get away. He said, 'It is as though he came with Wando's kingdom to let me see it, for I have never before seen those people my brother became ruler over. Nevertheless Renzi is a cheat. Now, of you who are princes, only Ndoruma will accompany me back to my court. Ngere, you go back to your home, and all you other princes also.' All these princes began to scatter, and Gbudwe also left. As for Gbudwe's war-leader, Basili, who had been shot, they carried him home to die.

II

It is presumably to Gbudwe as he was at about this time that most descriptions of his appearance given by men who frequented his court as boys and youths refer, though some descriptions I record must refer to him as he was some years earlier. I quote one of them, given by Kuagbiaru, who must have then been about seventeen or eighteen years of age.

Gbudwe was a short man, though not excessively short. He was short with the shortness of [his son] Gangura, though he was stout also, not, however, unpleasantly stout. He was stout with the stoutness of a man whose flesh is loose with it. His breasts protruded like those of a woman, but not altogether like a woman's for they were a man's breasts. His wrists were wrinkled [with fat], and his forearm was like a man's shank. His eyes were little protruding eyes, and they sparkled like stars. When he looked at a man in anger they were terrible; then they went grey like ashes.

His straw hat was woven with great skill and it had a wide brim all round it; and cowries were woven round the base of the crown, completely encircling it. He took two hat-pins, beaten out of white metal, and he stuck in one on one side and the other on the other side. His hat was marvellously fine, and when he wore it, it suited him splendidly, and he looked a great king indeed. When he approached people from afar you could not mistake Gbudwe. He was a marvellous prince.

Gbudwe never wore black-stained barkcloth, only red barkcloth and white barkcloth, which is that barkcloth which is soft. Gbudwe on account of his wearing his barkcloth short, wore it wide at the sides. He tied it to the top of his thigh so that it did not reach to his knees. He wore it short but it covered both flanks; and [when seating himself] he hitched it up so that the extremities of it spilled over on to his thighs. He took his red cloth which he had brought back with him from [captivity among] the Arabs and tied it round his middle so that the end of it spilled over his barkcloth.

He was on the whole light-coloured, but not excessively so. When he went into court his dogs took position on either side of him. He carried two spears in his hand, and the third thing he held was his curved ceremonial knife. Those who wanted to see him climbed up trees to see him, because other people shut out their view. A man who had not seen Gbudwe climbed a tree to have a look at him. Gbudwe was a fine-looking man. He would never file his teeth, they formed an unbroken line in his mouth, and they were white.

Other Azande have described him to me in much the same terms. They have said that the colour of his skin was dull copper, or, as Azande put it, the colour of the leaf of the *nonga* plant, and the skin was smooth and soft. His plump hands ended in long nails, which he is said to have dug into the necks of erring wives. He swung his arms in a swagger cultivated by princes. His facial features were more like those of Gangura (in 1928) than those of any other of his sons, especially in the little black moustache and short bristling beard turning to grey. His hair was grey-black like Gangura's and he resembled Gangura also in stature —though he was a little taller and also bulkier and stouter—and in loudness of voice and vehemence of speech. In his stoutness he resembled rather his son Rikita, though he was not so potbellied. His teeth were as white as those of his eldest son Basongoda in his young days. His legs were also like those of Basongoda, short and stumpy; or perhaps even more like those of his nephew Kanimara. I was told that when he was younger his hair was invariably dressed but that in his later years it was sometimes dressed but usually just cut short, the fashion adopted by his two eldest sons, Basongoda and Mange. When dressed, in the manner described in the text above, the skin of a monkey (*ngarangara*) was attached to the hoop (of the hat) so that it fell over the nape of his neck and shoulders. In wearing his bark-cloth short, so that his knees and part of his thighs were exposed, and as a close fit (*ko ni wi e mbikpimkipi, ko awinga domba te*), he did not follow the fashion of many princes of his day who wore their barkcloth loose and falling to the calf, or, in the case of some princes, such as Basongoda and Gumba, to the ankle. When threatening war he would pull the barkcloth right up his thighs.

He generally carried a curved ceremonial knife in his hand and would lay it across his knees as he sat in court, and he used it to assist himself in rising from his stool by pressing it on the ground. He once possessed a knife of this kind with a very fine handle of Mangbetu workmanship, but his courtiers so often and so pointedly admired it, saying, 'Gbudwe, what a fine knife, what a fine piece of craftsmanship!' that in despair he gave it away to one of them, and ever afterwards he used one with an ordinary wooden handle. Princes seldom carried a spear, but Gbudwe used to walk with one in his homestead, and once he killed a stray deer with it there. In his latter years he carried a spear of foreign craftsmanship which had been given to him by an Arab trader. He never smoked but would offer a pipe to others and let them smoke in his presence. Though fond of beer, he is said to have drunk it in moderation and never to have been seen intoxicated by his subjects.[1]

12

The forces of three European powers had by this time already entered, or were about to enter, Zandeland. As was said earlier, we need not here consider the French advance, beyond pointing out that by 1898 the French had a number of posts in Tembura's kingdom; for this probably facilitated later British penetration of his country, which served as a base for the British expedition against Gbudwe that was to lead to his death and the annexation of his kingdom. The Belgians also had established posts to the south-west of Gbudwe's domains—the French posts being to the north-west of them—and they had, after stiff opposition, defeated Ndoruma son of Ezo and occupied his country. We will later make some reference to Belgian activities in so far as they concern Gbudwe, in an account of his attack on their post at Mayawa. The British were last on the scene, but they were the first to clash with Gbudwe's people.

The battle of Omdurman took place in 1898, and the reconquest of the Sudan followed. The northern Bahr al-Ghazal was occupied by Anglo-Egyptian forces between 1900 and 1903. A delicate situation then developed in this part of central Africa, where Belgian, French, and British interests overlapped and might, without forbearance, lead to conflict. In 1901 two British officers, Sparkes Bey and Bimbashi Haynes, went on patrol to Tembura's country, where the king welcomed them and presented them with a vast store of ivory. It was found that he had about a thousand rifles and a body of troops moderately well trained by the French, who had been in his country for over six years.[2] As the Belgians were to occupy the old kingdom

---

[1] For the appearance of kings and princes in general see my paper 'Zande Kings and Princes', in *Anthropological Quarterly* (1957).

[2] Capt. E. S. Stephenson, *Sudan Intelligence Reports*, 1912, no. 210. This is not, however, mentioned by *The Bahr El Ghazal Province Handbook*, 1911, which gives the first patrol to visit Tembura as that commanded by Capt. Bethell, R.A., in June

of Ezo at about the same time and were in control, or partially
in control, of the Zande kingdoms in what was till recently the
Belgian Congo, and as the western Zande territories in what
was till recently French Equatorial Africa had been occupied
by the French, Gbudwe's kingdom was to be the last of the
Zande kingdoms to remain independent of European rule, as
it had been the last, at any rate of those with which we are concerned in this account, to succumb to the Egyptian Government.
The Anglo-Belgian pincers now began to close on it.

Capt. Stephenson tells us, in his report already cited, that
King Tembura had become rich and powerful and that there
were rumours that Gbudwe was jealous of him and had spoken
of having an Anglo-Egyptian post established in his country to
counteract Tembura's influence with that Administration.
There may have been some foundation for these rumours,
because we learn from the *Bahr El Ghazal Province Handbook*
(p. 59) that Gbudwe had sent an embassy to the Government
in 1902, though we are not told what was its purport. If he had
any such idea it was, however, belied, at any rate in the eyes of
the British, by his actions. The same authority[1] says that in
March 1903 'a friendly mission', under command of Bimbashi
Armstrong, set out to visit Gbudwe, but Armstrong was killed
by an elephant on the way, and Colour-Sergeant Boardman,
who proceeded with the patrol, was held up by the people of
Gbudwe's son Mange, and, being surrounded after crossing the
Jur river on 9 March, had to withdraw. In the following year
a force was dispatched to establish relations with Gbudwe's son
Rikita, who administered the most northerly part of his kingdom. Azande know the reception of this patrol as 'the war of the
scribe (*Bakepai* or *Bakewaraga*)', after the name by which they
designated its leader, or the person whom they took to be its
leader. I was told that the patrol came from the north (Tonj)
and, having reached the confines of Rikita's territory, its leader
announced that he was making a peaceful tour of the country
and asked Rikita for unimpeded transit. Rikita replied that it
was not for him to grant or deny transit, but for his father to

1904, when a post was established in his territory (p. 60). References to *Sudan
Intelligence Reports* have not been checked. I have had to rely on notes taken from
them in Khartoum many years ago.
  [1] Loc. cit.

make the decision. Now it seems that Gbudwe had repeatedly complained that Rikita had contact with the Arabs at Tonj, so when a messenger from his son reported what Bakepai had said, he answered angrily that he had had enough of Rikita's duplicity and that there was to be no more of this sort of conduct in Bazingbi's country. Truly, he said, he had not begotten sons, for the foreigner could insult him without protest. When Gbudwe's words were reported to his son, Rikita made a surprise attack on Bakepai, who was seriously wounded in the combat and taken back by the patrol, which beat a hasty retreat, to Tonj, where he died and was buried. Bagbandara, Gangura, and some other of Gbudwe's sons had arrived with their followers on the banks of the Sueh prepared for war, but they took no part in the fighting, which occurred on the border between the country Rikita himself administered and that administered on his behalf by the Bongo Toi.

Speaking of this incident *The Bahr El Ghazal Province Handbook* notes (p. 60): 'In February 1904, a force of three companies of the XV Sudanese, which was despatched in order to establish friendly relations with Sultan Rikita, met with opposition, and returned via Tonj and Rumbek to Shambe.' It is stated in Capt. E. S. Stephenson's report that this strong force was led by Sutherland Bey, Bimbashi Bethell, and Wood Bey. He says that it went via Tonj towards Yambio. It was attacked by Rikita and, Bimbashi Haynes being mortally wounded, it returned to Tonj.

In the same year there was a further clash between government troops and Azande of Gbudwe's kingdom (presumably some of Mange's people) who were raiding the Jur (Beli–Sofi peoples); and later they raided the Bongo. Taking all these incidents together, it might well have appeared to the authorities at Wau that Gbudwe, far from wishing to come to an agreement with the Government, and further still from intending to submit to it, was showing himself to be openly hostile; and so it did appear to them. As we shall see, in the following year a very strong force was sent against him.

13

In the same year (1904) that Rikita attacked the British patrol coming from the north, Gbudwe attacked, with disastrous consequences to himself, a Belgian fort in the south of his kingdom. This attack is known to Azande as 'the campaign of Mayawa', after the name of a river near which the fort was situated. A sketch of the background to this campaign must first be given.

We have earlier noted that the Arab ivory and slave traders began to penetrate into the Zande and Mangbetu kingdoms in the middle sixties, that during the following decade their trading-posts were being taken over by the Egyptian Government, and that Gbudwe's kingdom was till 1882 the only kingdom north of the Welle both determined and able to exclude traders and Government alike. But though the Government had taken over the trading-stations, the troops of the companies which originally owned them, the so-called 'Nubians', remained, and trading and slaving went on much as before, so that it was scarcely possible to say, in the chaotic entanglement of the time, who were in the employ of the Government and who were not. When the Mahdists gained control in the northern Bahr al-Ghazal and in a considerable part of Equatorial Province from 1883 to 1885, these Arabs of one sort or another were infected by Mahdist propaganda; and insubordination, mutiny, and defection were prevalent throughout the region. Most of these scavengers and parasites then withdrew with the Amir Karamalla to the north in 1885, and, as far as the Bahr al-Ghazal was concerned, an unwonted period of peace and freedom from oppression or the threat of it ensued. But Emin's retirement to the south had left Mahdist forces in occupation of the Nile and from their posts there (Shambe, Bor, and Lado) they were able to make incursions into what is now the Congo Republic, using the routes previously used by government patrols. These incursions only indirectly concern our story, and we need, therefore, only refer to them in so far as the relations of the Dervishes with the sons of Wando affected the further relations between Renzi, son of Wando, and Gbudwe, and ultimately between Gbudwe and the Belgians.

It very often happened in the history of African kingdoms that native dynastic and political rivalries became involved with the interests and ambitions of outsiders and with the struggle for dominance between them. So it happened in the kingdom of Wando. One of his sons, Ukwe, we learn from

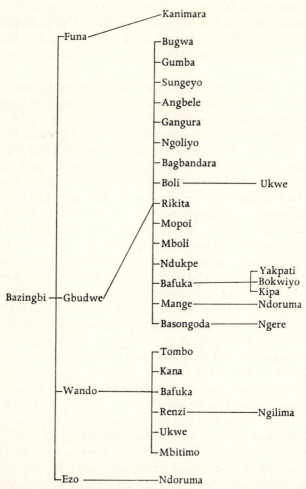

(The genealogy gives most of the names of Zande princes mentioned in the text.)

Junker, about 1880, rebelled against his father and appealed
to the Arabs (the representatives of the Egyptian Government
in the Mangbetu territories) for assistance. This was given, the
Arabs being only too pleased to turn all such disputes to their
own advantage, and Ukwe's elder brother Mbitimo was captured and held for a time in chains. His father sought refuge in
the bush and with his brother Ngoliyo, and finally, so Emin

tells us, in Makarakaland.[1] What happened after this, I do not rightly know. There are no European records—Junker, Casati, and Emin had all departed to Uganda—and my own researches were conducted in Gbudwe's old kingdom and not in Wando's, with which I had only a passing and casual acquaintance; but when the curtain goes up for the next scene we find Wando dead and a bitter feud in progress between Ukwe and his younger brother Renzi against a wider and even bitterer struggle between the Belgians and the Arabs.

According to Hutereau,[2] Mbitimo predeceased his father Wando. When Wando died, Renzi, who was on the Mebesina, tributary of the Yakuluku, wished to seize his father's inheritance and also to bring into subjection his father's brother Galia (Ngoliyo), who had been given a territory to rule over by Wando.[3] In his design to take over his father's territory Renzi was supported by his younger brother Bafuka, then on the Nanduku river, but was opposed by his elder brother Ukwe. Renzi brought in the Dervishes from Bor, on the Nile, to attack Ukwe They did not effectively occupy any territory but returned to the Nile with the booty they had pillaged in Ukwe's country. When the Belgians began to occupy the Welle (Uele) region, Ukwe submitted to them at once, hoping to enlist their support against Renzi. There then passed a period of some years during which the Belgians constantly forced back the incursions of the Dervishes, Ukwe helping the Belgians and Renzi the Dervishes. In September 1894 a Dervish force met near Dungu a Belgian reconnaissance from that post and defeated it, but in December of the same year a strong Dervish force was routed by Commandant Christiaens, who was wounded in the affray. In February 1895 Commandant Francqui organized at Dungu a

---

[1] Junker, op. cit., vol. ii, 1891, pp. 160, 172, 263, 268, 274, and 276. Mbitimo's country extended from Ngoliyo's eastwards along the lower courses of the Kibali and Duru. Ukwe's country was further north, on the middle courses of these rivers. Wando, with his youngest ruling son Renzi, governed at the time the northernmost section of his kingdom. Ukwe, aided by his Arab allies, had got possession of Mbitimo's territory and was aiming at getting possession of Renzi's and Wando's also.

[2] Op. cit., 1922, pp. 182–90. Hutereau gives much useful information, but it is necessary to say that his account is very often inaccurate, especially in the dating of events, where it is sometimes far off the mark.

[3] This territory 'comprenait la Boere, la Nabanda, affluent de la Boere, la Molabundu, et la Zangwa, affluents de la Babanda, la Nabambiso, affluent Boere, la Namona, affluent de la Singbi, affluent du Yubo' (ibid., p. 182).

column to occupy the banks of the Nile. The route of this column lay through the territories of Bafuka and Renzi, and, as it was advancing through the country of the former, its advance guard, a platoon of Hausa troops, fell into an ambush laid by Bafuka's people; the leader of the platoon, Frenet, and thirty-six Hausa were killed and eighteen Hausa were wounded. Commandant Francqui was also wounded. The column retreated to Dungu pursued by Azande, its rearguard having to fight two battles, at the villages of Kana and Tombo. Five months later a company under Lieutenants Zwinhufoud, Devenyns, and Laplume, accompanied by a contingent of Ukwe's warriors, marched against Bafuka but were unable to bring him to an engagement. However, Renzi and Bafuka seem to have changed sides shortly afterwards, for when Chaltin left Surur (Vankerckhovenville) in January 1897 for the Nile, Renzi and Bafuka with their warriors served with his force as auxiliaries. This force defeated the Dervishes and took Rejaf by assault.

What have the Azande to say about these events? Although they took place outside the kingdom of Gbudwe, they were of sufficient magnitude for his subjects to have been aware of them; and I quote two texts given me by them, the first referring to Bafuka's ambush and the second giving some account of the relations between Renzi, Ukwe, the Belgians, and the Dervishes.

The Belgians came and resided in Bafuka's country for many days. Bafuka said that he had not the slightest intention of receiving them. He admonished his subjects about them, that they should keep watch on the track going in the direction of where the Belgians were; if they saw them approaching they should come and tell him, and he would assail them on their route. They must not let their caravan use that track in any circumstances. Then the day came when the Belgians advanced in a column of file together with their porters, and they came against Bafuka with war. Some subjects of Bafuka ran to tell him, saying that while he was waiting the Belgians had arrived with a force to attack him. Bafuka called up all his subjects; and he sent messengers to Malingindo and to Kana and to Tombo to tell them that that which they had all declared they would fight in defence of their country had come. Let them all come; together they would deal with these foreigners. He sent a messenger to Kipa son of Renzi, telling him also of the state of affairs. All these men came, and Bafuka drew up his army in formation. It stretched to a great distance.

A scout hastened to tell Bafuka: 'Ai! Be very much on guard today. It will be today. Ai! Bafuka, it will be today.' Tombo said that he would go ahead to attack them. Malingindo said that for his part he would lead on the right wing. Kana said that for his part he would lead on the left wing. Kipa and Bafuka were, for their part, in reserve. They all drew up their companies in formation, and all was prepared. On their side, the Belgians began to advance, and they continued to advance, not knowing that the subjects of Bafuka already lay in ambush for them along the path, and they entered between the Azande as a single body [*ki ni limi a limo ndururu azande sa*]. When they reached a point opposite the senior companies, these rose suddenly to attack them wildly on all sides. That began the fight, and it went on for a long time. The subjects of Bafuka were killed like grass in number, and the Belgians were killed like grass also. They continued to fight till at dusk Bafuka's men put the Belgians to flight. The subjects of Bafuka took in booty a great number of the Belgian breach-loaders. It finished, and Bafuka returned to reside in his home. Renown of the engagement spread all over the countryside, that Bafuka had had a great battle with the Belgians. It passed from mouth to mouth till all heard of it. This event took place while Gbudwe was still alive; he heard of the fame of this fight.

The second text runs as follows:

Renzi was a son of Wando, who was a son of Bazingbi. He was a very powerful man and he did strong things, such as favouring the Europeans and doing good to foreigners. Above all, he did not wish to be in any way disloyal to the Belgians. That war the Belgians waged against Gbudwe, he was with them, for he wished to take Gbudwe's inheritance; that is why, when the Belgians came against Gbudwe with war, he also came after them to make war on Gbudwe. The Belgians greatly favoured him, and they gave him a wide area over which to rule, so that he was a great king in the inheritance of his father Wando.

He was a deceitful man, for he used to get up in the night and take off his fine barkcloth—that by which people recognized him—and wear instead just a small piece of old barkcloth. He then wandered by night over the country of his subjects, and if he saw some of them drinking beer, he sat behind them in the night just as though he were some ordinary young man. He went on drinking beer till he was well satisfied, when he began to speak ill of himself to them, saying, 'Oh that bad witch who is Renzi, why does he abuse people so? Oh, if only he would die!' If there was a man present who habitually criticized him, he would at once interrupt to abuse him soundly, for he would not know that he was present. People thus talked ill of him in his very presence, and when he left no one knew that it was he, for he came to them unknown.

That great war which Renzi fought against his elder brother Ukwe: after their father Wando died they wanted to dispute his inheritance between them, Ukwe saying that since he was the elder he ought to take the inheritance, but Renzi saying that it was not at all so, for even though Ukwe was the elder, he was not going to take the inheritance. Renzi consulted the poison oracle, asking it whether, as he was about to make war on Ukwe, he would defeat him and drive him from his father's kingdom. The oracle replied that it would not be so, he would not drive Ukwe out if he made war on him. He then asked the oracle a second question: if he, Renzi, went to fetch those *Abolomu* who were the Arab Dervishes, and they came and made war with Ukwe, would they drive him out? The oracle said to him 'Yes'—if he did this he would take the inheritance. He went to the Dervishes in the east and he said to them, 'There is a man here called Ukwe who wants to make war with you, you had better come and build a fort in Wando's kingdom.' For Renzi was a friend of the Dervishes. So they came and built a fort right in the centre of Wando's kingdom. They told Ukwe to come and submit to them, but he defied them and fled to the Belgians in the west and told them that the Dervishes wanted to take their country, the inheritance of Wando. The Belgians came and made war with the Dervishes, who were aided by Renzi. They fought for a long time, and the Dervishes defeated the Belgians. Renzi then consulted the oracle again as to how he should act to get possession of his father's kingdom: if he were to go and intrigue with the Belgians to bring them to challenge the Dervishes and Ukwe, would he then be able to take the kingdom of Wando? The oracle told him that if he acted thus he would defeat Ukwe.

Renzi left the Dervishes and went and appeared before the Belgians, and he said to them cunningly, 'Now, Ukwe is treacherous to you, saying that the Dervishes are stronger, since they defeated you before. Ukwe wants to join the Dervishes to make war on you Belgians.' When the Belgians heard this speech they prepared for war, and they advanced with Renzi; and while he remained in his home, they began to build their fort. When the Dervishes heard of the Belgian move they went to build a fort at the river Nzoro. The Belgians approached from one side and the Dervishes and Ukwe approached from the other side. They fought together for a long time, and the Belgians were exhausted, and the Dervishes were exhausted also. Then the Belgians brought Renzi and established him in the kingdom of his father Wando; and they told Ukwe to get out of that country and to go after the Dervishes, since he was a traitor. Renzi in this way took possession of the kingdom of his father Wando from that time, and he became a great monarch.

Another big war of Renzi's was with Gbudwe's son Gangura. For Renzi wanted to make war with Gbudwe all the time; but Gbudwe would not accommodate him. It was Gangura who got angry, for his province was on the boundary between Gbudwe and Renzi. Gangura went to make war on Renzi's son Bazugba, about twice; and then Renzi got angry, and he came and burnt all Gangura's huts and seized all his wives and took them off to his home. Gangura then attacked Renzi's son Bazugba and fought him and captured all his wives and burnt all his huts, and he brought back his wives and gave them to Gbudwe. From this time fighting ceased altogether between Gangura and Renzi.

I have quoted the whole of this text as it was taken down, but it is only the central part relating to Renzi, Ukwe, the Belgians, and the Dervishes that has any immediate bearing on the present account. We have to bear in mind that Gbudwe knew what the situation in the kingdom of Wando was, that (from about 1896) Renzi son of Wando and his brother Bafuka had recognized Belgian overlordship, were acting as allies to the Belgians, and were, if the Zande account is correct, as we may suppose it to be, receiving arms from them. His hostility to the Belgians was no doubt to some extent due to these considerations, for Zande kings naturally thought of intrusive forces in terms of their traditional relations with each other; so that just as Gbudwe's attitude to the Arab traders to the east of his kingdom had been influenced by his relations with Ngangi son of Muduba, and just as his attitude to the Egyptian Government had been influenced by his relations with Ndoruma son of Ezo, so his attitude to the Belgians was influenced by his relations with Renzi son of Wando. Hence the war between him and Renzi, which has already been noted, was regarded as one, at least to some extent, between him and Renzi assisted by the Belgians, who had begun supporting him some three years before it took place. Gbudwe's subjects thought that some *Amusungu*, the word they used to describe Belgian forces, might have been on that occasion taking part in the operation in

Renzi's support. This would not necessarily mean that they thought that Europeans were taking part in it, for the term *Amusungu* covered both the Belgian officers and their Negro troops. They do not definitely assert that this was the case, and it probably was not; but they may well have been correct in supposing that the Belgians were aware of Renzi's intentions and that he acted with their approval and their support in the matter of arms. Therefore, also, the further advance of the Belgians and their building of a fort on the Mayawa could not have been viewed by Gbudwe as unconnected with Renzi's ambitions, but rather, as an attempt on Renzi's part to obtain possession of Gbudwe's domains with Belgian aid.

My notes on the campaign of Mayawa are not as full or as clear as I would wish, but such as they are, I set them forth. It seems that the Belgian column, supported by Renzi's warriors, first advanced into the country of Ukwe son of Boli, who had fled for refuge to Renzi's court after having incurred Gbudwe's displeasure by his conduct in the Birisi campaign, leaving his province to be divided among Mboli (father of Dika), Ango or Banginzegino (Gangura's younger uterine brother), and Migida or Ngbimi (died in European times)—all sons of Gbudwe—and two of Gbudwe's commoner governors, Zai and Kpoyo. Azande say that it was Ukwe who incited Renzi to bring the Belgians to Gbudwe's kingdom.

The Belgian force[1] first drove away Mboli's companies and then defeated those of Ango, Migida, Zai, and Kpoyo, which had encamped in the neighbourhood of the enemy. Mboli, as soon as he had appreciated the situation, sent a messenger to his father to tell him that this was not a *basapu*, a raid, but was to be a *sungusungu vura*, a campaign.

The Belgians at first occupied a Zande homestead and erected a stockade around it, and placed poles slanting from the inside against the stockade, over which grew yams (*gbata gbara*). It was from the protection of this fort, and with trained rifle fire, that they defeated the border princes and commoner governors who first came against them. Gbudwe then sent a messenger to Mboli, telling him that no one was again to attack the fort; they

---

[1] Under command of Capt. Colin (A. de Calonne-Beaufaict, op. cit., p. 61). Colin had only 128 soldiers. Commandant Lemaire came to his assistance, and then Gbudwe's men withdrew (Art. 'Lemaire' in *Biographie Coloniale belge*, 1951).

were only to attack foraging parties. The Belgians in the meanwhile built another fort and one on a larger scale, some hundreds of yards square (as far as I could judge from descriptions of it), with a high stockade and a wide trench around it. The earth from the trench was thrown up against the beams of the stockade, but holes were left at various elevations for firing in lying, squatting, kneeling, and standing positions.

Gbudwe had also sent a messenger to Gangura, telling him not to go to war yet—he would consult the poison oracle first— but to cut and weave cane (*kate*) into baskets, for it was an *asua* year (these much-relished termites rise every second year from September to November). Gbudwe himself was equally leisurely. He was in no hurry to attack the Belgian post; and it is possible that he knew enough about the situation to know that it was hopeless. He is said to have told his inner circle of confidants that he would eat the *asua* termites first, because he had been warned by his poison oracle that he would not live to eat them again. Then, while the eleusine was ripening—some of it near the Belgian fort was harvested—the attack was launched in earnest. Most of Gbudwe's sons were present; though Basongoda, who sent two companies of warriors, was again left at home; and Rikita only arrived when his father was about to retreat. Some commoner governors—there were not many left at the end of Gbudwe's reign—were also present.

The most important of his sons to bring support was Mange, who arrived two days before the main attack began and made his camp to the east of the Mayawa. Mange certainly had not seen his father since his return from captivity in 1884, when some say that he had a short interview with him before returning to his own province; and if he did not see him then, as others say, he had not met his father for about a quarter of a century. Gbudwe now, warned by the poison oracle that he had but a short time to live, sent for Mange to come to his camp that he might see his son once more before he died. Mange sat on a stool before his father, not facing him but sideways. After his father had looked at him for a while, he in his turn sat sideways so that his son might see him without their eyes meeting. Then Mange rose and made a speech, threatening the enemy, but always keeping his eyes averted from the eyes of his father, standing sideways to him. Such formal shyness is usual between a king and his elder sons, but in Mange's case the uneasiness was increased by doubt of the son's loyalty, so Azande say. It will be remembered that when Gbudwe returned from captivity he had difficulty in persuading Mange to leave the province in the centre of his kingdom which he directly administered himself. Mange is said to have given his father more recent grounds for suspicion by negotiating with the Belgians and providing them with provisions; and he is said to have had his ulcerated leg treated by a Belgian doctor whom Azande named Nagumbira. This doctor is said to have departed in haste and horror when he saw that Mange's son Ndoruma was looking at him with his red eyes, thinking that no man's eyes could glow like that if he did not have murder in his heart. It may well have been the case that Mange had received medical treatment from the Belgians, for Commandant Lemaire's mission arrived at M'volo on the River Nam in December 1903, and when a British patrol reached Ire on the same river in January 1905 they found the Lemaire mission occupying a strongly built fort there and found that it had also established four posts in the neighbourhood of the Nile–Congo watershed.[1] Azande do not know that Mange intrigued with the Belgians, but they think that he may have done so because Mange's people did not suffer at their hands as Gbudwe's did when their country was occupied.

About this time, and before Gbudwe's attack on the fort, there took place an incident often mentioned by Azande. There was heavy rain, and some of Gbudwe's *aparanga*, unmarried warriors, tried to take refuge in the huts of his son Bagbandara's men. These, partly on account of some of them having their wives with them, but also on account of a feeling of resentment that the subjects of Gbudwe's sons had towards the subjects of their father, because they put on airs, at first insulted them and then struck them. A fight with spears ensued, and Batikpo killed Suma, one of Bagbandara's elders. Gbudwe was annoyed that courtesy had not been shown to his men, and Bagbandara had to pay him a heavy indemnity in spears.

Gbudwe's forces under his sons had now all arrived. Zegi had been the first to arrive, at the time of the weeding of the eleusine (*kombira molu*), and he was followed by Bagbandara and Gangura, who camped in the homestead of a man called Basesele,

---

[1] *The Bahr El Ghazal Province Handbook*, 1911, pp. 59–60.

where they were joined by Gbudwe himself. While Bagbandara was absent from his province, Renzi son of Wando, who had been assisting the Belgians in the construction of their fort, ravaged it. Gbudwe and his sons now formed a semicircle around the fort. At a council of war Gbudwe ordered his sons to attack the fort one after another, and not all together: first Gangura, then Bagbandara, then Kipa, then Zegi, and so on. Mange was to organize the attack from his side under his sons in the same manner. Bagbandara, jealous of the honour done to Gangura, disposed his companies by night and was the first to attack at dawn. Gangura had distributed porridge and *asau* termites to his men, and they were just about to eat when they heard sounds of fighting. This was a clash between Bagbandara's men and a party sent from the fort to obtain provisions from Renzi, the party withdrawing when attacked. Then one by one Gbudwe's sons hurled their men against the fort—Gangura, Kipa, Zegi, and so on—and one by one they withdrew with heavy casualties. The fight went on for two days, and it was a slaughter. The enemy were invisible behind their stockade, and all the Azande could do was to throw their spears over the top, hoping to strike someone on the other side; but as far as my informants knew, the garrison suffered no casualties, while the attackers were shot down in numbers as they rushed, half-blinded by powder smoke, to within a few yards of the stockade to hurl their spears at close range. Among those killed were a number of well-known men, including Nduga and Bangindi of the Andebile clan, Ndegu of the Agiti clan, and Bangau of the Avundua clan. At the end of the day the corpses were placed by twos and threes in holes and covered with earth. The women wailed and shrieked, and even Gbudwe's order to them to be quiet did not silence them. One informant said that he had some of them executed for having had sexual relations with their husbands in camp, which is forbidden, and so having brought about the disaster. At dawn on the third day Gbudwe ordered a retreat, and he told Rikita, who had just arrived on the scene, to cover it. He was old and tired and broken, and his men were dispirited at their defeat and losses.

After Gbudwe had returned to his home at Birikiwe, the Belgians built a new fort on the Hu river, in Mboli's (later Dika's) country, and they were there when the British entered

Gbudwe's kingdom. They built another one near the junction of the Yubo and the Lingasi in Ngindo's (Akoavongara's) country. The collapse was not only military, it was also a moral collapse. Bagbandara joined the Belgians and laid waste, with their aid, Basongoda's country from a post on the Nagbaka (Ngere's country). The Belgians sent two rifles to Gangura and invited him to submit. He did not commit himself, though he sent them provisions. Before he had made up his mind, the British appeared on the scene and he made his submission to them. (It was not till 1907 that the spheres of Belgian and British influence were clearly demarcated.)

14

When Gbudwe returned from Mayawa he was tired and despondent. Azande say that the poison oracle had long ago foreseen the arrival of another lot of *Abolomu* from the west and had told him that he would not survive their coming. This was a force, led by British officers, sent to subjugate Gbudwe from Wau, the capital of the Bahr al-Ghazal province. A certain Mbikara of the Abambura clan brought news of its approach to Gbudwe, who was in his eleusine gardens to the east of his home at Birikiwe, where later the British established the post which became known as Yambio, after Gbudwe's earlier name. When his followers returned from Mayawa they found that the eleusine had already ripened and its leaves withered, and Gbudwe had given instructions for his to be garnered at once and was supervising the harvesting of it. Mbikara said that Gbudwe's friends were approaching and were already in the uninhabited bush that separated his kingdom from what had been the kingdom of Ndoruma son of Ezo. The sons of Ndoruma were assisting the force in its passage, and King Tembura had welcomed it and had dispatched a contingent of riflemen of his own, consisting of Angbaga and members of other peoples the Azande of Gbudwe's kingdom consider barbarians, to accompany it.

Gbudwe did not expect war. It would seem that he had reason to suppose that the expedition would be favourably disposed towards him, and he spoke of them as his friends and gave orders that their advance was not to be opposed. It is improbable that, in any case, effective resistance could have been made, for his subjects had suffered too much at the hands of the Belgians to welcome a further engagement with a well-armed column. Gbudwe slept three nights in his gardens, and on the morning of the fourth day he returned to his home at Birikiwe. On the fifth day news came that the expedition had reached the country of his son Zegi, who, on being informed by scouts of its approach, had fled from his home with his wives and children. When the force arrived at his court they captured there two men, Danga of the Abangali clan and a son of Gangura of the Avungbadi clan, put cord round their necks, and led them with the column, apparently as guides. When Gbudwe heard that the force had reached the Baguga, a few miles to the west of Birikiwe, he left his home for his gardens once more. Here he received envoys from the British—a servant of King Tembura (who was his son-in-law) called Bilingi and three other men. They advised Gbudwe that he should at once send his son Gangura to meet the force, and Gangura was accordingly sent for and dispatched in the late afternoon with a number of youths, including several of the Belanda (*Abari*) colony which resided near Gbudwe's court, bearing maize and groundnuts as gifts. When Gangura and his personal attendant Libiru, one of my informants about these events, appeared together with Bilingi and the other envoys before the British commander they were placed under guard with cords round their necks. This was unexpected, as they had come in peace and bearing gifts. Gangura was then asked why his father had not come, and he replied that Gbudwe awaited his friends at his court and in the meanwhile had sent his son with provisions.

The British force broke camp in the early morning and advanced to Gbudwe's court, arriving there about 8 o'clock in the morning. They found a fair gathering of men awaiting them. Gangura ordered everyone to lay down his arms and to do as he was told; and he sent Lendiwa of the Abalingi clan to bring in maize. A diversion now took place. A man called Matadi, of the Abangbinda people and a subject of Gbudwe, mounted a mound and, brandishing his spear, shouted to Gangura, asking him why they should lay down their arms when he was bound a prisoner and when the other side had not laid down theirs. According to another version, Matadi acted thus on the orders of Gbudwe, who had been told by the poison oracle that if he did so, Gangura would escape. In this version, Matadi said, 'What a thing it is to see a son of Gbudwe with a cord round his neck. Shall we look upon him thus?' A British officer pointed at him and gave an order to a soldier, who shot him dead. All the subjects of Gbudwe present at once took flight, the only other of them to be shot being a certain Bagwiya. In the confusion that ensued, Gangura and Libiru snatched the cords round their necks from the hands of the soldiers who held them. Gangura preferred, he afterwards said, the risk of being shot to the ignominy of being in a column which captured his father, lest it should be said that it was he who had led the way to his father's refuge. The two men bolted into the bush, fired at as they ran, and afterwards they were pursued by soldiers and a party of Tembura's Angbaga. They were followed for the rest of that day and on the morning of the following day, when the chase was abandoned, they had reached, and hidden in, the forest of Karikai.

The patrol in the meantime sought out Gbudwe. They went to his gardens and from there to a small grass hut, of the kind Azande call *basura*, which had been erected for his shelter in the bush near by. Here they found Gbudwe alone, squatting in the entrance to the hut. He fired at the approaching soldiers, wounding one of them; and they returned his fire, and he was hit in the left arm (some say in the thigh also). He thereupon threw his rifle towards them, saying that he could fight no longer, but as the soldiers ran forward to capture him he produced a pistol from behind his back and with it killed three of them. Azande admit that, of course, all this is hearsay and conjecture, as none were present at the time save Gbudwe himself and members of the British force. Nevertheless, it is generally believed that this is more or less what happened, and that further, when Gbudwe was seized, his arm was bandaged and the soldiers tried to seat him on a donkey to return with him a prisoner. However, Gbudwe is said to have struck the donkey again and again in the face, so that they had to give up their attempt to transport him by this means and instead carried him on a stretcher to Birikiwe. There they reported to the British commander what had occurred, and he sat down and wrote it all on paper. Gbudwe meanwhile was under guard in a hut.

It is doubtful whether anyone remained with Gbudwe till
the end, though my informants thought that one of his wives,
a daughter of Tangili, was with him, because it was she who
brought, as far as they could remember or had heard, the news
of his death. All were agreed, however, that his grandson Ukwe
son of Boli was the only one of his kinsmen to see him after his
capture. Ukwe is the traitor of the story. He had defected at
Birisi some years before, had been driven by Gbudwe from the
district he administered, and had sought refuge with Renzi,
with whom he intrigued against Gbudwe. Afterwards, it is said,
he had fled to Basongoda's court. Azande say that Gbudwe
wished Basongoda to mutilate him and that he refused to do so,
though he refrained from giving him political office. When
Ukwe heard of the approach of the British force he hastened to
join it and to ingratiate himself with its commander, and Azande
think it was very possibly he who divulged Gbudwe's place of
refuge. Some even think that Ukwe may have murdered him.
They say that he asked to see Gbudwe and was allowed to do
so. He entered the hut where Gbudwe was under guard and
spent some time with him in the evening. Shortly after he came
out a soldier entered and found Gbudwe dead. But though it is
often said that Ukwe may have murdered his grandfather, no
one pretends that he can know what happened; and there is
another version of Gbudwe's death which says that he brought
it about by refusing all food and comforts, declaring that he had
no wish to endure a second captivity.

Gbudwe was buried at Birikiwe (Yambio) in a hastily dug and
shallow grave, on which was placed a pot. Some say that his head
was left sticking out of the top of the grave and was covered with
the pot. A Zande called Zai, who had held a minor commoner
governorship, was buried near by. He had been shot by a firing
party on the orders of the British commander. Azande are not
certain why he was shot (British reports say he misled Gbudwe
about their intentions). We can readily understand that no one
rightly knew what was happening at the time, or why it was
happening. My informants thought that one of the three British
officers was named Bonuoli (? Boulnois) and that the other two
were addressed as *saatube* (the Arabic *sa'adtu al-Bey*).

The British account is naturally somewhat different, since
the events were seen by them in a different perspective. The

official report states barely: 'An expeditionary force composed of four companies of the IXth and two companies of the Xth Sudanese, with detachments of artillery and mounted infantry, arrived at the village of the hostile Sultan Yambio on the 7th February 1905. The Sultan himself was wounded in endeavouring to escape, and died in hospital on the 10th idem.'[1]

In a recent account the late H. C. Jackson, relying on published and unpublished reports and correspondence, has supplied further details of the Yambio patrol.[2] His account, doubtless based on opinions held at the time, is open to criticism, especially with regard to its moral strictures on Gbudwe, who is pictured as a sadistic tyrant, guilty of every form of atrocity. This assessment of his character is without reasonable foundation. However, Mr. Jackson's relation is probably correct in its outline of events. He says that after many days march, the patrol reached Gbudwe's domain, but even when it was approaching his court 'the Sultan remained intransigent'. To avoid bloodshed, Lieut. Fell, R.N., volunteered to go forward to meet Gbudwe at his court, some six miles from the military camp.

After beating off a little opposition, he arrived at the outskirts and sent a message saying that he would come and talk with the Sultan provided that his bodyguard laid down their spears. The warriors obeyed his order, but rearmed immediately Fell and his little party started to approach. The Azande were then told that the troops would open fire unless the Lieutenant's order were properly carried out. The spearmen remained hostile so, after further warnings, two or three volleys were fired. Sultan Yambio's men, unable to stand up to disciplined rifle-fire—to which, of course, they were unaccustomed —fled into the bush. A few prisoners were taken by the patrol party, one of whom later went to Lieutenant Fell and offered to lead him to the Sultan's hiding-place. With this man as a guide, the patrol was able to find and capture the Sultan without meeting further opposition. As Sultan Yambio was found to be badly wounded in the wrist and knee, he was given immediate medical attention; but though his wounds were not considered to be dangerous, he died on the day of his capture, apparently from fear of the retribution which the future might hold for him.

Jackson also tells us that after Gbudwe's death the patrol returned to Wau—one of the officers, Captain Drake, being

[1] *The Bahr El Ghazal Province Handbook*, 1911, p. 60.
[2] H. C. Jackson, *Behind the Modern Sudan*, 1955, pp. 61–4.

badly mauled by a leopard on the journey—leaving Lieutenant Fell behind, apparently at Tembura, where he died of black-water fever about a year later.

We have an interesting comment on the patrol, which explains why so considerable a force was sent against Gbudwe, in what Father Geyer, the founder of Catholic missions in the Bahr al-Ghazal, says about it. That two earlier British patrols had been compelled to retreat had increased Gbudwe's renown as a redoubtable figure among the population of Wau, the capital of the province. Father Geyer, writing in February 1905, says that while Tembura stood by the Government, old Gbudwe did not attempt to conceal his intention not to submit. The Governor, Major Boulnois, early in that year therefore advanced with an imposing force through Tembura's country, where he made arrangements to protect his rear, and then marched against Gbudwe. Wau was full of rumours about the outcome. First it was rumoured that Gbudwe had been killed and his country occupied; then that the patrol had been defeated, that the victorious Azande were approaching Wau, that the Dinka people would rise in consequence, and that measures were being taken to protect the civilian population of the town. Then, at last, on 21 February a runner brought the news that Gbudwe had been mortally wounded and his country occupied. The Governor of the province fell sick and died shortly after the patrol took place.[1]

15

This is a short history, mostly dealing with external relations, of the kingdom of Gbudwe. This kingdom came to an end at Gbudwe's death, and my story is therefore finished. However, what happened in the following few years throws some light backwards on what happened before, and therefore adds to our understanding of it. A military administration was imposed, with its centre at Yambio (Birikiwe), but it probably—information about administration in these early years is meagre—amounted to little more than the maintenance of security and communications. We learn from Sudan Intelligence Reports that most of Gbudwe's sons were left as rulers of their provinces,

[1] Op. cit., pp. 193-4 and 244.

now, of course, responsible to the Anglo-Egyptian Administration and not to a native paramount. It was both evident and recognized that administration would have to be conducted through them.[1] In 1906 Rikita was taken to Khartoum in the hope that he would be impressed. In the following year Ukwe, who had been placed in Gbudwe's old district, was removed as he had 'proved himself useless'. There was no overt opposition to the Administration, but Bimbashi R. W. Hadow was doubtless correct when he said that the Zande 'was longing to get rid of us'.[2] The princes, although their position was weakened and their authority undermined, were still in the main supported by the loyalty of their subjects and were able to maintain some degree of passive resistance to the Administration; and there were complaints about them from every part of the country. King Tembura (d. 1914) was reported in 1910 as having become a useless drunkard, and in the following year his son Renzi was appointed to attend to his father's business. Captain E. S. Stephenson tells us that Mvuta or Toreh, son of King Ndoruma, gave much trouble to the Belgians (when the Congo–Sudan boundary was fixed, he elected to remain in the Sudan).[3] In 1910 Ndoruma's second son, Zubeir, was reported to be raiding and mutilating people; and when, in 1912, he was captured, he was sentenced to ten years' imprisonment. Then—to return to Gbudwe's kingdom—we learn from an Intelligence Report that in January 1914 Gbudwe's sons Mange, Basongoda, Gangura, Sasa, and others were reported to be assembling their men and to have announced their intention of wiping out the Equatorial company at Yambio. That the princes were all hostile to the Military Administration is beyond doubt, but we may question whether they contemplated armed revolt, for they had learnt that open resistance was futile. However, the Administration acted on the information received, and Mange, Basongoda, Mopoi, and Gangura were arrested by Lieutenant Bond, or on his instructions, and were sent as prisoners to Wau, where Basongoda died. The others were then sent to Omdurman, where Mange died in 1916. Gangura, who died recently, and Mopoi (d. 1928) were eventually released and returned to

---

[1] *Intelligence Report*, no. 201 (1911).
[2] Ibid., no. 169 (1908).
[3] Ibid., no. 210 (1912).

their homes. A good deal of discontent was noticed after the removal of these princes, but there was no serious disaffection of a political kind in Gbudwe's old kingdom after 1914. The Zande account of these events is somewhat different, but as it is peripheral to our story I do not give it here. Nor do I feel it necessary to pursue a relation of events further.

CHRONOLOGY OF EVENTS

Gbudwe's birth	*c.* 1835
War of Bazingbi's daughter (against Arab traders)	*c.* 1867
War against Ngima. Gbudwe succeeds his father	*c.* 1868–9
Fight against Abu Guroon's (Arab) company	*c.* 1869
Fight with 'Abd al-Sammad's and Ghattas' (Arab) companies	1870
Campaign against Ngangi	*c.* 1875
War with the Egyptian Government. Capture of Gbudwe	1881–2
Return of Gbudwe from captivity	1884
Gbudwe's war with Wando (*Karikai*)	*c.* 1885–7
Campaign against the Dervishes	1898
Gbudwe's war with Renzi (*Birisi*)	*c.* 1899
Attack on British patrols	1904
Attack on Belgian post (*Mayawa*)	1904
British expedition against Gbudwe. Gbudwe's death	1905
Exile of Gbudwe's sons	1914

XVII

GBUDWE'S BORDER RAIDS

AZANDE distinguish between a *sungusungu vura*, a campaign, lasting from several days to several weeks, and a *basapu*, a border raid or affray.[1] Gbudwe fought a number of such campaigns between about 1867 and 1905, the year of his death.[2] The wars, as has been shown already, were for the most part national events which, since the whole of Gbudwe's kingdom participated in them, are known to all his subjects old enough to have taken part in them. In this chapter some description is given of the many border affrays which took place more or less regularly and in which the marcher lords of the kingdom attacked, or defended themselves against, the marcher lords of adjacent kingdoms. Information about these affrays could only be obtained in any detail, if at all, in the districts where they took place and from those who took part in them.

In order to discover, if only approximately, how frequently these border raids took place, as well as to understand how they were conducted, I took down descriptions of those which occurred in some of the southern provinces of Gbudwe's kingdom, where it was bordered for most of its extent by the kingdom of Wando, later ruled by his son Renzi, who during his father's lifetime administered on his behalf the area with which we are concerned. Most of the information I collected relates to one province, that of Gbudwe's son Ndukpe and later of Ndukpe's brother Gangura, for it was there I chiefly lived when in Zandeland.

It is not easy to present a detailed map of these provinces on either side of the border and to do so would certainly require more topographical knowledge than I possess. Even a sketch like the one presented opposite is adequate to show the provincial governors on either side of the border only at one period of time, for the areas changed hands at death or deposition, and

[1] See Chap. XIII.   [2] See Chap. XVI.

GBUDWE

G	B	U	D	W	E

Bagbandara son of Gbudwe

Bazo

Suma son of Renzi

Ndukpe son of Gbudwe (then his brothers Gangura and Zegi)

Yakpati son of Renzi

Zengendi (then Ngoliyo son of Gbudwe)

Bafuka son of Gbudwe (then his son Kipa and other sons)

Bawili son of Renzi (then his brother Malingindo)

RENZI

Basongoda son of Gbudwe

Bafuka son of Wando

Borugba son of Gbudwe

Ngoliyo son of Bazingbi

WANDO

N
W+E

GBUDWE'S SOUTHERN MARCHES.

when this happened provincial frontiers might be changed. It is sufficient, however, to show the relative dispositions during the last fifteen years of Gbudwe's life of those marcher lords with whom we are chiefly concerned, that is from 1890 to 1905.

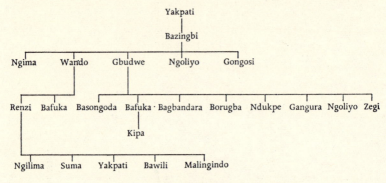

PRINCES MENTIONED IN THIS CHAPTER.

Ndukpe's province lay towards the sources of the Yubo and the Uze. Most of it was originally administered for Gbudwe by a commoner governor, Gundusu of the Angbadimo clan. There came a time when Gbudwe, as Zande kings are said to have been accustomed to do, drove some of his adult sons from his court, accusing them of adultery with his wives; and one of them, Ndukpe, went to reside in Gundusu's country, where he was later given two wives by his father. He slowly began attracting followers to himself from among Gundusu's subjects—a habit of young princes in the territories of commoner governors —and eventually Gbudwe transferred Gundusu to a province in the east of his realm (where Gami was in the 1920s) leaving the country he had formerly administered to be taken over by Ndukpe; though some of his former subjects appear to have been taken over by another commoner governor, Bazo of the Akowe clan. Ndukpe is said to have later also taken over the country of a commoner governor called Bamboti, adjacent to that of Gundusu. Bamboti had been removed to a district further east.

Gundusu's occupation of this province was too long ago for any of my informants to say what border affrays he might have engaged in. Ndukpe took over his country round about 1890, and it seems to have been two or three years later that he had his first clash with his opposite number in the province of Renzi, son of the aged King Wando. The information about this and his other fights was given me by two of his subjects who took part in them: Banvuru and Basingbatara. Ndukpe was at the time living in his first court on the Nambia, tributary of the Uze, and he hoed his maize cultivation in the wood called Karikai. This wood used to be in the territory of Renzi, whose subjects had slowly been pressed southwards along the streams by Gbudwe's subjects, who made the border very uncomfortable for them. Renzi's son Yakpati said that it was an insult for Ndukpe to hoe his cultivation in his father's territory, and he ordered an attack on Ndukpe's warriors, who were encamped at Karikai to hoe their master's maize cultivation. The attack was of the kind Azande call a *tame basapu*, a daylight surprise attack. Now it happened that a man called Bie, an elder of the Abambura clan, was on some errand of his own when he spotted Yakpati's men in hiding. Instead of giving the alarm at once, he wisely kept silence and continued on his way as though he had not seen them. When well out of sight, he ran back to warn Banvuru and the other leaders of the companies of young warriors of the impending attack. Messengers were sent to rouse the men of neighbouring provinces, while Ndukpe's men went to meet Yakpati's men and engaged them. Azande say of such an engagement, when the opposing forces are met in combat, *vura kongo*, and in illustration they interlace their fingers. Ndukpe's men suffered no casualties but two important men were killed on Yakpati's side: Ngongara, his *putabenge* or operator of the poison oracle, and Ngbatuyo, a subject of Renzi sent to Yakpati by his father to assist him in the administration of his district. When Ndukpe himself arrived on the scene the fight was over. He ordered a large fire to be made and the corpses of the two enemy dead to be thrown on top of it. The place reeked with the smell of their burning flesh and hair; and they threw more wood on the bodies. Ndukpe did this to strike terror into the hearts of Yakpati's people (*ka ba iliwa a ku bangili avuru Yakpati*). After this fight Ndukpe moved his court to Karikai wood.

Not long afterwards Ndukpe raided some of Renzi's[1] subjects just across the border, a raid known as 'the raid of Gbudwe's wife'. One of Gbudwe's wives and his cook (*negbindi*), Nazikpo

[1] Wando had died in 1892 or 1893.

of the Abanzuma clan, had run away from him to Wando's country, and Gbudwe told Ndukpe to 'close the path' by which she had fled. Kuagbiaru was my main informant about this raid. Ndukpe, whose court was then on the Nakarongo, tributary of the Mbomu, went with his companies of warriors to the home of an elder, called Kongobina, near the border, on

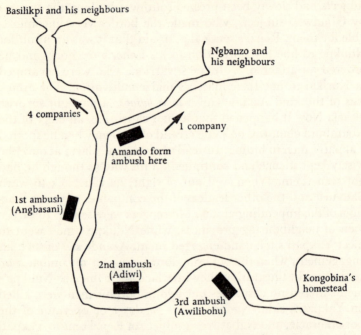

SKETCH 20. THE RAID OF GBUDWE'S WIFE.

the stream Dingbili, tributary of the Duru. From there he sent before dawn his five companies of unmarried warriors across the frontier. One company, the Amando, under Banvuru (Andogo clan) was to attack the homestead of a man called Ngbanzo (Agiti clan) and the homesteads of his neighbours, and the other four companies were to attack the homesteads of Basilikpi (Akangani clan) and his neighbours. The two parties separated at the junction of their respective paths. Since the objective of the single company was nearer than that of the other four, they had orders to wait till the others had attacked before rushing their own objective. Meanwhile three companies of married warriors (the Angbasani, the Adiwi, and the Awilibohu) were stationed in ambushes at intervals between the junction of the paths and Ndukpe's headquarters in Kongobina's homestead.

The four companies burnt Basilikpi's huts, but the people of the homestead were unharmed because they were sleeping in another hut, near by but hidden in the bush. Kuagbiaru said that they may have been warned of the raid by the poison oracle. It is a common practice for those who live near a frontier (*ti ngba piyo*) to build a secret hut in the bush for use if they have reason to fear that they may be attacked; and they frequently consult the poison oracle to discover whether a raid is pending. When Basilikpi's family saw their homes in flames they at once fled, giving the alarm, which spread from homestead to homestead across the countryside, summoning all able-bodied men to the scene of action. The four companies hastily retreated with their booty and, though they were pursued to the edge of the cultivations, they were not attacked because the enemy had not yet mustered sufficient strength to risk an engagement. On the other hand, they were gathering in strength so rapidly that the attackers decided to beat a hasty retreat and not to take the risk of pillaging and burning any further homesteads. The only person injured was one of the raiders, a certain Malimbia (Abangosi clan). This man, in his greed for booty, lagged behind when his companions withdrew and became separated from them. Two of the defenders, who had crept through the grass under cover of night, saw that he was alone and speared him.

The Amando company in the meanwhile changed their plan. The occupants of the homesteads which were their objective had been alerted by the alarm and had prepared themselves to meet an assault. Moreover, Banvuru feared that, should the other four companies retreat beyond the junction of the paths, his line of retreat would be cut and he might be ambushed. He therefore decided not to rush the homesteads in the face of an alerted enemy but to withdraw hastily from his position and to station his men in ambush near where the path forked. This move was highly successful, for Ngbanzo and his neighbours came running down the path to join Basilikpi and his friends and fell into the ambush, losing five of their warriors, including Ngbanzo himself, to the spears of the Amando company. The men of this company, after having cut off the genitals of the enemy dead, now retreated to the first ambush prepared according to plan, that of the Angbasani company. The Angbasani began to quarrel with the Amando, accusing them of having disobeyed orders, and in the resulting confusion, and threatened by the rapidly increasing force of the enemy, who were pouring in from homesteads all along the border, the Angbasani deserted their post and retired, together with the companies of unmarried warriors, instead of covering the withdrawal of these companies as they should have done. The combined companies withdrew past the second and third ambushes to where Ndukpe was waiting for news of the raid. The pursuit was not, however, continued. Just as they reached Ndukpe, Malimbia collapsed, and the spear he had dragged with him in his flight was drawn out of his body. Kuagbiaru said that since he was one of the Amadi people, who are skilled in the use of medicine, he was able, after being carried home, to treat his wound successfully.

Banvuru was apprehensive lest Ndukpe should punish him for disobeying orders, but the prince, since the manœuvre was successful, agreed that it had been justified in the circumstances. On the other hand, he expressed displeasure with the Angbasani for having deserted their post, and they had to pay him a heavy fine in spears.

In the same year there took place Ndukpe's third and last border affray. It was not, however, either initiated by him or directed against him. He became involved in it in support of his brother Bagbandara. Renzi son of Wando was stung by the raids of Gbudwe's sons across the border, and he resented also the settlement of Gbudwe's subjects in what he regarded as his territory. He consulted the poison oracle about Ndukpe and was told by it not to proceed against him. He then asked the oracle about Bagbandara, and it told him that it would be all right for him to invade the territory of that prince, whose court at that time was on the Bimikuru, tributary of the Badi. Renzi's force was under the command of his eldest son Ngilima, whose men were supported by those of his brothers Suma, Yakpati, and others. Ndukpe was at the time on a visit to his father, but as he had said that Bagbandara was his friend and was to be aided if attacked, Mabu, Ndukpe's consulter of oracles, Bazo, his company commander, and Dinde, a noble left in charge of his province during his absence, led his warriors to Bagbandara's aid as soon as they heard the *tatangba*, the cries of warning. The attack had fallen on the home of Bagbada (Abaiwo clan), and when they arrived they found that Renzi's men had killed two of Bagbandara's men in the fighting and then, having had the better of the affair, had retired and taken up a position on the stream Soro, whose waters flow into the Duru, to await a counter-attack. Before this was delivered, one of Ndukpe's riflemen, a certain Sakondo of the Amengbaya clan, crept with his rifle along the stream and shot and killed two of Ngilima's riflemen, who, it was later discovered, were his kinsmen. A general mêlée then developed in the middle of the stream in which Ndukpe lost two men and Ngilima five men, including Ngewe, who had been sent by Renzi to observe the raid and to report to him on it. As the enemy finally retreated in haste, the two sons of Gbudwe claimed the victory. The enemy was not pursued because Ndukpe's representatives did not care to take the responsibility of ordering pursuit in the absence of their master. Two other frontier governors, Kipa and Zengendi, arrived with their followers to assist Bagbandara after the fighting had ended.

The fight just described probably took place in 1897 or 1898. Eleusine was springing up in the gardens at the time: it had ripened when Ndukpe died on a visit to his father's court, and Bagbandara and Kpoyo, one of Gbudwe's confidants, were sent to kill his wives. I was told that some thirty of them were killed.

Gbudwe gave Ndukpe's province to his younger uterine brother Gangura, who in his turn gave part of it to a still younger uterine brother, Zegi. In the translation of the Zande text which follows it would appear that Gangura's first fights were raids on the courts of his opposite numbers Yakpati and Suma, but I have no information about these raids in my notebooks other than that contained in the text. Then, probably in 1900, he had to meet an attack by Renzi. Gangura's court at the time was near the source of the Mbomu, between the source of that river and the source of the Dingbili, and it was the season when the eleusine reddens in the gardens. In the previous year Renzi had been defeated by Gbudwe in a lengthy campaign, and to restore his prestige he organized a large-scale daylight surprise attack on Gangura's home and court. Gangura

had just finished a big hunting battue (*tuwa*) which had been
unusually successful, and he was celebrating his good fortune
by giving his subjects a feast of porridge, meat, and beer at his
court. He had received intelligence of an impending attack by
Renzi but had reason to believe that it was to be directed against
either Bafuka or Bagbandara and not against himself. He sent
messengers to warn his brothers but did not take precautions
to guard his own border. Some of his wives were collecting the
remainder of their ground-nut harvest at a considerable distance from his court together with their young children, some
female servants, and a few boy pages, when they were surprised
by Renzi's force about 10 o'clock in the morning and were
threatened with death were they to give the alarm. Among the
party were Gangura's eldest son and the child's mother. Renzi's
men then proceeded by an unfrequented route to Gangura's
court, which was about three hours' march from the border,
and arrived there at midday. No one saw them and therefore no
alarm was given. They surprised several of the revellers of the
night before, who were still befuddled with beer. Five of them
were speared before the others realized what was happening.
Gangura was sleeping in a hut in his private enclosure and,
being awakened by the noise, ran out to see what had occasioned
it. Seeing Renzi's men in occupation of his court he ran back to
get his rifle. They shouted to him that they had not come to
kill him but to take him in bonds to Renzi, who could please
himself in what he did with him. Gangura opened fire and shot
one man in the shoulder. Renzi's men returned the fire and one
of their bullets struck Gangura in the sole of his foot. Whereupon
he plunged into the thick undergrowth at the head of the
Mbomu river, where it would have been difficult to find him
and impossible to capture him without loss of life, since he was
both armed and in cover. So, instead of pursuing him, Renzi's
men occupied themselves in wrecking his home. They burnt
all his huts, both those in his court and those in his private
enclosure, and his granaries, together with the eleusine and
ground-nuts stored in them. They stole his hens, speared his
dogs, and smashed his great wooden gong with a log. They
captured some fifteen of his wives and three of his rifles. They
then departed with their spoil—women, rifles, hens, spears,
baskets of ground-nuts, gourds containing oil, and other spoil—

and made their way back in triumph to Renzi's kingdom. Their retreat was covered by Renzi himself, who had been waiting in ambush with many of his warriors to fall on Gangura's men if they should attempt pursuit. After the first surprise the alarm had spread over the countryside, and Gangura's warriors began to pour into his devastated court from all sides, eager to give pursuit. It was, however, abandoned before they reached Renzi's ambush because no one knew whether Gangura was alive or dead and they had no orders from him to engage the enemy. It was also felt that Renzi would not have made so daring an attack if the poison oracle had not assured him of a successful withdrawal.

After this defeat Gangura moved his court to the Nagbaka, tributary of the Uze, where he stayed for two years, and then to the Nawo, tributary of the Dingbili, tributary of the Duru; from there he organized an attack, a *tame basapu*, on the court of Yakpati son of Renzi to avenge his earlier disaster. This was in about 1903. His companies advanced stealthily in single file along a little-frequented path, abstaining from attacking any of the scattered homesteads they passed lest the alarm be given. But in spite of these precautions Yakpati had received warning of the raid and had fled from his home with his wives and children and most of his possessions. There was, however, some fighting in his court in which one of Gangura's men and two of Yakpati's men were killed. The raiders then burnt and razed Yakpati's huts and returned home.

Later in the same year Suma, son of Renzi, aided by his brother Yakpati, made a sudden descent at night on the territory of Zegi (Mbitimo), Gangura's younger brother. Their men were seen and the alarm was given (*tatangba ni poi*), so, after killing one of Zegi's subjects and burning some homesteads, they hastily made for home, withdrawing their ambushes (*anguru*) as they met them in their retreat. While they were returning home, Zegi had collected his fighting force, and his brothers Gangura, Bagbandara, and Ngoliyo, all frontier princes, came to his assistance. Gangura's men were the first on the scene and they followed the enemy till they came to the junction of the paths which led to the courts of Suma and Yakpati respectively. Here they waited for the men of the other princes to arrive and for Gangura to arrange the order of advance (*kwadi li vura*). Ngoliyo's men were the first to arrive and were told to pursue Suma's force. This movement was to prevent Suma's men from returning and taking the main force, going in the direction of Yakpati's court, in the rear. As Ngoliyo had only two companies of his own, Gangura lent him a company, the *Awili Rungesi,* under the command of Ngawe of the Akpura clan, and they were later joined by one of Kipa's companies, the *Awili Gine* under Ingida of the Abambura clan. Suma's warriors turned and put up a short fight against this detachment in which two of their company leaders (*abalivura*) were killed and Gangura's company commander Ngawe was speared through the shoulder, later dying of his wound. (Gangura ordered Ngbakume to be put to death for having caused his death by witchcraft, and he honoured Ngawe by sending a leopard-skin for him to be buried on.) After this encounter both sides departed to their homes.

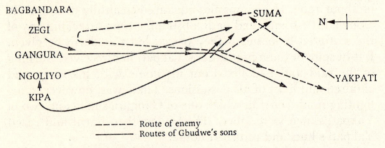

SKETCH 21. GANGURA'S RAID ON YAKPATI.

In the meanwhile the main body of Gangura's men, together with Zegi's, took the path to Yakpati's country. They advanced across country as a body, each company by the side of the next (and not in a single column of file)—a formation only possible when the grasses are short. They pillaged and burnt about ten enemy homesteads, but there was no fighting as the enemy offered no resistance. In addition to other spoil, they carried away much of the eleusine from the granaries and a wooden gong. Bagbandara's warriors and the rest of Kipa's forces had remained in reserve in Gangura's country.

Probably also in the same year Gangura made a surprise night raid (*basapu*) into Suma's country. At the time of weeding

eleusine he had received intelligence from one of his spies
(a *bomoi*), Kangada of the Abakpoto clan, who had observed every
stage in the preparation of the beer, that a feast was about to be
held in the home of Bangbandili of the Agiti clan, a commoner

SKETCH 22. GANGURA'S NIGHT RAID INTO SUMA'S COUNTRY.

who had been given administrative office by Suma almost on
the boundary between his province and Yakpati's;[1] and Gangura had consulted his poison oracle about this feast and had
been told that if he raided it his raid would be successful.
Gangura set out by night with the entire fighting strength of

[1] This is doubtless the reason why in the text given later the raid is said to have
been on Yakpati's territory.

his province. Kangada led and was followed by the riflemen,
these by the companies of youths, and these by the companies
of elders. They arrived at the home of a man called Bazilikpi,
of the Agbaku clan, where they waited for a while. While they
were waiting, Gangura told his men that they were to cut off
not the ears of the slain but their genitals, because people cheated
claiming that two ears were evidence that they had slain two
men, whereas both ears came from the same victim. No one, he
said, had more than one set of genitals; but ears would be
allowed in the case of slain women. The force then moved
forward to just outside the homestead in which the feast was
taking place. They were so near to it that they could see and
hear one of the feasters mocking Gangura, boasting that they
had held their dance on his border and cared nothing for him.
Mabu raised his rifle and shot the man. At the report the other
riflemen began to fire, the dancers panicked and sought safety
in the thick undergrowth of a near-by stream, and Gangura's
spearmen rushed in to kill. They killed ten men and two women,
suffering no loss themselves. Gangura, who had remained at
some distance in the rear, then sent a messenger to order withdrawal, saying, *ngama ni de ki ga*, 'the serpent bites and makes
off'. Before withdrawing they burnt the huts and collected what
spoil they could. The spoil was rich in weapons, because Suma's
men had fled without their spears and shields, having had no
time to pick them up; but not in other things, because Gangura's
men also had no time to search huts and granaries for goods,
for the alarm was being given on every side and at any moment
there might be a counter-attack. So they burnt the huts and
granaries, cut off the genitals and ears of the slain, and withdrew to a short distance, where they remained in position till
about 8 o'clock from desire for a fight, hoping to engage the
enemy in a real battle (*bakumba vura*). Then, there being no sign
of immediate attack, and on reiterated orders from Gangura,
they retired together with the companies of married warriors
who had been posted in the rear to cover their retreat. It is said
that Suma's people were so horrified by the mutilation of their
dead that they lost heart and for that reason refrained from
pursuit. Gangura had the captured spears bound in bundles
and the genitals and ears put in a bag, and he sent them to his
father Gbudwe, who was much amused and congratulated

Gangura on his valour. Gbudwe's courtiers celebrated the event by an evening of speech-making in which they praised Gbudwe and boasted of their past deeds and also of what they would accomplish against their king's enemies in the future (*selekpo vura*).

The following text given by Kuagbiaru, at one time Gangura's page and later a leader of one of his military companies, gives an account of his master's relations with the marcher lords of Renzi's kingdom opposite his province.

Renzi was the son of Wando who was towards the west. He wanted to make war on Gbudwe, and he sent his army against Gbudwe, and Gbudwe overcame him. Then Gbudwe blackened the names of his sons, saying: 'Alas! My sons, you were present when a man scratched me, but it was as though you had not been present.' When he had lapsed into silence, Gangura said to Bafuka, 'Why do we let the prince [Renzi] make weaklings of us? We are here with you on the frontier, so we had better attack this fellow Renzi.' Gangura then went after Renzi's son Yakpati, whose territory lay between his own and that of Renzi. Gangura made war against him and drove him away and burnt his residence and captured his many wives, all of whom he brought back and presented to Gbudwe. Gangura then made war on Renzi's son Suma, whose home was on the River Soro, which river was the boundary between the province of Bagbandara and that of Gangura. Gangura joined forces with Ngoliyo, and they made war on Suma. Ngoliyo's warriors killed two of Suma's elders, whose names were Umbadi and Kpakana; these two men were Suma's elders. They brought back with them many women captives and presented them to Gbudwe. After this Renzi lost patience, saying, 'Why do the sons of Gbudwe treat my sons ill like this?' He began to practise deception, letting it be known that he was going to make war on Bagbandara, so that Gangura thought that he was in fact going to raid Bagbandara. Renzi then divided his war companies, and while some of them went against Bagbandara, he himself began to advance by stealth on Gangura. As Gangura knew nothing of this move, he was giving a feast to which a very great number of men had come to drink beer. They were intoxicated all night long, and it was not till close on daybreak that they dispersed to get some sleep.

Renzi advanced through the night and arrived near Gangura's home, and he took possession of his camp,[1] and he slept there. At the

---

[1] A camp site in the bush, perhaps a site at one time occupied by Gangura's men when assembling for a raid.

first light of dawn Renzi appeared against Gangura in the company of many of his subjects.[1] Just as Gangura rose from sleep he saw Renzi's war party close by. He seized one of his rifles which was propped against a tree, and he fled. When Renzi's men saw him they shot at him with their rifles and they hit him in the heel. He continued in flight till he reached the end of the gardens, where he stopped to fire at them with his rifle. He hit one of Renzi's elders in the head,[2] and he at once fell to earth dead. His name was Gutenge. Renzi then turned back to Gangura's court. He captured every one of Gangura's wives, and he burnt all his huts and his three large granaries full of millet. He then departed, taking all Gangura's wives with him. The subjects of Gangura followed after him only a little way; and Gangura said: 'It is no matter, let us leave him alone, for he has consulted the poison oracle [about the success of his foray].' So they turned back. They sent a messenger to Gbudwe and told him all that had happened. However, Gbudwe said: 'It is of no consequence: Renzi consulted the poison oracle about his affairs. But, Gangura, do not stop worrying the sons of Renzi in any circumstances.'

Gangura consulted the poison oracle about his chances with regard to Yakpati son of Renzi, and the oracle told him that if he went forward he would defeat Yakpati. So Gangura went up against him and he killed many of his subjects, for they were attending a feast which was being held in that territory. He captured many women, and he slew also many people; and the women he captured were about equal in number to those captured from him earlier. He gave them all to Gbudwe, together with the many spoils pillaged in Yakpati's country, for he burnt all the homesteads there, and he drove Yakpati into the bush. After this it was all finished between them. The Belgians began to occupy the country and to prohibit war altogether.

I now very briefly list the border affrays of two other sons of Gbudwe with border provinces: Bafuka (and his son Kipa) and Bagbandara. Bafuka's province was to the west of Ndukpe's (Gangura's). He was one of the more senior of Gbudwe's sons and was already governing his province as early as 1880. Part of it had earlier been administered by a commoner governor, Ongosi, who had been deprived of his position by Gbudwe. When Bafuka was settled in his territory he turned on his neighbour Gongosi son of Bazingbi and drove this uncle of his out

---

[1] Other accounts say that Renzi was not himself present but in support in the rear.
[2] Others say in the shoulder.

of his domains, on the excuse, Azande say, that he had told his subjects to eat ground-nuts in their shells (*sisi awande*) in his court. Bafuka placed his eldest son Kipa in Gongosi's deserted home on the Anzara, tributary of the Yubo, and gave him his province. From there Kipa later moved to take over the province of his uncle Mboli, to whom his father Bafuka had given it but whom he afterwards expelled from it.[1]

When my chief informant about this part of Gbudwe's kingdom, Zaba, who was in my day white-bearded, was summoned to act as one of Bafuka's pages, his master's court was on the Angmongoyero, tributary of the Sueh. He had already engaged in several raids and counter-raids across the border, but the first that Zaba witnessed was an attack on the country of Ngoliyo son of Bazingbi, who had been given a district to rule over by his elder brother Wando.[2] In this raid Bafuka's men surprised four of Ngoliyo's men who were returning from gathering the oracular poison *benge* to the south of the Uele river. They killed them and sent the *benge* to Gbudwe. The next of Bafuka's raids was against the territory of a commoner governor of Wando's who held his court on the Mbuele river. This took place shortly after Gbudwe had returned from captivity in 1884. Bafuka was defeated, and it is said that he was the first to flee and was followed by his men in disorder. In a third raid Bafuka and his son Kipa, who by this time had part of his father's kingdom to administer, attacked the country of Yakpati son of Renzi. The raid is said to have been fairly successful, one of Renzi's subjects, Sana, being killed. This took place round about 1888. Then, shortly after Gbudwe's war with the Dervishes in 1898, Bafuka raided the country of Bangodiya, son of Welegine, of the Agiti clan, a commoner who held a governorship in Renzi's kingdom. Many of Bangodiya's followers were killed, and many of their women were captured and sent to Gbudwe. Bafuka died a few days after the conclusion of Gbudwe's war with Renzi near the hill Birisi and therefore probably in 1899.

His province was then administered by his sons under the eldest, Kipa. Kipa had, during his father's lifetime, been raided

[1] See Chap. X.
[2] At that time Bafuka's province must have extended further to the west of Ngoliyo's province or must have extended further to the east than is shown on my sketch-map.

by a son of Renzi called Bawili, who made an attack on his court on the Masumbu river, tributary of the Yubo, round about 1883. There were no casualties on either side. Two years later Kipa made a counter-raid into Bawili's country; his court being then on the Masangani river, tributary of the Yubo. Shortly after this, Bawili committed adultery with one of his father's wives and was, on the orders of his father, displaced and emasculated by his eldest brother Ngilima. His province was given to another brother, Malingindo. He attacked the home of one of Kipa's subjects, Mai of the Akenge clan, who lived near the border. This raid took place shortly after Bafuka's death. Gangura came to assist his nephew in repelling the attack but did not reach the scene of action in time to help him. Kipa's company commander Ingida killed one of Malingindo's men. Kipa's men had no casualties.

Bagbandara's province was to the east of that of Ndukpe (later Gangura) and, being the elder, he had been given a province before him. This province had earlier been administered by a commoner governor, Mai, who had been killed in the war between Gbudwe and Wando at Karikai in about 1886. Later in the same year Bagbandara's first affray took place. He was drinking beer in the evening with some of his subjects and, when intoxicated, began to threaten war against Wando's son Renzi. My informant Banvuru was present on this occasion, for he had been sent by Ndukpe to ask his brother for a present of straw hats. Bagbandara decided in his cups to make a surprise raid by night on one of Renzi's commoner governors. As the bush grasses were high, his men had to advance along paths into Renzi's country, and it was on one of these paths that the fighting took place, Bagbandara losing two men in it and returning crestfallen. He next made a surprise attack on the home of one of Renzi's subjects called Bukpanda, whom his warriors killed. Later Renzi's sons Suma and Yakpati made a border raid on the home of Mambeli, a subject of Bagbandara. Bagbandara came to help him but was defeated and forced to retire. Then Renzi's eldest son Ngilima attacked Bagbandara—a raid which has already been described in giving an account of Ndukpe's fights. Finally, after Gbudwe's defeat at the hands of the Belgians at Mayawa in 1904, Renzi, who was aiding them, raided Bagbandara's country and burnt his home and court.

The account given above of the border forays of four of Gbudwe's sons and marcher lords may be incomplete and have other deficiencies but at least it gives some indication of the frequency of these raids and of their scope. We have to remember that the other marcher lords were also conducting raids or resisting them on the border between their territories and the territories of the marcher lords of the kingdom of Wando who lived opposite them. I can give no details of these raids—I had little opportunity to collect information about them—but they certainly occurred all along the southern frontier of Gbudwe's kingdom. Indeed, if we consider this frontier alone, and leave the other frontiers out of consideration, it is evident that a border raid on one or other section of it must have taken place with such frequency that we may say that they were annual events. It is true that they were usually very small-scale affairs, involving sometimes no casualties and perhaps never more than a dozen or so, but they were sufficiently frequent to keep the border provinces of the kingdoms of Gbudwe and Wando in a state of constant alertness and the two kingdoms in a permanent state of hostility.

APPENDIX

THE ORIGIN OF THE RULING CLAN, THE AVONGARA

A HISTORY of the Azande, as we have seen, is mainly an account of dynastic rivalries and wars, of the conquest and subjugation of other Negro peoples, and of their struggles to maintain their independence against Arabs and Europeans. The verbal traditions in which these events are recorded may be accepted as in the main reliable for as far back as the generation of the sons of Tombo and Mabenge, the two Zande kings from whom every member of the noble Avongara clan appears to trace his descent, that is, some six generations back from the present time. Little is known about Tombo and Mabenge, and even less about their father Ngura, although he is undoubtedly a historical figure. Before him the names in the genealogy are names and nothing more. Nobody pretends to know anything about the men whom the names designate, and there is no agreement about the order in which they should be placed. Any noble or any well-informed commoner can, however, tell you one or other version of the story of how the mythological ancestor of the ruling Avongara clan came to acquire authority. I commence by giving three versions taken down from three men in the old kingdom of Gbudwe. I shall then give the versions recorded by some earlier writers on the Azande and, finally, I shall discuss some of the chief features of the myth. The first of the versions for which I am myself responsible was given by a noble, Tembura, son of King Ngangi, a senior man who already had a family at the time of King Gbudwe's death in 1905. Like the two other versions, it was written down for me by my Zande clerk Reuben, son of Prince Rikita.

In the past it was the Angbapio clan who were the nobles of this country, only at that time the title 'noble' [*gbia*] did not exist. When a man did something wrong they just talked about it, so that the matter was not straightened out. They called them Angbapio because when people came to make cases before them they sat on top of a big termite-mound weaving their nets. That is why they called them Angbapio, for it was nets [*pio*] that pleased [*ngba*] them.[1]

---

[1] See Chap. IV for a discussion of this and the folk-etymology of clan names in general.

A certain Ngbapio man went and arrived at a mound, the mound being sodden and clean [there was a hole in it which had no cobwebs or other obstructions at its entrance]. He saw this entrance to the mound, that it had the appearance of a man having frequently sat there. He twined his rope well and he arranged his snare at the mouth of this den, and when it was ready he went home; and he said nothing to anybody about it. Early next morning he rose to go and inspect his snare. While he was on his way, that man who habitually slept in this mound was about to come out of it. The owner of the snare meanwhile was on his way and, as he looked round, he saw the man seated. He came and questioned him, but he did not reply. He took the man and went with him to his home, and he waited, but no one heard speech from him. The name of that man was Kongolikate. Kongolikate grew up until such time as they gave him a wife. Then his wife was with child. When he was dying he said to her that if she bore her child he was to be called by the name of Basenginonga; and if anyone were to call him by another name she was not to accept it. Till this child grew up to man's estate people called him by many names, but his mother did not accept them, for his father had said of him that no one was to give him a name, and when his father had said this he had died, his son still being in his wife's womb. It was only as he was dying that he spoke to his wife, for no one had ever heard him speak except his wife, and she only as he was dying. When this son was born the people called him by many names, but his mother accepted none of them, saying, 'The name of this child is on my lips; his father named him to me'; and the people pressed her in vain to tell it to them, but she would not do so, for her husband had said to her that she was to tell it to no one until such time as the child had grown up with his fellows. She heeded what her husband had said to her. When the child grew up and reached the age at which her husband had said they might name him, his mother then named him by the name of Basenginonga, as his father had named him. Moreover, when his father was dying he told his wife that when she bore him his child he was not to eat things away from his fellows; everything the child should do [by way of providing food], she should make it big for him and his friends.

The child grew up, and he wandered with his friends. He killed many tree-rats and brought them home and handed them to his mother. She cooked them nicely and prepared three bowls of porridge and gave them to him, and the lad called all the sons of his maternal uncles, and they came and ate the meal all together. Many boys came to reside with him because he gave them food frequently.

When anyone called the lad he answered *aba*, 'Yes, father', and his reply of assent was *i gbia*, 'Yes, master'. When anyone sent him on an errand he never refused. Everybody liked him. Always the word *gbia* alone was on his lips, so people called him by the name *Gbia*, for that was what he said to people all the time, the word *gbia* being always on his lips. His maternal uncles sat in their courts to hear cases; and they said that while that man's case was good, the other man's case was good also. For his part, the lad sat on their termite-mound, and he said to his maternal uncle, 'Do not settle the case thus, my maternal uncle; say that because that man has wantonly committed adultery with the wife of the other, let him pay to the other twenty spears, since he wantonly had congress with her, for he knew that she was a man's wife when he had congress with her.' All the people began to cry aloud with great clamour, saying, 'Oh this boy who is always saying *gbia* so that they called him *Gbia* to mock him! However, he settles cases well, so we will speak our cases before him alone, for he settles cases correctly.' So it was that they said that he was noble [*gbia*]. The stock of the nobles [*agbia*] commenced from that time. However, it must be said that people have many different stories about how the nobles originated. One man has one story and another man has a different story; for there is nobody who really knows for certain. That is why there are many different stories of their origin.

The second version was taken down from Kuagbiaru, one of my regular informants. Kuagbiaru had been brought up as a page at the court of Prince Gangura, one of whose company commanders he afterwards became, and he was therefore very conversant with affairs of the nobles.

This is about the name of the Avongara. Ngara[1] was a very powerful man indeed; there was no one who could press his head to the ground [in wrestling]. He overcame everyone everywhere, and his renown was therefore on men's lips. No one passed his home without his molesting them. For he desired to take dominance from the Abakundo, for they were the rulers at that time.

A man arose to send a boy to go and purchase meat. The boy went and arrived in the centre of Ngara's home, and he passed on ahead to purchase meat for his master. He purchased meat and started to return. The boy continued on his way home and arrived at Ngara's homestead. Ngara asked the boy, saying to him, 'To whom are you taking meat?' The boy replied that it was for his master, who had sent him to go and buy it. Ngara set on the boy and gave him a sound hiding, and he took his meat away from him. The boy continued on his way and reached the home of his master, and he told his master what had happened and finished the story. His master told the boy that they would go along together. They went on their way and reached Ngara's home, and he said to Ngara, 'You there, so this is the way you act here!' Ngara started to go up to him to contend with him. They continued to wrestle for a time, and the man ran with Ngara to the ground. He then bound Ngara with cord and took him away. He took him to the country of the Abakundo, saying [to the people on the way], 'Friend, that man who was always beating people, namely Ngara; it is he whom I am removing.' All the people ran to the path to see him, and they said that he was the binder of Ngara [*vo-ngara*].

The Abakundo used to be the rulers. It was their custom, when they killed an animal, to put it in a granary for two days; then they began to

---

[1] Reuben wrote Ngora throughout. I have altered this to Ngara because this is more in accordance with the sense of the story. *Ngara* means 'strength'. The *a* sound tends to take on the value of *o* after the syllable *vo*.

cook it, when it was very high [*kundo*]. This man Vongara, when he killed
his animal, took a great pot and cooked the whole of it and cooked porridge
to go with it. He then called all the people to come and eat this meat. He
continued frequently to act in this manner. The people attended his court
more than they attended on the Abakundo. The Abakundo did not know
how to hear cases properly, but when people made cases before Vongara he
settled them correctly. He said that that person who did wrong to another
must give spears to that other in compensation. He began the custom of
paying compensation for the benefit of the people. He began to establish an
outer and an inner court for the people. He chose his courtiers, those who
were to eat porridge in the inner court, and he gave them their porridge
by themselves; and he gave another lot to the many people in the outer
court. People began to come to him in numbers from all directions. The
title of nobles [*agbia*] then persisted, which is the same as Avongara.

The third text was taken down from Bangili, son of Ndaku.
Bangili was very knowledgeable about the affairs of princes and
court etiquette, as his father had been before him.

In the past the Abakundo and the Angbapio clans were like ruling nobles
of this country. The Abakundo were so called because whenever they killed
an animal they put its flesh in a granary for two days, and then they ate it.
This is why they were called Abakundo. As for the Angbapio, their main
interest was the weaving of nets; the weaving of nets was sweeter to them
than hearing court cases. This is why they were called Angbapio, because
nets appealed to them more than anything else. These two clans arranged
their homes well but they did not at all know how to settle cases. A man
would bring his case before them and they would just say, 'While your
cause is good, his cause is also good.' This appeared to be most unsatisfactory to the people.

There was a source of a stream near by, and this source was always full of
voices of men, only these men were ghosts of the dead. On a certain day a
man appeared from there; and he held in his hands a harp and two knives.
He continued to come forward, and when he had reached the path he took
hold of a wild custard-apple tree. A certain man of the Angbapio clan
rose, saying that he would go to have a look at this man who was standing
by the wild custard-apple tree. The Ngbapio man said to him, 'Friend,[1]
where do you come from? What is your name?' The man replied, 'Friend, a
nobleman [*gbia*] am I, and my name is Digene.' This Ngbapio man said to
him, 'Come, let us go to the homestead', and he asked him further, saying,
'Friend, what is your clan?' He replied, 'Friend, I am a sister's son to the
Abakundo and a nobleman of the canoe [*gbia ni kurongbo*].'[2] They continued
on their way and arrived at the homestead; and there the Ngbapio man
related everything to the people. They cooked porridge and invited him to
partake of it, but he refused and sat on top of a termite-mound, playing on

---

[1] The Zande word is *dami*, an old-fashioned, even archaic, usage retained
because the story is in the distant past. The modern equivalent is *nda*.

[2] I believe this to be in reference to the Zande myth of origin of men, which tells
how mankind emerged from a sort of canoe.

his harp. The wife of his maternal uncle asked, saying, 'Who is this man they are pressing to partake of porridge?' A child told her that it was that man whom they had brought from the source of the stream and who said that he was a nobleman [*gbia*]. She roasted four large sweet potatoes, prepared them nicely, and sent a child with them to him. He asked for water, and he washed his hands well till they were clean; then he took one of the sweet potatoes and he ate it, and ate it all. But he did not eat a second one.

They went on dwelling together till one day he said to them, 'Let us hunt tree-rats'; but before this the people did not know their name as *akuru* [tree-rats], but as *agbiro* [insects]. He told them that their name was not *agbiro* but *akuru*. They went after tree-rats and killed them in great numbers. He said to the others, 'It is better to dry them well first in the sun, so that they are dried; then people can come tomorrow to eat them to their hearts' content, for we do not eat ours on the day on which they died.' At day-break he said to his maternal uncle's wife, 'Friend, I want you to cook a fine big lot of porridge.' She cooked a fine big lot of porridge and presented it to him. He summoned the people to come to eat it, that is, those who were elders. He sat near by with the little boys. People began to speak cases before his uncle, and he entered into the discussion to give verdicts. He said that one man had done ill wantonly to another and that he must pay twenty spears for having had intercourse with his wife. After this incident the people made him their prince for the future, and they made their cases before him alone. But some people say that the hearing of cases at court began among small boys with regard to porridge. The boys began to quarrel and they came to where he was to tell him about it. He said to one who had wronged another, 'Your cause is not good, why did you strike him first?' The hearing of cases at court began with this incident, and it continued. Whenever people started quarrelling among themselves they went to make a case before him.

It was Digene who began fighting fights with the *nonga* fruit. He collected a great many stalks of the *nonga* and took them and distributed them among all his young men, part of them standing to one side and the rest of them on the other side, and they began to pelt each other. Warfare began with this, and men fought each other in war. He began the custom of distributing war-spears by cutting spears out of the *bilingba* shrub, very many of them, and distributing them among all his followers, to each in turn a bundle of four. So the custom of distributing war-spears began, princes distributing real war-spears to their subjects.

He [Digene] begat a son, Basenginonga; Basenginonga begat Kongolikate; Kongolikate begat Monopiko; Monopiko begat Korongbanda and Nyasiyo. However, since Nyasiyo did not give good judgements the people got tired of him, and only Korongbanda remained with a following. Korongbanda begat Bazia; Bazia begat Gbandi; Gbandi begat Monogbandi; and Monogbandi begat Ngura.

The sense of these stories is clear. They present a picture of the past as Azande think of it. In ancient days, before they were welded together by the Avongara, the Ambomu clans—which later under Avongara leadership conquered and assimilated so many foreign peoples, the resultant amalgam being the Azande people—lived along streams as autonomous local groups: Abakundo, Angbapiyo, Agbambi, Akalinga, Agiti, Angumbi, Akurungu, Angbadimo, Aremete, etc. There were no ruling houses, and disputes within a clan were settled by heads of families, while the elders of two clans met if there was a dispute between them, and tried to settle it. Then appeared, as the myth relates, a man who gained precedence by his wisdom and liberality and whose descendants have established themselves as a ruling dynasty over the Ambomu and other Azande. This man's name has already been given as Kongolikate, Vongara, and Digene. I have heard him called Gine also; and it will be seen later that he is referred to by other names. In some accounts I have been told that he was found by Nyorobe, the head of a big Abakundo family, but in others Nyorobe was given as the name of the Abakundo girl he married. The accounts I was given seldom listed his descendants to Ngura in exactly the same order, though almost every informant gave Gbandi or Monoghandi as Ngura's father, as do almost all of the genealogies listed by other authorities.

Of these the earliest is the explorer Wilhelm Junker, who in 1882 wrote that: 'The Zandehs all claim descent from a certain Kelliso through Kaegobeli, Gorro, Baendi, Ngura I, and Ngura II, father of Mabenge and Tombo, whose two diverging lines have already been noticed.'[1] Junker's information was collected in either what was the Belgian Congo or what was French Equatorial Africa. Hutereau's information—he was a Belgian official—was mostly gathered in the Belgian Congo, probably mainly in 1911 or 1912. He says that the original Zande clans occupied the basin of the Shinko, where they lived in independent groups along streams and without chiefs, their affairs being conducted by heads of families. The Avongara, whom he calls Avurngura, are a fairly recently formed clan. There were quarrels in the clan of the Akegobili which provoked the departure of Kliso, who installed himself among the Abakundo. He was a great hunter and very generous in allowing others to enjoy the fruits of his chase. Also he gave good counsel, which was accepted, so that disputes were settled without recourse to violence. His authority grew and he was able to transform the political organization of the people, consolidating them under his authority. He acquired many wives; and people worked willingly in his cultivations, knowing that they would receive food in return; and he possessed many spears, given to him by those to whom he had been of service. In another legend recorded by Hutereau a man of the Akegobili clan married a girl of the Abakundo clan whose name was Kliso, and she bore a son called

[1] Op. cit., vol. iii, 1892, p. 185.

Kurangbwa. At the death of his father, Kurangbwa quitted his paternal group and went with his mother to live near both the Akegobili and the Abakundo, hunting equally with both. He used to prepare an abundance of food for all who cared to come and eat it. At this time the Abakundo used to keep their meat till it was very high before eating it. Some Abakundo who had feasted on fresh meat at Kurangbwa's home left their clan to come and live with him. Thus was formed a clan with Kurangbwa as their leader. The two legends now converge. The son of Kliso or of Kurangbwa, Bakliso, was his father's heir. With his supporters, he attacked the neighbouring Zande clans and defeated them and put his sons to rule over them. The nobles claim that it was Bakliso who took the name of Vurngura, but Hutereau thought that it was more logical to suppose that it was not until after the death of Ngura, the fifth of the dynasty, that this was done. (He thought that the word he spells Avurngura was composed of the two words *avura*, 'followers of', and Ngura, the name of the king; but this is faulty etymology both with regard to sound and sense, as Fr. Vanden Plas has shown.)[1] Thus Hutereau's genealogy runs: Kliso or Kurangbwa-Bakliso-Goro-Bwendi-Ngura. Such collaterals as are shown in it have no recorded lines of descent.[2]

De Calonne, also an administrator, collected his material in the Belgian Congo in the years prior to 1915, in which year he died. Both Hutereau's and de Calonne's books were published post-humously, but Hutereau's seems to have required little editing while de Calonne's was in parts very scrappy. He gives several legends of the origin of the royal clan. The ancient Avongara were called Akegobili, Agundagunda, or Akulubwa. One of the Akulubwa beat in wrestling Ngura (de Calonne's spelling Gura), who used his superior strength to pillage all who passed through his territory; hence the name Avungura (his spelling), 'those who bound Ngura'. Another legend says that one of the Akulubwa, called Basenginonga, was hunting far from home, lost his way for several weeks, and escaped a bush fire by hiding in a burrow of an ant-bear. As he came out of it, he was seen by some women of the Abakundo clan and made prisoner; whence the legend of the Akegobili coming out of a termite-mound. He distinguished himself as a hunter and became rich. Following the custom of the Abakundo, his master was about to be put to death for adultery, when he persuaded the people to accept compensation instead and himself paid it. For this service he was freed and given a wife, by whom he had a son, who soon distin-

---

[1] V. H. Vanden Plas, 'Quel est le nom de famille des chefs Azande?', *Congo*, 1921, pp. 1–10.

[2] Op. cit., pp. 140–6 and 151.

guished himself. When the Abakundo killed a beast they hid it in their granaries and later ate it secretly. The young man, on the contrary, when he had meat was most liberal with it; and besides being hospitable, he listened attentively when cases were discussed. By these means he gathered a following around him, at which Ngura, chief of the Abakundo, took umbrage. But, Ngura being beaten in a wrestling match by the young man, his subjects left him; whence the name taken by the new chief, Sukulukpwata, 'he who fights the old fight'. Another legend recorded in this confused account says that Diwitiroko commanded the Azande, who had fled before pale men called Azudia. His descendants, Monabwendi (Monogbandi) and Gura (Ngura), were installed to the north of the present region of Bangaso. Yet another legend says that the Avongara were anciently called Akegobili or Agundagunda. They arrived at the country of the Abakundo, whose chief was Gara (Ngara). Pressed by hunger, they wished to collect the fruit of the *banga* tree, but Gara forbade them until they had beaten him in wrestling. One of them overcame him.

These legends recorded by de Calonne[1] can scarcely be more than odd notes found among his papers by his editor Col. Bertrand. He also gives a number of different records of descent down to Ngura (his Gura), information which he must have jotted down at different times and in different places. I record them because they demonstrate what others have also learnt by experience, that the genealogy of the royal clan from the founder to Ngura, or perhaps we should say Gbandi or Monogbandi, is confused and quite useless for any historical purpose. After Ngura, however, he noted, as the rest of us have noted, that there is general agreement in the relation of genealogies. The different lists he took down from different informants are given on the following page.

My old friend Major P. M. Larken, who administered the Azande for over twenty years, first in Tembura District and then in Yambio District of the Bahr al-Ghazal Province of the Anglo-Egyptian Sudan, recorded prior to 1923 the myth of the founder of the Avongara royal house, taken down from informants in Tembura District. Two princes already dead by 1923, Kangua and Mabiko, told Major Larken that a long time ago the Azande inhabited the country between the Were and Bima rivers. There were no paramount chiefs and the clans lived independently of each other. One day a hunting party consisting of members of the Abakundo, Angbapiyo, and Avurunaze clans went into the forest to set their game nets. In the undergrowth they found a small naked boy with one leg buried in

[1] Op. cit., pp. 27–34.

DIFFERENT GENEALOGIES RECORDED BY DE CALONNE

#						
1.	Wara	Diwitiroko	Gunda Gunda	Nyarobe	Goro	Kliso
2.	Goro	Banduma	Kigobili	Bwendi	Lukaku	Goro
3.	Gura N'Gisa or Gura I	Bwendi or Monabwendi	Bwendi	Gura	Bwendi or Monabwendi	Bwendi
4.	Kulangura or Gura II	Gura	Gura	..	..	Gura I
5.	..	..	..	..	..	Gura II (?)

#						
1.	Kigobili	Diwitiroko	Kliso	Sukulupwata	Tunga Manga or Basenginonga	Gunda Gunda
2.	Nyeke	Nyeke	Gunda Gunda	Goro or Wara	Boduduma	Kegobili
3.	Bwendi	Banduma	Kegobili	Monabwendi	N'Dugwa	Goro or Wara
4.	Gura	Bwendi	Bwendi	Gura	Kunadio	Bwendi
5.	..	Gura	Gura	..	Bwendi	Monabwendi
6.	..	..	..	..	Gura	Gura

the ground. He was growing out of the ground like a *nonga*, an oval-shaped bulb about two inches long which grows with its top half exposed. The Abakundo claimed to have been the first to have seen him, but this was disputed by the Avurunaze, who challenged the Abakundo to prove their claim by pulling the boy's leg out of the ground. This they failed to do, whereas the Avurunaze succeeded in freeing the boy. The party then took him home, and he was brought up by the Avurunaze. When he had learnt to talk and was asked how he came to be alone in the forest, 'He replied sometimes that he had dropped from the sky, and sometimes that he had come out of the earth. No trace could be found of his parents and the accepted idea was that the Almighty had made him and put him where he was found.' At this time the clans were at enmity and there were no means of settling disputes between man and man, even when they were members of the same clan. 'The Bokundeu [Aba kundo] used to put their meat away until it got smelly, and then eat it among themselves, issuing no invitations to the Ngbwepiu [Ang-bapiyo] or Vurunaze [Avurunaze]. The Ngbwepiu were equally exclusive, while the Vurunaze were even more selfish than either, as they not only refused to invite their neighbours to eat with them, but went so far as not to share their food with anybody, each man devouring his own, and not lifting his head from the pot till it was empty.' The foundling, Basenginonga, acted differently. When he had meat he invited everyone to come and eat it with him, which appealed greatly to the people, and they elected him their ruler and gave him a wife from the Avurunaze. To begin with he ruled over only the three clans who had found him, but as his fame spread other people left their clans and came and settled under him, and as his power increased he conquered the other clans and foreign peoples also. Basenginonga appeared eleven generations ago. When he died his son Senginonga succeeded him, and his son Piko succeeded him. Piko's grandson was Mabenge.[1]

Another (unpublished) account, by Bimbashi Stevenson, also a British administrator and also in Tembura District, written in 1911, gives much the same information as that provided by Major Larken. One of these accounts is evidently taken from the other. A third genealogy taken down in Tembura District is in a report (also unpublished) by Captain J. E. Tracy Philipps, at one time Commissioner for the District. It runs as follows: Basenginonga-Turugba-Wara-Yombe-Bakpinga (Gbwandi)-Ngura.

Fr. Vanden Plas, a Dominican missionary, spoke Zande, as did Major Larken and Captain Philipps, and he was co-author with

---

[1] P. M. Larken, 'Zande Notes', *Sudan Notes and Records*, 6, 1923, pp. 241-2.

Mgr. Lagae of an excellent Zande grammar and dictionary. He cites a text about the origin of the Avongara, written in the Belgian Congo and probably by a Zande school boy, and gives literal and free translations of it. My own free translation is as follows:

This is how in the past the Akulangba took authority from the Abakundo. Once upon a time, the Abakundo being the rulers, a man called Basenginonga of the Akulangba and sister's son to the Abakundo lived on the right bank of the Mbomu. He crossed the river and came to the home of his maternal uncle of the Abakundo, where he passed some months. Every day, when his uncle settled disputes he sat and listened to the cases. One day two men brought their dispute before his uncle, and when they had finished stating their case his uncle gave the verdict that they were both in the right. They returned to their homes. Now, their sister's son Basenginonga considered the matter and asked whether the verdict of his uncle was just. His uncle's followers replied that they could make no sense of it. Whereupon Basenginonga said that it would not do. Since one of the men had seduced the wife of the other he must pay the husband ten spears, because he had seduced his wife. The Azande agreed with Basenginonga. Therefore the Azande brought their cases before the sister's son, and since it was so, the Abakundo said, as he was their sister's son, he might remain with them to settle cases for the Azande. So the Azande all subjected themselves to him.

Fr. Vanden Plas says that in the genealogy he presents from Basenginonga to Ngura (his Ngula) the names before Ngura may be collaterals which have got inserted into a single line of descent and that, whether this be so or not, they should be treated with reserve (we agree). It runs: Basenginonga-Turugba-Wara-Yombe-Gbwandi-Ngula (with a number of brothers, given by one informant only and presented with great reserve).[1]

Mgr. Lagae, also a Dominican Father, besides being co-author of the Zande grammar and dictionary, is the author of an ethnographical treatise on the Azande. In this treatise he cites a text written by Édouard Yérépiya, son of Prince Bafuka. My own free translation of this text is as follows:

The name Avongara originated in this way. There was a man called Ngara who ill-treated the people, and there was no one able to resist him, no one to bind him. Basenginonga built himself a home. This man came and appeared in Basenginonga's homestead. Basenginonga threw himself on him and bound him and laid him bound on the ground, there being no one with him to help him bind him. So when the Azande heard about it they said, 'Basenginonga has bound [vo] Ngara', and they said 'The binder of Ngara is he.' That name [Vongara] stuck to him. When he begat children people said that they were the children of Vongara [Avongara]. This story continued to be remembered in association with the nobles.[2]

[1] C. R. Lagae and V. H. Vanden Plas, op. cit., vol. i, pp. 38–9. This list is the same as that given by Capt. Philipps and, here again, one may have been taken from the other.   [2] Op. cit., p. 14.

Mgr. Lagae comments that Ngara had given himself this name, which means 'the force', because no one was able to overcome him, and he adds that the eponym of the Avongara is not Gura or Ngura, as Hutereau supposed, but Vongara. Mgr. Lagae also says that besides this name of Avongara, one speaks of the royal clan under the names of Akulangbwa, Akegobili, and Abalingi. He thinks that Abalingi is the name of Basenginonga's clan. Akulangbwa and Akegobili, says Mgr. Lagae, are sobriquets which conform little to the picture of the founder of the dynasty. *Kula* is an archaic word equivalent to *kara*, 'to return' or 'to twist'; *ngbwa* means 'mouth' or 'word'. The expression alludes to the habit nobles have of changing their minds. Akegobili signifies, he was told, those who go round a termite-mound slyly (*a-ke-go-bili*) and alludes to the fact that the nobles are sometimes well disposed to you in appearance but secretly hostile.[1] Today the nobles only call themselves Avongara.[2]

Now, it is clear that we can do nothing to bring these different accounts into a single story or to decide which of the many genealogies is the correct one. We have just to accept that there is no agreement about the order of names from the founder of the royal clan to Gbandi or Monoghandi; and as far as the relation of events is in question, we can put little trust in tradition before the time of Ngura's grandsons, the sons of Tombo and Mabenge, for what little has survived about either of the kings is manifest legend, e.g. the legend of the miracles performed by Mabenge's witch-doctor.[3] It may be that the same persons are given in different genealogies under different names. It may be also that some names and some incidents in the stories have a regional distribution and are possibly the product of ethnic divergences: for example, to the best of my recollection I have never met a member of the Avurunaze clan which figures in the myth recorded by Major Larken in the old kingdom of Tembura, nor have I ever heard it mentioned in connection with the origin of the Avongara or in any other connection. But these are no more than possibilities. We can never be certain; nor can we extricate ourselves from the confusion of names and mythical events: Ngara was a leader of the Abakundo and he was also a man who wished to take their authority from them; and Nyarobe was an important member of the Abakundo clan, was a daughter of that clan, and was also the founder of the Avongara. However, that is not

---

[1] The word is sometimes used by Azande to refer to women, to indicate their deceitfulness.

[2] Op. cit., pp. 14–15.

[3] De Calonne, op. cit., pp. 29–30. Hutereau, op. cit., pp. 161–2, is certainly in error in linking the legend with Bazingbi, Mabenge's grandson. See also the author's *Witchcraft, Oracles and Magic among the Azande*, 1937, pp. 196–9.

to say that the myth cannot at all be elucidated. Indeed, when we reflect on the various versions of the story of the origin of the Zande royal house we cannot fail to notice three elements in them, a consideration of which explains some of their features. These are legend, popular etymology, and the dramatization in a story of persons and events of the main functions Azande associate with royal office.

A mysterious origin, if not required by the logic of genealogies, fits into it very easily. Every man was begotten by another, so that a line of ancestors is indefinite and could not be retained in the memory. Consequently, unless a people have written records or unless there are court heralds whose duty it is to learn by heart and recite the names of the ancestors, African lines of descent, even of royal houses, often do not go back very far. And this is doubtless the reason why we find among peoples who attach some importance to lines of descent that the lines from the founder of a clan to the present generation are approximately the same length and that, it would seem, they remain at that length, the names of ancestors dropping out as the names of new generations are added. When we reach the founder, there is only a choice between people admitting to themselves that the names of earlier ancestors are unknown and rounding off the genealogy with a mysterious origin of the founder. To admit that the earlier ancestors are unknown involves people in the predicament of a supposed line of nameless ancestors stretching from son to father indefinitely into the past without there being collaterals at any generation. In the case of the myth we are examining, another predicament has to be overcome. The Avongara rule the Azande as an aristocratic class. The founder of the dynasty has, therefore to drop from heaven, spring from the ground, appear from a ghost-infested stream, or be found in a termite-mound, or he is figured as a member of some clan which has no existence except in this context, the Akulangba, the Akegobili, or Agundagunda. Otherwise he would have to be presented as a member of a commoner clan, a situation not to be envisaged. Mgr. Lagae, it is true, says that the clan of Basenginonga was Abalingi, a clan which does not exist at the present time. I have never myself heard this suggested, and as none of our other authorities mention the Abalingi, I think we must conclude that in this matter Mgr. Lagae must have been misinformed and that his statement would not find any support among the Azande themselves, whether nobles or commoners. However, although the myth provides a rational solution to this problem, it is necessary to add that the Azande themselves do not think that they know that what is said about the origin of Basenginonga (or whatever he was called) is a true account in the sense that the lines of their kings from Tombe and Mabenge are true. They only think that it could be true, for it is what their fathers told them. They are reserved when asked whether they believe the story they have told you and will not answer either 'yes' or 'no', just as they will not say whether they believe that Ture, the hero of their folk-tales, ever existed or never existed. People say that he was a real person and their fathers used to say the same, so maybe he was.[1] This being the case, the fact that different versions give different origins does not incommode anybody: as the first of my texts has it, 'One man has one story and another man has a different story; for there is nobody who really knows for certain. That is why there are many different stories of their [the nobles'] origin.' A very sensible observation, and one that allows for acceptance of all the stories. Furthermore, Azande do not feel that it matters at all where Basenginonga came from. That is not the significant part of the myth; and this was clear from the emphasis placed on certain features in it every time I heard the stories of the origin of the nobles related, features stressed also in most of the versions recorded by others, namely the acceptance of Basenginonga's authority on account of certain qualities of personality, in particular liberality and good judgement.

Popular etymology is also very evident in the myth. It might be thought that possibly the Angbapiyo did in fact get their name from their fondness for making nets, the Abakundo from their taste for high meat, were it not that, as I have shown earlier,[2] very many Zande clan names could not possibly have originated in the manner Azande say they did originate in the stories they relate to account for them. In part, at least, the stories are attempts to explain the names, and nothing more. Consequently we do not have to seek further for certain characteristics of the myth than a desire to have a rational derivation of names, and we need not attribute any other significance to them. In the stories the Angbapiyo were making nets and paying more attention to that than hearing cases, not because net-making has anything to do with the rest of the story, but because the name of the clan sounds to Azande like *ngba*, 'to be good', and *piyo*, 'nets'; and the Abakundo kept their meat till it was high, not because it is necessary for the story that they should have done so— they could have eaten it secretly without doing that—but because the final syllables of the word are the same as, or resemble to Zande ears, the word *kundo*, 'to be high (meat)'. The whole story of the founder of the royal clan having overcome and bound a man called Ngara is, I am convinced, nothing more than a story invented to account for the name Avongara. Azande are of the opinion, no

---

[1] See Evans-Pritchard, *The Zande Trickster*, 1967, pp. 24–5.
[2] See Chap. IV.

doubt a right one, that all clan names must have had a meaning and that therefore the story of how a certain clan received its name is contained in the name—it is a kind of sociological doctrine of signatures. They have therefore at some time or other invented a story or several stories to explain the name; and this has produced some curious results. It must be said that Azande themselves realize that these stories only tell us how the various clans might have got their names, for they recognize that it cannot be known for certain how they got them. They have a critical, even in many cases sceptical, attitude in all such matters. Even the man who tells you the story accounting for a clan name will often add that he does not vouch for its authenticity; it is what he has heard others say.

Now, in the name Avongara the *A* is the plural prefix, *vo* is interpreted as being the verb 'to bind', and since in the structure of the name what was bound was *ngara*, there must have been a man of this name. Hence, since the royal clan are called Avongara, they must be descendants of a man who bound Ngara. It is because the story is nothing more than an imaginative effort to explain the origin of a word that it is a more or less pointless story, a story in which the incidents are determined by sounds rather than by the logic of a situation it is supposed to elucidate, the relationship of the royal clan to commoners. In reality, the *vo* in Avongara is probably a second plural prefix and has nothing whatsoever to do with the verb 'to bind'.[1] Some of the picturesque incidents in the myth are also just a play upon sounds. The founder of the royal house is usually called Basenginonga. The word cannot be made to mean anything intelligible; but the last two syllables, *nonga*, could mean an earth-fruit, so the ancestor of the clan gets pulled out of the earth, in which one of his legs is stuck, on account of his name, or part of it, and he also starts war by teaching the young men mock fighting with stems of the same plant. Kongolikate is also a word which cannot, I think, be broken down into a sentence with intelligible meaning, but the verb *kongo* means 'to be caught' or 'to be entangled', and it may very well be that the first version of the myth I have recorded, in which the founder of the dynasty is caught in a snare from which he is unable to extricate himself, is derived from that fact. We might reach a similar conclusion about the name Bakulukpwata and possibly about other names of the founder.[2]

The chief significant points in the myth are those which attribute to the ancestor of the Avongara the qualities Azande emphasize as

[1] See Chap. IV.

[2] De Calonne (op. cit., p. 33) says that Kliso owes his name to the red fruit of the *kliso* or *nungaw*. For *nungaw* we should perhaps read *nonga*. If this is so, *kliso* may be a second name in some parts of Zandeland for the red *nonga* fruit.

those distinguishing nobles and which are to a student of their political organization the basic functions of the ruling clan. These are, first, the settlement of disputes by clear judicial decisions, especially in cases of adultery, always of major importance to Azande, and secondly, liberality, especially in the distribution of food. Basenginonga attracts a following because the Angbapiyo and the Abakundo are unable, as he is able, to give clear decisions, and all the clans, unlike him, hide their game and eat in secret and away from their fellows. Minor points which mirror the Zande representation of their rulers are cleanliness and economy in eating, care in the preparation of food, eating apart from commoners, and a certain distinction and withdrawal from common touch. The founder is also, in one version, the inventor of war, who distributes among his followers the weapons of war. In the myth the founder of the royal clan acts exactly as a king or prince acts today. He listens attentively to cases and gives unambiguous verdicts; he provides food for his followers at court, fresh, well cooked, and in quantity; and he makes war and distributes weapons to be used in it.

A further point in the myth or myths to which attention may be directed is the mother's brother-sister's son relationship. This is, of course, imposed by the logic of the story. Either the founder must be somebody's sister's son or, if he had a mysterious origin, his son must be, for his lineage to be established. But there may be more to the stressing of the *wili dewili*, sister's son, relationship, generally with reference to the widespread and numerically important Abakundo clan, than just the logic of the story. The founder of a royal dynasty taking over authority from the people of his mother is so common a motif among African peoples that we should make more than a passing reference to it. It presents, however, a very difficult and complex problem, to which insufficient attention has been paid and which cannot be considered in any detail here. It would seem that the mother's brother-sister's son relationship expresses in its political representation a neutral, and therefore arbitrative, position of a ruling dynasty to the commoner clans whom they rule. In other words, the sister's son-mother's brother relationship stressed in the myth does not, it may be suggested, express a sister's son relationship to a particular clan, though in the story it has of course to be a particular clan, but to commoner clans in general. It is an expression in the myth of a sister's son relationship of nobles as such to commoners as such, of rulers to those whom they rule and among whom they adjudicate.

The dramatization and personification of royal functions, as seen by the Azande, need not, of course, be merely, and only, a throwing-back into the past and into a mythological form of present practice, and we do not have to conclude that the story of Basenginonga has no historical value at all. It could be that the myth, which with regard to these functions is credible, is a statement, in however picturesque a way, suitable to a dramatic story of what actually occurred. Here we face a problem which is for the most part insoluble.

If we suppose that Basenginonga (let us take his name for that of the founder of the clan) was a real person, whose origin is unknown, and that he established his authority over the Ambomu clans—which in the hands of his descendants became an unbridgeable gulf between the class of nobles and the class of commoners—we have to ask how he could have established his authority. To this question there is, I think, an answer of a kind. The evidences in Zande accounts of the past tend to show that in early times the kings did not have such absolute power and did not control so centralized an organization as their descendants had at the time of European penetration of their country. Their authority could have grown slowly, therefore, in the course of more than a century of conquest and domination of foreign peoples; and this is more or less what Azande themselves say, and what they say is strengthened by the observation that the kings tend to exercise most despotic rule on the peripheries of the area of conquest. It is true that the genealogy from Basenginonga to Gbandi raises doubts whether everything said about the royal clan, including the existence of Basenginonga, is not entirely unacceptable. Did none of the progenitors of Ngura have more than one son who left heirs? Here again there is an answer of a kind. We often observe in the study of the royal genealogies of other African peoples the same phenomenon of bifurcating branches to a certain point of depth and then a single line of ancestors to the founder of the royal house, and it is possible that what has happened is a compression of the genealogies into a form appropriate to a developing political situation. The ruling dynasties are all descended from Tombo and Mabenge, and other persons of noble birth of collateral lines who lack high political office might have grafted their ancestors into one or the other of these two lines of descent in order to identify themselves more closely with the ruling houses. This is possible, though there

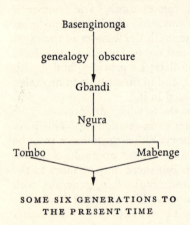

Basenginonga

genealogy | obscure

Gbandi

Ngura

Tombo   Mabenge

SOME SIX GENERATIONS TO
THE PRESENT TIME

is an objection to the explanation. In my day the sons of the ruling princes in the old kingdom of Gbudwe all knew their lines of descent back to Mabenge, the father of Yakpati, the father of Bazingbi, that is, three generations back to Bazingbi and five generations back to Mabenge, and we know from early travel accounts that the lines they trace are true. Therefore, if the princes of my time gave me a correct statement of their line of descent to five generations back, why should not the princes of Junker's time have done the same for him? Now, five generations from the old princes whom he consulted about the history of their clan takes us back well beyond Ngura, from whom all Avongara trace their descent. If there had been other lines of descent, Junker might be expected to have heard of them because he was deeply interested in, and a persistent inquirer into, Zande history, and furthermore had travelled widely in Zandeland to pursue his inquiries. He does not mention any other lines, and no one else, so far as I am aware, has ever met a Vongara who did not trace his descent from either Tombo or Mabenge, both sons of Ngura. It is, of course, possible that the lines of collateral issue from Avungara earlier than Ngura, if there were any, died out. However, the names, or some of them, between Ngura and Basenginonga may be those of collaterals without descendants whose names must have become displaced in the genealogy, or they may be different names of the same persons which have in course of time come to stand for different persons, or they may be fictions required by the imagination to make a break between the historical ancestor of all Avongara, Ngura, and the mythopoeic figure of Basenginonga. Certainly, as we have seen, there is no agreement about the names or their order. This is the part of the line of descent, therefore, which allows for manipulation, where names can be dropped out as new names come into circulation in each new generation. Thus I was usually given only two names, very occasionally more, between Basenginonga and Ngura, whereas earlier inquirers, as we have seen, were sometimes given four names. To Ngura the descent of the nobles is too well known to be altered, whether deliberately or inadvertently, and its stability is maintained also by the political relations the genealogy represents, as well as being a record of descent; while the name of Basenginonga is a fixed point required by lineage logic. In between, not only do names probably drop out, but what we know in general about lineages suggests that the dropping out is inevitable. But the fact that the genealogy from the founder of the royal dynasty to Gbandi is of no historical value does not by itself exclude the possibility of its foundation by some individual.

The alternative to accepting that Basenginonga was an Mbomu individual, or even a foreigner, who in some way established his authority over the Ambomu people is to accept that the Avongara of today are the descendants of an Mbomu clan which somehow achieved dominance over the rest of the Ambomu, or of a foreign people who did that. But if they were a Mbomu group—Akulangba[1] or whatever it might be—what has happened to their descendants other than those in the genealogy of the descendants of Ngura? Individuals and even odd lines may get inserted into a tree of descent at a lower point than that at which they originated, though I have already given a reason for believing that this may not be the case with the genealogy of the Avongara, but it is difficult to believe that a group large enough to have imposed its will on a whole people could be so merged into a line of descent of such shallow depth (even shallower in Junker's time). De Calonne suggests that they were 'a small nucleus of strangers who created a social crystalization in an amorphous milieu',[2] and another writer says that they may be 'the survival of a race who conquered the Azande'.[3] But if they were strangers they could scarcely have dominated the Ambomu people unless they were a very large group, and if they were such a group, we are again faced with the problem of what happened to their descendants; or unless they were culturally vastly superior to the Ambomu, and there seems to be no evidence for such a group having appeared in Central Africa at the time the genealogical indications point to. Major Larken goes even further. He says that the Avongara have their own customs—incest and sacrifice of slaves on the death of one of them—and their own language. It must, however, be said that the marriage of close relations and sacrifice of slaves are not uncommon among aristocracies, and Major Larken, though he feels certain that they had a language,[4] in his day still known in part to some of them, is not able to produce any evidence for there having been one. When pressed, his informants usually produced the jargon of reversed syllables spoken as a game by the sons of princes at court. The only words of the language he remembers having obtained are

---

[1] Gore also gives Akurangba as another name for the Avongara in his *Zande and English Dictionary*, 1952 edn., p. 81, the letters *l* and *r* being (for him) interchangeable symbols in writing Zande. It could be the same word as that used in the expression *gbia ni kurongbo*, 'nobleman of the canoe', as mentioned earlier in one of my own texts. Mgr. Lagae's derivation of this word has already been given. It is possible, though I have no evidence to support the suggestion, that the word sounds to Azande like *akulu ngba*, 'tree-rats are good', and this would account, following the construction of Zande etymology, for the founder hunting tree-rats in two of the texts.

[2] Op. cit., p. 14.

[3] *The Bahr El Ghazal Province Handbook*, 1911, p. 26.

[4] Larken, op. cit., 1926, p. 241; also op. cit., 1923, pp. 241–2. See also Evans-Pritchard, 'A Zande Slang Language', *Man*, 1954, no. 289.

dua, 'yes', *durati*, 'no' (surely a very long word for 'no'), and *dimo*, 'bow'. Apart from the fact that there would seem to be no point in Avongara seeking to hide an almost dead language, other considerations weigh heavily against there having been one. Zande princes live isolated lives, spending most of their time in their private quarters in the company of their wives and daughters and small sons —all other males, except small pages when summoned, whether noble or commoner are rigidly excluded—and I find it difficult to see with whom they could have talked a Vongara language; and certainly had they taught it to their small sons, or had these sons later talked it among themselves at court, commoners could not fail to know at least that there was such a language; but though I have asked many of them about it, including those who as small boys had been familiar with the domestic and public life of princes, they not only all denied that the Avongara ever spoke any other language than Zande, save the jargon I have mentioned, but were clearly astonished that anyone could suppose otherwise. Moreover, if, as we have some grounds for believing, all Avongara correctly trace their descent from Ngura, there could not have been a Vongara language. None of the early travellers, who usually resided at royal courts and might, therefore, in spite of their slight acquaintance with the Zande tongue, have noticed if a non-Zande tongue was spoken at them, has mentioned that any language was spoken by the Avongara other than that spoken by all Azande, nobles and commoners alike.

So, on the evidences we possess—which are, it is true, slender, negative, and of course, not in the strict sense historical—I conclude that we would be right to choose the first alternative as the less unlikely, though with great reserve, that a man called Basenginonga or by some other name may have been a real person—in spite of some unacceptable traditions of his origin—who established some sort of pre-eminence over the Ambomu people which his descendants developed into the complete domination of the Avongara in historic times; though how many generations ago he lived and from what stock he came we have no means of ascertaining. If de Calonne's information is correct, we can, however, say that when the Azande began their migrations south-eastward and penetrated the Uele basin they were not yet ruled, or not yet entirely ruled by the Avongara, for he says that they migrated in two waves, an earlier (possibly late seventeenth century) one consisting of the Abele, the Abwameli, the Angada, and probably the Abagwa, and a later one led by the Avongara.[1] If this evidence is accepted, it adds weight to the view that the ascendancy of the Avongara was of relatively recent

---

[1] Op. cit., p. 102.

date and a process of slow development, and also to the view that, if that is the case, it may have had a beginning in the personal ascendancy of some individual.

If we cannot say when the royal house came into being, neither can we say from what stock it originated. It is perhaps not surprising that legend has here obliterated memory, giving the founder either a mysterious origin or making him a member of a clan which has no existence and may be presumed never to have existed, for Zande clans are legion, are of many different ethnic origins, and are widely dispersed and intermingled, and, with the exception of the Avongara, the members of a clan have no genealogical knowledge of their relationships. We know that, in fact, new clans have come into being through a split-off from the parent stem, though we do not know how this took place. In these circumstances it is probable that, if a man were to decide to call his family by a different name, his link with his original clan might easily be forgotten in course of time. We can only surmise what might have happened. There can be no verification.

It may further be suggested that, as has so often happened, it was a succession of successful wars which confirmed and increased the authority of the Avongara, however it may have come about in the first instance. The Azande under Avongara leadership were generally victorious on account of their superior political organization. It was only when they came up against peoples with similar statal organs that they were unable to master them. Those who held their own against them were the Abandiya to the west of Zandeland and the Mangbetu to the south-east of it. These peoples speak of the Azande as the Avongara, the name of their royal house; and the Azande speak of the two ethnic conglomerations similar to their own by the names of their royal houses, Abandiya and Mangbetu. In the case of the Abandiya we are faced with much the same difficulties in trying to elucidate the origin and early history of their ruling clan as in the case of the Avongara. Their ancestor was a certain Gaki. Between Gaki, a mythological figure, and Pobe or Pwobe (who corresponds to Ngura in Avongara tradition, as being the king from whose two sons Gobenge and Mwanda it would seem that almost all the present-day aristocracy trace their descent) there are recorded in a single line of descent six ancestral names of persons about whom either nothing is known or about whom there are only scraps of information, probably of a legendary kind. A study of Abandiya traditions therefore sheds little light on those of the Avongara.

The case of the Mangbetu is, in spite of their tangled history, more helpful, for it shows that it is not unreasonable to suppose that an individual can, through his ability and character, in the barbarous conditions obtaining, become the leader and his descendants the unquestioned rulers of a whole people or of a number of peoples brought by him and his successors into political association. That it is reasonable to suppose this, can be shown by many examples in history; but the Mangbetu one is the most appropriate to our present discussion, since they are adjacent to the Azande and are in a number of respects similar to them in culture and institutions. A conglomeration of peoples were ruled by the royal family of the Mangbetu, whose name is given by other peoples to rulers and ruled alike. This family seems to have been pretty well exterminated in the wars in which they became involved after 1870. Now, in that year Schweinfurth met the Mangbetu king Munza, of whom he has left us a fascinating picture,[1] but the point of interest is that this King Munza appears to have been only the grandson of Nabiembwale or Nabiembali, a man of the Mabiti clan who founded the Mangbetu royal dynasty and gave to it the new family or clan name of Mangbetu. Unfortunately, we do not learn this from Schweinfurth, who is silent on the history of the royal house; but we have to remember that the authorities who vouch for the fact, Hutereau and de Calonne,[2] were making their inquiries at the end of the last century and in the opening years of the present century, when the history of the royal house must have been well known to their informants, for the period was only a generation after the death of Munza and only three generations after the founder of the royal dynasty (who may have been a Vongara). This is scarcely time for the circumstances attending the rise of the Mangbetu dynasty to have been erased from the people's memory or to have become seriously distorted or falsified. And if Nabiembwale could make himself ruler of the Medje people and as their ruler bring other peoples under his sway, why could not Basenginonga make himself ruler of the Ambomu? But I must repeat that one can only surmise what may have happened; there can be no certainty because there are no means of verification.

[1] Though doubtless an exaggerated one: see Czekanowski, op. cit., vol. i, p. 179.
[2] Hutereau, op. cit., pp. 266 et seq.; de Calonne, op. cit., pp. 125 et seq.

BIBLIOGRAPHY

ANDERSON, R. G., 'Some tribal customs in their relation to medicine and morals of the Nyam-Nyam and Gour peoples inhabiting the Bahr el Ghazal', *Fourth Report of the Wellcome Tropical Research Laboratories*, 1911.

ANON., 'M. M. Nillis and de la Kéthulle on the borders of Darfur', *The Geographical Journal*, 1896.

ANTINORI, O., 'Viaggi di O. Antinori e C. Piaggia nell'Africa Centrale', *Bollettino della Società Geografica Italiana*, i, 1868.

Bahr El Ghazal Province Handbook, The, Anglo-Egyptian Handbook Series 1, Khartoum, 1911.

BALFOUR, H, 'Thorn-lined Traps in the Pitt-Rivers Museum, Oxford', *Man*, xxxii, 1932, 77.

BAUMANN, H., 'Die materielle Kultur der Azande und Mangbetu', *Baessler-Archiv*, Berlin, 1927.

—— 'Likundu. Die Sektion der Zauberkraft', *Zeitschrift für Ethnologie*, 1928.

BAXTER, P. W. T., and BUTT, A., *The Azande and Related Peoples of the Anglo-Egyptian Sudan and Belgian Congo*, London, 1953.

BETHELL, BIMBASHI A. B., *Sudan Intelligence Reports*, no. 122, 1904.

Biographie coloniale belge, Art. 'Lemaire', vol. ii, 1951.

BROCK, R. G. C., 'Some notes on the Zande peoples as found in the Meridi District', *Sudan Notes and Records*, i, 1918.

—— 'The Zande Tribe', *Sudan Notes and Records*, i, 1918.

BROWNE, W. G., *Travels in Africa, Egypt, and Syria from the year 1792 to 1798*, London, 1799.

BURROWS, G., *The Curse of Central Africa*, London, 1903.

—— 'On the Natives of the Upper Welle District of the Belgian Congo', *Journal of the Royal African Institute*, 1899.

BURSSENS, H., *Les Peuplades de l'Entre-Congo-Ubangi*, London, 1958.

CALONNE-BEAUFAICT, A. DE, *Azande*, Bruxelles, 1921.

CAPENNY, S. H. F., 'The Khedivic possessions in the basin of the Upper Ubangi', *The Scottish Geographical Magazine*, 1899.

CARMIGNANI, RENZO, *Il cannibalismo degli Asandè*, Roma, 1954.

CASATI, GAETANO, *Ten Years in Equatoria and the Return with Emin Pasha* (trans. Hon. Mrs. J. Randolph Clay and I. Walter Savage Landor), 2 vols., London and New York, 1891.

CHAILLÉ LONG, COL. C., *Central Africa: Naked Truths of Naked People*, London, 1876.

CLINE, W., *Mining and Metallurgy in Negro Africa*, Menasha, Wisconsin, 1937.

CRAFFEN, E., and COLOMBO, E., 'Les Niam-Niam', *Revue internationale de sociologie*, no. 11, 1906.

CZEKANOWSKI, JAN, *Wissenschaftliche Ergebnisse der deutschen Zentral-Afrika-Expedition, 1907–1908, unter Führung Adolf Friedrichs Herzog zu Mecklenburg*, Bd. 6, 2: *Forschungen in Nil-Kongo-Zwischengebiet*, Leipzig, 1924.

EMIN PASHA, *Emin Pasha in Central Africa, being a Collection of his Letters and Journals*, edited and annotated by Professor G. Schweinfurth, Professor F. Ratzel, Dr. R. W. Felkin, and Dr. G. Hartland, London, 1888.

EVANS-PRITCHARD, E. E., 'The Bongo', *Sudan Notes and Records*, xxi, 1929.

—— 'The Mberidi and Mbegumba of the Bahr el Ghazal', *Sudan Notes and Records*, xiv, 1931.

—— 'The non-Dinka peoples of the Amadi and Rumbek Districts', *Sudan Notes and Records*, xx, 1937.

—— *Witchcraft, Oracles and Magic among the Azande*, Oxford, 1937.

—— 'A Zande Slang Language', *Man*, liv, 1954, 289.

—— 'Zande Historical Texts', *Sudan Notes and Records*, xxxvi–xxxviii, 1955–7.

—— 'A history of the kingdom of Gbudwe', *Zaïre*, x, t. i, t. ii, 1956.

—— 'Zande Clan Names', *Man*, lvi, 1956, 62.

—— 'Zande Totems', *Man*, lvi, 1956, 110.

—— 'The origin of the ruling clan of the Azande', *Southwestern Journal of Anthropology*, xiii, 1957.

—— 'Zande Border Raids', *Africa*, xxviii, 1957.

—— 'Zande Warfare', *Anthropos*, lii, 1957.

—— 'The Zande royal court', *Zaïre*, xi, t. i, t ii, 1957.

—— 'Zande kings and princes', *Anthropological Quarterly*, xxx, 1957.

—— 'The Ethnic composition of the Azande of Central Africa', *Anthropological Quarterly*, xxxi, 1958.

—— 'An historical introduction to a study of Zande society', *African Studies*, xviii, 1958.

—— 'The distribution of Zande clans in the Sudan', *Man*, lix, 1959, 24.

—— 'Zande Cannibalism', *Journal of the Royal Anthropological Institute*, xc, 1960.

—— 'Zande clans and settlements', *Man*, lx, 1960, 213.

—— 'A contribution to the study of Zande culture', *Africa*, xxx, 1960; 'A Further Contribution', etc., xxxiii, 1963; 'A Final Contribution', etc., xxxv, 1965.

—— 'The organization of a Zande kingdom', *Cahiers d'études africaines*, iv, 1960.

—— 'The ethnic origin of Zande office-holders', *Man*, lx, 1960, 141.

—— 'Zande clans and totems', *Man*, lxi, 1961, 147.

—— *The Zande Trickster*, Oxford, 1967.

GESSI PASHA, ROMOLO, *Seven Years in the Sudan* (*Sette anni nel Sudan egiziano*, Milano, 1891), 1892.

GEYER, F. X., *Durch Sand, Sumpf und Wald*, Leipzig, 1914.

GIORGETTI, F., *Our African Missions*, vol. vii, no. 6, 1952.

—— 'Il cannibalismo dei Niam Niam', *Africa*, April 1957.

—— *La Superstizione Zande* (private circulation), Wau, 1958 (printed edn., Bologna, 1966).

GORE, CANON E. C., and MRS., *Zande and English Dictionary* (1st edn., 1931), London, 1952.

GRAER, A. M. DE, 'L'art de guérir chez les Azande', *Congo*, 1929.

HADDOW, BIMBASHI R. W., *Sudan Intelligence Reports*, no. 169, 1908.

HADDOW, BIMBASHI R. W., *Sudan Intelligence Reports*, no. 210, 1912.

HEUGLIN, M. TH. V., *Reise in das Gebiet des Weissen Nil und seiner westlichen Zuflüsse in den Jahren 1862–1864*, Leipzig und Heidelberg, 1869.

—— (Extracts from letters, trans. M. Mare) 'Travels in the Sudan in the Sixties', *Sudan Notes and Records*, 24, 1941.

HILL, R., *A Biographical Dictionary of the Anglo-Egyptian Sudan*, London, 1951.

HOLT, P. M., *The Mahdist State in the Sudan, 1881–1898*, Oxford, 1958.

HUTEREAU, A., 'Notes sur la vie familiale et juridique de quelques populations du Congo belge', *Annales du Musée du Congo belge*, ser. 3, 1909.

—— *Histoire des peuplades de l'Uele et de l'Ubangi*, Bruxelles, 1922.

IRVINE, F. R., *A Text-book of West African Agriculture*, London, 1934.

JACKSON, H. C., *Behind the Modern Sudan*, London, 1955.

JONES, W. O., *Manioc in Africa*, Stanford, California, 1959.

JUNKER, WILHELM, *Travels in Central Africa during the years 1875–1878* (trans. A. H. Keane), London, 1890.

—— *Travels in Central Africa during the years 1879–1883* (trans. A. H. Keane), London, 1891.

—— *Travels in Central Africa during the years 1884–1886* (trans. A. H. Keane), London, 1892.

KROLL, H., 'Die Haustiere der Bantu', *Zeitschrift für Ethnologie*, 1929.

LAGAE, C.-R., *Les Azande ou Niam-Niam*, Bruxelles, 1926.

—— and VANDEN PLAS, V. H., *La Langue des Azande*, 2 vols., Ghent, 1921–2.

LARKEN, P. M., 'Zande Notes', *Sudan Notes and Records*, vi, 1923.

—— 'An Account of the Zande', *Sudan Notes and Records*, ix, 1926.

—— 'Impressions of the Azande', *Sudan Notes and Records*, x, 1927.

LELONG, M. H., *Mes Frères du Congo*, 2 vols., Alger, 1946.

LOTAR, L., *La Grande Chronique de l'Uele*, Bruxelles, 1946.

—— 'Souvenirs de l'Uele', *Congo*, t. i, t. ii, 1931.

MacMICHAEL, H. A., *The Sudan*, London, 1954.

MAES, J., 'La Sanza du Congo Belge', *Congo*, t. i, 1921.

—— and BOONE, O., *Les Peuplades du Congo belge*, Bruxelles, 1935.

MARNO, E., *Reise in der egyptischen Aequatorial-Provinz und in Kordofan in den Jahren 1874–1876*, Leipzig und Heidelberg, 1879.

MECKLENBURGH-SCHWERIN, ADOLF FRIEDRICH A. H., HERZOG V., *From the Congo to the Niger and the Nile*, London, 1913.

MERRILL, E. D., *The Botany of Cook's Voyages*, Waltham, Mass., 1954.

PELLEGRINETTI, A., *Le memorie di Carlo Piaggia*, Firenze, 1941.

PETHERICK, J., *Egypt, the Sudan and Central Africa*, Edinburgh and London, 1861.

PETHERICK, MR. and MRS., *Travels in Central Africa*, 2 vols., London, 1869.

PIAGGIA, C., *Dell'arrivo fra i Niam-Niam e del soggiorno sul Lago Tzana in Abissinia*, Lucca, 1877. See also Antinori, O., and Pellegrinetti, A.

PONCET, J., *Le Fleuve blanc*, Paris, 1863.

SANTANDREA, S., 'Il gruppo Ndogo del Bahr El-Ghazal', *Annali-Lateranensi*, 1938.

—— 'Little-known tribes of the Bahr el Ghazal Basin', *Sudan Notes and Records*, xxvii, 1946.

SANTANDREA, S., *Bibliografia di studi africani della Missione dell' Africa Centrale*, Verona, 1948.

SCHLIPPE, P. DE, *Shifting Cultivation in Africa*, London, 1956.

SCHNELL, R., *Plantes alimentaires et vie agricole de l'Afrique noire: Essai de phytogéographie alimentaire*, Paris, 1957.

SCHWEINFURTH, GEORG, *Im Herzen von Afrika*, 1878 and 1922 edns., Leipzig; trans. E. E. Frewer, *The Heart of Africa*, 2 vols., London, 1873.

—— 'Das Volk der Monbuttu in Central-Afrika', *Zeitschrift für Ethnologie*, 2, 1873.

—— *Linguistische Ergebnisse einer Reise nach Centralafrika*, Berlin, 1873 (3).

—— *Artes Africanae*, Leipzig and London, 1875.

SELIGMANN, C. G., and B. Z., *Pagan Tribes of the Nilotic Sudan*, London, 1932.

SLATIN PASHA, RUDOLF C., *Fire and Sword in the Sudan*, London, 1896.

STEPHENSON, CAPT. E. S., *Sudan Intelligence Reports*, no. 210, 1912.

STRUCK, B., 'An Unlocated Tribe on the White Nile', *Journal of the African Society*, 1908.

Sudan Intelligence Reports, no. 201, 1911.

THURIAUX-HENNEBERT, A., *Les Azande dans l'histoire du Bahr el Ghazal et de l'Equatoria*, Bruxelles, 1964.

TOTHILL, J. D. (ed.), *Agriculture in the Sudan*, London, 1948.

TUCKER, A. N., 'The Tribal Confusion around Wau', *Sudan Notes and Records*, 14, 1931.

—— *The Eastern Sudanic Languages*, vol. i, London, 1940.

—— and BRYAN, M. A., *Handbook of African Languages*, Part 3, *The Non-Bantu Languages of North-Eastern Africa*, London, 1956.

VAN BULCK, G., and HACKETT, P., 'Oubangui to Great Lakes', *Linguistic Survey of the Northern Bantu Borderland*, vol. i, London, 1956.

VANDEN PLAS, V. H., *La Langue des Azande*, vol. i, *Introduction historico-géographique*, Ghent, 1921.

—— 'Quel est le nom de famille des chefs Azande', *Congo*, i, 1921.

VAN GELUWE, H., *Mamvu-Mangutu et Balese-Mvuba*, London, 1957.

VON WIESE, CAPT., in Mecklenburgh-Schwerin, A. F. A. H., Herzog v., *From the Congo to the Niger and the Nile*, London, 1913.

W(HEATLEY), M. J., 'The Belanda', *Sudan Notes and Records*, 6, 1923.

Yambio District Records (mimeographed), n.d., circulated by A. T. T. Leich.

INDEX

Note: only the names of the most important Azande, authorities and topics relating to the kingdom of Gbudwe are listed